A HISTORY OF CIVIL LITIGATION

A HISTORY OF CIVIL LITIGATION

POLITICAL AND ECONOMIC

PERSPECTIVES

FRANK J. VANDALL

OXFORD

UNIVERSITY PRESS

OXFORD
UNIVERSITY PRESS

Oxford University Press, Inc., publishes works that further Oxford University's objective of excellence in research, scholarship, and education.

Oxford   New York
Auckland   Cape Town   Dar es Salaam   Hong Kong   Karachi
Kuala Lumpur   Madrid   Melbourne   Mexico City   Nairobi
New Delhi   Shanghai   Taipei   Toronto

With offices in
Argentina   Austria   Brazil   Chile   Czech Republic   France   Greece
Guatemala   Hungary   Italy   Japan   Poland   Portugal   Singapore
South Korea   Switzerland   Thailand   Turkey   Ukraine   Vietnam

Library of Congress Cataloging-in-Publication Data

Vandall, Frank J.
    A history of civil litigation : political and economic perspectives / Frank J. Vandall.
      p. cm.
    Includes bibliographical references and index.
    ISBN 978-0-19-539191-6 (alk. paper)
    1. Liability (Law)—United States—History. 2. Strict liability—United States—History.
3. Products liability—United States—History. 4. Corporate power—United States.
5. Legislation–United States.
I. Title.
    KF1250.V36 2011
    346.03—dc22

                                                                2010031840

1 2 3 4 5 6 7 8 9
Printed in the United States of America
on acid-free paper

To Sheila, Megan, Josh, Keegan, Madison, and Emma for their continuing support, inspiration, and sunshine.

CONTENTS

ACKNOWLEDGMENTS

I thank David Bederman, Bill Buzbee, Rich Freer, Andrew Popper, Polly Price, Christopher Robinette, Paul Rubin, Ani Satz, Robert Schapiro, George Shepherd, Joanna Shepherd, and Randall Strahan for their valuable comments on portions of the manuscript.

I also appreciate the research assistance of Anna Diehn and Dena Bouchard.

I am indebted to Marianne D'Souza for her dedication, organizational skills, and professional assistance.

I would like to thank the copyright holders of the following works who permitted their inclusion in this book:

Vandall, Frank J., *Strict Liability* 1–12, 17–25, 29–34, 36 (1989), reprinted by permission of Greenwood Press;

Vandall, Frank J., "A Preliminary Consideration of Issues Raised in the Firearms Sellers Immunity Bill", 38 *Akron Law Review* 113, 113–32 (2005);

Vandall, Frank J., "Undermining Torts Policies: Products Liability Legislation", 30 *American University Law Review* 673, 679–703 (1981);

Vandall, Frank J., "Judge Posner's Negligence–Efficiency Theory: A Critique", 35 *Emory Law Journal* 384, 387 (1986);

Vandall, Frank J., "A Critique of the Restatement (Third) Apportionment as It Affects Joint and Several Liability", 49 *Emory Law Journal* 565 (2000);

Vandall, Frank J., and Vandall, Joshua F., "A Call for an Accurate Restatement (Third) of Torts: Design Defect", 33 *University of Memphis Law Review* 910, 915–18, 926–44 (2003);

Vandall, Frank J., "Constructing a Roof before the Foundation is Prepared: The Restatement (Third) of Torts: Products Liability Section 2(b) Design Defect", 30 *University of Michigan Journal of Law Review*, 261, 262, 265–79 (1997);

Vandall, Frank J., "'Design Defect' in Products Liability: Rethinking Negligence and Strict Liability", 43 *Ohio State Law Journal* 61, 72–86 (1982);

Vandall, Frank J., "Reallocating the Costs of Smoking: The Application of Absolute Liability to Cigarette Manufacturers", 52 *Ohio State Law Journal* 405–35 (1991);

Vandall, Frank J., "The Legal Theory and the Visionaries that Led to the Proposed $368.5 Billion Tobacco Settlement", 27 *Southwestern University Law Review* 473–85 (1998);

Vandall, Frank J., "The Restatement (Third) of Torts, Products Liability Section 2(b): Design Defect", 68 *Temple Law Review* 167, 186 (1995);

Vandall, Frank J., "Constricting Products Liability: Reforms in Theory and Procedure", 48 *Villanova Law Review* 843, 851–74 (2003).

Finally, I would like to thank Dean David Partlett of Emory University School of Law for granting me a sabbatical in order to finish the book.

INTRODUCTION

This book describes the expansion of civil liability from 1466 to 1980 and the cessation of that growth in 1980 when corporations realized they could affect the content of the law. It evaluates the creation of tort causes of action during the period 1400–1980, then specifically considers reevaluation and limitation of these developments from 1980 to the present. A keystone case is *MacPherson v. Buick Motor Co.* (1916), because it rejects transparent and unmanageable legal fictions and adopts negligence as a foundational cause of action. During the period 1916–1944, the courts used numerous causes of action (such as express and implied warranty, fraud, and negligence) to accomplish justice and provide a means for injured consumers to recover.

The book will use products cases and policies for much of its argument. The policies supporting the more than 500- year expansion in tort liability were forcefully presented by Judge Roger Traynor in a products case, *Escola v. Coca Cola Bottling Co.* (1944):

> . . . I believe the manufacturer's negligence should no longer be singled out as the basis for a plaintiff's right to recover in cases like the present one. In my opinion it should now be recognized that a manufacturer incurs an absolute liability when an article that he has placed on the market, knowing that it is to be used without inspection, proves to have a defect that causes injury to human beings . . . . Even if there is no negligence, however, public policy demands that responsibility be fixed wherever it will most effectively reduce the hazards to life and health inherent in defective products that reach the market. It is evident that the manufacturer can anticipate some hazards and guard against the recurrence of others, as the public cannot. Those who suffer injury from defective products are unprepared to meet its consequences. The cost of an injury and the loss of time or health may be an overwhelming misfortune to the person injured, and a needless one for the risk of injury can be insured by the manufacturer and distributed among the public as a cost of doing business. It is to the public interest to discourage the marketing of products having defects that are a menace to the public. If such products nevertheless find their way into the market, it is to the public interest to place the responsibility for whatever injury they may cause upon the manufacturer, who, even if he is not negligent in the manufacture of the product, is responsible for its reaching the market . . . .
>
> . . . It is needlessly circuitous to make negligence the basis of recovery and impose what is in reality liability without negligence. If public policy demands that a manufacturer of goods be responsible for their quality regardless of negligence there is no reason not to fix that responsibility openly. . . .

. . . As handicrafts have been replaced by mass production with its great markets and transportation facilities, the close relationship between the producer and consumer of a product has been altered. Manufacturing processes, frequently valuable secrets, are ordinarily either inaccessible to or beyond the ken of the general public. The consumer no longer has means or skill enough to investigate for himself the soundness of a product, even when it is not contained in a sealed package, and his erstwhile vigilance has been lulled by the steady efforts of manufacturers to build up confidence by advertising and marketing devices such as trade-marks . . . .

. . . Consumers no longer approach products warily but accept them on faith, relying on the reputation of the manufacturer or the trade mark.

These policies can be summarized as a shift from a balanced playing field (negligence) to one favoring injured consumers. However, the strict liability foreshadowed by Traynor was not adopted until 1962 when he wrote the majority opinion in *Greenman v. Yuba Power Products*, basing the doctrine on the policies earlier stated in *Escola*. The American Law Institute quickly followed Traynor's lead and in 1964 adopted strict liability in Section 402A of the *Restatement (Second) of Torts*. From 1964 to 1980 almost all states adopted a strict liability cause of action for defective products. This wave of adoption was the most rapid and dramatic expansion in consumer protection in over five hundred years. Corporate America was bloodied, but not knocked out by these expansions in liability.

The wake-up call for product consumers was the adoption in 1980 and proliferation of the statute of repose. This was followed by numerous reforms in tort theory and civil procedure that eventually reduced both the plaintiff's chances of winning and the size of the settlement or verdict.

The unique focus of the book will be first to argue that civil justice no longer rests on historic foundations such as fairness and impartiality, but has shifted to power and influence. Reform in the law, both legislative and judicial, is today driven by financial interests—not precedent or a neutral desire for fairness or to "make it better." Second, the book will examine the role of persuasive agencies, such as the American Law Institute, in reforming and shaping civil justice. Never has it been less true that we live under the rule of law. Congress and the courts make the law, but they are driven by those who have a large financial stake in the game.

The medium for the story presented will be reality in fact—not theory and not philosophy. Examples used to make points will be taken from both actual cases and enacted legislation. The following six chapters will consider these concepts: First, Chapter 4 will explore the development of civil liability from 1466 to 1916. The earliest reported torts case is *Anonymous* in 1466. It appears to rest on absolute liability as it reasons:

At your request I accompany you when you are about your own affairs; my enemies fall upon and kill me, you must pay for my death. You take me to see a wild beast show or that interesting spectacle, a mad man; beast or mad man kills me; you must pay. You hang up your sword; someone else knocks it down so that it cuts me; you must pay. In none of these cases can you honestly swear that you did nothing that helped to bring about death or wound.

Up to 1850, there are few reported torts cases. The most important one, *Weaver v. Ward* (1616), seemed to be stating settled law when it held that if the defendant causes direct injury, he is liable, but if the defendant causes an indirect injury, the plaintiff has the burden of showing negligence.

A foundational case in torts is *Brown v. Kendall* (1850). The facts are trivial, but the holding is enormously important. The defendant was trying to separate dogs by beating them with a stick. While backing up, he hit the plaintiff in the eye. The judge rejected 384 years of settled law by holding:

> In these discussions, it is frequently stated by judges, that when one receives injury from the direct act of another, trespass will lie. But we think this is said in reference to the question whether trespass and not case will lie, assuming that the facts are such that some action will lie. These *dicta* are no authority, we think, for holding, that damage received by a direct act of force from another will be sufficient to maintain an action of trespass, whether the act was lawful or unlawful, and neither willful, intentional, or careless . . . .

The judge then birthed the negligence cause of action:

> The court are of opinion that these directions were not conformable to law. If the act of hitting the plaintiff was unintentional, on the part of the defendant, . . . then the defendant was not liable, unless it was done in the want of exercise of due care, adapted to the exigency of the case, and therefore such want of due care became part of the plaintiff's case, and the burden of proof was on the plaintiff to establish it . . . .

The privity concept was adopted in *Winterbottom v. Wright* (1842), which holds that a person can only recover in a product case if that person is in a contractual relation with the defendant. But as privity often proved too harsh, the courts developed numerous "legal fictions" such as the concepts of invitation, fraud, and imminently dangerous product to allow a plaintiff not in privity to sue. However, by 1916, the list of "fictions" became unmanageable, and the New York Court of Appeals in the precedent-setting case of *MacPherson v. Buick Motors* adopted negligence as the foundation for products cases:

> We hold, then, that the principle of *Thomas v. Winchester* is not limited to poisons, explosives, and things of like nature, to things which in their normal operation are implements of destruction. If the nature of a thing is such that it is reasonably certain to place life and limb in peril when negligently made, it is then a thing of danger. Its nature gives warning of the consequences to be expected. If to the element of danger there is added knowledge that the

thing will be used by persons other than the purchaser, and used without new tests, then irrespective of contract, the manufacturer of this thing of danger is under a duty to make it carefully. That is as far as we are required to go for the decision of this case . . . . We are dealing now with the liability of the manufacturer of the finished product, who puts it on the market to be used without inspection by his customers. If he is negligent, where danger is to be foreseen, liability will follow.

Chapters 2 and 3 deal with the explosion in strict liability from 1916 to 1980. When the courts found negligence to be awkward, expensive, and ineffective as applied to products cases, they adopted the concept of strict liability, which holds the seller liable for a defective product even if the injured consumer cannot show negligence. Strict liability was adopted by case law in California in *Greenman v. Yuba Power Products* (1962); in 1964, it became the core of Section 402(A) of the *Restatement (Second) of Torts*.

However, this explosive expansion of products liability over a mere eighteen years peaked in 1980. The shot fired over the bow of the consumers' ship took the form of a complex defense concept: the statute of repose. The first such act was adopted in 1980, holding that a cause of action fails if the injury occurs more than ten years after the sale of the product. This should have been a warning to consumers that their 580 year march to the courthouse had hit a large pothole.

Chapter 4 discusses the legal reforms emanating from the corporate boardroom from 1980 to the present. Beginning around 1980, corporate America realized damage awards and lawsuits had become a cost of production: if they could be diminished, profits would increase. Because most tort cases begin in the state courts, lobbyists worked the state legislatures to develop laws favorable to their clients' financial interests. The reform measures adopted in the courts and legislatures from 1980 to the present include expanded preemption, elimination of joint and several liability, reduction in punitive damages, severe requirements for qualifying witnesses as experts, reduced availability of class actions, and caps on noneconomic damages—along with Section 2(b) of the *Restatement (Third) of Torts: Products Liability*.

Corporate lobbyists working through the state legislatures played a well-recognized tune, but the attack did not stop with the legislatures. The corporate attorneys were creative and insightful in realizing the American Law Institute was a respected voice in American justice—and one ripe for the picking. This new and important beachhead was essential to rewriting the law of products liability (the most financially important tort) in Section 2(b) of the *Restatement (Third) of Torts* (1997).

Chapter 5 indicates how corporations write the law. The theme of this chapter is that in those areas where corporations have an interest (always true with products), they determine the law. This point will be illustrated with three socially important examples: tobacco, gun policy, and SUV roll-over indexes.

Tobacco Litigation: For approximately fifty years, tobacco manufacturers were able to brag they had never paid a penny in damages for cancer caused by smoking. The statement was true. But then the states sued them for damages caused to the states. In 1996 a settlement was reached in which the tobacco manufacturers agreed to pay $206 billion to the states.

Immediately after the settlement, Congress authorized substantial payments to assist beleaguered tobacco farmers. Today, it remains legal to manufacture and sell tobacco, which kills over 400,000 Americans per year.

Gun Policy: To quash the numerous suits brought by states, survivors, and victims of shootings, Congress passed a bill immunizing the manufacturers and sellers of handguns. This directly benefited the gun industry while preventing the states and injured victims from obtaining justice. Whatever gun manufacturers might be able to do to make handguns safer is now blocked from view even though today, guns are used in the killing of approximately 18,000 people each year. However, the Second Amendment has never been interpreted to hold the manufacturers of defective guns cannot be sued or that the sale of guns cannot be regulated.

Sport Utility Rollover Index: Because SUVs have a center of gravity higher than a car's, they tend to roll over with disastrous results. Some SUVs also have a higher center of gravity than others and roll over more easily. This rollover tendency is a matter of math and physics, so it would be a relatively simple task to develop an index showing the relative likelihood of each SUV to rollover . Such an index would help consumers decide whether to purchase a high-index SUV. But manufacturers realized that if consumers knew the risk, they might not purchase an SUV. Unsurprisingly then, the National Highway Traffic Safety Administration (NHTSA) rejected the rollover index proposal.

In these frequent rollovers, numerous SUVs also have a tendency for their roofs to collapse, often causing death. NHTSA adopted a meaningless roof-crush standard (proposed by the industry) that does little to protect passengers. The point of this chapter is to show that when corporate or financial interests are at stake, legislation or regulation will strongly tend to protect those interests.

Chapter 6 extends what we have learned. It takes the arguments of the preceding chapters and apply them to contemporary events. For example, it will consider what the book has to say in regard to the bailouts of Wall Street, the banks, Chrysler, and General Motors along with regulatory failures.

1. THE DEVELOPMENT OF CIVIL LIABILITY
1466–1916

Civil causes of action that are commonly known as torts began to develop from 1400 to 1850. The first lesson to be learned in examining the history of civil liability is to recognize the enormous disagreement concerning the reliability of the available evidence and the conclusions that can be drawn from it. However, this chapter will make clear substantial agreement exists on two points: first, the foundation of tort law is absolute liability, not negligence, and second, strict liability has been expanding since approximately 1850.

A. THE PERIOD 1400–1850

The key element of the civil law of antiquity was that if the plaintiff was able to show causation in fact, the defendant was absolutely liable. Negligence or fault was not an issue:

> At your request I accompany you when you are about your own affairs; my enemies fall upon and kill me, you must pay for my death. You take me to see a wild beast show or that interesting spectacle, a mad man; beast or mad man kills me; you must pay. You hang up your sword; someone else knocks it down so that it cuts me; you must pay. In none of these cases can you honestly swear that you did nothing that helped to bring about death or wound.[1]

This short statement constitutes a summary of civil (tort) law up to the year 1300.[2]

Although court reports begin to become available from 1300 through 1850, there is substantial disagreement over their legal import. Little can be said about personal injury law before 1800 because there are only a few reported cases: "The meager quality of the English and American evidence counsels caution in making any dramatic assertions about pre-nineteenth century tort doctrine."[3] In discussing research into personal injury laws of this period, Professor Fifoot states: "To ransack the Year Books for large statements of doctrine made in

---

1. Wex S. Malone, *Ruminations on the Role of Fault in the History of the Common Law of Torts*, 31 LA. L. REV. 1, 3 (1970).

2. *Id.* at 9.

3. Gary T. Schwartz, *Tort Law and the Economy in Nineteenth-Century America: A Reinterpretation*, 90 YALE L.J. 1717, 1722 (1981).

irrelevant circumstances by judges barely conscious of their significance is neither a pleasing nor a profitable task."[4]

An argument can be made that prior to 1850, there was no liability. Professor
Rabin states: "[T]he focus on a dominant tension between strict liability and fault
seems misplaced. To the contrary, I will argue that fault liability emerged out of
a world-view dominated largely by no-liability thinking."[5] There are several reasons for this suggestion that no liability existed before 1850:

> Throughout the "heyday of negligence," the common law courts wrestled
> with issues that forced a choice between powerful no-liability principles and a
> fledgling doctrine of fault liability. Gradually the no-liability principles-immu-
> nities, privileges, and no-duty consideration imported from other conceptual
> systems (property, contract and such)—retreated, like a melting glacier in a
> hostile environment, before the successive onslaughts of fault and, later strict
> liability rules.[6]

Professor Rabin's theme is that industrialization forced an expansion of
liability:

> [I]n this period of rapid modernization, industrial growth and the fault
> principle typically worked in combination to *expand* liability rather than to
> limit it . . . .
>
> Viewed against a parsimonious early common law, then, it is the steadily
> growing compensatory influence of the fault principle, rather than its insulat-
> ing effect, that emerges as the notable characteristic of industrialization.[7]

Prosser's view is that strict liability reigned before 1850. In this period, the
remedies for wrongs depended upon the issuance of writs. There were two principal writs: trespass, and trespass on the case.

> Writs in trespass were confined to forceable acts in breach of the King's peace.
> The writ of trespass on the case developed out of a practice of applying to the
> Chancellor, in cases where no writ could be found in the Registrar to cover
> the plaintiff's claim, for a special writ, in the nature of trespass, drawn to fit
> the particular case. . . .
>
> [I]n its earlier stages trespass was identified with the view that liability
> might be imposed without regard to the defendant's fault.[8]

---

4. CECIL HERBERT STUART FIFOOT, HISTORY AND SOURCES OF THE COMMON LAW: TORT AND
CONTRACT 189 (1949).

5. ROBERT L. RABIN, PERSPECTIVES ON TORT LAW 44 (2d ed. 1983).

6. *Id.* at 68.

7. *Id.* at 69.

8. WILLIAM LLOYD PROSSER, JOHN W. WADE, & VICTOR E. SCHWARTZ, CASES AND MATERIALS
ON TORTS 2–3 (6th ed. 1976).

Professor Malone's theory is that liability up to about 1800 was absolute: "The imposition of virtual no-fault liability in both Trespass and Trespass on the Case in England continuously throughout the Middle Ages and, in fact, up until the nineteenth century . . . reflected the ethical, social and economic needs of the times. . . ."[9] The absolute liability theory was first recorded in the 1466 case of *Anonymous*, [10] in which the judge concluded, "In my opinion if a man does a thing he is bound to do it in such a manner that by his deed no injury or damage is inflicted upon others."[11]

It was the mid-1800s before the modern concept of negligence emerged. Before that time, it meant merely a breach of duty or custom: "It is conceded everywhere that negligence, meaning a failure to use the care of a reasonable prudent man, is a much later development. This mythical creature did not make its appearance in English tort law until the nineteenth century was well underway."[12]

Fault was not mentioned until the case of *Weaver v. Ward* in 1617.[13] While the plaintiff and the defendant were skirmishing in a military exercise, the defendant fired his rifle and injured the plaintiff. The defendant was held liable in trespass, but the court stated: "[N]o man shall be excused of a trespass . . . except it may be judged utterly without his fault."[14] It must be noted, however, that "for nearly three hundred years after the case was decided we do not find a single English decision in which a defendant charged with accidental shooting manages to escape liability through the loopholes of *Weaver v. Ward*—'utterly without his fault'. . . ."[15]

B. THE PERIOD 1850–1916

From 1850 through 1900 there was an emergence of negligence as well as a continued growth in strict liability doctrines. These important legal developments were spawned by the Industrial Revolution.

Brown v. Kendall (1850)[16] is the foundational case in the development of negligence theory. It involved a man separating fighting dogs by beating them with a stick. He backed up while doing so and hit the plaintiff in the eye. The court rejected the trespass action and made new law by holding that to win, the plaintiff must show either negligence or intent. Thus, the plaintiff's trespass

---

9. Malone, *supra* note 1, at 24.

10. Anonymous, Y.B. 5 Edw. 4, fol. 7, pl. 18 (K.B. 1466).

11. *Id.*

12. Malone, *supra* note 1, at 18.

13. Weaver v. Ward (1617) Hobart 134, 80 Eng. Rep. 284 (K.B.).

14. *Id.*

15. Malone, *supra* note 1, at 18–19.

16. 60 Mass. (6 Cusn.) 292 (1850).

argument resting on strict liability failed. *Brown v. Kendall* is a unique case for several reasons. First, the facts are too weak to support a theory that was ostensibly developed to protect industry. Plain and simple, it was a dog-fight case involving injury to a third party, not a suit against an industry such as a railroad or manufacturer. *Brown v. Kendall* was also wrong in regard to the law at that time. Judge Shaw rejected the plaintiff's contention that he could win in trespass (because the essence of an action in trespass was strict liability):

> In these discussions, it is frequently stated by judges, that when one receives injury from the direct act of another, trespass will lie. But we think this is said in reference to the question, whether trespass and not case will lie, assuming that the facts are such, that some action will lie. These *dicta* are no authority, we think, for holding that damage received by a direct act of force from another will be sufficient to maintain an action of trespass, whether the action was lawful or unlawful, and neither willful, intentional, or careless.[17]

The law before 1850 was the opposite of what Judge Shaw stated it to be. Shaw's cavalier statement of the law has been criticized:

> To be sure, Shaw was correct in pointing out that many of the cases decided during the preceding century involved merely the question of whether or not the plaintiff had properly sued in trespass or in case as a purely procedural matter. But he did not mention the older precedents which indicated that an unintended but harmful contact . . . was actionable trespass in itself.[18]

The *Brown v. Kendall* decision is sometimes explained as having been decided in order to subsidize the newly developing industries in the United States. That rationalization is never mentioned in the case, however. The subsidy theory is described as follows: "[A] consistent theory of liability based on fault was developed to confer on industrial enterprise an immunity from liability for accidental harm to others. Apparently, the idea was to tax enterprise with the cost of only those damages avoidably caused."[19] Professor Horwitz is more forceful in arguing for a subsidy basis of negligence:

> [Common] law doctrines appeared to present a major cost barrier to social change. . . . In an undeveloped nation with little surplus capital, elimination or reduction of damage judgments created a new source of forced investment, as landowners whose property values were impaired without compensation in effect were compelled to underwrite a portion of economic development. . . .

---

17. *Id.* at 295.
18. Charles O. Gregory, *Trespass to Negligence to Absolute Liability*, 37 Va. L. Rev. 359, 366 (1951).
19. *Id.* at 382.

Under the pressure of damage judgments, American courts before the Civil War began to change legal rules in order to subsidize the activities of great works of public improvement [such as] . . . "factories, machinery, dams, canals and railroads."[20]

However, the subsidy theory has not been accepted by everyone. Professor Gary Schwartz read every nineteenth-century personal injury case in two states and concluded: "[T]he New Hampshire and California case law resists the claim that the nineteenth century negligence system can properly be characterized or disparaged as an industrial subsidy."[21] He found the "New Hampshire Supreme Court held railroads liable to passengers for 'even the smallest neglect.' If a railroad car derailed, the California Supreme Court declared a presumption of negligence on the railroad's part. . . ."[22] In New Hampshire the subsidy theory lacked any basis in fact: "There were no suits brought by any injured employees against their employers, and no tort claims of any sort brought against the textile factories. . . . With respect to the textile industry, therefore, the tort law subsidy thesis is not so much false as irrelevant."[23]

In apparent disregard of the subsidy theory, both strict liability and negligence expanded after 1850 with the two doctrines growing together. The 1849 New York case of *Hay v. Cohoes Co.*[24] was an influential early American decision. While involved in construction on his own land, the defendant set off a substantial explosion, and the plaintiff's house was damaged by flying fragments of stone and debris. Clearly the physical invasion of the plaintiff's property was not intentional, and there was no evidence of negligence in setting off the blast. However, the highest court in New York held the plaintiff should nonetheless recover. In evaluating *Hay v. Cohoes*, Professor Gregory concluded: "A fair reading of the opinion shows that the defendant was held liable on some . . . notion of absolute liability. . . ."[25] New York recently reaffirmed the decision in *Hay v. Cohoes*: "[C]ases in our own court . . . had held . . . that a party was absolutely liable for damages to neighboring property caused by explosions."[26]

In 1866 the keystone strict liability case of *Rylands v. Fletcher*[27] was decided. The defendants, owners of a mill, had a reservoir constructed on nearby land. When the reservoir was being filled, the water leaked into connecting

---

20. MORTON J. HORWITZ, THE TRANSFORMATION OF AMERICAN LAW, 1780–1860, at 70–71 (1977) (*quoting* Losee v. Buchanan, 51 N.Y. 476, 484 (1873)).

21. Schwartz, *supra* note 3, at 1773.

22. *Id.* at 1743.

23. *Id.* at 1737.

24. 2 N.Y. 159 (1849).

25. Gregory, *supra* note 18, at 371.

26. Spano v. Perini Corp., 250 N.E. 2d 31, 33 (N.Y. 1969).

27. (1865) 3 H. & C. 774 (Ex.), *rev'd*, [1866] L.R. 1 Exch. 265, *aff'd*, [1868] L.R. 3 H.L. 330.

passageways and flowed into the plaintiff's nearby coal mines. The defendant was not at fault based on negligence because he had hired an independent contractor to build the reservoir. Therefore, the plaintiff brought an action in strict liability. The court held:

> We think that the true rule of law is, that the person who for his own purposes brings on his lands and collects and keeps there anything likely to do mischief if it escapes, must keep it in at his peril, and, if he does not do so, is prima facie answerable for all the damage which is the natural consequence of its escape.[28]

Although *Rylands v. Fletcher* was at first rejected in the United States, it has been gradually accepted.[29] Over more than one hundred years it has been applied to a diverse set of facts, including drilling for natural gas and overflowing sludge ponds.[30]

From 1850 to 1900 the United States saw a growth in negligence along with the continued expansion of strict liability. It also witnessed the deciding of the famous case of *Rylands v. Fletcher* and the twisting and molding of negligence to accomplish strict liability. The railroads played an important role in the development of tort law by providing two essential ingredients: injuries, and a party with enough assets to be worth suing. During this period the railroads crisscrossed the country, breaking, burning, and killing as they went. Industries, towns, injuries, and recoveries all grew larger: "The railway injury rate doubled between 1889 and 1906. At the turn of the century, industrial accidents were claiming about 35,000 lives a year, and inflicting close to 2,000,000 injuries."[31]

After 1900, liability expanded in favor of the injured party; this section will examine that development. Manufactured products (such as automobiles, machinery, and food) began to appear and cause injury. Products liability is the subject of the most complete and pervasive expansion in legal theory. Growth also occurred in the areas of abnormally dangerous activities, res ipsa loquitur, and negligence per se. The continued deterioration of immunity defenses has also worked to expand the liability of persons who had formerly been protected from suit.

Products liability had begun in 1837 in the case of *Langridge v. Levy*,[32] in which a father purchased a rifle for his son who was subsequently severely injured

---

28. [1866] L.R. 1 Exch. 265, 279.
29. *See* WILLIAM P. KEETON ET AL., PROSSER AND KEETON ON THE LAW OF TORTS 549 (5th ed. 1984).
30. *Id.* at 549–50.
31. LAWRENCE M. FRIEDMAN, A HISTORY OF AMERICAN LAW 422 (1973).
32. (1837) 150 Eng. Rep. 863, 864 (Ex.).

while using it. The court held the seller of the gun liable in fraud based on these facts:

> At the trial . . . it appeared that in June, 1833, the plaintiff's father saw in the shop of the defendant, a gun-maker in Bristol, a double-barrelled gun, to which was attached a ticket in these terms:—"Warranted, this elegant twist gun, by Nock, with case complete, made for his late Majesty George IV.; cost 60 guineas: only 25 guineas." He went into the shop, and saw the defendant and examined the gun. The defendant (according to Langridge's statement) said he would warrant the gun to have been made by Nock for King George IV., and that he could produce Nock's invoice. Langridge told the defendant he wanted the gun for the use of himself and his sons, and desired him to send it to his house at Knowle, about two miles from Bristol, and that they might see it tried. On the next day, accordingly, the defendant sent the gun to Langridge's house by his shopman, who also on that occasion warranted it to be made by Nock, and charged and fired it off several times. Langridge ultimately bought it of him for 24l, and paid the price down. Langridge the father and his three sons used the gun occasionally; and in the month of December following, the plaintiff, his second son, having taken the gun into a field near his father's house to shoot some birds, putting in an ordinary charge, on firing off the second barrel, it exploded and mutilated his left hand so severely as to render it necessary that it should be amputated. There was conflicting evidence as to the fact of the gun's being an insecure one, or inferior workmanship. Mr. Nock, however, proved that it was not manufactured by him. The defendant also denied that any warranty had been given. The learned Judge left the jury to say, first, whether the defendant had warranted the gun to be made by Nock, and to be a safe and secure one; secondly, whether it was in fact unsafe or of inferior materials or workmanship and exploded in consequence of being so; and thirdly, whether the defendant warranted it to be a safe gun, knowing that it was not so. The jury found a general verdict for the plaintiff. . . .[33]

Later in 1850, the concept of privity emerged.[34] In *Winterbottom v. Wright*, an injured driver of a mail coach sued the person who had a contract to repair them. In rejecting the driver's claim, the court reasoned:

> The contract in this case was made with the Postmaster-General alone. . . . If we were to hold that the plaintiff could sue in such a case, there is no point at which such actions would stop. The only safe rule is to confine the right to recover to those who enter into the contract: if we go one step beyond that, there is no reason why we should not go fifty. The only real argument in favor

---

33. *Id.*
34. Winterbottom v. Wright (1842) 152 Eng. Rep. 402, 405 (Ex.).

of the action is, that this is a case of hardship; but that might have been obviated, if the plaintiff had made himself a party to the contract. Then it is urged that it falls within the principle of the case of *Levy v. Langridge*. But the principle of that case was simply this, that the father having bought the gun for the very purpose of being used by the plaintiff, the defendant made representations by which he was induced to use it. There a distinct fraud was committed on the plaintiff; the falsehood of the representation was also alleged to have been within the knowledge of the defendant who made it, and he was properly held liable for the consequences. How are the acts of that case applicable to those of the present? Where is the allegation of misrepresentation or fraud in this declaration: It shews nothing of the kind. Our judgment must therefore be for the defendant.[35]

Privity, as developed in *Winterbottom*, meant that to bring suit, a plaintiff must be in contract with the defendant; if the person bringing the suit was not in contract, that person could not sue. However, shortly after the privity concept appeared, the courts began to develop legal fictions to skirt it.[36]

A legal fiction is a statement that something is true when, in fact, it is false.[37] In *Huset v. J.I. Case Threshing Machine Co.*, the court stated three exceptions [fictions] to the privity rule:

> The first is that an act of negligence of a manufacturer or vendor which is imminently dangerous to the life or health of mankind, and which is committed in the preparation or sale of an article intended to preserve, destroy, or affect human life, is actionable by third parties who suffer from the negligence. . . . The leading case upon this subject is *Thomas v. Winchester*, 6 N.Y. 397, 57 Am.Dec. 455. . . . In all these cases of sale the natural and probable result of the act of negligence—nay, the inevitable result of it—was not an injury to the party to whom the sales were made, but to those who, after the purchasers had disposed of the articles, should consume them. Hence these cases stand upon two well-established principles of law: (1) That everyone is bound to avoid acts or omissions imminently dangerous to the lives of others, and (2) that an injury which is the natural and probable result of an act of negligence is actionable. It was the natural and probable result of the negligence in these cases that the vendees would not suffer, but that those who subsequently purchased the deleterious articles would sustain the injuries resulting from the negligence of the manufacturers or dealers who furnished them.

---

35. *Id.*

36. *See* Huset v. J.I. Case Threshing Mach. Co., 120 F. 865, 870 (8th Cir. 1903).

37. *See* BLACK'S LAW DICTIONARY 894 (7th ed. 1990) (defining legal fiction as a "situation contrived by the law to permit a court to dispose of a matter").

The second exception is that an owner's act of negligence which causes injury to one who is invited by him to use his defective appliance upon the owner's premises may form the basis of an action against the owner. *Coughtry v. Globe Woolen Co.*, 56 N.Y. 124, 15 Am. Rep. 387. . . .

The third exception to the rule is that one who sells or delivers an article which he knows to be imminently dangerous to life or limb to another without notice of its qualities is liable to any person who suffers an injury there from which might have been reasonably anticipated, whether there were any contractual relations between the parties or not. *Langridge v. Levy*, 2 M. & W. 519, 4 M. & W. 337. . . .[38]

These fictions included fraud, invitation, extra-hazardous or extraordinarily dangerous products, and abnormally dangerous products.[39] In *Coughtry v. Globe Woolen Co.*, the owner of a building was sued for negligently constructing a scaffold that resulted in injury to a contractor's employee; it is an example of the "invitation exception."[40] *Thomas v. Winchester*, in which a druggist sold deadly poison mislabeled "extract of dandelion,"[41] is an example of the "inherently dangerous product exception."[42] The facts of *Thomas v. Winchester* are as follows:

Action in the supreme court, commenced in August, 1849, against Winchester and Gilbert, for injuries sustained by Mrs. Thomas, from the effects of a quantity of extract of belladonna, administered to her by mistake as extract of dandelion. . . .

RUGGLES, Ch. J. delivered the opinion of the court. This is an action brought to recover damages from the defendant for negligently putting up, labeling and selling as and for the extract of *dandelion,* which is a simple and harmless medicine, a jar of the extract of *belladonna,* which is a deadly poison; by means of which the plaintiff Mary Ann Thomas, to whom, being sick, a dose of dandelion was prescribed by a physician, and a portion of the contents of the jar, was administered as and for the extract of dandelion, was greatly injured.

The facts proved were briefly these: Mrs. Thomas being in ill health, her physician prescribed for her a dose of dandelion. Her husband purchased what was believed to be the medicine prescribed, at the store of Dr. Foord, a physician and druggist in Cazenovia, Madison County, where the plaintiffs reside. . . .

The defendant was a dealer in poisonous drugs. Gilbert was his agent in preparing them for market. The death or great bodily harm of some person

---

38. *Huset,* 120 F. at 870–71.
39. *See infra* notes 40–43 and accompanying text.
40. 56 N.Y. 124 (1874).
41. 6 N.Y. 397 (1852).
42. *Id.*

was the natural and almost inevitable consequence of the sale of belladonna by means of the false label. . . .

The defendant's negligence put human life in imminent danger. Can it be said that there was no duty on the part of the defendant to avoid the creation of that danger by the exercise of greater caution?[43]

The fictions developed by the courts allowed them to avoid the concept of privity when they felt application of the fiction would accomplish justice. The impact of the fiction was that a person not in privity was nonetheless able to sue and recover against the seller of the product.[44]

The case of *MacPherson v. Buick Motor Co.* (1916)[45] is a watershed, marking the collapse of the doctrine of privity and a shift to the concept of negligence in products litigation.[46] The facts in *MacPherson* were:

The defendant is a manufacturer of automobiles. It sold an automobile to a retail dealer. The retail dealer resold to the plaintiff. While the plaintiff was in the car it suddenly collapsed. He was thrown out and injured. One of the wheels was made of defective wood, and its spokes crumbled into fragments. The wheel was not made by the defendant; it was bought from another manufacturer. There is evidence, however, that its defects could have been discovered by reasonable inspection, and that inspection was omitted. There is no claim that the defendant knew of the defect and willfully concealed it. The case, in other words, is not brought within the rule of *Kuelling v. Lean Mfg. Co.*, 183 N.Y. 78, 75 N.E. 1098, 2 L.R.A., N.S., 3030, 111 Am.St.Rep. 691, 5 Ann.Cas. 124. The charge is one, not of fraud, but of negligence. The question to be determined is whether the defendant owed a duty of care and vigilance to any one but the immediate purchaser.[47]

Cardozo wrote for the majority:

We hold, then, that the principle of *Thomas v. Winchester* is not limited to poisons, explosives, and things of like nature, to things which in their normal operation are implements of destruction. If the nature of a thing is such that it is reasonably certain to place life and limb in peril when negligently made, it is then a thing of danger. Its nature gives warning of the consequences to be expected. If to the element of danger there is added knowledge that the thing will be used by persons other than the purchaser, and used without new

---

43. *Id.* at 405–09.

44. *See* Greenman v. Yuba Power Prods., Inc., 377 P.2d 897, 900–02 (Cal. 1963).

45. 111 N.E. 1050 (N.Y. 1916).

46. *See id.* at 1051–53 (discussing concept of negligence as it relates to product liability and noting that manufacturers of dangerous products are under a duty of care to make products carefully).

47. *Id.* at 1051.

tests, then, irrespective of contract, the manufacturer of this thing of danger is under a duty to make it carefully. That is as far as we are required to go for the decision of this case. There must be knowledge of a danger, not merely possible, but probable. . . . We are dealing now with the liability of the manufacturer of the finished product, who puts it on the market to be used without inspection by his customers. If he is negligent, where danger is to be foreseen, a liability will follow.[48]

A careful reading of *MacPherson* makes clear the fictions had expanded to such an extent that they had consumed the privity rule. *MacPherson* began a new conceptual approach in products liability: a shift from the technical concept of privity and the application of legal fictions to the more expansive and flexible concept of negligence.

---

48. *Id.* at 1053–55.

2. THE DISSATISFACTION WITH NEGLIGENCE: Policies Supporting Strict Liability 1916–1980

From 1916 through 1944, the courts struggled with various theories such as negligence, fraud, express warranty, and implied warranty in products liability cases. The results were unsatisfactory because the consumers constantly lost cases they should have won. The judicial frustration with these adverse results was articulated by Justice Traynor in his concurring opinion in *Escola v. Coca-Cola* in 1944[1] in which he argued that recovery in products liability cases should rest upon absolute liability.[2] His reasons for departing from negligence theory were founded upon social policy: "[T]he risk of injury can be insured by the manufacturer and distributed among the public as a cost of doing business. It is to the public interest to discourage the marketing of products having defects that are a menace to the public."[3] However, this theory lay dormant from 1944 until 1963.

In the early 1960s, a woman purchased a Shopsmith for her husband. While he was using the lathe attachment to this product, a block of wood came loose and hit his head. This led to the foundational case of *Greenman v. Yuba Power Products* (1963)[4] in which the California Supreme Court adopted the strict liability theory suggested in *Escola*. The court held: "The purpose of such liability is to insure that the costs of injuries resulting from defective products are borne by the manufacturers that put such products on the market rather than by the injured persons who are powerless to protect themselves."[5] The trend in the reasoning and holding to the courts since *Greenman* has been to rely upon strict liability and to remove barriers to recovery in cases involving products. The courts have emphasized the social policy reasons for their decisions with one distinction: the policies emphasized have been those favoring consumer recoveries, such as loss shifting, availability of insurance, and ease of prevention.[6]

---

1. Escola v. Coca-Cola Bottling Co., 150 P.2d 436, 440 (Cal. 1944) (Traynor, J., concurring).

2. *Id.* at 440–44.

3. *Id.* at 441.

4. Greenman v. Yuba Power Prods., Inc., 59 Cal. 2d 57 (Cal. 1963).

5. *Id.* at 63. The absolute liability called for in *Escola* and the strict liability adopted in *Greenman* are the same. Cause-in-fact must be shown, and assumption of risk is a defense. The core issue in strict liability is defect. (See Chapter 3).

6. *See Greenman*, 59 Cal. 2d 57; Henningsen v. Bloomfield Motors, 32 N.J. 358 (N.J. 1960); Phillips v. Kimwood Mach. Co., 269 Or. 485, 492 n.6 (Or. 1974).

In doing so, the courts have engaged in an inquiry weighted at the beginning in favor of the consumer rather than a neutral balancing of interests. For example, in a 1978 California case,[7] *Baker v. Lull*, the court held that once the plaintiff proves the product's design proximately caused his injury, he has established a prima facie case, and the burden of proof shifts to the manufacturer to show the benefits of the existing design exceed the costs of avoiding the problem. The growth in strict liability represented in *Greenman* and *Escola*, as well as the emphasis on policies that favor the consumer, permitted Judge Guido Calabresi to conclude: "Today, in product liability, the risk is initially placed on the producer and remains there unless complex circumstances, more powerful than user fault, justify a shift in riskbearing from producer to user."[8]

From 1944 to 1972, two different products liability theories developed. One was negligence, based essentially on the reasonable-person concept. The other was strict liability, resting firmly on the theory the loss should be shifted from the injured consumer to the seller. At some point, these two conceptual frameworks had to meet. This occurred in the 1972 California case of *Cronin v. J. B. E. Olson Corp.*,[9] in which the California Supreme Court rejected the negligence line of authority and set the stage for defining defect. In the court's view, the "unreasonably dangerous" test sounded of negligence and would require the plaintiff to prove absence of reasonable care, which had been disavowed in *Greenman*. The *Cronin* court emphasized the plaintiff need only prove a "defect" and that strict liability is not negligence.[10]

Since *Cronin*, the growth of strict liability in the products area has been dramatic. For example, the action has been applied to airplanes, automobiles, leased trucks, buses, steam vaporizers, drugs, and perfume.[11] It has also been adopted in almost every state.[12] The class of plaintiffs has expanded to include donees,

---

7. Barker v. Lull Eng'g Co., 573 P. 2d 443 (Cal. 1978): "[O]nce the plaintiff makes a prima facie showing that the injury was proximately caused by the product's design, the burden should appropriately shift to the defendant to prove, in light of the relevant factors, that the product is not defective." *Id.* at 455.

8. Guido Calabresi, *Product Liability: Curse or Bulwark of Free Enterprise*, 27 CLEV. ST. L. REV. 313, 319 (1978).

9. 501 P. 2d 1153 (Cal. 1972).

10. *Id.*

11. *See* Cintrone v. Hertz Truck Leasing & Rental Serv., 212 A.2d. 769 (N.J. 1965) (leased trucks); Dreisonstok v. Volkswagenwerk, A.G., 489 F.2d 1066 (4th Cir. Va. 1974) (buses); McCormack v. Hankscraft Co., 154 N.W.2d 488 (Minn. 1967) (steam vaporizor); (Moran v. Faberge, Inc., 332 A.2d. 11 (Md. 1975) (perfume).

12. *See* John F. Vargo, *The Emperor's New Clothes: The American Law Institute Adorns a "New Cloth" for Section 402A Products Liability Design Defects—A Survey of the States Reveals a Different Weave*, 26 U. MEM, L. REV. 493 (1996) (Part III provides a survey of the various states' strict liability laws).

third parties, and bystanders.[13] The class of defendants has also expanded enormously to include sellers, retailers, wholesalers, manufacturers, and component-part suppliers.[14] In short, there is neither a product nor a seller who is clearly beyond the reach of a strict liability action.[15]

The provisions of the *Restatement (Second) of Torts*, Section 402A [strict liability] have become the core of the products liability expansion. In 1992, Professors Henderson and Twerski stated:

> Only rarely do provisions of the American Law Institute's Restatements of the Law rise to the dignity of holy writ. Even more rarely do individual comments to Restatement sections come to symbolize important, decisive developments that dominate judicial thinking. Nevertheless, Section 402A of the *Restatement (Second) of Torts* is such a provision. Literally thousands upon thousands of products liability decisions in the past twenty-five years have explicitly referred to, and come to grips with, that section.
>
> Among products liability followers one need only identify an issue as presenting "a comment *k* problem," to capture instantly the essence of the relevant debate and incorporate nearly thirty years of legal controversy, development and refinement.
>
> [S]ection 402A has achieved the status of sacred scripture. . .[16]

The next two sections (addressing abnormally dangerous activities and res ipsa loquitur) deal with legal concepts that adopt or mirror strict liability. They are presented to give a full treatment of the strict liability concept.

A. ABNORMALLY DANGEROUS ACTIVITIES

Strict liability for abnormally dangerous activities involving land has also expanded, growing from cases involving fire and trespassing animals to cockroach extermination, blasting, pile driving, crop dusting, and aviation ground damage. In a suit against the Cities Service Company, strict liability was also applied to the escape of phosphate slime from a sludge pond.[17]

---

13. *See* Frank J. Vandall, *"Design Defect" in Products Liability: Rethinking Negligence and Strict Liability*, 43 Ohio St. L.J. 61, 77 (1982). *See also* Restatement (Second) of Torts § 402A, note O.

14. *See* Restatement (Second) of Torts § 402A, Comment f.

15. However, Congress has protected gun manufacturers from certain suits. S. 1805, Protection of Lawful Commerce in Arms Act (2003).

16. James A. Henderson & Aaron D. Twerski, *A Proposed Revision of Section 402A of the Restatement (Second) of Torts*, 77 Cornell L. Rev. 1512, 1512 (1992).

17. Cities Serv. Co. v. State, 312 So. 2d 799 (Fla. Dist. Ct. App. 2d Dist. 1975).

The theory underlying abnormally dangerous activities has been refined: now it is clear the reason for strict liability is to shift the loss to the injurer: "The question, in other words, was not *whether* it was lawful or proper to engage in blasting but *who* should bear the cost of any resulting damage—the person who engaged in the dangerous activity or the innocent neighbor injured thereby."[18]

The theory of abnormally dangerous activity had been applied to the manufacturer of a "Saturday night special" firearm. In the case of *Richman v. Charter Arms Corp.*,[19] a person used a handgun to rob, rape, and murder a third-year medical student. The trial court held the manufacturer could be liable to the parents of the decedent on the basis the manufacture and sale of Saturday night specials was an abnormally dangerous activity.[20] However, the case was reversed on appeal,[21] with the appellate court reasoning the theory of abnormally dangerous activities must be limited to torts involving the use of land. Blasting is the classic example of an abnormally dangerous activity.[22]

B. RES IPSA LOQUITUR

Elements of strict liability are contained within the doctrine of res ipsa loquitur, whose theory is that the event itself speaks of the defendant's negligence. Plaintiffs can take their case to the jury if they present circumstantial evidence from which the jury may infer the defendant was negligent. Res ipsa is applied when the court feels the plaintiff should recover, but the court is not ready to embrace the doctrine of strict liability. Res ipsa, then, is strict liability in negligence clothing.[23] From the time a barrel of flour fell from a window above a shop in 1863, res ipsa has been applied to a missing airplane (1967),[24] a car that left the road and struck a culvert (1967),[25] and most dramatically to a team of doctors and nurses who insisted they knew nothing about an injury to an

---

18. Spano v. Perini Corp., 25 N.Y. 2d 11 (N.Y. 1969).

19. 571 F. Supp. 192 (E.D. La. 1983).

20. *Id.* at 209.

21. Perkins v. F. I. E. Corp., 762 F. 2d 1250 (5th Cir. 1985).

22. *See* Vandall, *supra* note 13, at 70. ("Evidently the goal of the Restatement reporter, in drafting section 520, was to limit the scope of strict liability essentially to blasting cases. That is, the danger from very few activities (blasting, nuclear power) cannot be eliminated through reasonable care.")

23. *See* Charles O. Gregory, *Trespass to Negligence to Absolute Liability*, 37 Va. L. Rev. 359, 383 (1951).

24. Cox v. Northwest Airlines, Inc., 379 F. 2d 893 (7th Cir. 1967), *cert. denied*, 389 U.S. 1044 (1968).

25. Johnson v. Foster, 202 So.2d 520 (Miss. 1967).

anesthetized patient (1944).[26] In the products area, res ipsa has also been applied to an exploding bottle of soda.[27]

Historical analysis makes clear that personal injury law rests upon a foundation of absolute liability, and that since 1900 the development of legal theory in dealing with products has been toward strict liability and away from negligence. If there is a debate as to theory, it is narrow and extends to the reliability of fragmentary case law before 1850. This debate does not affect the conclusion that feudal law rested upon absolute liability and that since the beginning of the twentieth century, doctrinal growth has been in the area of strict liability. This is especially accurate in the area of products liability law. Historically, then, the importance of negligence has been overstated, and the foundational role of strict liability is clear.

C. THE LAW'S DISSATISFACTION IN REGARD TO THE THEORY FOR RESOLVING PRODUCTS CASES

The reasons courts have adopted strict liability fall under four headings. First, the judges were frustrated with the results under commercial law. Second, the courts concluded the results under negligence were unjust. Third, at the same time, the courts were developing specific policy reasons for favoring strict liability. Fourth (although this was not a conscious goal), the courts developed strict liability to provide medical assistance in the absence of uniform health care.

1. Dissatisfaction with Commercial Law

The commercial law's express and implied warranties, disclaimers, limitations, and notice requirements[28] were found to leave the consumer without a recovery in a very large number of cases. For example, Professor James stated: "Warranty is a case in point. This was fashioned to serve commercial needs in a commercial context, and however well or ill adapted it is to that end today, its technicalities and limitation reflect those needs. If it occasionally happens to fit the needs of accident law, that is pure coincidence."[29]

One of the main issues in *Greenman v. Yuba Power Products* was whether the notice provision of the Uniform Commercial Code was controlling. That is, must the plaintiff give notice to the defendant of his intent to sue within a set period

---

26. Ybarra v. Spangard, 154 P.2d 687 (Cal. 1944).

27. Escola v. Coca-Cola Bottling Co., 150 P.2d 436, 436 (Cal. 1944) (Traynor, J., concurring)

28. *See, e.g.,* Greenman v. Yuba Power Prods., Inc., 59 Cal. 2d 57 (Cal. 1963).

29. Fleming James Jr., *Products Liability* (pt. 2), 34 Tex L. Rev. 192, 227–28 (1955).

of time?[30] In rejecting the notice requirement, the California Supreme Court stated:

> The notice requirement of Section 1769 . . . is not an appropriate one for the court to adopt in actions by injured consumers against manufacturers with whom they have not dealt. . . . "As between the immediate parties to the sale [the notice requirement] is a sound commercial rule, designed to protect the seller against unduly delayed claims for damages. As applied to personal injuries, and notice to a remote seller, it becomes a booby-trap for the unwary. The injured consumer is seldom 'steeped in the business practice which justifies the rule. . . .' [I]t will not occur to him to give notice to one with whom he has no dealings." . . . We conclude, therefore, that even if plaintiff did not give timely notice of breach of warranty to the manufacturer, his cause of action based on the representations contained in the brochure was not barred.[31]

In a much-quoted statement the *Greenman* court further held: "The remedies of injured consumers ought not to be made to depend upon the intricacies of the law of sales."[32]

The American Law Institute stated, in a comment to Section 402A of the *Restatement (Second) of Torts*, that strict liability is separate and apart from the provisions of the Uniform Commercial Code and the Sales Act:

> The rule stated in this Section is not governed by the provisions of the Uniform Sales Act, or those of the Uniform Commercial Code as to warranty; and it is not affected by limitations on the scope and content of warranties, or by limitation to "buyer" and "seller" in those statutes. Nor is the consumer required to give notice to the seller of his injury within a reasonable time after it occurs, as is provided by the Uniform Act. The consumer's cause of action does not depend upon the validity of his contract with the person from whom he acquires the product, and it is not affected by any disclaimer or other agreement, whether it be between the seller and his immediate buyer, or attached to and accompanying the product into the consumer's hands.[33]

Prosser indicated that reliance upon the term *warranty* was the root of the problem with the Uniform Commercial Code:

> Although the writer was perhaps the first to voice it, the suggestion was sufficiently obvious that all of the trouble lay with the one word "warranty". . . . Why not, then, talk of the strict liability in tort, a thing familiar enough in the law of animals, abnormally dangerous activities, nuisance, workman's

---

30. *Greenman*, 59 Cal. 2d 57.
31. *Id.* at 62.
32. *Id.* at 64.
33. RESTATEMENT (SECOND) OF TORTS § 402A (1965).

compensation, libel, misrepresentations, and respondeat superior, and discard the word "warranty" with all its contract implications?[34]

2. Negligence Leads to Unjust Results

In an early products case, *Escola v. Coca-Cola*[35] (1944), Judge Traynor in his concurring opinion argued for the adoption of absolute liability against manufacturers in his concurring opinion. This was because cases that should have been won were being lost by injured consumers. However, this call-to-arms was not to be met with action in California until *Greenman v. Yuba Power Products* (1963).[36] In that case California adopted strict liability against manufacturers of products, but rejected Traynor's phrase "absolute liability."

After *Greenman*, the American Law Institute adopted Section 402(a) of the Restatement (1965). This is perhaps the most widely adopted statement of strict liability, which provides: "One who sells any product in a defective condition unreasonably dangerous to the user or consumer or to his property is subject to liability for physical harm thereby caused to the ultimate user or consumer. . . ."[37] This language created the threshold problem of whether a product must be defective, unreasonably dangerous, or both defective and unreasonably dangerous. What, for example, is the difference between *defect* and *unreasonably dangerous?*

This semantic battle raises the question of how the phrase "unreasonably dangerous" happened to appear in the *Restatement (Second)* Section 402A provision of strict liability. The explanation is that when Professor Prosser drafted Section 402A, he suggested the words "unreasonably dangerous" as the test for strict liability.[38] The word "defect" was added later to the Restatement draft to show that something must be wrong with the product.[39] To clarify, the drafters of the Restatement never intended for liability to apply to manufacturers of whiskey, cigarettes, or butter.[40] Although these are dangerous products, it could be argued there is nothing "wrong" with them in that they function as intended.

Cronin v. J. B. E. Olson Corp. (1972) faced squarely the question of whether a product must be both defective and unreasonably dangerous.[41] The California

---

34. William L. Prosser, *The Fall of the Citadel (Strict Liability to the Consumer)*, 50 MINN. L. REV. 802 (1966).

35. Escola v. Coca-Cola Bottling Co., 150 P.2d 436, 436 (Cal. 1944) (Traynor, J., concurring).

36. Greenman v. Yuba Power Prods., Inc., 59 Cal. 2d 57 (Cal. 1963).

37. RESTATEMENT (SECOND) OF TORTS § 402A (1965).

38. 38 ALI PROCEEDINGS 87–88 (1961).

39. *Id.*

40. *Id.*

41. 501 P. 2d 1153 (Cal. 1972).

Supreme Court held the plaintiff must only prove the product is defective, not that it is also unreasonably dangerous. The court reasoned:

> The result of the [unreasonably dangerous] limitation . . . has burdened the injured plaintiff with proof of an element which rings of negligence. . . . [I]t has been observed that the Restatement formulation of strict liability in practice rarely leads to a different conclusion than would have been reached under laws of negligence. . . .[42]

The court went on to firmly reject the unreasonably dangerous requirement of the *Restatement (Second)* Section 402A:

> Of particular concern is the susceptibility of Restatement section 402A to a literal reading which will require the finder of fact to conclude that the product is, first, defective and, second, unreasonably dangerous. . . . A bifurcated standard is of necessity more difficult to prove than a unitary one. . . . We think that a requirement that a plaintiff also prove that the defect made the product "unreasonably dangerous" places upon him a significant increased burden and represents a step backward in the area pioneered by this court.[43]

In short, the *Cronin* court felt the "unreasonably dangerous" phrase smacked of negligence, which would create an inappropriate burden on the plaintiff. The *Cronin* case makes it clear that with strict liability, the courts are trying to distance themselves from negligence and to favor the consumer, while at the same time reducing the consumer's burden of proof. The scales were being tilted in the consumer's favor.

3. Specific Policy Reasons for Strict Liability

The policies that have been adopted by the courts in holding manufacturers and sellers of products strictly liable to consumers are fundamental and far-reaching. The following is an analysis of the seven arguments supporting the adoption and expansion of strict liability.

a. Loss Shifting The theory behind loss shifting is that the seller is ordinarily in a better position than the consumer to cover the damages.[44] The seller can raise the price of the goods to cover the damages, and the costs of the damages will therefore be spread among the various consumers. One response on the part of the sellers to the loss-shifting argument is that it will put them out of business. However, if strict liability is adopted widely, after a period of time all sellers will be subject to it, and no seller will have an advantage over another. That is, in the short run, it may be true the first seller subjected to a large judgment based

---

42. *Id.*

43. *Id.*

44. Escola v. Coca-Cola Bottling Co., 150 P.2d 436 (Cal. 1944) (Traynor, J., concurring).

on strict liability will be at a disadvantage, but after its competitors are also subject to damage suits based on strict liability, their advantage will be eliminated. The point of loss shifting, then, is that the seller is better able to bear the loss than the innocent consumer and, after a period of time, will be able to pass the loss on to consumers in the form of higher prices.[45]

It is also true, however, that if a seller is unable to bear the damages and must go out of business, other sellers who exercise more care will absorb the market abandoned by the defendant. In this way, loss shifting will encourage sellers to study and implement safety requirements.[46]

The concept of elasticity of the demand curve should also be considered at this point. Elasticity manifests how responsive the amount demanded is to a change in price.[47] If the demand for a product is very elastic, a small increase in price will lead to a substantial loss of total revenue. On the other hand, if the demand for a product is inelastic, a small increase in price will lead to only a parallel small loss in total revenue. The point is the impact of an increase in the price of a product brought on by the adoption of strict liability will depend upon the elasticity of the demand curve the manufacturer or seller faces.

b. Safety The second reason for subjecting sellers to strict liability is to protect human life and health.[48] The theory is that if the sellers are held strictly liable, they will exercise a high degree of care in order to avoid injury and damage suits, because for those subject to a large number of suits, the price of their products will soon rise and they will no longer be able to compete. Another way of saying this is that sellers who exercise care will not likely be subject to suit and, therefore, will be able to charge lower prices and obtain more business. In this way, strict liability encourages safety and protects the health of the consumer.

c. Superior Knowledge One of the key reasons for holding sellers strictly liable is they have knowledge of the defect and are treated by the law as experts. The courts have suggested that because of superior knowledge on the part of the product manufacturer, it makes sense to hold the manufacturer liable as compared to the uninformed consumer.[49]

In a market where both the seller and the consumer have perfect knowledge, this argument would have little weight. But in the real world, consumers often know very little about the safety of their purchases. Thus, superior knowledge is a strong argument for holding sellers strictly liable. For example, the young man who was severely burned in the Pinto crash had no idea he was riding in a car

---

45. A. MITCHELL POLINSKY, AN INTRODUCTION TO LAW AND ECONOMICS 98 (1983).

46. *Id.*

47. PAUL A. SAMUELSON, ECONOMICS 353 (11th ed. 1980).

48. *See Escola,* 150 P.2d 436, *infra,* note 54.

49. *See* Borel v. Fiberboard Paper Prods., 493 F.2d 1076 (5th Cir. 1973), *cert. denied,* 419 U.S. 869 (1974).

that would explode if hit from behind.[50] The same can be said of the teenage girls burned to death in the Indiana Pinto accident.[51] Also, the parents who placed a steam vaporizer on a chair had no knowledge the water inside the vaporizer would become super-heated and scald their young child[52] when the child apparently tripped and fell into the chair while walking to the bathroom in the middle of the night. Finally, few automobile purchasers realize some car roofs are likely to collapse in a rollover crash.[53]

d. Insurance Because of the availability of insurance, the courts have held it makes more sense to place the loss on the manufacturer or seller rather than the innocent consumer.[54] Judge Traynor stated in *Escola v. Coca-Cola:* "The cost of an injury and the loss of time or health may be an overwhelming misfortune to the person injured, and a needless one, for the risk of injury can be insured by the manufacturer and distributed among the public as a cost of doing business."[55]

e. Economic Analysis of Strict Liability If it is accurate to suggest economics rely on the functioning of the market, it is valid to argue the prices upon which the market depends must reflect all of the costs,[56] one of which is damages. That is, if the damages caused by a product are not reflected in the price, the product will be underpriced and too much of it will be consumed.

From an economic point of view, negligence results in the product being underpriced and leads to overconsumption.[57] For example, if a ten-speed bicycle costs $200, a certain number of ten-speed bicycles will be purchased. However, if that price were to reflect all of the injuries caused by ten-speed bicycles, the price would be higher, perhaps $225 or $230. The theory is that if the bicycle were priced to reflect the actual damages caused, the socially correct number of bicycles would be purchased and the market would function efficiently.[58] Another way to say this is that with bicycles priced at $200, too many are consumed, with strict liability adjusting the price upward so the correct number of bicycles will be purchased.

Professor Polinsky summarizes the economic argument in favor of strict liability and against negligence as follows: "In essence, the rule of strict liability

---

50. *See* Grimshaw v. Ford Motor Co., 119 Cal. App. 3d 757 (Cal. 1981).

51. *See* LEE PATRICK STROBEL, RECKLESS HOMICIDE: FORD'S PINTO TRIAL 27 (1980).

52. *See* McCormack v. Hankscraft Co., 154 N.W.2d 488 (Minn. 1967).

53. *See* Turner v. General Motors Corp., 514 S.W. 2d 497 (Tex. Civ. App. Tex. 1974).

54. Escola v. Coca-Cola Bottling Co., 150 P.2d 436 (Cal. 1944) (Traynor, J., concurring).

55. *Id.*

56. *See* Steven Shavell, *Strict Liability Versus Negligence*, 9 J. LEGAL STUD. 1 (1980); POLINSKY, *supra* note 45.

57. POLINSKY, *supra* note 45.

58. *Id.*

induces efficient behavior because it forces the injurer . . . to take into account all of the adverse effects of his behavior on the victim. . . ."[59] He concludes strict liability is especially appropriate when a third party is injured (common in products cases):

> When the victim is a third party, the argument for using a strict liability rule is strengthened relative to the argument for using a negligence rule. . . . Under strict liability, the price of the product will equal its full cost, including the expected accident losses *to third parties*. Consumers will therefore purchase the correct amount. . . . [T]he problem with the negligence rule, that it encourages too much output, is generally worse when the victim is a third party.[60]

A leading opponent of strict liability is Judge Posner, who theorizes that as compared with negligence, strict liability is inefficient:

> A negligence standard differs from strict liability in that under negligence the injurer is liable only for those accidents that he could have avoided at a lower cost than the expected accident cost. . . . The difference between strict and negligence liability is that under the former system injurers must pay the losses of victims of accidents that are not worth preventing, whereas under the latter system injurers have no duty to pay victims of such accidents.[61]

Professor Polinsky argues: "Under strict liability, producers will be fully insured by liability insurance, and under negligence, consumers will be fully insured by first-party accident insurance."[62] This makes sense, because insurance is not readily available to consumers to cover products liability losses.[63] Generally the consumer is unaware of the defect in the product and does not sense the need for insurance.

A novel theory of strict liability has been suggested by Judge Posner. As it is a challenge to traditional notions of strict liability, it must be examined closely. Posner's concept of strict liability is: "If the expected loss . . . cannot be reasonably averted by taking greater care but can be by an adjustment in the activity level, an economic case for strict liability is made out."[64] Several points should be noted. First, this definition of strict liability is contrary to the cases. In a common strict liability case such as blasting, the goal of the courts is not to alter the level of activity. Instead, it is the opposite: blasting is highly valuable to society and to be

---

59. *Id.* at 39.

60. *Id.* at 103.

61. RICHARD A. POSNER, TORT LAW (CASES AND ECONOMIC ANALYSIS) 4, 5 (1982).

62. POLINSKY, *supra* note 45, at 100.

63. *See id.*

64. POSNER, *supra* note 61, at 477, 511.

encouraged.[65] The goal of strict liability is not to reduce the level of activity but simply to spread the inevitable losses.[66]

Second, there is no reason strict liability will lead to a change in the level of activity. Indeed, all that flows from a strict liability action is damages, which is also what results from a negligence action. Defendants in negligence actions may decide to reduce their level of activity, as may defendants who are held strictly liable. The calculation of damages is based on the losses the plaintiff has suffered,[67] not whether the defendant was sued in strict liability or negligence.

Judge Posner challenges the traditional rationale for strict liability (loss shifting) on two grounds. First, "there is an element of conjecture involved in supposing that taking a concentrated loss off the back of the victim of some accident and dividing it up into many small losses to customers or shareholders will increase total utility."[68] Professor Calabresi takes the contrary position, stating the party "in the best position to make the cost-benefit analysis between accident costs and accident avoidance costs"[69] should bear the loss. In this way, defendants will soon adjust their conduct.[70] Also, Calabresi notes that placing the entire loss on one person is not efficient.[71]

Second, Posner argues "there is an alternative . . . method of loss spreading available to potential victims besides strict liability; they can buy insurance."[72] But Professor Calabresi suggests this is invalid to the extent there is little deterrence value in placing the loss on the victims[73] as they only rarely are able to make changes in the conduct causing the injury. For example, few consumers have the ability to modify an automobile to make it safer (e.g., less likely to roll over). To purchase insurance, the consumer must first be aware of the risk, but in products cases, the consumer is often uninformed in regard to the dangerous nature of the product and thus does not know insurance is needed.

f. Distance from the Manufacturer Over the last 160 years, society had become more complicated and impersonal. The wagon maker no longer lives next door. A Chevrolet product may have its origin in China. Other products are manufactured around the world such as in Germany, Japan, Korea, China, and

---

65. *See* Spano v. Perini Corp., 25 N.Y. 2d 11 (N.Y. 1969).

66. *Id.*

67. *See* W. P. Keeton et al., Prosser and Keeton on the Law of Torts 165 (5th ed. 1984).

68. Posner, *supra* note 61, at 517.

69. Guido Calabresi & Jon T. Hirschoff, *Toward a Test for Strict Liability in Torts*, 81 Yale L. J. 1060 (1970).

70. Guido Calabresi, The Costs of Accidents: A Legal and Economic Analysis 68–94 (1970).

71. *Id.* at 39–45.

72. Posner, *supra* note 61, at 517–18.

73. Calabresi, *supra* note 70, at 55.

Yugoslavia. Justice Traynor reasons this social and marketing distancing is in part responsible for the growth in strict liability:

> As handicrafts have been replaced by mass production with its great market and transportation facilities, the close relationship between the producer and consumer of a product has been altered. Manufacturing processes, frequently valuable secrets, are . . . inaccessible to or beyond the ken of the general public. The consumer no longer has means or skill enough to investigate for himself the soundness of a product . . . and his . . . vigilance has been lulled by the steady efforts of manufacturers to build up confidence by advertising and marketing devices such as trademarks. . . . The manufacturer's obligation to the consumer must keep pace with the changing relationship between them. . . .[74]

g. Strict Liability Avoids Universal Health Care One additional important policy has received little attention but is in need of careful examination. In the United States, strict liability functions in part as a substitute for socialized medicine. It has developed to allow injured consumers to purchase medical treatment that might otherwise be unavailable.

By contrast, the British National Health Service pays for a citizen's every medical necessity.[75] If an Englishman breaks his leg playing football, walking down steps in his home, or riding in a car that crashes because of a defective part, his medical treatment is provided without charge by the National Health Service[76] (although there is a slight charge for prescription drugs). There are also certainly delays for elective as well as non-emergency surgery (e.g., a person who wants to have a hip socket replaced may have to wait as long as eighteen months).

If, because of the broken leg, the driver loses two months' work, a portion of lost wages will be covered by British Social Security. These payments are scaled in relation to the wages earned. They are substantial and may continue for the rest of the injured person's life. Indeed, the Social Security payments to an injured person over the remainder of his life could be greater than the recovery at trial.[77] Prosthetic devices and rehabilitative services are also covered by the National Health Services.

In conclusion, the United States has embraced strict liability, in part, to make certain the victim is compensated for personal injuries. Britain accomplishes the same goal by means of a welfare state and universal health care.

---

74. Escola v. Coca-Cola Bottling Co., 150 P.2d 436, 440 (Cal. 1944) (Traynor, J., concurring).

75. Interview with Professor A. L. Diamond, Director of the Institute for Advanced Legal Studies, London, England (Mar. 17, 1984).

76. A. L. Diamond, 1 Royal Commission on Civil Liability and Compensation for Personal Injury 48 (1978).

77. *Id.* at 76.

As this is being written, Congress has passed a universal health care system in the United States.[78] Litigation of personal injury claims arising from defective products will somewhat decrease as victims will have their injuries treated under the health care system. The pressure for litigation and strict liability will be reduced. Thus, universal health care will accomplish de facto tort reform: fewer suits because health care expenses have been paid.

---

78. *See* http://www.whitehouse.gov/Issues/Health-Care.

3. THE CORE ISSUE IN STRICT LIABILITY:
An Appropriate Test for Defect

A. THE EMERGENCE OF STRICT LIABILITY

The goal of strict liability is to afford the victim easier access to powerful manu-facturers and sellers than was available under the existing negligence regime. In Chapter I, we examined the keystone case of *MacPherson v. Buick Motors*. The next critical case after *MacPherson* is *Escola v. Coca-Cola Bottling Co.*[1]

Escola was decided in 1944 by the Supreme Court of California.[2] A waitress had gone to a storage area to obtain a bottle of Coca-Cola; when she picked it up, the bottle exploded in her hand.[3] Up to that point it was a routine exploding bottle case, but the court dealt with the problem of absence of control on the part of the manufacturer by applying res ipsa loquitor.[4] The importance of *Escola* is Justice Traynor's concurring opinion where he argues that manufacturers should be held to the standard of strict liability.

The purpose of the strict liability cause of action was to make it easier for the consumer to recover against a manufacturer for injury from a defective product:

> [T]he manufacturer's negligence should no longer be singled out as the basis of a plaintiff's right to recover in cases like the present one. In my opinion it should now be recognized that a manufacturer incurs [strict liability] when an article that he has placed on the market, knowing that it is to be used without inspection, proves to have a defect that causes injury to human beings.[5]

Justice Traynor explained the reasons for strict liability in product cases in the following terms: "[P]ublic policy demands that responsibility be fixed wherever it will most effectively reduce the hazards to life and health inherent in defective products that reach the market."[6]

Traynor had to wait eighteen years (until 1962) to turn his concurring opinion in *Escola* into law. This opportunity arrived in *Greenman v. Yuba Power Products, Inc.*[7] In *Greenman*, the plaintiff's wife had given him a Shopsmith, "a combination

1. Escola v. Coca-Cola Bottling Co., 150 P.2d 436 (Cal. 1944) (Traynor, J. concurring).
2. *Id.*
3. *Id.* at 437.
4. *Id.* at 438–40.
5. *Id.* at 440.
6. *Id.* at 440–41.
7. 377 P.2d 897 (Cal. 1963).

power tool that could be used as a saw, a drill, and [a] wood lathe."[8] In 1957, while the plaintiff was using his Shopsmith as a lathe for turning a large piece of wood, the wood suddenly flew off the lathe and hit him in the face, causing serious injury.[9] Justice Traynor used the case as an opportunity to implement his far-reaching concept of strict liability for products, saying "[T]he liability is not one governed by the law of contract warranties but by the law of strict liability in tort."[10] He explained the new doctrine of strict liability:

> Implicit in the machine's presence on the market, however, was a representa-
> tion that it would safely do the jobs for which it was built. Under these cir-
> cumstances, it should not be controlling whether plaintiff selected the
> machine because of the statements in the brochure, or because of the
> machine's own appearance of excellence that belied the defect lurking beneath
> the surface, or because he merely assumed that it would safely do the jobs
> it was built to do. It should not be controlling whether the details of the
> sales from manufacturer to retailer and from retailer to plaintiff's wife were
> such that one or more of the implied warranties of the sales act arose. "The
> remedies of injured consumers ought not be made to depend upon the intri-
> cacies of the law of sales." To establish the manufacturer's liability it was
> sufficient that plaintiff proved that he was injured while using the Shopsmith
> in a way it was intended to be used as a result of a defect in design and manu-
> facture of which plaintiff was not aware that made the Shopsmith unsafe for
> its intended use.[11]

The trial court's verdict in favor of the plaintiff and against the manufacturer was affirmed.[12] Thus, in 1962 the California Supreme Court created strict liabil-ity. This came about because Justice Traynor viewed negligence as wasteful of both the consumer's and the court's resources. He concluded it was inefficient to have the plaintiff sue the seller, the seller sue the distributor, the distributor sue the wholesaler, and the wholesaler sue the manufacturer: "It is needlessly circuitous to make negligence the basis of recovery and impose what is in reality liability without negligence. If public policy demands that a manufacturer of goods be responsible for their quality regardless of negligence there is no reason not to fix that responsibility openly."[13]

The commercial world Justice Traynor anticipated in 1944 has now become a reality. For example, today vehicles are made in many foreign countries as well

---

8. *Id.* at 898.

9. *Id.*

10. *Id.* at 901.

11. *Id.* (internal citations omitted).

12. *Id.* at 902.

13. Escola v. Coca-Cola Bottling Co., 150 P.2d 436, 441 (Cal. 1944) (Traynor, J., concurring).

as the United States. As consumers know little about the design and construction of the product, they must rely on the manufacturer:

> As handicrafts have been replaced by mass production with its great markets and transportation facilities, the close relationship between the producer and consumer of a product has been altered. *Manufacturing processes, frequently valuable secrets, are ordinarily either inaccessible to or beyond the ken of the general public.* The consumer no longer has means or skill enough to investigate for himself the soundness of a product . . . and his erstwhile vigilance has been lulled by the steady efforts of manufacturers to *build up confidence by advertising and marketing. . . .*[14]

Following closely on the heels of *Greenman* came Section 402A of the *Restatement (Second) of Torts* (1965). The Reporter for that provision was Dean William Prosser. Section 402A provides:

> One who sells any product in a defective condition unreasonably dangerous to the user or consumer or to his property is subject to liability for physical harm thereby caused to the ultimate user or consumer, or to his property, if (a) the seller is engaged in the business of selling such a product, and (b) it is expected to and does reach the user or consumer without substantial change in the condition in which it is sold. The rule stated in Subsection (1) applies although (a) the seller has exercised all possible care . . . (b) the user or consumer has not bought the product from or entered into any contractual relation with the seller.[15]

Section 402A of the *Restatement (Second) of Torts* is the most successful section of the Restatement, having been cited over three thousand times from 1964 to 1992.[16] Almost thirty years after the passage of Section 402A, Professors Henderson and Twerski were able to say: "Only rarely do provisions of the American Law Institute's Restatements of the Law rise to the dignity of holy writ."[17]

In 1972, ten years after the adoption of strict liability in *Greenman*, the Supreme Court of California was met with a challenging case in *Cronin v. J.B.E. Olson Corp.*[18] In *Cronin*, the driver of a delivery van was hit in the back of the head by a bread tray that slipped forward because of a broken hasp.[19] This occurred

---

14. *Id.* at 443 (emphasis added) (citations omitted).

15. RESTATEMENT (SECOND) OF TORTS § 402A (1965).

16. *See* James A. Henderson, Jr. & Aaron D. Twerski, *A Proposed Revision of Section 402A of the Restatement (Second) of Torts*, 77 CORNELL L. REV. 1512, 1512 n.1 (1992) (citing a letter to the authors dated October, 11 1991 from Marianne M. Walker, A.L.I. Restatement Case Citations Editor).

17. *Id.* at 1512.

18. 501 P.2d 1153 (Cal. 1972).

19. *Id.* at 1155.

while the driver was passing another vehicle and resulted in the bread van crashing.[20] The issue before the *Cronin* court was whether the product must have an unreasonably dangerous defect for strict liability to apply.[21] Specifically, the question was whether Section 402A's requirement that a product be "unreasonably dangerous" was part of California law, or whether the product merely needed to be found "defective" to come within strict liability in California.[22] After examining the issue carefully, the California Supreme Court held Section 402A was not part of California law, and that the state's law of strict liability only required the product be shown to be defective.[23] The court adopted this approach because "unreasonably dangerous" sounded of negligence, and negligence was more difficult for the injured consumer to prove than defect and strict liability.[24] However, the court left open the question of how *"defect"* is defined.[25] As defect is the core issue in a products liability case based on strict liability, we will now consider it.

B. THE SEVERAL TESTS FOR DEFECT

Several tests have been developed to define the keystone element in strict liability: *defect*. In evaluating the various tests, it will be helpful to ask whether they are responsive to the underlying precedential policy as stated by the New Jersey Supreme Court in *Henningsen v. Bloomfield Motors*: "[T]he burden of losses consequent upon use of defective articles is borne by those who are in a position to either control the danger or make an equitable distribution of the losses when they do occur."[26]

1. Section 402A: "Defective Condition Unreasonably Dangerous"

The American Law Institute (ALI) is composed of law professors, judges, and practitioners; its primary mission is to draft restatements of the common law. The ALI adopted Section 402A of the *Restatement (Second) of Torts* in 1963. The Restatement's test for strict products liability provides "[o]ne who sells any product in a *defective* condition *unreasonably dangerous* to the user or consumer or to his property is subject to liability for physical harm thereby caused to the ultimate user or consumer. . . ."[27] The drafters used the term "unreasonably

---

20. *Id.*
21. *Id.* at 1156.
22. *Id.* at 1163.
23. *Id.*
24. *Id.*
25. *Id.*
26. Henningsen v. Bloomfield Motors, Inc., 161 A.2d 69, 81 (N.J. 1960).
27. RESTATEMENT (SECOND) OF TORTS § 402A (1965) (emphasis added).

dangerous" to make it clear that the product must be defective and that a manufacturer will not be liable for a product that may be somewhat dangerous but not defective, such as alcohol.[28] The term "unreasonably dangerous" has caused a great deal of dissatisfaction with the Restatement formulation.[29]

Specifically, the Restatement test has been criticized on two grounds. First, it has been described as misleading because the term "unreasonably dangerous" suggests to the jury the product must be more than dangerous.[30] Second, it implies the plaintiff must prove the defendant has been negligent.[31] Defenders have attempted to respond to these criticisms by suggesting the terms *unreasonably dangerous* and *defective* mean the same thing and should not be interpreted to suggest either that the plaintiff must prove negligence or that something more than mere dangerousness of the product must be shown.[32]

The question then arises as to why Dean Prosser, the Restatement reporter, used the phrase "unreasonably dangerous" in Section 402A rather than "defect," which would have more accurately reflected the developing case law. Some insight comes from the ALI Proceedings in 1961. The following is a discussion between Reed Dickerson and Prosser on a draft of Section 402A (Food):

Professor Dickerson: . . . I would think that if he [the purchaser] showed that it [the product] was unreasonably dangerous, it would per se be legally defective, and it is only gilding the lily to add the word "defective." . . .

Dean Prosser: Mr. Dickerson has stated an original point of view which I first brought in to the Council of the American Law Institute in connection with this section. ". . . food in a condition unreasonably dangerous to the consumer" was my language. The Council then proceeded to raise the question

---

28. *Id.* Comment I states:

Many products cannot possibly be made entirely safe for all consumption, and any food or drug necessarily involves some risk of harm, if only from over-consumption. Ordinary sugar is a deadly poison to diabetics and castor oil found use under Mussolini as an instrument of torture. That is not what is meant by "unreasonably dangerous" in this Section. The article must be dangerous to an extent beyond that which would be contemplated by the ordinary consumer who purchases it, with the ordinary knowledge common to the community as to its characteristics. Good whiskey is not unreasonably dangerous merely because it will make people drunk, and is especially dangerous to alcoholics: but bad whiskey, containing a dangerous amount of fuel oil, is unreasonably dangerous.

29. *See* Barker v. Lull Eng'g Co., 573 P.2d 443 (Cal. 1978); Cronin v. J.B.E. Olson Corp., 501 P.2d 1153 (Cal. 1972).

30. *See Barker*, 573 P.2d at 451.

31. *See Cronin*, 501 P.2d at 1162.

32. W. Page Keeton, *Products Liability and the Meaning of Defect*, 5 St. Mary's L.J. 30, 32 (1973); John W. Wade, *On the Nature of Strict Tort Liability for Products*, 44 Miss. L.J. 825, 829–38 (1973).

of a number of products which, even though not defective, are in fact dangerous to the consumer—whiskey, for example [laughter]: cigarettes . . . and they
raised the question whether "unreasonably dangerous" was sufficient to protect the defendant against possible liability in such cases.

Therefore, they suggested that there something must be [sic] wrong with
the product itself, and hence the word "defective" was put in: but the fact that
the product itself is dangerous, or even unreasonably dangerous, to people
who consume it is not enough. There has to be something wrong with the
product.

. . . "Defective" was put in to head off liability on the part of the seller of
whiskey, on the part of the man who consumes it and gets delirium tremens,
even though the jury might find that all whiskey is unreasonably dangerous
to the consumer.[33]

This brief interchange makes it clear Prosser originally drafted Section 402A
using the "unreasonably dangerous" test and only added the "defect" test at the
urging of the ALI Council. Why however did he ignore the developing strict liability language of the cases and use instead the old negligence phrase "unreasonably dangerous"? One may suggest that because Prosser was such a central
figure in the analysis and development of negligence law, he used the "unreasonably dangerous" test because he was familiar with it and had found it to be
workable.[34]

The "unreasonably dangerous" test was never considered by the ALI in terms
of products in general. Dean Wade recalls the phrase "unreasonably dangerous"
was never discussed by the Torts Section of the ALI as it might be applied to
inedible products[35]—it was only debated in its application to food.[36] Nonetheless,
Section 402A was extended to all products. The ALI realized that once the
Michigan Supreme Court applied strict liability to cinder blocks, it could not be
confined to food.[37]

2. The Risk-Benefit Test

The reason for the risk-benefit test is that strict liability is not insurance and any
evaluation of a design hazard must necessarily involve the weighing of danger
against utility.[38] This means that just because there is an injury does not mean

---

33. Discussion between Reed Dickerson and Dean Prosser, 38 A.L.I. Proc. 76, 87–88
(1961).

34. *See generally* WILLIAM L. PROSSER, HANDBOOK OF THE LAW OF TORTS 139–205 (4th ed.
1971).

35. Wade, *supra* note 32, at 831.

36. *Id.*

37. Spence v. Three Rivers Builders & Masonry Supply, Inc., 90 N.W.2d 873 (Mich. 1958).

38. *See* W. Page Keeton, *Products Liability—Design Hazards and the Meaning of Defect,*
10 CUM L. REV. 293, 313 (1979); Wade, *supra* note 32, at 835.

the defendant needs to pay. Dean Page Keeton was a leading proponent of the risk-benefit test:

> A product is defective if it is unreasonably dangerous as marketed. It is unreasonably dangerous if a reasonable person would conclude that the magnitude of the scientifically perceivable danger *as it is proved to be at the time of trial* outweighed the benefits of the way the product was so designed and marketed.[39]

Risk is determined by the likelihood of harm, the seriousness of the harm, and the nature of the danger.[40] Benefit, on the other hand, is determined by the need for the product, the feasibility of a safer design, and the availability of substitute products.[41] Dean Keeton noted the test closely paralleled negligence, but distinguished the risk-benefit analysis from negligence "primarily because, as proposed, the danger in fact as proven at trial determines whether a product is good or bad. This difference would seem to be obvious."[42]

3. The *Barker v. Lull* Tests

The California Supreme Court developed a bifurcated test for defect in *Barker v. Lull*:

> [A] product may be found defective in design, so as to subject a manufacturer to strict liability for resulting injuries, under either of two alternative tests. First, a product may be found defective in design if the plaintiff establishes that the product failed to perform as safely as an ordinary consumer would expect when used in an intended or reasonably foreseeable manner. Second, a product may alternatively be found defective in design if the plaintiff demonstrates that the product's design proximately caused his injury and the defendant fails to establish, in light of the relevant factors, that, on balance, the benefits of the challenged design outweigh the risk of danger inherent in such design.[43]

The rationale for this definition is to continue the California theory the term "unreasonably dangerous" unfairly burdens the injured plaintiff with proof of an element that rings of negligence.[44] A second reason is "it is simply impossible to

---

39. Keeton, *supra* note 32, at 37–38. *See* Wade, *supra* note 32, at 830–38. *But see* Donaher et al., *The Technical Expert in Products Liability Litigation*, 52 Tex. L. Rev. 1303, 1307 (1974).

40. Keeton, *supra* note 38, at 314.

41. *Id.*

42. *Id.* at 314–15.

43. Barker v. Lull Eng'g Co., 573 P.2d 443, 455–56 (Cal. 1978).

44. *Id.* at 456.

eliminate the balancing or weighing of competing considerations in determining whether a product is defectively designed or not."[45]

The *Barker v. Lull* test raises several issues. First, as Dean Wade has noted, the expectations of the ordinary consumer creates problems: "[I]n many situations . . . the consumer would not know what to expect, because he would have no idea how safe the product could be made."[46] One case suggests a solution: it holds the "consumer expectation" test makes sense because it is the consumer's expectation of performance, not how the product works, that is key.[47] Other courts weigh the risk-utility of the product when applying the consumer expectation test.[48]

Second, the most substantial problem is the use of the phrase "proximate cause" in the second prong of the test as the term is unclear and superfluous.[49] Findings of proximate cause and defect involve the same policy inquiries and balancing, and it is repetitious and misleading to ask whether the defect was the proximate cause of the damage. The social policy question is asked initially when the court weighs the various factors to see whether the product is defective.[50] It is confusing to the court, the jury, and the attorneys to ask the same policy questions again, but under a different label. However, because the term "proximate cause" is vague, the trial court is given some flexibility in deciding whether to send the case to the jury.

4. Negligence with Imputed Knowledge

The Oregon Supreme Court developed a test for strict liability based upon a modification of the traditional negligence approach:

> A . . . defective article would be one which a reasonable person would not put into the stream of commerce *if he had knowledge of its harmful character*. The test, therefore is whether the seller would be negligent if he sold the article *knowing of the risk involved*. Strict liability imposes what amounts to constructive knowledge of the condition of the product.[51]

---

45. *Id.*

46. Wade, *supra* note 32, at 825, 829.

47. Brethauer v. General Motors Corp., No. 1 CA-CV 07-0530, 2009 WL 820120, at *7 (Ariz. Ct. App. Mar. 31, 2009).

48. John F. Vargo, *The Emperor's New Clothes: The American Law Institute Adorns a "New Cloth" for Section 402A Products Liability Design Defects—A Survey of the States Reveals a Different Weave*, 26 U. Mem. L. Rev. 493, 540 (1995–1996) (referring to this approach as a "Modified Consumer Expectation Test").

49. *See* Leon Green, The Rationale of Proximate Cause 758–59 (1927).

50. *See* Wade, *supra* note 32, at 837–41.

51. Phillips v. Kimwood Mach. Co., 525 P.2d 1033, 1036 (Or. 1974).

This test was embraced by both Deans Wade and Keeton;[52] however, the two disagree on whether it is a test of negligence. Dean Wade said, "It may be argued that this is simply a test of negligence,"[53] while Dean Keeton states, "Since the test is not one of negligence, it is not based upon the risks and dangers that the makers should have, in the exercise of ordinary care, known about."[54] The Oregon court added "[t]he Wade and Keeton formulations of the standard appear to be identical except that Keeton would impute the knowledge of dangers to the manufacturer at the time of trial, while Wade would impute only the knowledge existing at the time the product was sold."[55]

The most obvious problem with the test is the use of the term *negligence*. The courts have consistently held strict liability is not a matter of negligence.[56] In addition, the imposition of constructive knowledge by the Oregon court is not new—this is often done when circumstantial evidence is strong enough to permit an inference the manufacturer had knowledge of the defect, even though it insists it had no knowledge.[57] The "negligence with imputed knowledge" test for defect would require the plaintiffs to prove negligence. This is contrary to the cases and to the fundamental reasons supporting strict liability.[58] The imputed knowledge test can be critical, however, when the manufacturer of a drug (such as DES) argues it did not know of the risk at the time of sale. In a case such as DES, the manufacturers' knowledge may be imputed.

5. The Communicative Tort

Dean Leon Green suggested a solution to the strict liability quagmire, proposing "a communicative tort action based on the duty to inform or to give reliable information, set off distinctly from the . . . negligence action based on the duty of care."[59] A seller will be held liable under this action if a defective product injures a consumer because of the absence of a warning or adequate instructions.[60] In short, sellers will be taken at their word.[61] The reason for the duty to warn is the

---

52. *See* W. Page Keeton, *Manufacturer's Liability: The Meaning of "Defect" in the Manufacture and Design of Products*, 20 Syracuse L. Rev. 559, 568 (1969); John W. Wade, *Strict Tort Liability of Manufacturers*, 19 Sw. L.J. 5, 15–16 (1965).

53. Wade, *supra* note 52.

54. Keeton, *supra* note 52.

55. *See* discussion in *Phillips*, 525 P.2d at 1036 n.6.

56. *See, e.g.*, Barker v. Lull Eng'g Co., 573 P.2d 443 (Cal. 1978); Cronin v. J.B.E. Olson Corp., 501 P.2d 1153 (Cal. 1972).

57. *See* William L. Prosser, *The Fall of the Citadel (Strict Liability to the Consumer)*, 50 Minn. L. Rev. 791, 840–45 (1966).

58. *See Barker*, 573 P.2d 443; *Cronin*, 501 P.2d 1153.

59. Leon Green, *Strict Liability Under Section 402A + 402B: A Decade of Litigation*, 54 Tex. L. Rev. 1185, 1188 (1976).

60. *Id.* at 1191.

61. *Id.*

"corporate seller's command of all the media of communications to support his aggressive [ad] campaigns."[62]

Dean Green performed an invaluable service by pointing the courts toward one of the most critical elements of products liability: information (or lack of information) communicated by the seller. However, it is unlikely the courts will fully adopt the communicative tort because it is drafted in unfamiliar language. In addition, the amount of information communicated by the seller has little impact on a case brought by a bystander or donee.[63] In some cases, however, the nature of the warning or instructions is determinative.[64] Much of Green's theory has been adopted in the area of pharmaceutical litigation when the issue is whether the drug manufacturer adequately warned of the drug's risk.[65] Today, the drug manufacturer will be held liable if it fails to warn of a material risk in the product. The Norplant litigation is an example.

6. The Cheapest Cost Avoider

Judge Guido Calabresi has done much to clarify fundamental concepts in strict liability through the application of economic analysis.[66] In applying these principles, he has found the cost-benefit test (as put forward by Judge Learned Hand) is flawed: "The present Learned Hand test tends to make injuries richer at the expense of victims."[67] Calabresi argues the purpose of strict liability is not merely

---

62. *Id.* at 1190.

63. Some of the most conceptually difficult products liability cases are those brought by bystanders. *See, e.g.,* Elmore v. American Motors Corp., 451 P.2d 84 (Cal. 1969).

64. *See* Borel v. Fibreboard Paper Tool Corp., 493 F.2d 1076 (5th Cir. 1973), *cert. denied,* 419 U.S. 869 (1974); Burch v. Amsterdam Corp., 366 A.2d 1079 (D.C. Cir. 1976); Michael v. Warner/Chilcott, 579 P.2d 183 (N.M. Ct. App. 1978).

65. *E.g.,* Perez v. Wyeth Labs., Inc., 734 A.2d 1245 (S. Ct. N.J., 1999).

66. *See generally* GUIDO CALABRESI, THE COSTS OF ACCIDENTS (1970); Guido Calabresi & Jon T. Hirschoff, *Toward a Test for Strict Liability in Torts,* 81 YALE L.J. 1055 (1972).

67. Calabresi & Hirschoff, *supra* note 66, at 1077. Professor Calabresi has criticized sellers for suggesting a products liability crisis exists. The sellers want to shift the loss to the consumers or the government, but Professor Calabresi argues this violates a basic principle of economics: that taking risks is what corporations do best. Guido Calabresi, *Product Liability: Curse or Bulwark of Free Enterprise,* 27 CLEV. ST. L. REV. 313, 321 (1973). Professor Posner appears to define strict liability as absolute liability: "Even if strict liability had no effect whatever on safety, it would have an economic effect: it would compel the manufacturer to insure consumers against accidents resulting from nonnegligent defects in his products." RICHARD A. POSNER, ECONOMIC ANALYSIS OF LAW 137 (2d ed. 1977). He then criticizes strict liability (thus defined) because it fails to balance cost against benefit. In products cases, Professor Posner clearly prefers the negligence approach as set forth by Learned Hand. In an apparent oversight, Posner evaluates contributory negligence and mishandling as defenses to strict liability, but fails to consider the economic impact of assumption of risk in products liability cases. *Id.* at 137–42. *But see id.* at 127–28.

to accomplish distributional goals.[68] The reason for the trend toward strict liability (as in respondeat superior, ultra hazardous activity liability, and worker's compensation) is based "at least in part on a desire to accomplish better primary accident cost reduction."[69]

To achieve accident cost reduction, Calabresi points toward the following test:

> The strict liability test we suggest does not require that a government institution make such a cost-benefit analysis. It requires of such a institution only a decision as to which of the parties to the accident *is in the best position to make the cost-benefit analysis between accident costs and accident avoidance costs and to act on that decision once it is made.* The question for the court reduces to a search for the cheapest cost avoider.[70]

For example, "a violinist is the best evaluator of the relative advantages and costs of working in a steel mill, with regard to the suffering he will feel if he loses his hand. . . ."[71] In contrast, an SUV manufacturer can best predict the likelihood and costs of SUV rollovers.

By setting forth an economic test for strict liability, Calabresi has performed a substantial service. Products liability suits usually pit a relatively unsophisticated consumer or user against a knowledgeable seller.[72] In these cases, the cheapest cost avoider is almost always going to be the seller. Clearly, the "cheapest cost avoider" test argues the powerful should generally be held liable.

7. Absolute Liability

Strict products liability is not absolute liability because the corporation does not pay for all the damages it causes. Likewise, strict liability is not "enterprise liability" or insurance. One approach to products liability might be to hold the seller liable for all injuries to the consumer caused by the product. Absolute liability was first suggested as a basis for products liability by Justice Traynor in *Escola v. Coca-Cola:* "In my opinion it should now be recognized that a manufacturer incurs an absolute liability when an article that he has placed on the market, knowing that it is to be used without inspection. proves to have a defect that causes injury to human beings."[73] Traynor's reason for absolute liability was that "the risk of injury can be insured by the manufacturer and distributed among the public as a cost of doing business."[74]

---

68. Calabresi & Hirschoff, *supra* note 66, at 1077.
69. *Id.* at 1075.
70. *Id.* at 1060.
71. *Id.* at 1069.
72. *Id.*
73. 150 P.2d 436, 440 (Cal. 1944).
74. *Id.* at 441.

However, the far-reaching and unknowable scope of absolute liability has led the courts and the commentators to reject it. Calabresi, for example, concluded: "Strict liability has never meant that the party held strictly liable is to be a general insurer of the victim no matter how or where the victim comes to grief."[75] In like manner, Keeton reported, "[T]he product must be defective as marketed in order to subject the manufacturer to liability."[76] No court dealing with products liability has followed Traynor's position on absolute liability.[77]

Under strict liability the seller is not absolutely liable, is not an insurer, and is not liable for all injuries caused by the product. The central question in a products liability case is the scope of liability, and the answer to the question of scope of liability is determined by the concept of defect.[78]

C. COMPARATIVE FAULT

A layman might assume incorrectly that once the product is determined to be defective, the case is over. Before 1978, the rule was that if plaintiffs were negligent to any degree, they could not recover. However, comparative fault permits the plaintiff to recover even if the plaintiff is negligent to some extent. The theory behind comparative fault is that the jury should weigh the wrongful act of the plaintiff against the wrongful act of the defendant in determining damages.[79] The issue in this section is whether comparative fault should be applied in strict liability cases as it will examine the application of comparative fault to strict liability to determine if it effects a change in the definition of defect. However, this is not the place to evaluate all of the various defenses to a strict liability action (such as assumption of risk and contributory negligence) as that has been done elsewhere.[80]

An analysis of comparative fault begins with contributory negligence (i.e., the plaintiff was careless to some degree). Historically, contributory negligence was not recognized as a defense to strict liability because strict liability did not rest

---

75. Calabresi & Hirschoff, *supra* note 66, at 1056. "General insurance was not the rule in classical instances of strict liability, such as ultrahazardous activities, or in legislatively mandated instances, such as workmen's compensation, and it is not the rule in the recent instances of application such as products liability." *Id.*

76. Keeton, *supra* note 32, at 33.

77. *See,* e.g., Barker v. Lull Eng'g Co., 573 P.2d 443, 446 (Cal. 1978); Phillips v. Kimwood Mach. Co., 525 P.2d 1033 (Or. 1974).

78. Keeton, *supra* note 32, at 33.

79. *See* Daly v. General Motors Corp., 575 P.2d 1162 (Cal. 1962).

80. *See generally* David G. Epstein, *Products Liability: Defenses Based on Plaintiff's Conduct,* 1968 UTAH L. REV. 267; Dix W. Noel, *Defective Products: Abnormal Use, Contributory Negligence, and Assumption of Risk,* 25 VAND. L. REV. 93 (1972).

upon negligence.[81] However, contributory negligence was a complete defense to negligence. By contrast, assumption of risk (the victim knew the risk and voluntarily assumed it) in certain forms was accepted as a defense to strict liability.[82] The Uniform Comparative Fault Act was drafted in 1977, and contemporaneously several state supreme courts have applied comparative fault in strict liability actions.[83] These developments raise the question of whether this application of comparative fault to a strict liability cause of action reshapes strict liability into negligence.[84]

Several reasons have been suggested for refusing to apply comparative fault to a strict liability action.[85] First, "apples and oranges" cannot be compared. That is, comparative fault means comparative negligence and is only applicable in a negligence action. One cannot compare the conduct of the plaintiff, under comparative fault, with the defect of a product, which in a strict liability action does not rest on negligence.[86] The second objection is that if comparative fault is applied to strict liability, "a manufacturer's incentive to produce safe products will . . . be reduced or removed."[87] One of the purposes of strict liability is to prevent defective products. If the manufacturer is not held strictly liable or if the damages are reduced, the incentive to avoid defective products will also be reduced.

The California Supreme Court responded to these contentions in *Daly v. General Motors Corp.*[88] In reply to the "apples and oranges" argument, the court stated:

> We think it clear that the adoption of a system of comparative negligence should entail the merger of the defense of assumption of risk into the general scheme of assessment of liability in proportion to fault in those particular cases in which the form of assumption of risk involved is no more than a variant of contributory negligence.[89]

The court added "fixed semantic consistency . . . is less important that the attainment of a just and equitable result."[90]

In dealing with the argument that comparative fault will reduce the manufacturer's incentive to produce safe products, the court held the manufacturer

---

81. Devaney v. Sarno, 311 A.2d 208, 209 (N.J. Super. Ct. App. Div. 1973).
82. *Id.* at 209–10.
83. *See, e.g., Daly,* 575 P.2d 1162. John W. Wade, *Products Liability and Plaintiff's Fault—The Uniform Comparative Fault Act,* 29 Mercer L. Rev. 373 (1978).
84. *See Daly,* 575 P.2d 1162, 1181 (Mosk, J., dissenting).
85. *See generally id.*; Wade, *supra* note 83, at 376–81.
86. *Daly,* 575 P.2d 1162.
87. *Id.* at 1169.
88. *Id.* at 1162.
89. *Id.* at 1167, (quoting Li v. Yellow Cab Co., 532 P.2d 1226, 1241 (Cal. 1975)).
90. *Id.* at 1168.

cannot avoid its responsibility for selling defective products even when the plaintiff's conduct has contributed to his injury.[91] Indeed, "its exposure will be lessened only to the extent that the trier finds that the victim's conduct contributed to his injury."[92] In answering the objection that jurors cannot compare plaintiff's negligence with defendant's strict liability, the court looked at the maritime doctrine of "unseaworthiness" and found it to be analogous to the application of comparative fault to strict liability.[93] The court further found "[n]o serious practical difficulties appear to have arisen even where jury trials are involved."[94] The California Supreme Court's conclusion is buttressed by the position taken by the Uniform Comparative Fault Act that comparative fault should apply whether the action is based on negligence or strict tort liability.[95]

Comparative fault should apply to the doctrine of strict liability. The most compelling reason for this is presented by Wade: "Why is it desirable to transfer to the other users of the product—all innocent—the cost of that part of the plaintiff's injury that is attributable to his own fault?"[96] As to the practical difficulties of the jury comparing "apples and oranges," one response is that the members of the jury must merely close their eyes and do it.[97] Finally, the most substantial reason for applying comparative fault to strict liability is fairness.[98] There is no reason the manufacturer should be burdened with losses suffered by the consumer when those losses are attributable to a careless act or assumed risk on the part of the consumer.[99]

However, one caution has to be raised in considering this issue. In the United States, we lack a universal health care system and, therefore, to whatever extent the plaintiff in a products liability suit is at fault, and has his or her damages reduced under comparative fault, the plaintiff may be forced to rely upon Medicare, Medicaid, or welfare for assistance.[100] All consumers do not have

---

91. *Id.* at 1169.

92. *Id.*

93. *Id.* at 1170.For decades, seamen have been permitted to recover from shipowners for injuries caused by defects that render a vessel "unseaworthy.". . . As noted by many courts, the concept of "unseaworthiness" is not limited to or affected by notions of the shipowner's fault or due care, but applies to any deficiency of hull, equipment, or crew, regardless of cause, which renders the ship less than reasonably fit for its intended purposes. . . . Nonetheless, comparative principles have been made applicable to suits brought under the "unseaworthiness" doctrine (a form of strict liability), and the degree to which plaintiff's own negligence contributes to his injuries has been considered in determining the amount of his recovery. *Id.*

94. *Id.* at 1170.

95. Wade, *supra* note 83, at 374.

96. *Id.* at 379.

97. Aaron D. Twerski, *The Use and Abuse of Comparative Negligence in Products Liability*, 10 IND. L. REV. 797, 806 (1977).

98. *See* Wade, *supra* note 83, at 379. *Compare with* Twerski, *supra* note 97, at 798–800.

99. Daly v. General Motors Corp., 575 P.2d 1162,(Cal. 1978).

100. *See* Calabresi, *supra* note 66, at 284–85.

sufficient insurance to cover injuries that may occur in dealing with defective products, even if those injuries may be brought about by their own fault.

The doctrine of comparative fault should apply regardless of whether the cause of action is negligence or strict liability.[101] Further, it should apply regardless of the particular test for defect.[102] Comparative fault does not change strict liability into negligence as long as the jury is clearly instructed to first apply strict liability theory to the seller to determine liability.[103] After answering that question, the jury should then calculate damages by looking at the nature of the plaintiff's conduct as compared to the defect in the product.[104]

Comparative fault favors the injured consumer, not powerful manufacturers and sellers. It prevents the negligent plaintiff from being dismissed because of a mere scintilla of fault. Instead the case goes to the jury and the victim may still recover something.

D. THE ROLE OF THE COURT AND THE JURY UNDER STRICT LIABILITY

1. The Court

Defect is initially for the court to decide. The effectiveness of a Jeep's roll bar,[105] the placement of a Pinto's gas tank,[106] the strength of the front end of a Volkswagen bus,[107] and the top speed of a Chevrolet[108] are issues of design defect for the judge. Whether the case goes to the jury depends on whether reasonable persons could differ. Of course, if reasonable persons could differ or there are questions of fact involved in the case such as whether the explosion resulted from the gas tank hitting the differential or from a bystander lighting a match, such questions of fact are left to the jury.[109] However, if the defect question is such that "reasonable minds could not differ," the court directs a verdict on the issue for the plaintiff or the defendant. For example, if the court found the lack of visibility of a child's bike could be cured by a fifty-cent reflector, the court could direct a verdict for the

---

101. Wade, *supra* note 83, at 374.

102. *See supra* text accompanying notes 26–80.

103. *See Daly,* 575 P.2d 1162.

104. *Id.*

105. *See* Leichtamer v. Am. Motors Corp., 424 N.E.2d 568 (Ohio 1981); Turner v. Gen. Motors Corp., 514 S.W.2d 497 (Tex. Civ. App. 1974).

106. Grimshaw v. Ford Motor Co., No. 19-77-61 (Orange County (Cal.) Super. Ct., Mar. 30, 1978); Roy J. Harris, *Why the Pinto Jury Felt Ford Deserved $125 Million Penalty,* WALL ST. J., Feb. 14, 1978, at 1; Connie Bruck, *How Ford Stalled the Pinto Litigation,* AM. LAW., June 1979, at 23.

107. Dreisonstok v. Volkswagenwerk, A.G., 489 F.2d 1066 (4th Cir. 1974).

108. In Schemel v. General Motors Corp., 384 F.2d 802 (7th Cir. 1967), the court apparently wanted to avoid deciding the appropriate maximum speed for a car, with the goal being to avoid an administrative quagmire.

109. *See* GREEN, *supra* note 49, at 475.

plaintiff on the question of defect.[110] However, if the court has doubts about whether the product is defective, the question of defect should be given to the jury.

The test for whether the product is defective usually involves a balancing of operative factors. First, the court in applying strict liability must consider the reasons behind it: to shift the loss from the consumer to the seller and to provide the loss be borne by the person who created it.[111] Second, the court should weigh: (1) the product's utility, including style or aesthetic appeal;[112] (2) alternative designs;[113] (3) substitute products;[114] (4) likelihood of injury;[115] (5) nature of the injury;[116] (6) cost of making the product safer;[117] (7) availability and effectiveness of warnings;[118] (8) ability of the seller to obtain insurance or otherwise carry the loss;[119] (9) impact upon society of finding the product defective;[120] and (10) experimental nature of the product.[121] This is not an exhaustive list, and the court may consider other factors it deems relevant based on the facts of the specific case.

---

110. *See* Schwinn Sales South, Inc. v. Waters, 190 S.E.2d 815 (Ga. Ct. App. 1972).

111. This policy was enunciated in Greenman v. Yuba Power Prods., Inc., 377 P.2d 897 (Cal. 1963) and in Escola v. Coca-Cola Bottling Co., 150 P.2d 436 (Cal. 1944).

112. For example, see *Dreisonstok*, 489 F.2d 1066, for a discussion of the boxy V.W. van.

113. *See, e.g.,* Grimshaw v. Ford Motor Co., No. 19-77-61 (Orange County (Cal.) Super. Ct., Mar. 30, 1978) (the controversy over the location of the Pinto gas tank); McCormick v. Hankscraft Co., 154 N.W.2d 488 (Minn. 1967) (a steam vaporizer with a lid that fell off); Ellis v. Rich's Inc., 212 S.E.2d 373 (Ga. 1975) (a fondue pot handle that permits the pot to rotate when hot and filled with oil).

114. For example, is there a substitute for Red Dye No. 2 as a food coloring? Are there other less dangerous additives that accomplish the same result? In contrast, there is no substitute for blood. Hines v. St. Joseph's Hosp., 527 P.2d 1075 (N.M. Ct. App. 1974).

115. For example, there is a substantial likelihood of injury from a vaporizer with a non-locking lid. *McCormick*, 154 N.W.2d 488.

116. If there is an injury, will it be minor or serious? For example, jagged threads on a drum of gasoline are likely to produce an explosion causing serious injuries. Gulf Refining Co. v. Williams, 185 So. 234 (Miss. 1938).

117. *See* Schwinn Sales South, Inc. v. Waters, 190 S.E.2d 815 (Ga. Ct. App. 1972) (noting that for a few cents, the manufacturer could place reflectors on a child's bike).

118. The seller may be liable for failure to include an adequate warning. *See* Crane v. Sears Roebuck & Co., 32 Cal. Rptr. 754 (Cal. Ct. App. 1963); Incollingo v. Ewing, 282 A.2d 206 (Pa. 1971). *See generally* Dix W. Noel, *Products Defective Because of Inadequate Directions or Warnings*, 23 S. L.J. 256 (1969); Twerski et al., *The Use and Abuse of Warnings in Product Liability—Design Defect Litigation Comes of Age*, 61 CORNELL L. REV. 495 (1976).

119. *See* Greenman v. Yuba Power Prods., Inc., 377 P.2d 897 (Cal. 1963); Henningsen v. Bloomfield Motors, 161 A.2d 69 (N.J. 1960). *See generally* CALABRESI, *supra* note 69, at 39–60, 103–25, 168–284, 313–14.

120. *See* GREEN, *supra* note 49, at 757. *See generally* Schemel v. Gen. Motors Corp., 384 F.2d 802 (7th Cir. 1967).

121. For example, "It is also true . . . of many new or experimental drugs as to which, because of lack of time and opportunity for sufficient medical experience, there can be no

No priority is given to the ten factors. This is not intended to be an exclusive list, and the weight allocated to each factor will vary with the particular case. For example, the key factors in deciding whether a child's bicycle should have factory-installed reflectors may be the cost of the reflectors and likelihood of injury;[122] prevention and cost are both involved in deciding whether a forage wagon should have protective covers on the conveyor belt;[123] and the utility (cargo-carrying ability) of the Volkswagen "bus" is the most important element in deciding whether the engine should be in the front or rear.[124]

2. The Jury

There is little agreement on the formulation of jury instructions covering defect.[125] Several approaches have been suggested. First, a list of factors might be submitted to the jury as the ones they should weigh in deciding whether the product was defective.[126] This approach has been criticized on the basis the jury is not sophisticated enough to handle the subtle issues involved in weighing these complex factors.[127] Second, the jury might simply be asked: "Was the product defective?"[128] A third approach emerged in *Barker v. Lull*,[129] in which the California Supreme Court was faced with an important issue: whether the trial court could define defect, or whether it must ask the jury to determine "[W]as the product defective?"[130] The court responded that the charge to the jury in a strict liability case has two elements:

> [I]n design defect cases, a court may properly instruct the jury that a product is defective in design if (1) the plaintiff proves that the product failed to perform as safely as an ordinary consumer would expect when used in an intended or reasonably foreseeable manner, or (2) the plaintiff proves that the product's design proximately caused injury and that defendant fails to prove,

---

assurance of safety . . . but such experience as there is justifies the marketing and use of the drug notwithstanding a medically recognizable risk." RESTATEMENT (SECOND) OF TORTS § 402A cmt. k (1965). Of course, with any experimental product, clear and detailed warnings of risks would be necessary.

122. *See generally* Schwinn Sales South, Inc. v. Waters, 190 S.E.2d 815 (Ga. Ct. App. 1972).

123. *See* Winnett v. Winnett, 310 N.E.2d 1 (Ill. 1974).

124. Dreisonstok v. Volkswagenwerk, A.G., 489 F.2d 1066 (4th Cir. 1974).

125. *See* Barker v. Lull Eng'g Co., 573 P.2d 443, 452–53 (Cal. 1978); Phillips v. Kimwood Mach. Co., 525 P.2d 1033, 1040–41 (Or. 1974); Keeton, *supra* note 34, at 35–36.

126. Wade, *supra* note 52, at 17. Wade's list is similar to the list of factors just presented.

127. *See generally* GREEN, *supra* note 49, at 1218–20; Keeton, *supra* note 39.

128. Cronin v. J.B.E. Olson Corp., 501 P.2d 1153, 1162 (Cal. 1972).

129. *Barker*, 573 P.2d 443.

130. *Id.* at 446.

in light of the relevant factors, that on balance the benefits of the challenged design outweigh the risk of danger inherent in such design.[131]

From *Barker,* the charge to the jury could be (1) did "the product perform as an ordinary consumer would expect," or (2) did the defendant "prove, in light of the relevant factors, that on balance the benefits of the challenged design outweigh the risk of danger inherent in such design."[132]

From 1963 to 1996, the most successful tests for defect in a products liability case based on strict liability were first, risk-utility; second, consumer expectation; and third, negligence with imputed knowledge.[133] None had a clear majority.

3. Cases Applying the *Restatement (Second)* § 402A

The following cases are presented to demonstrate an application of the principles discussed above. An example of a case that arose after the passage of *Restatement (Second) of Torts* § 402A is *Mueller & Co. v. Corley.*[134] The plaintiff's breast implant ruptured and she sued the manufacturer. The defendant argued the reasonable expectations of the plaintiff's doctor in suggesting the implant should control. This was rejected on appeal, when the court adopted the test of the reasonable consumer:

> The defective condition in the prosthesis in question rendered it unreasonably dangerous to Mrs. Corley, not to her physician, Dr. Leeves. The appropriate question for the jury, therefore, was whether the defective condition was one which was not contemplated by the user, the "ultimate consumer." Restatement (2d) of Torts § 402A (1965). The trial court properly keyed its instructions to the mind of the person who would be injured by the dangerous condition of the product.[135]

The second case involves the application of § 402A to a difficult set of facts: the severe brain damage to a two-year-old child who almost drowned in an above-ground pool. The parents argued the pool was defective because it lacked a self-latching gate. In rejecting the suit by the parents, the Wisconsin Supreme Court stated:

> Comment g to section 402A of Restatement, Torts 2d, defines "defective condition" in part as follows:
>
> **Defective condition.** The rule stated in this Section applies only where the product is, at the time it leaves the seller's hands, in a condition not

---

131. *Id.* at 452.
132. Keeton, *supra* note 38, at 302–05.
133. *See* Vargo, *supra* note 48.
134. 570 S.W.2d 140 (Tex. Civ. Appeal 1978).
135. *Id.* at 145.

contemplated by the ultimate consumer, which will be unreasonably danger-ous to him.

[T]he test in Wisconsin of whether a product contains an unreasonably dangerous defect depends upon the reasonable expectations of the ordinary consumer concerning the characteristics of this type of product. If the average consumer would reasonably anticipate the dangerous condition of the prod-uct and fully appreciate the attendant risk of injury, it would not be unreason-ably dangerous and defective. This is an objective test and is not dependant upon the knowledge of the particular injured consumer, although his knowl-edge may be evidence of contributory negligence under the circumstances.

* * *

Based upon the principles discussed above, we conclude that the swimming pool described in plaintiff's complaint does not contain an unreasonably dan-gerous defect. The lack of a self-latching gate certainly falls within the cate-gory of an obvious rather than a latent condition. Equally important, the average consumer would be completely aware of the risk of harm to small children due to this condition, when the retractable ladder is left in a down position and the children are left unsupervised. We conclude, therefore, that plaintiff's second amended complaint fails to state a cause of action.[136]

E. AN EMBRACE OF NEGLIGENCE

Numerous products liability cases are brought under a negligence cause of action.[137] A leading proponent of negligence is Judge Posner, who criticizes the theory of strict liability for failing to maximize the joint value of the interfering activities, and argues negligence leads to the most efficient result.[138] Posner's thesis touches upon fundamental theories of negligence, strict liability, and economics. It therefore deserves attention, particularly as applied to products liability cases.

To prove his point, Posner uses "the now familiar example of the railroad engine that emits sparks which damage crops along the railroad's right of way."[139] He concludes:

The value-maximizing solution may turn out to involve changes by both par-ties in their present behavior: for example, the railroad may have to install a good but not perfect spark arrester and the farmer may have to leave an

---

136. Vincer v. Esther Williams All-Aluminum Swimming Pool Co., 230 N.W.2d 794, 797–99 (Wis. 1975) (emphasis added) (citations omitted).

137. *See* Dreisonstok v. Volkswagenwerk, A.G., 489 F.2d 1066 (4th Cir. 1974).

138. Richard A. Posner, *Strict Liability: A Comment*, 2 J. LEGAL STUDIES 205 (1973).

139. *Id.*

unplanted buffer space between the railroad right of way and his tilled fields. Or, the value-maximizing solution may involve changes by the railroad only, by the farmer only, or by neither party.[140]

However, there are several important reasons Posner's negligence theory should be rejected in dealing with defective products. First, the consumer may not know of the defect. (The tendency of some Ford Explorers to roll over is an example.) Second, the victim may be unable to avoid the injury (prescription drugs). Third, often the victim is a third party, not the purchaser, and can do nothing. (The plaintiff may be a passenger in the defective car, or have received the defective product as a gift). Fourth, the product may have injured thousands or hundreds of thousands of victims and, therefore, negotiating a change in design is costly (drugs, tobacco). Fifth, defective products often cause personal injury, not merely property damage, as is the case with sparking trains.

Powerful sellers quickly recognized negligence favored them because the victim had to prove it—and that is a heavy burden. What may not be quite so obvious grows out of the goal of negligence: to put both parties at equal advantage. A study of negligence indicates the law struggles to place each party on equal footing. The predictable result is victims are often going to lose. There are several reasons: First, many victims will not have sufficient funding to bring a suit, and an attorney may refuse to take the case on contingency. Second, the damages may be too small to be worth suing (however, adding up large numbers of small damages may equal a great savings to sellers). Third, the victim may lack the time or be unable to find qualified experts to bring a suit. Fourth, the victim may be unable to discover evidence of negligence.

CONCLUSION

Strict liability in products cases grew out of actions against businesses and corporations related to the purpose of the enterprises: selling products. In contrast, negligence was developed largely to handle disputes between individuals. When a corporation was a defendant in a negligence suit, the activity at issue usually was incidental to the purpose of the enterprise (e.g., a train hitting a cow or setting a field on fire).[141]

In deciding strict products liability cases, the courts very early recognized they were dealing with the powerful: sellers, manufacturers, wholesalers, and retailers.[142] They sensed vague and hard-to-prove negligence terminology was inadequate for dealing with these well-asseted defendants; therefore, they

---

140. *Id.* at 206.
141. Anderson v. Minneapolis, St. P. & S. St. M. Ry. Co., 179 N.W. 45 (Minn. 1920).
142. *See* PROSSER, *supra* note 34, at 244–70.

adopted strict liability for cases involving defective products.[143] Beginning in 1964, the courts placed losses upon sellers by means of strict liability. In the period 1964–1992, strict liability was cited in thousands and thousands of published court opinions.[144] During this time almost every state adopted some form of strict liability for defective products.[145] The doctrine has been applied to all sorts of products: cars,[146] trucks,[147] airplanes,[148] above-ground swimming pools,[149] motorcycles,[150] breast implants,[151] and pharmaceuticals.[152] However, this explosion in strict liability did not go unnoticed by the powerful sellers and manufacturers; their rapid and dramatic response to this frontal attack will be examined in Chapter 4.

---

143. This is a fair description of the defendants discussed *supra* in text accompanying notes 1–25.

144. *See supra* note 16 and accompanying text.

145. *Id.* at 1529 (noting that in 1992, at least thirty-eight states had passed statutes dealing with products liability law).

146. *E.g.*, Bennett v. Matt Gay Chevrolet Oldsmobile, Inc., 408 S.E.2d 111 (Ga. App. 1991).

147. *E.g.*, Gonzales v. Carmenita Ford Truck Sales, Inc., 238 Cal. Rptr. 18 (Cal. Ct. App. 1987).

148. *E.g.*, Nachtsheim v. Beech Aircraft Corp., 847 F.2d 1261 (7th Cir. 1987).

149. *E.g.*, Richardson v. Clayton & Lambert Mfg. Co., 634 F.Supp. 1480 (N.D. Miss. 1986).

150. *E.g.*, Andrews v. Harley Davidson, Inc., 796 P.2d 1092 (Nev. 1990).

151. *E.g.*, Artiglio v. Sup. Ct., 27 Cal. Rptr. 2d 589 (Cal. Ct. App. 1994).

152. *E.g.*, Grinnell v. Charles Pfizer & Co., 79 Cal. Rptr. 369 (Cal. Ct. App. 1969).

4. LEGAL REFORM EMANATES FROM THE CORPORATE BOARDROOM, 1980–PRESENT

Recent reforms in theory and procedure put forward by the powerful have changed the way victims' attorneys view products cases. Once the poster child for judicial activism, products liability litigation has been dismantled piece by piece. These broad-spectrum reforms dramatically affect practically every facet of a modern products case, from the need for an expert witness to the amount and types of damages recoverable. A task of this chapter is to demonstrate large numbers of reforms to theory and procedures have dramatically affected the value of the products case[1] so that today the victim's attorney must reject all but the largest casess. In this way, corporate America (through the courts, legislatures, and agencies) has rewritten civil justice.

A. CONSTRICTIONS IN LEGAL THEORY

Section 402A is the most cited section of any Restatement.[2] Following its adoption in 1963, there were approximately seventeen years of expansion in strict liability and victims' access to the courts. However, corporations soon began a counterattack. The retrenchment in products liability began in the early 1980s with state legislation.

There have been numerous recent constrictions to strict liability theory, especially in the fundamental concepts of design defect and warning.[3] The original purpose of strict liability was to benefit consumers and prevent them from

---

1. Frank J, Vandall, *Constricting Products Liability: Reforms in Theory and Procedure*, 48 VILL. L. REV. 843 (2003).

2. James A. Henderson, Jr. & Aaron D. Twerski, *A Proposed Revision of Section 402A of the Restatement (Second) of Torts*, 77 CORNELL L. REV. 1512, 1512 (1992) (recognizing vast amounts of literature have been devoted to the field of products liability, focusing specifically on Section 402A of the Second Restatement). *See id.* at 1512–13 (indicating Section 402A has been cited by "thousands of products liability decisions").

3. *See, e.g.*, Barker v. Lull Eng'g Co., 573 P.2d 443, 452–53 (Cal. 1978) (providing that the first line of inquiry for design defects cases is whether the product performed as safely as an ordinary consumer would expect if the product were used in an intended and reasonably foreseeable manner; the second line is whether the benefits of the challenged design outweigh the risk of danger inherent in the design); Anderson v. Owens-Corning Fiberglass Corp., 810 P.2d 549, 553 (Cal. 1991) (following design defect test as laid out in *Barker*).

having to prove negligence.[4] There are three bases for holding a seller strictly liable: if the product contains a manufacturing defect, if there is a design defect, or if the manufacturer fails to provide an appropriate warning.[5]

In regard to design defect, the courts, impressed with the power of the manufacturers and sellers, have moved away from the original concept of strict liability as developed in *Escola, Greenman,* and the *Restatement (Second) of Torts* section 402A. Some courts have shifted to a negligence definition of design defect.[6] This shift is exemplified by contrasting *Barker v. Lull*[7] with *Anderson v. Owens Corning*

---

4. *See,* e.g., Escola v. Coca-Cola Bottling Co., 150 P.2d 436 (Cal. 1944) (Traynor, J., concurring) ("Those who suffer injury from defective products are unprepared to meet its consequences"). Traynor went on to comment:

> It is to the public interest to discourage the marketing of products having defects that are a menace to the public. If such products nevertheless find their way into the market it is to the public interest to place the responsibility for whatever injury they may cause upon the manufacturer, who, even if he is not negligent in the manufacture of the product, is responsible for its reaching the market.

Id. at 462. Traynor's concurrence found it significant that mass production of most public goods had all but eradicated the close relationship once held between manufacturer and consumer. *See id.* at 467. ("The consumer no longer has means or skills enough to investigate for himself the soundness of a product. . . ."). *Id.*

5. *See* McLaughlin v. Michelin Tire Corp., 778 P.2d 59, 82 (Wyo. 1989) (Urbrigkit, J., dissenting) ("A product may be defective in three ways: (1) manufacturing flaw; (2) defective design; (3) absence or inadequacy of warnings regarding the use of the product.").

6. *See,* e.g., Chaulk v. Volkswagen of Am., Inc., 808 F.2d 639, 641 (7th Cir. 1986) (relating action for design defect to ordinary negligence). The appellate court in *Chaulk* reversed the judgment of the district court and held the plaintiffs were entitled to a new trial on the issue of negligence regarding the manufacturer's faculty design of the latch system on its 1977 Volkswagen Rabbit. *See id.* at 643 (providing court's holding). This latch system was designed in a manner that caused it to release on impact from a side collision; as a result, the plaintiff was ejected from the car. *See id.* at 640 (discussing facts of a case); *see also* Parke-Davis & Co. v. Stromsodt, 411 F.2d 1390, 1399 (8th Cir. 1969) (holding a drug manufacturer was negligent as it gave inadequate warnings about the product); Sterling Drug, Inc. v. Yarrow, 408 F.2d 978, 994 (8th Cir. 1969) (finding a manufacturer liable for failing to use reasonable efforts to warn consumers); DeRosa v. Remington Arms Co., Inc., 509 F. Supp. 762, 766 (E.D.N.Y. 1981) ("[T]he New York Court of Appeals has recently made its recognition . . . of [the] process . . . of a negligence-type balancing into a cause of action in strict liability for design defect"); WILLIAM L. PROSSER & W. PAGE KEETON, PROSSER AND KEETON ON THE LAW OF TORTS § 99, 697 (5th ed. 1984) (noting that negligence is the standard for recovery in failure-to-warn cases). *But see* Ellen Wertheimer, *Unknowable Dangers and the Death of Strict Liability: The Empire Strikes Back,* 60 U. CIN. L. REV. 1183, 1185 (1992) (stating plaintiffs' recovery under strict liability "depends not upon the manufacturer acting negligently, but upon the manufacturer making the product and the product causing injury").

7. 573 P.2d at 455 (finding plaintiff need not prove negligence, but must rather make a prima facie showing the injury was caused by defendant's product).

Fiberglass Corp.[8] *Barker* indicated the defendant will be held strictly liable if the risks of the design exceed the benefit. *Anderson* required "knowledge" to be part of the test for strict liability: the seller must be shown to have known of the risk at the time of sale. Traditionally knowledge has been an element of negligence. The impact of this shift toward a negligence test for strict liability is to make it more expensive for consumers to prove their cases because the burden of showing negligence is heavier than for strict liability.[9] Thus, this shift to negligence helps to insulate the seller.

In 1982, the court in *Beshada v. Johns-Manville Products Corp.*[10] held a manufacturer could be strictly liable for failure to provide a warning even if the manufacturer did not know of the defect in the product and the need for a warning. This dramatically favored the consumer because only the absence of a warning of a material defect needed to be shown. The powerful were galvanized into action by this frontal attack and immediately fired back.

Since 1982, New Jersey and many other states have tended to move away from strict liability and have adopted a negligence test for warning.[11] Today, a manufacturer is only held liable for failure to provide an appropriate warning if it knew or should have known of the defect in the product and foresaw the need for a warning.[12] In the early strict liability cases such as *Beshada*, knowledge was not a requirement. This is because knowledge rings of negligence. Professor Ellen

---

8. 810 P.2d at 559 (holding manufacturer may present state-of-art defenses against strict liability lawsuit).

9. *See* John F. Vargo, *The Emperor's New Clothes: The American Law Institute Adorns a "New Cloth" for Section 402A Products Liability Design Defects—A Survey of the States Reveals a Different Weave*, 26 U. Mem. L. Rev. 493, 556 (1996) (providing jurisdictional interpretations of appropriate strict liability tests, and noting elimination of the consumer expectation test will force the plaintiff to present evidence of reasonable alternative design, which will drive up the cost of the case).

10. 447 A.2d 539, 546–47 (N.J. 1982) (holding manufacturer's state-of-art defense was not applicable).

11. *See, e.g.*, Richter v. Limax Intern, Inc., 45 F.3d 1464, 1468 (Kan. 1995) ("Kansas applies the sane test to whether a manufacturer met his duty to warn under negligence as it does under strict liability.").

12. *See, e.g.*, Karjala v. Johns-Manville Prods. Corp., 523 F.2d 155, 159 (8th Cir. 1975) (stating that manufacturer is said to possess the skills of an expert in the field and thereby has the duty to warn of any dangers); Borel v. Fiberboard Paper Prods. Corp., 493 F. 2d 1076, 1106 (5th Cir. 1974) (imposing liability for failure to adequately warn); Balido v. Improved Mach., Inc., 105 Cal Rptr. 890, 898–901 (Cal. Ct. App. 1972) (indicating manufacturer's warning regarding product's lack of safety devices or controls may be found to be inadequate if the consumer is likely to disregard warnings); Seley v. G.D. Searle Co., 423 N.E.2d 831, 836 (Ohio 1981) (holding the drug manufacturer could not be held strictly liable, despite fact that ingestion of drug caused the plaintiff to have a stroke, if the drug manufacturer provided warning with medication that reasonably disclosed to medical profession risks associated with use of such medication); Berkebile v. Brantley Helicopter

Wertheimer makes clear in her outstanding article that "knowledge" is indeed a negligence test for warning.[13]

The exception to the embrace of negligence is Alaska, which breathed new life into a warning cause of action based on strict liability. In *Shanks v. Upjohn Co.*,[14] a pilot committed suicide after taking a prescription calmative that lacked a warning. The court held the case could go to the jury even thought it was not clear the manufacturer knew of the risk of suicide that called for a warning.[15] However, the failure of other states to adopt a negligence test for warning means that manufacturers will continue to be held liable in failure-to-warn cases.[16]

Products liability has also been limited by the dramatic judicial expansion of the concept of preemption.[17] This theory posits that if there is a federal statute or regulation providing a standard, it preempts and replaces the conflicting state law.[18] The growth in preemption since around 1985 has been so rapid and

---

Corp., 337 A.2d 893, 902 (Pa. 1975) (noting adequacy of warning depends upon the seriousness of danger and whether consumer can reasonably appreciate that danger).

13. *See* Wertheimer, *supra* note 6, at 1202–05 (arguing the failure-to-warn doctrine, without imputation of knowledge, is reducible to ordinary negligence on the part of the manufacturer).

14. 835 P.2d 1189, 1192 (Alaska 1992) (reciting facts of case).

15. *See id.* at 1200 (finding the jury was entitled to hear plaintiff's strict liability claim even though the plaintiff could not show that defendant knew of danger posed by product).

16. *See* Anderson v. Owens-Corning Fiberglass Corp., 810 P.2d 549, 559 (Cal. 1991) (holding the manufacturer could not be held liable for the plaintiff's injuries unless the manufacturer knew at the time of manufacture or distribution that its product was harmful and that it failed to warn the consumers of such dangers); Wertheimer, *supra* note 6, at 1208 (noting failure-to-warn cases present a problem for defendants because a "warning is always feasible").

17. *See* Burke v. Dow Chem. Co., 797 F. Supp. 1128, 1132 (E.D.N.Y. 1992) (stating that if a court invokes federal preemption, a plaintiff may not have recourse); *see also* Jones v. Rath Packing Co., 430 U.S. 519, 532 (1977) (holding California law that conflicted with federal regulations regarding packaging and shipment of meat was invalid due to preemption doctrine); Moss v. Parks Corp., 985 F.2d 736, 740–41 (4th Cir. 1993) (holding products liability claims against paint thinner manufacturer were expressly preempted when plaintiff sought label requirements inconsistent with federal regulations); Barbara L. Atwell, *Products Liability and Preemption: A Judicial Framework*, 39 BUFF. L. REV. 181, 188–91 (1991) (concluding there had been compliance with federal regulation such that state law claim was preempted and "there is generally no basis for compensating the victim . . ."); Marc S. Klein et al., *State Product Liability Law and the "Realpolitik" of Federal Preemption*, CA11 ALI-ABA 23, 25 (1995) ("In the past decade, federal preemption has emerged as a very potent limitation on state product liability law").

18. *See* Phillip H. Corby & Todd Smith, *Federal Preemption of Products Liability Law: Federalism and the Theory of Implied Preemption*, 15 AM. J. TRIAL ADVOC. 435, 448 (1992) (citing the *Hines v. Davidowitz* Theory developed in Hines v. Davidowitz, 312 U.S. 52

dramatic that it is possible to suggest to defense attorneys that practically every time they find a federal statute or federal regulation providing a standard, they may argue the federal standard preempts any conflicting state statute or common law rule.[19] The leader of this judicial attack on state causes of action has been the U.S. Supreme Court.

An example of federal preemption is automobile airbags, with the federal courts striking down state cases that held a manufacturer of an automobile strictly liable if it failed to provide them.[20] The courts have ruled the federal statute allowing the manufacturer to choose either a mechanical seat belt or air bags was sufficient, and the manufacturer could not be held strictly liable if it selected the mechanical "decapitator" approach.[21] A second area expanding preemption involves pesticides.[22] As the Federal Insecticide Fungicide and Rodenticide Act

---

(1941) for proposition that state law is preempted when it stands in the way of full objectives of Congress); *see also* Louisiana Pub. Serv. Comm'n v. FCC, 476 U.S. 355, 369 (1986) ("Pre-emption may result not only from the action taken by Congress itself; a federal agency acting within the scope of its congressionally delegated authority may pre-empt state regulation."); Mulhern v. Outboard Marine Corp., 432 N.W.2d 130, 134 (Wis. Ct. App. 1988) (finding federal preemption of matter deprives plaintiff from seeking redress under state law).

19. *See*, e.g., Geier v. Am. Honda Motor Co., Inc., 529 U.S. 861, 867–69 (2000) (holding federal safety requirements for automobiles preempted plaintiff's design defect lawsuit based on failure of car manufacturer to install driver's-side air bags). *But see* Medtronics, Inc. v. Lohr, 518 U.S. 470, 503 (1996) (concluding the Medical Device Amendments of 1976 did not preempt the plaintiff's common law claims).

20. *See*, e.g., Porkorny v. Ford Motor Co., 902 F.2d 1116, 1123 (3d Cir. 1990) (holding the state claim that the van was defectively designed because it failed to be equipped with air bags was preempted by federal statute); Schwartz v. Volvo N. Am. Corp., 554 So. 2d 927 (Ala. 1989) (holding the National Traffic and Motor Vehicle Safety Act preempts any state claims for failure to install air bags); Boyle v. Chrysler Corp., 501 N.W. 2d 865, 867 (Wis. Ct. App. 1993) (indicating compliance with the federal act preempts state law claims based on the absence of air bags)

21. Hunter v. Gen. Motors Corp., 1988 WL 288972, *8 (D. Conn. 1988) (holding the National Traffic and Motor Vehicle Safety Act preempts state law by giving manufacturers options on how to meet safety requirements). In a crash, drivers who forgot to fasten the lap belt were often decapitated by the shoulder strap. *See* Miles v. Ford Motor Co., No. 05-99-01258-CV, 2001, WL 727355, at *7 (Tex. App. 2001) (providing factual claims made by plaintiffs that passive seat belt system had decapitated dummies during institutional motor tests)

22. *See* Papas v. Upjohn Co., 926 F.2d 1019, 1024 (11th Cir. 1991), *vacated* by 504 U.S. 1215 (1992) (holding the Federal Insecticide, Fungicide and Rodenticide Act (FIFRA) preempts any state-law claims in regards to warnings); Kennan v. Dow Chem. Co., 717 F. Supp. 799, 805 (M.D.Fla. 1989) (holding congressional intent to create a comprehensive system for pesticide labeling was adequate to preempt contradictory state regulations); Fitzgerald v. Mallinckrodt, Inc., 681 F. Supp. 404, 409 (E.D. Mich. 1987); (denying recovery in tort when the federal government has preempted state regulation through enactment of

(FIFRA) sets up standards for pesticides, several decisions have held these pre-empt conflicting state law.[23]

A third important expansion in the concept of preemption is in tobacco litiga-tion. In the famous *Cipollone v. Liggett Group, Inc.*[24] case, Rose Cipollone smoked for over forty years, finally dying of lung cancer. The case spanned seven years of litigation and involved thirteen federal decisions, including two appeals to the U.S. Supreme Court.[25] The Court held that even though there was no express language in the relevant federal statute, there was express preemption of the plaintiff's allegation of failure to provide an appropriate warning.[26] In this case, preemption protected the powerful tobacco manufacturers from challenge.

The plaintiff's attorney in the *Cipollone* case is rumored to have expended mil-lions of dollars in this suit against the cigarette manufacturers.[27] The case stands for the rule that if you sue a large manufacturer, it is going to spend millions of dollars to defend and force you to spend a like amount[28]—the concept of justice will not save you. Rose Cipollone died, her husband (the next plaintiff) died, then her son took over the case and finally voluntarily discharged the suit.[29] The point is that bringing a products liability case is often enormously expensive, and if the law is not in the plaintiff's favor going in (as in *Cipollone*), the risk of spending millions of dollars and losing is substantial.

In contrast to *Cipollone*, however, several recent cigarette cases have been brought based on fraud.[30] The attorneys argued the cigarette manufacturers

---

FIFRA); Davidson v. Velsicol Chem. Corp., 834 P.2d 931, 936 (Nev. 1992) (ruling FIFRA implicitly preempts state tort claims based on a failure to adequately label pesticide)

23. *See Papas*, 926 F.2d at 1023 (providing congressional language banning contradic-tory state labeling requirements).

24. 505 U.S. 504, 508 (1992) (discussing facts of case).

25. *See* Cipollone v. Liggett Group, Inc., 693 F. Supp. 208 (D.N.J. 1998), *aff'd in part, rev'd in part*, 893 F.2d (3d Cir. 1990), *aff'd in part, rev'd in part*, 505 U.S. 504 (1992) (noting jury's attribution of eighty percent responsibility to Mrs. Cipollone barred plaintiff's recovery on failure-to-warn claim).

26. *See Cipollone*, 505 U.S. at 524–30 (holding federal statute disallowed plaintiff's defect claim due to manufacturer's failure to provide warning on cigarette carton).

27. *See* Carl T. Bogus, *War on the Common Law: The Struggle at the Center of Products Liability*, 60 Mo. L. Rev. 1, 58 (1995) (detailing breadth of *Cipollone*) (citing Henry J. Reske, *Cigarette Suit Dropped*, A.B.A. J., Feb. 1993, at 30).

28. *See* Stephen Koepp, *Tobacco's First Loss: A Landmark Verdict is Likely to Spawn Many More Suits Against the Industry*, Time, June 27, 1988, at 50 (reporting that in recent years cigarette manufacturers are estimated to have spent anywhere between six hundred mil-lion and three billion dollars).

29. *See* Charles S. Griffith, III, Note, *The Legacy of the Marlboro Man*, 24 N. Ky. L. Rev. 593, 599–600 (1997) (providing background factual information regarding *Cipollone*) (citing Reske, *supra* note 27, at 30).

30. *See, e.g.*, Falise v. Am. Tobacco Co., 94 F.Supp.2d 316 (E.D.N.Y. 2000) (setting forth plaintiff's argument that defendant tobacco manufacturer fraudulently misled public

defrauded the consumers by suggesting cigarettes were safe and failing to disclose they knew cigarettes were addictive and would kill a certain percentage of the consumers if used exactly as intended.[31]

Perhaps the expansion of the doctrine of preemption has bottomed out. In March 2009, the U.S. Supreme Court held in *Wyeth v. Levine* that the approval of a warning label by the Food and Drug Administration did not preempt a state cause of action claiming the warning should have been stronger.[32] Under Vermont law, Wyeth's warning was held to be flawed, and the plaintiff was awarded $79 million.[33]

Two examples of the control corporations have over Congress, state legislatures, and agencies are tobacco and firearms. As with Nero, it is as if the federal and state legislatures are fiddling as thousands of citizens die—they have left the survival of individual citizens to the will of the powerful and the courts. In regard to tobacco, Congress has not adopted any meaningful laws holding tobacco manufacturers liable for providing a lethal product. Just the opposite is true: Congress expressly provided that the Food and Drug Administration (FDA) and the Consumer Product Safety Commission lacked authority to deal with the deadly aspects of tobacco.[34] Tobacco is the most dangerous product in the world because it takes the lives of more than 400,000 people each year. It would seem obvious the Consumer Product Safety Commission would have jurisdiction over tobacco, but the enabling act expressly provides the Commission lacks such authority.[35] The powerful tobacco manufacturers worked to make sure nothing of importance would be done by the Commission in regard to tobacco. However, this has changed somewhat as one of President Obama's first acts was to give the FDA limited power to regulate tobacco.[36]

---

regarding effects of smoking); *see also* Castano v. Am. Tobacco Co., 961 F.Supp. 953, 956 (E.D.La., 1997) (noting plaintiff's contentions that tobacco manufacturer fraudulently failed to inform consumers of addictive nature of nicotine).

31. *See, e.g., Falise,* 94 F. Supp. 2d at 328 (acknowledging arguments made by plaintiffs that tobacco manufacturers had actual knowledge of lethal consequences of smoking).

32. Wyeth v. Levine, 129 S. Ct. 1187, 1204 (U.S. 2009).

33. *Id.* at 1189.

34. *See, e.g.,* FDA v. Brown & Williamson Tobacco Corp., 529 U.S. 120, 142 (2000) (holding that Congress clearly intended to "exclude tobacco products from the FDA's jurisdiction") (citing Consumer Product Safety Commission Improvements Act of 1976, Pub.L. 94-284, § 3(c), 90 Stat. 503 (codified at 15 U.S.C. § 1261(f)(2))). Congress has adopted legislation "that eliminates the agency's (Consumer Product Safety Commission) authority to regulate tobacco and tobacco products. *See Brown & Williamson,* 529 U.S. at 151 (denoting congressional action to remove authority from CPSC).

35. *See id.* at 127–28 (finding that tobacco kills over three million people each year worldwide, and 400,000 in the United States alone).

36. Family Smoking Prevention and Tobacco Control Act, H.R. 1256/S.982; Signed into law by President Obama on June 22, 2009. The Act grants authority to the FDA to

Congress and the state legislatures have failed to deal with another epidemic: handgun violence.[37] Although a large number of regulations deal with firearms, these are only window dressing as they concern only the mechanical details of firearms purchase and ownership.[38] Even the Brady Bill, enacted on the heels of President Reagan's shooting, fails to confront the major issue, which is the saturation of the country with firearms.[39] In failing to address this epidemic of eighteen thousand deaths per year, Congress and state legislatures have tacitly approved the large number of violent and unnecessary deaths of children, spouses, and strangers.[40] Through omission, they have substantially contributed to the death of the inner cities (as claimed by Bridgeport, Connecticut, in its suit against the gun manufacturers).[41] This is dramatic evidence of the state and federal legislative embrace of the powerful.

The almost complete control of the state legislatures by the gun lobby is illustrated by the failure to respond to this epidemic other than the instantaneous reaction of the Georgia legislature in passing an act that forbids cities to sue the manufacturers of firearms for civil damages.[42] At a Pepperdine Law School

---

regulate the marketing, manufacturing, and sale of tobacco products, but the agency lacks the power to ban the products.

37. *See* Frank J. Vandall, *Economic and Causation Issues in City Suits Against Gun Manufacturers*, 27 Pepp. L. Rev. 719, 719 (2000) ("[T]he epidemic of [gun] violence has been largely ignored by American society. . . .").

38. *See* Frank J. Vandall, *O.K. Corral II: Policy Issues in Municipal Suits Against Gun Manufacturers*, 44 Vill. L. Rev. 547, 547–52 (1999) (chronicling deleterious effects of gun ownership).

39. *See* Brendan J. Healy, *Plugging the Bullet Holes in U.S. Gun Law: An Ammunition-Based Proposal for Tightening Gun Control*, 32 J. Marshall L. Rev. 1, 21 (1998) ("Perhaps the biggest weakness in Brady is the ease with which it can be circumvented . . . Brady has a neglible effect on those who already own guns, those who purchase their guns using a strawman, those who steal guns and those who purchase guns on the secondary market"); *see also* James B. Jacobs & Kimberly A. Potter, *Keeping Guns Out of the "Wrong" Hands: The Brady Law and the Limits of Regulation*, 86 J. Crim. L. & Criminology 93, 104 (1995) ("Brady supporters may have underestimated the ease with which the regulatory scheme can be circumvented and they may have overestimated the ability of government agencies to enforce these regulations.").

40. *See* Vandall, *supra* note 37, at 719 (documenting mortality rates due to gun violence).

41. *See* Vandall, *supra* note 38, at 549 ("The city of Bridgeport, Connecticut, for example, is suing [gun manufacturers] for the cost of deterioration of the city."). Bridgeport ultimately lost in the courts. *See Cincinnati Has a Shot*, Columbus Dispatch, June 18, 2002, at 8A (describing the *Bridgeport* case).

42. *See* H.B. 189, 145th Gen. Assembly, Reg. Sess. (Ga. 1999) (reserving civil action against gun manufacturers to state discretion). Only nine days after Atlanta sued, the Georgia Legislature barred such suits. *See* Vandall, *supra* note 38, at 556 (discussing the efforts of gun manufacturers in lobbying the Georgia legislature) (citing Kathy Pruitt, *Blocking of Gun Suit Now Law*, Atlanta J.-Const., Feb. 10, 1999, at B1).

symposium, a lawyer for the National Rifle Association (NRA) was proud to state that while attending a gun convention in Atlanta, NRA representatives were able to walk across the street and instantly persuade the Georgia legislature to pass the above-mentioned prohibitive legislation.[43] The courts were equally impressed with the power of the gun industry and avoided holding gun sellers liable up to 2005, at that time Congress outlawed most damage suits against gun manufacturers.[44]

The Brady Bill was a step forward and has allegedly been successful in preventing gun sales to more than two hundred thousand criminals, but its critical failure is that it still permits every day the sale of firearms to thousands of citizens.[45] This continues the clear and foreseeable danger of children obtaining firearms from their parents or others and shooting their parents or other children, as well as spouses using handguns to kill each other, and the large number of shootings of total strangers in the United States. As of February 2009, there are no cases that hold a gun manufacturer liable for such regularized shootings.[46]

B. PROCEDURAL RETRENCHMENTS: THE PRESENTATION OF THE PRODUCTS CASE IN THE COURTROOM

Procedure is the grease of the civil litigation process. It determines key issues such as where to sue, the qualifications of expert witnesses, and whether a number of victims can join together in one suit. Quite often procedural issues determine the outcome of the case. Almost all of these procedural retrenchments were determined by the courts—and the changes tend to favor corporate defendants.

The purpose of this section is to demonstrate that various recent modifications in the law related to discovery, presentation of evidence, punitive damages, and need for an expert witness have helped to bring about a dramatic increase in the costs of litigating a products liability case. It follows that the more expensive

---

43. *See* Vandall, *supra* note 37, at 722 n. 53 (reporting Governor Roy Barnes signed a bill into law blocking the City of Atlanta's lawsuit against gun manufacturers, potentially bringing an end to the legislative battle over the right of any local government to bring a products liability suit against gun manufacturers) (citing Kathy Pruitt, *supra* note 42, at B1).

44. Protection of Lawful Commerce in Arms Act, Pub. L. No. 92, 119 Stat. 2095 (2005).

45. *See* Healey, *supra* note 39, at 21 (noting ability of gun holders to circumvent system); Timothy D. Lytton, *Lawsuits Against the Gun Industry: A Comparative Institutional Analysis*, 32 CONN. L. REV. 1247, 1255 (2000) ("Illegal sales at the retail level are quite common.").

46. For a further discussion of cases supporting the fact no gun manufacturer has yet to be held liable for gun violence, see *supra* notes 37 and 38.

the process, the fewer the number of people who will be able to sue. Fewer suits translate into increased profits for the powerful.

One of the most costly developments in the litigation of a products liability case is the almost absolute requirement of having an expert in every case.[47] This was made crystal clear by the Supreme Court in the 1993 case *Daubert v. Merrell Dow Pharmaceuticals.*[48] *Daubert* involved Bendectin, which was a calmative given to pregnant women.[49] The mothers of children who were born with congenital birth defects brought suits, alleging these defects were caused by the mothers consuming Bendectin during the period when the fetus was forming limbs.[50] The children displayed missing and shortened limbs as well as incomplete neurological development in some cases.[51] After many years of intermediate appeals, the Supreme Court held the trial judge was the gatekeeper who had the power to evaluate the credentials of expert witnesses, as well as whether their testimony would be of value to the jury.[52] Following *Daubert*, numerous courts rejected the plaintiff's proposed expert witness.[53]

However, some assumed *Daubert* was limited to scientific and technology-based cases and would not be applied to nontechnical cases.[54] This flawed assumption was corrected by the U.S. Supreme Court in the 1999 case of *Kumho Tire Co., Ltd. v. Carmichael,*[55] in which *Daubert* was held to apply to nontechnical cases.[56] In *Kumho*, a tire on a minivan exploded, and the plaintiff's expert testified the tire was defectively designed. The Court ruled that as the gatekeeper function of the trial court applied to nonscientific testimony, the trial court could reject the expert witness on the basis he was insufficiently trained or experienced.[57] The significance of the *Kumho* decision is the expert witness requirement now

---

47. *See, e.g.,* 735 Ill. Comp. Stat. 5/2-623 (1997) (requiring certificate of merit from an expert in all products liability actions). This statute was held unconstitutional in Best v. Taylor Mach. Works, 689 N.E.2d 1057 (Ill. 1997).

48. 509 U.S. 579, 584 (1993) (establishing standards for admission of expert witness testimony).

49. *See id.* at 582 (explaining use of Bendectin).

50. *See id.* (discussing Bendectin as a potential teratogen).

51. *See id.* (listing various birth defects).

52. *See id.* (holding trial judge must determine whether expert's reasoning or methodology is valid and can be applied to the facts at hand).

53. *See, e.g.,* Weisgram v. Marley Co., 528 U.S. 440, 457 (2000) (holding the court may exclude "erroneously admitted" evidence through exclusion of experts).

54. *But see* Kumho Tire Co., Ltd. v. Carmichael, 526 U.S. 137, 141 (1999) (explaining trial judges' "gate keeping" duties).

55. *See id.* at 152 (granting trial court increased "latitude in deciding how to test an expert's reliability").

56. *See id.* at 151 (declining to limit standards for experts to scientific or technical fields).

57. *See id.* at 153 (allowing expert to be rejected based on methodology employed when making decisions and/or on qualifications).

applies to all cases, scientific as well as nonscientific.[58] *Daubert,* in conjunction with *Kumho,* stands for the rule the plaintiff's expert will be carefully scrutinized in all products cases. The impact on a products case is that the price of a lawsuit has increased by the cost of finding an expert whose qualifications can withstand this scrutiny and extended trial preparation. Assuming the cost of such an expert is approximately $25,000, *Daubert* and *Kumho* have arguably increased the cost of presenting a products case by this amount. Also, although *Daubert* involves a rule for handling federal cases, it has expanded to state cases. When a plaintiff's assets are limited, each increase in the cost of litigation further restricts the opportunity for the injured consumer to sue and further insulates the manufacturer.

Another critical development that has constricted the litigation of products liability cases is the broad refusal by the courts to embrace the class action concept embodied in the Federal Rules of Civil Procedure,[59] which provide:

> One or more members of a class may sue or be sued as representative parties on behalf of all only if (1) the class is so numerous that joinder of all members is impracticable, (2) there are questions of law or fact common to the class, (3) the claims or defenses of the representative parties are typical of the claims or defenses of the class, and (4) the representative parties will fairly and adequately protect the interest of the class.[60]

As illustrated by the language of the rule, small but numerous products liability cases precisely meet the test. For instance, the most obvious product for a class action suit is tobacco. The injured smoker should be able to join with other injured smokers as a class and sue the tobacco manufacturers. Tobacco naturally meets the requirements of a class action[61] because there are many victims and common facts.[62] Specifically, the numerous victims all smoked cigarettes for varying periods of time with the same product (tobacco) being involved.[63]

---

58. *See id.* (providing example of expert witness requirement being applied in a nonscientific manner).

59. *See* Martin L.C. Feldman, *Predominance and Products Liability Class Actions: An Idea Whose Time Has Passed?,* 74 TUL. L. REV. 1621, 1627 (exploring that courts have cautioned it is necessary to strictly adhere to the requirements of class certification under the Federal Rules).

60. FED. R. CIV. P. 23(a) (setting forth requirements for class actions to ensure fair and adequate representation for all parties).

61. Vandall, *supra* note 1, at 866. *See also* Castano v. Am. Tobacco Co., 160 F.R.D. 544, 555 (E.D. La. 1995) (indicating unique nature of product makes tobacco amenable to class action).

62. Vandall, *supra* note 1, at 866. *See also Castano,* 160 F.R.D. at 555 (acknowledging large numbers of victims and similarity of facts are requisites to class action suits).

63. Vandall, *supra* note 1, at 867. *See also Castano,* 160 F.R.D. at 555 (citing common injury cause of action as cigarette addiction).

In most, each smoker contracts one of four forms of cancer and is seriously injured or dies.[64]

This was the basis of a Louisiana class action lawsuit where the lower district court certified the class by holding the class action provision applied to cigarette smokers.[65] However, the district court certification was rejected by the Federal Court of Appeals. Judge Smith, quoting Judge Posner, wrote:

> One Jury . . . will hold the fate of an industry in the palm of its hand . . . That kind of thing can happen in our system of civil justice. . . . But it need not be tolerated when the alternative exists of submitting an issue to multiple juries constituting in the aggregate a much larger and more diverse sample of decision-makers. That would not be a feasible option if the stakes to each class member were too slight to repay the cost of suit . . . But this is not the case . . . Each plaintiff if successful is apt to receive a judgment in the millions . . . With the aggregate stakes in the tens or hundreds of millions of dollars, or even in the billions, it is not a waste of judicial resources to conduct more than one trial, before more than six jurors . . . ."[66]

Clearly what Judge Smith means is it is appropriate for a powerful corporation to cause the deaths of over four hundred thousand lives a year (over three million worldwide), but it is not appropriate for the consumers who are injured or killed to take these tobacco manufacturers to court as a class in order to shift the loss, raise the price, and deter the manufacturing of such a product.[67] Posner wants the powerful corporations to take on the consumers one by one.

An exception to the historical cigarette class action prohibition is the case in Florida brought by numerous nonsmoking airline flight attendants who argued the smoke in airplanes caused their lung cancer.[68] The court certified the flight attendants as a class, and they recovered a small amount. Perhaps the court was motivated to certify the class because the plaintiffs agreed to reject damages based on their physical injuries, accepting only punitive damages that would go toward research and prevention.[69]

---

64. Vandall, *supra* note 1, at 867. *See also Castano*, 160 F.R.D. at 548 (noting that smoker must have suffered serious injury or death to be in class, but recognizing the widow of a smoker may serve as plaintiff).

65. Vandall, *supra* note 1, at 867. *See also Castano*, 160 F.R.D. at 561 (E.D. La. 1995) (certifying class action pursuant to Fed. R. Civ. P. 23(b) and 23(c)(4)).

66. Castano v. Am. Tobacco Co., 84 F.3d 734, 748 (5th Cir. 1996) (quoting directly from Judge Posner's decision regarding fee or loss shifting).

67. *See id.* at 752 (reversing and remanding district court's decision to certify class with instructions that district court dismiss class complaint).

68. *See* Broin v. Phillip Morris Cos., Inc., 641 So. 2d 888, 892 (Fla. App. 1994) (reasserting class action allegations).

69. *See* John Pacenti, *Flight Attendants Seek Approval of $349 Million*, Assoc. Press, Jan. 26, 1998, at 1–2, *available at* 1998 WL 7379727 (reporting settlement that called for $300 million for medical research and $49 million for legal fees and expenses).

Another class action brought by thousands of Florida smokers reached a jury verdict of $145 billion in the summer of 2000.[70] The lawsuit was brought on behalf of five hundred thousand Floridians against five of the nation's largest cigarette manufacturers[71] by a Miami pediatrician alleging smoking caused his emphysema. The tobacco manufacturers responded by stating no scientific proof exists that smoking causes any particular illness and that the public is well aware smoking is risky. The jury rejected the industry's claims and found for the smokers on all counts.[72] However, this apparent victory for smokers was thrown out for technical reasons.[73]

If fairness were the key factor in products litigation, courts would work to make certain corporate defendants do not use their wealth to bludgeon the victims. But courts do not. Most products liability suits involve defendants who are large American or foreign corporations. No products suit against such a defendant is going to be inexpensive.[74] A preferred tactic used by well-asseted opponents in all types of litigation is to make the victim to spend large amounts of money in litigation.[75] In these cases, the defendant manufacturer forces the plaintiff's attorney to spend a huge amount in prosecuting the case.[76] Perhaps the best example is the *Cipollone* tobacco case, where it is estimated the plaintiff's attorney spent approximately $6 million preparing and presenting the case.[77] In *Cipollone*, it became clear the defendants' goal was to "paper the plaintiff to death."[78] The cigarette manufacturers used the discovery process to drag out the

---

70. *See* News Service Wire, *Re B&W Statement*, REG. NEWS SERV., July 17, 2000, *available at* 2000 WL 24184584 (reporting jury award was ten times net worth of companies being sued).

71. The suit was brought against R.J. Reynolds, Brown & Williamson, Lorillard Tobacco, Philip Morris, and Ligget Group, Inc. *See id.* (referring to defendants in the case).

72. *See id.* (relating that jury's decision was exclusively in favor of class of smokers and included total judgment of $272.11 billion against tobacco companies).

73. "[T]he Florida Supreme Court upheld the lower court's decision to throw out the $145 billion in damages awarded by a jury in the case known as Engle v. Liggett." Robert Walberg, *MSN Monday*, July 6, 2006.

74. *See* News Service Wire, *supra* note 70 (noting many tactical weapons used by large corporate defendants in product liability cases).

75. *See id.* (recognizing financial burdens of litigation may prevent plaintiffs from bringing and sustaining suits).

76. *See, e.g.*, Cipollone v. Liggett Group, Inc., 505 U.S. 504, 506 (1992) (acknowledging some obstacles to class actions brought against large corporations).

77. *See id.* (providing an example of how time-consuming and expensive products liability cases can be).

78. *See id.* (setting forth types of strategic delays defendants in product liability cases may employ); *see also* Bogus, *supra* note 27, at 58 (noting exhaustion is a powerful weapon for large corporate defendants).

case and increase the cost of litigation.[79] Large corporate defendants often adopt the posture that the victim must "prove everything," which is enormously expensive.[80] These tactics were victorious in *Cipollone* because, after the plaintiff died, the plaintiff's son voluntarily discontinued the case.[81] This dismissal followed multiple federal *Cipollone* cases .[82]

In support of these developments, tort reform (decreasing the opportunity to sue) and corporate insulation is most evident in three areas: discovery, punitive damages, and statutes of repose. The impact of discovery and factors affecting punitive damages are discussed below.

Protracted discovery in products cases has helped to expand the cost of litigation. An article by Professors George Shepherd and Morgan Cloud argues discovery is the primary reason for the explosion in the costs of litigating all cases—including products cases.[83] The authors reason that, as it is risky for either side to forego lengthy discovery, many cases have now become prohibitively expensive.[84] They conclude discovery has "weighted the scales of justice against some of society's most vulnerable groups," and that this increased financial burden has made litigation unaffordable for many people.[85] The obvious beneficiaries of expensive discovery are the powerful, who can afford it.

One way to deter corporations who engage in willful misconduct is to punish them with extra-damages called punitive damages. But plaintiffs in products liability suits must face the risk that even if they are successful in winning punitive damages, large portions of the award may be taken away from them. In the

---

79. *See Cipollone,* 505 U.S. at 506 (recognizing that more than nine years of litigation had passed since the original complaint had been filed).

80. *See* Elizabeth Gleick, *Tobacco Blues: The Tobacco Industry Has Never Lost a Lawsuit but a New Billion Dollar Legal Assault and a High-Ranking Defector May Change That,* TIME, Mar. 11, 1996, at 54 (noting the Liggett Group had already spent $75 million defending the lawsuit and was prepared to spend even more).

81. *See* Bogus, *supra* note 27, at 58 (quoting Henry J. Reske, *Cigarette Suit Dropped,* A.B.A.J., Feb. 1993, at 30, and noting that after the death of the parents, neither the son nor attorneys "wanted to continue the fight").

82. *See, e.g., Cipollone,* 505 U.S. at 506 (setting forth the history of the case). A Florida attorney, Woody Wilner, has discovered a way to dramatically reduce the costs of litigating a tobacco suit: he does not attend the tobacco manufacturers' depositions of the plaintiff. *See* Howard Erichson, *Informal Aggregation: Procedural and Ethical Implication of Coordination Among Counsel in Related Law Suits,* 50 DUKE L.J. 381, 390 (2000) (noting strategies employed by successful plaintiff's attorney).

83. *See* George B. Shepherd & Morgan Cloud, *Time and Money: Discovery Leads to Hourly Billing,* 1999 U. ILL. L. REV. 91, 126–29 (examining transformations in legal proceedings due to discovery rules).

84. *See id.* at 98 (theorizing the uncertainty of discovery costs has increased stakes and forced litigants to cover all bases).

85. *Id.* (suggesting that increasing the cost of discovery effectively precludes poorer segments from suits).

case of *BMW v. Gore*,[86] involving fraud on the part of BMW in failing to inform consumers the manufacturer had repainted portions of brand-new BMWs, the plaintiff recovered a $2 million punitive damage award in the state court.[87] However, on appeal the U.S. Supreme Court held the award violated the Fourteenth Amendment.[88]

In deciding whether a punitive damage award is excessive and in violation of the Fourteenth Amendment, the Court indicated it would look at three factors.[89] One is the nature of the injury:[90] is it based on economic loss or personal injury? The value of the BMW was decreased because of the new paint job, which is an economic loss. (Because many products liability cases involve personal injury, a victim may be able to argue the holding in *BMW*, resting on economic loss, does not apply.) The second factor is the ratio of punitive damages to out-of-pocket losses.[91] The Court suggested a ratio of four-to-one, or perhaps in extreme cases ten-to-one, might be appropriate, but anything larger (beyond a single digit ratio) is suspect.[92] Finally, the Court suggests the amount of punitive damages should bear some relationship to the criminal penalty for that type of conduct, and in the *BMW* case the most that could be awarded as a fine was $10,000.[93] The Court sent a $79 million punitive award in a cigarette case back to the state court for reconsideration.[94] This remand of the case suggests that punitive awards in personal injury cases will not escape emasculation by the Supreme Court.

Another way to benefit the powerful is to permit punitive awards, but then take some of it away. Several states, such as Georgia, have statutes that return a large percentage of the punitive damages obtained in a products liability case to the state.[95] The Georgia statute provides that seventy-five percent of the punitive damage award goes to the state rather than the victim.[96] Instead of slapping the

---

86. 517 U.S. 559 (1996).

87. *See id.* at 568–71 (imposing punitive damages to further states' legitimate interests in punishing unlawful conduct and deterring repetition).

88. *See id.* at 573–75 (stating that because of the Fourteenth Amendment, punitive damages may not be "granted disproportionate[ly]").

89. *See id.* at 576–85 (defining in general three aggravating factors that must be present for a punitive damages award).

90. *See id.* at 575 (stating "some wrongs are more blameworthy than others").

91. *See id.* at 580–81 (declaring "exemplary damages must bear a reasonable relationship to compensating damages").

92. *See id.* (endorsing various "reasonable" ratios).

93. *See id.* at 582–83 (rejecting impulse for categorical approach but precluding awards that "raise a suspicious judicial eyebrow").

94. Phillip Morris v. Williams, 549 U.S. 346 (2007).

95. *See* GA. CODE ANN § 51-12-5.1(e)(2) (2002) (stating "seventy-five percent of . . . punitive damages, less . . . costs . . . shall be paid into state's treasury").

96. *See id.* (stating Georgia law with respect to punitive damages).

hands of the defendant for producing a defective product that maims or kills, the hands of the victim's attorney are slapped for obtaining justice for the client. The message from the legislature to Georgia attorneys is clear: Do not take products cases. Do not represent injured consumers. This is concrete evidence of the legislature's affection for the powerful corporations.

The powerful realize numerous factors affect the calculations by the plaintiff's attorney in deciding whether to accept a products case. The impact of the theoretical and procedural reforms since 1980, is plaintiffs' attorneys will likely refuse to accept many modest-sized products liability cases because they believe they will lose the case or even if they win, the victory will not cover their out-of-pocket expenses. There are several possible solutions to this virtual closing of the courthouse doors to modest products cases.

First, follow the "superfund" model for toxic spills and assess the corporations that produce the largest amount of recurring damage and the most severe losses in products cases. The money would be used to fund a program that would provide justice in modest products cases.[97] The Comprehensive Environmental Response, Compensation and Liability Act of 1980 (CERCLA) has become widely referred to as "superfund" because it "establishes a multi-billion dollar 'hazardous substance response trust fund'" as a means of financing governmental cleanups of hazardous chemical waste spills and sites.[98] CERCLA is funded in part by the government's ability to recover the costs of any response or remedial actions taken when there is an actual or threatened release of a hazardous or toxic substance at a disposal site. Under section 107(a), CERCLA allows the government to name as parties to recovering the costs of the cleanup the owner or operator of the facility, the persons who arranged for the disposal, the persons in charge of the treatment or transportation of the toxic materials, and the transporters of such hazardous wastes.[99] This provision places ultimate liability on the

---

97. *See* 42 U.S.C. §§ 9601(11), 9604 (Dec. 11, 1980) (establishing "trust fund" for receipt of penalties); 26 U.S.C. § 9507 (Dec. 11, 1980) (delineating powers and functions of "Hazard Substance Superfund"); *see also* United States. v. Bestfoods, 524 U.S. 51, 55–56 (1998) (noting CERCLA holds responsible the parties who polluted).

98. Douglas F. Brennan, *Joint and Several Liability for Generators Under Superfund: A Federal Formula for Cost Recovery*, 5 UCLA J. Envtl. L. & Pol'y 101, 105–06 (1986) (citing CERCLA, 42 U.S.C. § 9631) (stating CERCLA allows remedial and abatement actions).

99. *See id.* (citing United States v. A & F Materials Co., Inc., 582 F. Supp. 842, 845 (S.D. Ill. 1984) (restating test of liability); *see also* United States v. Ward, 618 F. Supp. 884, 895 (E.D.N.C. 1985) (providing an interpretation of CERCLA statute). The general test for whether a defendant is liable under Section 107(a) is whether the defendant(s) decided to put the waste into the hands of a facility that contains hazardous waste. *See id.* (acknowledging CERCLA statute to hold generators of hazardous waste strictly liable for disposal of by-products).

chemical manufacturers.[100] Thus Congress, through CERCLA, has provided a means by which the financial burdens of hazardous waste cleanups rest on the responsible chemical industry.[101]

The second approach might be modeled after the "black lung" act that reimburses expenses for coal miners who have developed black lung disease.[102] The trigger for payment is a certification by a doctor that the damage the miner suffered was caused by inhalation of coal dust.[103] The purpose of the "Black Lung" Act of 1972 is to provide compensation for claimants who became disabled due to pneumoconiosis contracted while mining.[104] The act requires proof of three things for a claimant to recover: (1) disease or pneumoconiosis;[105] (2) causation;[106] and (3) disability, defined as an inability to engage in coal mine employment (or its functional equivalent) caused by pneumoconiosis.[107] The "Black Lung" Act suggests there could be a stated threshold and compensation for modest products injuries. This would shift the loss from the victim to the corporation.

A third possible solution is to enact a special victim-of-products court that would provide simplified procedures such as limitations on discovery and a restriction on damages to less than $100,000. This could be modeled after the popular small claims courts,[108] which developed in the early 1900s in response to the expense and insufficiencies of the regular courts.[109] Proponents of the

---

100. *See Ward,* 618 F. Supp. at 895 (citing 42 U.S.C. § 9607(a)(3) (1982)) (stating generators of hazardous material cannot escape liability by disregarding the method by which their products were disposed of).

101. *See id.* (citing United States v. A & F Materials Co., Inc., 578 F. Supp. 1252) (D.C. Ill. 1984) (holding liability cannot be avoided by characterizing the transaction as a sale).

102. *See* William S. Mattingly, *Blacklung Update: The Evolution of the Current Regulations and the Proposed Revolution,* 100 W. Va. L. Rev. 601, 602 (1998) (discussing recent changes and interpretations of Black Lung Benefit Acts).

103. *See* Timothy F. Cogan, *Is the Doctor Hostile? Obstructive Impairments and the Hostility Rule in Federal Black Lung Claims,* 97 W. Va. L. Rev. 1003, 1006 (1995) (explaining that to be covered under the Black Lung Act, claimant must show that inability to perform coal mine employment was due to pneumoconiosis).

104. *See* 30 U.S.C. § 901 (1988 and Supp. V. 1993) (noting the purpose and intent of the Black Lung Benefits Act).

105. *See* Pittston Coal Group v. Sebben, 488 U.S. 105, 114 (1988) (paraphrasing statute).

106. *See id.* (indicating detrimental condition must have been caused by coal mine employment).

107. *See id.* (defining total disability).

108. *See, e.g.,* Ca. Civ. Pro. Code § 116.120 (West 2003) (setting forth general provisions on small claims divisions); Colo. Rev. Stat. Ann. § 13-6-401 (West 2002) (setting forth procedures and requirements of small claims divisions).

109. *See* Arthur Best et al., *Peace, Wealth, Happiness and Small Claims Courts: A Case Study,* 21 Fordham Urb. L.J. 343, 346 (1994) (describing Colorado small claims court).

movement believed a society should have an accessible and effective forum for asserting legal rights. The formal procedures in the regular courts were often unreasonably time-consuming and expensive,[110] thereby closing the courthouse doors to many injured persons.[111]

Small claims courts were developed to solve these problems by opening the courthouse doors to the injured citizen with a small claim.[112] These courts serve three purposes: "(1) fair resolution of civil disputes; (2) deterrence of violent self-help by disputants; and (3) identification of recurring social problems that might be proper subjects for legislative or administrative action."[113] Small claims courts do not require the parties to have legal expertise.[114] Claimants are able to resolve their legal problems for a small fee in a trial that lasts only a few minutes.[115] Of course, many of the procedures and details of the small claims court would have to be redesigned for products cases.

The conclusion is inescapable that the unnecessary, multifaceted tort "reforms" over the last thirty-some years have been extremely successful in benefiting the powerful.[116] The constriction in tort theory and civil procedure has left victims having substantial (but not litigable) damages with no forum for relief. The loss has been left on the innocent victim. This has resulted in huge windfall profits for manufacturers to the extent of victims' injuries multiplied by the number of occurrences.

---

110. *See id.* at 347 (citing Roscoe Pound, *Administration of Justice in the Modern City*, 26 HARV. L. REV. 302 (1913) (advocating heightened accessibility of courts to promote social justice).

111. Best, *supra* note 109, at 347 (citing Eric H. Steele, *The Historical Context of Small Claims Courts*, 1981 AM. B. FOUND. RES. J. 293) (indicating court formalities cause difficulties for litigants using the court system to collect small debts without having attorneys, thus increasing the cost of litigation).

112. *See* Best, *supra* note 109, at 347 (intending small claims court to be solution that created greater access to the court system).

113. *See id.* at 344 (discussing function of small claims court).

114. *See id.* (citing ARTHUR BEST, WHEN CONSUMERS COMPLAIN 10 (1981) (recognizing small claims courts serve a valuable purpose by not requiring petitioners to have legal expertise).

115. *See id.* Best, *supra* note 109, at 349 (citing Committee Hearings on S.B. 52 Before the Senate Committee on Judiciary (Feb. 9, 1976)).

116. There never was a demonstrated need for these retrenchments and reforms. *See* Thomas A. Eaton & Susette M. Talarico, *A Profile of Tort Litigation in Georgia and Reflections on Tort Reform*, 30 GA. L. REV. 627, 654 (1996) (pointing to the success of Georgia's multifaceted tort reforms); *see also* Mark Curriden, *Juries on Trial*, DALLAS MORNING NEWS, May 7, 2000, (acknowledging the effect of tort reform on juries).

C. OTHER LEGISLATION DESIGNED TO IMPEDE THE VICTIM'S ACCESS TO THE COURTS

Over forty years ago, Dean Prosser wrote that the citadel of privity was no longer a barrier to a plaintiff's recovery in products liability cases.[117] Today, he would be disappointed because a new type of "citadel" in the form of state legislative enactments is being erected to protect manufacturers and suppliers from tort liability.

This section will outline and analyze the legislative objectives of these reforms and compare them to the fundamental policies of products liability law. Part 1 focuses on the various state legislative enactments. Part 2 suggests these reforms are contrary to the underlying goals of fundamental torts policies and have altered the traditional role of the courts in products liability lawsuits.

1. State Legislative "Reforms" of Products Liability Law

a. The Impetus for Legislative Change Historically, the driving force in the constricting of victims' access to the courts has been the powerful sellers and the insurance industry. Manufacturers and insurance companies insisted the products liability insurance problem was of acute proportion during the period 1977–1980.[118] The insurance premiums manufacturers had to pay were argued to be

---

117. *See* William L. Prosser, *The Fall of the Citadel*, 50 Minn. L. Rev. 791 (1966).

118. One author has suggested:

In recent years, manufacturers have been charged dramatically increased fees for product liability insurance. Some manufacturers have testified during the last eighteen months that they may have to go out of business because of their high insurance rates. Insurance companies have claimed that there is a product liability "crisis" and that it is caused by the products liability legal system. They have demanded immediate legislative protection for manufacturers' interests in lawsuits. They have claimed that pro-consumer product liability legal doctrines result in unfair harassment of business by injured persons and that opportunistic consumers and money-hungry lawyers are gaining windfall wealth from responsible manufacturers. They have followed these claims with nationwide advertising campaigns for products liability "reform."

Anita Johnson, *Products Liability "Reform": A Hazard to Consumers*, 56 N.C.L. Rev. 677, 678 (1978) (footnotes omitted). *See* John W. Bell, *Averting a Crisis in Products Liability: An Evolutionary Process of Socioeconomic Justice*, 65 Ill. B.J. 640 (1977); Michel A. Coccia, *Wake Up, Industry, Before It's Too Late*, 1968 Ins. L.J. 501; Harvey W. Rubin, *The Impact of Tort Reform on the Products Liability Crisis: A Reinsurance Viewpoint*, 1978 Ins. L.J. 421; Symposium, *Products Liability: Toward Balancing the Scales*, 11 Akron L. Rev. 593 (1978). In contrast to the crisis theory, Professor Calabresi believes our "free enterprise society" requires manufacturers to bear the risks of the present product liability system. Guido Calabresi, *Product Liability: Curse or Bulwark of Free Enterprise?*, 27 Clev. St. L. Rev. 313, 322–23 (1978). He argues that in a free enterprise society, it is natural for both manufacturers and consumers to seek to avoid accident costs. That consumers wish to avoid these costs is not important, but that manufacturers also wish to do so is of greater concern because "it represents an unwillingness of the private sector to take on the function of

high, with some manufacturers claiming the alleged high rates could force them out of business.[119] Insurance companies asserted a products liability "crisis" existed and requested state legislative protection of manufacturers' interests.[120] These allegations caused a number of state legislatures to conduct inquiries.

For example, the Utah legislature found evidence in 1977 that vindicated the claims of manufacturers and insurance companies.[121] It determined the number of suits, judgments, and settlements arising from defective products had increased substantially. Because of these changes, insurance companies greatly raised the cost of products liability insurance. Furthermore, these increased insurance costs were passed on to the consumer and "certain product manufacturers [were] discouraged from continuing to provide and manufacture such products" because of the high cost and possible unavailability of products liability insurance.[122]

As a result of manufacturers' and insurance companies' complaints and official governmental findings (both on the state and federal level), many state

---

bearing incentives to innovate and thus to diminish those costs which cannot be given an actuarial basis." *Id.* In other words, manufacturers should bear the costs and risks of accidents as manufacturers are in the best position to manage present risks and diminish future accidents through improvements and innovations in their products. *Id.*

119. *Id.*Johnson, *supra* note 118, at 678.

120. *Id.*

121. UTAH CODE ANN. § 78-15-2 (1977).

122. UTAH CODE ANN. § 78-15-2(1) (1977). As a result of these determinations, the legislature enacted a statute designed to alleviate "the adverse effects" the present products liability system is generating in the manufacturing industry. *Id.* § 78-15-2(2).

In 1977, the Interagency Task Force on Products Liability, under the direction of the U.S. Department of Commerce, prepared an intensive study of products liability problems. Although the study revealed the problem was not of "crisis" proportions, it found many businesses were unable to obtain products liability insurance and that the increased cost of available insurance had "made a substantial impact on the price of many products." The Task Force attempted to define the problem and to provide insight into the new state legislative reforms. It concluded a number of small businesses must choose between foregoing product liability insurance or purchasing it at very high premiums. In most industries studied, product liability premiums appeared to have risen substantially from 1974 to 1976. The industries most severely affected by the increased insurance costs were engaged in the manufacture of industrial chemicals and certain consumer goods (such as pharmaceuticals, automotive parts, and medical devices). The problem of expensive insurance for smaller firms in all industries is less severe.

The Task Force identified three causes of the recent rise in products liability insurance premiums: insurance ratemaking procedures, the tort-litigation system, and unsafe manufacturing practices. Several less substantial causes were inflation, consumer and worker awareness, increases in the number and complexity of products, and product misuse. Finally, the Task Force stated it was uncertain whether the total number of pending claims in the industries studied had increased from 1970 to 1975. Department of Commerce, *Federal Interagency Task Force on Product Liability* (November 1, 1977).

legislatures instituted new laws designed to alleviate the alleged crisis. These modifications took many forms. Some were merely codifications of old common law impediments to a plaintiff's recovery; others were new but moderate changes, and one was a radical departure from the traditional torts reparations system, but all of the state legislative changes had one point in common, they benefited the powerful sellers. The most important changes are discussed below.

b. A Radical Change: The Statute of Repose Statutes of repose constituted the first shot fired by "reformers"[123] across the bow of the consumers. Over a period of more than twenty-five years, numerous states adopted statutes of repose.[124] These statutes dramatically alter the torts system by providing a fixed period of time after the original sale (usually five to twelve years) in which a products liability suit must be brought.[125] Indiana's statute is typical:

> [A]ny product liability action must be commenced with two [2] years after the cause of action accrues or within ten [10] years after the delivery of the product to the initial user or consumer; except that if the cause of action accrues more than eight [8] years, but not more than ten [10] years after the initial delivery, the action may be commenced at any time within two [2] years after the cause of action accrues.[126]

---

123. *See* Berry *ex. rel.* Berry v. Beech Aircraft Corp., 717 P.2d 670, 677 (Utah 1985) (commenting "[a] number of states have enacted . . . statutes of repose"). *But see* Lankford v. Sullivan, Long & Hagerty, 416 So.2d 996, 1003 (Ala. 1982) (striking down statute as being "arbitrary and capricious").

124. *See* Johnson, *supra* note 118, at 680 (noting harshness of rule).

125. Statutes of repose are similar to statutes of limitations in that each preludes an action at some point after injury has occurred. Although the purpose of the statute of limitations is to avoid unfairness to the defendant by not allowing a lawsuit when it is difficult to gather evidence, the purpose of the statute of repose is to protect a manufacturer or supplier from excessive liability. This is inherently unfair to an injured plaintiff. *Cf.* UTAH CODE ANN. § 78-15-1(3) (purpose of statute of repose is to give plaintiffs a reasonable time to bring suit while limiting that time in order to achieve reasonable and accurate calculation of insurance premiums).

Another important distinction between statutes of limitation and of repose is that the former fixes a time period in which an action must be brought that commences when the cause of action *accrues*. In contrast, the time period in which actions must be brought under statute of repose is not related to the accrual of any cause of action. Rosenberg v. Town of North Bergen, 61 N.J. 190, 199, 293 A.2d 662, 666 (1972).

Ten states have adopted statutes of repose. COLO. REV. STAT. § 13-21-403(3) (SUPP. 1978); CONN. GEN. STAT. § 52-55a(a) (1980); FLA. STAT. ANN § 95.031(2) (Harrison 1977); GA. CODE ANN. § 105-106(b)(2) (Cum. Supp. 1980); ILL. ANN. STAT. ch. 83, § 22.2(d) (Smith-Hurd Supp. 1966–1979); IND. CODE ANN. § 34-4-20A-5 (Burns Cum. Supp. 1980); NEB. REV. STAT § 25-224(2) (Cum. Supp. 1978); ORE. REV. STAT ch. 30 § 905 (1977); TENN. CODE ANN. § 23-3703(a) (Supp. 5, 1979); UTAH CODE ANN. § 78-15-3(1) (1977).

126. IND. CODE ANN. § 34-4-20A-5 (Burns Cum. Supp. 1980). There is no definition of the "initial user or consumer." Thus, it might be argued a retailer is an "initial user" under

This reform bars certain claims before the injury occurs.[127] It is indisputable "some victims of injury from an old defective product will be prevented from suing to collect damages."[128] However, most products liability litigation does not involve extremely old products as 97 percent of bodily injuries occur within five years of purchase.[129] Although there are several classes of cases on which a statute of repose will have a devastating impact,[130] it will not affect the vast majority of claims.

In addition, although wholesalers and retailers doing business intrastate will benefit significantly from statutes of repose, manufacturers will receive only limited relief. Their products will continue to be subject to the laws of the non-statute of repose states in which their products are marketed, and their insurance rates for interstate products will continue to be based on national statistics.[131] Accordingly, manufacturers would support widespread adoption of products liability legislation imposing a statute of repose.[132]

---

this statute, which could conceivably bar claims before the consumer has even purchased the product. In contrast, the Georgia's statute of repose mandates a ten-year limitation period starting on "the date of the first sale for use or consumption." GA. CODE ANN. § 105-106(b)(2) (Cum. Supp. 1980).

127. Comment, *State Legislative Restrictions on Product Liability Action*, 29 MERCER L. REV. 619, 628 (1978). *See also* Comment, *The Statute of Limitations in Strict Products Liability Actions*, 24 BUFFALO L. REV. 447 (1975); Comment, *Statutes of Repose in Products Liability: The Assault upon the Citadel of Strict Liability*, 23 S.D.L. REV. 149 (1978); Comment, *Products Liability—Accrual and Limitations of Actions*, TENN. L. REV. 335 (1968); Note, *Statutes of Limitations: Their Selection and Application in Products Liability Cases*, 23 VAND. L. REV 775 (1970); Note, *Economic Loss from Defective Products*, 4 WILLAMETTE L.J. 402 (1967).

128. Duane J. Gingerich, *The Interagency Task Force "Blueprint" for Reforming Product Liability Tort Law in the United States*, 8 GA. J. INT'L & COMP. L. 279, 288 (1978) (citing U.S. DEP'T OF COMMERCE, INTERAGENCY TASK FORCE ON PRODUCT LIABILITY, FINAL REPORT VII-25 (1977) [HEREINAFTER CITED AS TASK FORCE FINAL REPORT]

129. Johnson, *supra* note 118, at 690.

130. The new statutes would bar suits for injuries that are first observable many years after the purchase of the product. For example, a suit against a pharmaceutical manufacturer whose product caused birth defects that became apparent only after the child reached puberty would be barred by the typical statute of repose. These statutes also would bar suits based on defects in durable goods (such as workplace machinery) because such suits are usually instigated long after sale. *Id.* at 690–91.

Statutes of repose create a disincentive for manufacturers to ensure the long-term safety of their products because they receive total immunity for product-related injuries after the repose period has passed. *Id.*

131. Comment, *When the Product Ticks: Products Liability and Statutes of Limitation*, 11 IND. L. REV. 693, 710 (1978).

132. *Id.* at 711. *See also* Comment, *Choice of Law: Statutes of Limitation in the Multistate Products Liability Case*, 48 TUL. L. REV. 1130 (1974). In contrast to manufacturers, the wholesalers and retailers located within a statute-of-repose state will receive the full benefit of the statute.

However, statutes of repose may violate constitutional provisions of equal protection and due process. Attacks on products statutes will be patterned on earlier constitutional challenges to architects' and builders' statutes of repose[133]— an issue that remains unsettled.[134] Two cases involving these statutes, *Rosenberg v. Town of North Bergen*[135] and *Kallas Millwork Corp. v. Square D. Co.*,[136] illustrate the ways in which a court might decide a constitutional challenge to the typical products liability repose statute.

Rosenberg did not involve a defective product, but rather a personal injury suit against a contractor who had paved the roadbed upon which the plaintiff sustained her injuries.[137] The plaintiff alleged the New Jersey statute of repose[138]

---

133. A prototypical example of a statute of repose for architects and builders provides:

No person shall have a cause of action against any person performing or furnishing the design, planning, supervision, observation of construction, or the construction of an improvement to real property for recovery of damages . . . after *x* years have elapsed from the time of the initial occupancy after completion of construction of such improvement to real property.

U.S. DEP'T OF COMMERCE, INTERAGENCY TASK FORCE ON PRODUCT LIABILITY: FINALREPORT OF THE LEGAL STUDY 9 (1977) [HEREINAFTER CITED AS TASK FORCE LEGAL STUDY]. For a general discussion of these statutes, see Comment, *Limitation of Action Statutes for Architects and Builders—Blueprints for Non-Action*, 18 CATH. U. L. REV. 361 (1969).

134. Eleven states have upheld the constitutionality of these statutes: Smith v. Allen-Bradley Co., 371 F. Supp. 698 (W.D. Va. 1974); Grissom v. North Am. Aviation, Inc., 326 F. Supp. 465 (M.D. Fla. 1971); Carter v. Hartenstein, 248 Ark. 1172, 455 S.W.2d 918 (1970); Carr v. Mississippi Valley Elec. Co., 285 So. 2d 301 (La. App. 1973); Reeves v. Ille Elec. Co., 170 Mont. 104, 551 P.2d 647 (1976); Nevada Lakeshore Co. v. Diamond Elec. Inc., 89 Nev. 293, 511 P.2d 113 (1973); O'Connor v. Altus, 67 N.J. 106, 335 A.2d 545 (1975); Rosenberg v. Town of North Bergen, 61 N.J. 190, 293 A.2D 662 (1972); Josephs v. Burns, 260 Ore. 493, 491 P.2d 203 (1971); Freezer Storage, Inc. v. Armstrong Cork Co., 234 Pa. Super. Ct. 441, 341 A.2d 184 (1975); Good v. Christensen, 527 P.2d 223 (Utah 1974); Yakima Fruit & Cold Storage Co. v. Cent. Heating & Plumbing Co., 81 Wash. 2d 528, 503 P.2d 108 (1972).

Five states have held these statutes to be unconstitutional: Bagby Elevator & Elec. Co. v. McBride, 292 Ala. 191, 291 So. 2d 306 (1974); Fujioka v. Kam, 55 Hawaii 7, 514 P.2d 568 (1973); Skinner v. Anderson, 38 Ill. 2d 455, 231 N.E.2d 588 (1967); Saylor v. Hall, 497 S.W.2d 218 (Ky. 1973); Kallas Millwork Corp. v. Square D Co., 66 Wis. 2d 382, 225 N.W.2d 454 (1975).

135. 61 N.J 190, 293 A.2d 662 (1972).

136. 66 Wis. 2d 382, 225, N.W.2d 454 (1975).

137. Specifically, the plaintiff sued for personal injuries sustained as a result of a fall while walking across a highway. The roadbed of this highway had been repaved in 1935 to provide (on either side of the center line) three contiguous lanes of concrete. Sometime before the accident, two lanes had parted, leaving a fissure between them in which the plaintiff caught her heel and fell. The defendant was the contractor who had paved the highway. Rosenberg v. Town of North Bergen, 61 N.J. 190, 193 293 A.2d 662, 663 (1972).

138. N.J. STAT. ANN § 2A:14-1.1 (West Cum. Supp. 1980).

violated both the federal and the state constitutions. First, she claimed the statute deprived her of due process[139] because it barred her cause of action before it even arose. Second, she argued the classification of persons entitled to the benefits of the statute violated the New Jersey Constitution, which forbids the legislature to enact any private, special, or local law granting to any corporation, association, or individual an exclusive privilege, immunity, or franchise.[140]

The court rejected both arguments. With respect to the due process claim, the court stated "[t]he legislature is entirely at liberty to create new rights or abolish old ones as long as no vested right is disturbed."[141] On the classification claim, the court found that because contractors had become subject to extensive potential liability, the statute was a reasonable legislative method to protect them from suits arising from acts long past.[142] As the statute of repose encompassed so large a class of persons,[143] the court could find no exclusion from the class to justify plaintiff's allegation the law was "special" and in violation of the state constitution.[144] Moreover, the court held the statute did not violate the equal protection clause of the U.S. Constitution[145] because the classification bore a reasonable relationship to the relevant statutory purposes.[146]

The Wisconsin Supreme Court's decision in *Kallas Millwork* (also not involving a product) contrasts with *Rosenberg*.[147] Plaintiff Kallas Millwork had occupied property adjacent to that owned by Square D. Kallas Millwork alleged that sometime between 1945 and 1952, ITT Grinnell Corp. negligently installed a high pressure water line on Square D's premises. In 1968, the water line ruptured and the effluent water caused substantial damage to Kallas Millwork's property.

---

139. Although the court did not state the precise due process provision under which the plaintiff sued, it is apparent the plaintiff's claim arose under the due process clause of the New Jersey Constitution. N.J. Const. art. I, para. 1.Few courts, if any, have held products liability statutes of repose to be violative of either the state or federal due process clause. Task Force Legal Study, *supra* note 133, at 11.

140. N.J. Const. art. IV, § VII, para. 9(8).

141. *Rosenberg*, 61 N.J. at 199–200, 293 A.2d at 667. The court's rationale was that the statute, rather than barring the plaintiff's cause of action before it arose, prevents as she had alleged "what might otherwise be a cause of action" from ever accruing. Thus, the plaintiff who is injured more than ten years after the allegedly negligent act has *no* cause of action for redress. *Id.*

142. *Id.* 61 N.J. at 199–200, 293 A.2d at 667–68.

143. The class established by the statute included "any person performing or furnishing the design, planning, supervision of construction, or construction of such improvement to real property." *Id.* 61 N.J. at 201, 293 A.2d at 668 (citing N.J. Stat. Ann. § 2A:14-1.1 (West Cumm. Supp. 1980)).

144. *Rosenberg*, 61 N.J. at 190, 293 A.2d at 668 (citing N.J. Const. art. IV, § VII, para. 9(8)).

145. U.S. Const. amend. XIV, § 1.

146. *Rosenberg*, 61 N.J. at 190, 293 A.2d at 668.

147. 66 Wis. 2d 382, 225 N.W.2d 454 (1975).

The defendant asserted the lawsuit was barred by the Wisconsin designers' and contractors' six-year statute of repose.[148]

The plaintiff responded by arguing that by singling out a group of contractors, builders, and architects for protection while excluding others similarly situated, the statute of repose denied equal protection of the law to the excluded group.[149] The court agreed the statute violated the constitutional principles of equal protection.[150] This holding was premised on its determination the statute of repose creates unjust results by allowing an injured party to recover against persons other than those protected by the statutory class while denying recovery against a contractor or an architect (when either or both might have been responsible for the defective condition causing the injury).[151]

However, although decisions on the issue of the constitutionality of products liability statutes of repose have gone both ways, it is likely they will often survive future challenges.[152] In addition to these radical statutes, states have passed a

---

148. This statute is codified in WIS. STAT. ANN § 893.89 (West. Cum. Supp. 1980).

149. The court alluded to both the federal and the state constitutions. U.S. CONST. amend. XIV, § 1; WIS. CONST. art. 1, § 1.

150. Kallas Millwork Corp. v. Square D Co., 65 Wis. 2d 382, 391, 225 N.W.2d 454, 459–60 (1975). The court stated the test of constitutionality under the equal protection clause of either the U.S. or the Wisconsin Constitution is whether there exists any rational and reasonable justification for the legislative classification. "[I]f the classification is arbitrary and has no reasonable purpose or reflects no justifiable public policy [then] the classification [will] be held violative of constitutional guarantees of equal protection." Id. 65 Wis.2d at 388, 225 N.W.2d at 458. After reviewing two cases from other states in which the courts struck down analogous statutes on equal protection grounds, Fujioka v. Kam, 514 P.2d 568 (Haw. 1973) and Skinner v. Anderson, 39 Ill. 2d 455, 231 N.E.2d 588 (1967), the court determined the legislative protection given by the statute was unreasonable. The court noted persons other than builders, contractors, and architects also might be held liable for injuries resulting from a defective condition, but they were afforded no statutory protection. Not only are these persons (such as owners or those in control of the premises) subject to suit, but they also are barred from seeking indemnity from the contractor or architect. 66 Wis. 2d at 388–89, 225 N.W.2d at 458–59.

The court also suggested the statute might offend a Wisconsin constitutional provision that there be "a certain remedy in the laws for all injuries. . . ." WIS. CONST. art. 1, § 9, cited in 66 Wis. 2d at 393 n.1, 225 N.W.2d at 460 n.1.

151. Kallas, 66 Wis.2d at 391, 225 N.W.2d at 459.

152. TASK FORCE LEGAL STUDY, supra note 133, at 10–11. The Task Force noted that no court had held a statute of repose for architects and builders unlawful on due process grounds. Id. at 11. Moreover, products liability statutes of repose should not be held to violate equal protection principles unless the state legislature limits the application of these statutes to certain classes of defendants. Id. at 10. However, the Task Force stated that even if application of the statute is limited to a certain class, it should not be unlawful if the classification is a reasonable one. Id. at 10–11 (e.g., classification of manufacturers of capital goods). See Lankford v. Sullivan, Long & Hagerty, 416 So.2d 996, 1001 (Ala. 1982) (challenging statute under Alabama's equal protection clause); see also Kennedy v.

large number of legislative constrictions that will have cumulatively have a substantial impact on products liability suits. Such statutes deal with governmental standards, traditional defenses, and evidence. All benefit the sellers.

c. Further Alterations to the Products Liability System

i. Compliance with Governmental Standards At common law, compliance with governmental standards may be a factor considered by a court in determining whether a manufacturer has acted with due care.[153] However, the compliance-with-governmental-standards statute goes further to create a presumption the product is not defective or unreasonably unsafe, and accordingly, is a significant defense to a products liability claim.[154] For example, the Tennessee statute provides:

> Compliance by a manufacturer or seller with any federal or state statute or administrative regulation existing at the time a product was manufactured and prescribing standards for design, inspection, testing, manufacture, labeling, warning, or instructions for use of a product shall raise a rebuttable presumption that the product is not in an unreasonably dangerous condition in regard to matters covered by these standards.[155]

Although these statutes only rarely would offer a complete defense to a products liability suit, manufacturers may prevail when they otherwise would have lost due to plaintiff's failure to rebut the statutory presumption. Additionally, litigation of issues concerning governmental compliance might be avoided in cases in which the plaintiff prevailed on another theory.[156]

Arguably, this type of state legislation will discourage manufacturers from developing safer products because it encourages them to lobby instead for weaker regulations.[157] The effectiveness of manufacturers in influencing administrative

---

Cumberland Eng'g Co., 471 A.2d 195, 197 (R.I. 1984) (examining challenge of statute on state and federal equal protection grounds).

See also Vandall, *supra* note 1, at 869–70 (discussing radical changes caused by statute of repose).

153. Johnson, *supra* note 118, at 687. *See also* WILLIAM L. PROSSER, HANDBOOK OF THE LAW OF TORTS 203–04 (4th ed. 1971).

154. Only Utah and Tennessee have adopted such statutes. TENN. CODE ANN. § 23-3704 (Supp. 5, 1979); UTAH CODE ANN. § 78-15-6(3) (1977). *Cf.* KY. REV. STAT. ANN. § 411.310 (Baldwin Supp. 1979) (presumption that product is free of defects arises eight years after manufacture or five years after sale).

155. TENN. CODE ANN. § 23-3704 (Supp. 5, 1979).

156. TASK FORCE LEGAL STUDY, *supra* note 133, at 130.

157. Many manufacturers have the power to influence the formation of government standards to ensure they will be subject to less stringent requirements. Agencies often adopt regulations that are "rubber-stamped" versions of voluntary standards already practiced by the industry. There will be no incentive to improve products as the existing practice is acceptable. Johnson, *supra* note 118, at 687–88.

agencies to adopt certain safety standards is well-known.[158] Manufacturers thus may prefer to have agencies rather than courts set standards.[159]

ii. *The State-of-the-Art Defense* At common law, the custom of the industry is merely evidence of due care rather than a controlling factor. In the final analysis, due care is determined by the courts rather than by industry.[160] In contrast, state-of-the-art statutes make a manufacturer's compliance with technological feasibility an absolute defense to a products liability suit.[161] One such statute reads:

> Whenever the physical harm is caused by the plan or design of the product, it is a defense that the methods, standards, or techniques of designing and manufacturing the product were prepared and applied in conformity with the generally recognized state of the art at the time the product was designed or manufactured.[162]

The state-of-the-art defense has been adopted to deter courts from requiring manufacturers to make products accident-proof without regard to the expense involved.[163] However, after examining the issue, the Task Force rejected the

---

158. *See* Mark Green & Ralph Nader, *Economic Regulation vs. Competition: Uncle Sam the Monopoly Man*, 82 YALE L.J. 871, 876 (1973); Forward to Mark J. Green, *Nader Group Report on Antitrust Enforcement: A Summary*, 4 ANTITRUST L. 7 ECON. REV. 1 (1970).

159. Johnson, *supra* note 118, at 689. Another reason is that manufacturers are seeking protection from the unpredictable decision making of courts and juries. *Id.*

160. The T.J. Hooper, 60 F.2d 737, 740 (2d. Cir. 1932). *See* PROSSER, *supra* note 153, at 167–68, 644–45. In *T.J. Hooper,* a tugboat and its barges were lost at sea because the tugboat operator did not have a radio. At that time, it was not industry practice for tugboats to carry radios. Judge Hand ruled, however, that it was the court's duty to define due care, and because some tugboats did carry radios, the court could find the failure to have a radio was negligent. 60 F.2d at 740.

161. Arizona, Indiana, Kentucky, Nebraska, and Tennessee have enacted state-of-the-art defense statutes. ARIZ. REV. STAT § 12-683(1) (Supp. 1957-1980) (state-of-the-art when product first sold); IND. CODE ANN. § 34-4-20A-4(b)(4) (Burns Cum. Supp. 1980) (state-of-the-art when product was designed or manufactured); KY. REV. STAT. ANN § 411.310(2) (Baldwin Supp. 1979) (state-of-the-art when product was designed, prepared, or manufactured); NEB. REV. STAT § 25-21, 182 (Cum. Supp. 1978) (state-of-the-art when product was "first sold to any person not engaged in the business of selling such product"); TENN. CODE ANN. § 23-3705(a) (Supp. 5, 1979) (state-of-the-art when product was first placed on the market).

162. IND. CODE ANN. § 34-4-20A-4(b)(4) (Burns Cum. Supp. 1980). Although "state of the art" is not defined in this statute, Nebraska defines it as "the best technology reasonably available at the time." NEB. REV. STAT § 25-21, 182 (Cum. Supp. 1978).

163. Johnson, *supra* note 118, at 685. It is unclear what factors are required to persuade a court in a products liability suit that an alternative design or manufacturing process would have prevented the defect and resultant injury. *Id.* Thus, ten proponents of the state-of-the-art statute argue that legislatures, not courts, should judge the "delicate tradeoffs" necessary to design and manufacture a safe product. *See, e.g.,* Richard A. Epstein, *Products Liability: The Gathering Storm,* REGULATION, Sept.–Oct. 1977, at 15, 18.

state-of-the-art proposal because it would reduce manufacturers' incentive to develop a safer product.[164]

iii. Misuse The common law rule is that manufacturers and suppliers will not be liable in a products liability action for injuries caused by unforeseeable misuse[165] or alteration[166] of their products by the consumer or user. Misuse gives the defendant seller two bites at the apple, because it is the same as the defense of assumption of risk. Having two defenses that are essentially the same strengthens the hand of the powerful. A few states have adopted the misuse or alteration defenses while several have adopted both.[167]

However, these "reforms" may only codify the common law. For example, examination of the Arizona statute[168] reveals both the misuse and alteration provisions use the words "proximate cause" and "reasonably foreseeable," the terms

---

164. Task Force Legal Study, *supra* note 133, at 103. Moreover, the defense precludes inquiry into other reasonable manufacturing alternatives.

> The effect of instituting a state-of-the-art defense is to exonerate the manufacturer from liability, even where it could have utilized a different design or method of testing that was feasible (in terms of practicality and technology) at the time the product was marketed. Stated otherwise, no liability would exist when the product conformed to industry standards, even where the standard of the industry was one of negligence.

Id. at 110.

165. Task Force Legal Study, *supra* note 133, at 35. *See also* Prosser, *supra* note 153, at 668; Reinstatement, *supra* note 12 § 402A, comment h.

166. Prosser, *supra* note 153.

167. Ariz. Rev. Stat § 12-683(2), (3) (Supp. 1957-1980) (alteration; misuse); Conn. Gen. Stat § 52-572/(1980) (misuse); Ga. Code Ann § 105-106(b)(1) (Cum. Supp. 1980) (misuse); Ind. Code Ann. § 34-4-20A-4(b)(2), (b)(3) (Burns Cum. Supp. 1980) (misuse; alteration); Ky. Rev. Stat. Ann. § 411.320(2) (Baldwin Supp. 1979) (alteration); Ore. Rev. Stat. Ann § 30.915 (1977) (alteration); Tenn. Code Ann. § 23-3708 (Supp. 5, 1979) (misuse and alteration); Utah Code Ann. § 78-15-5 (1977) (misuse and alteration).

168. Arizona's statute provides:

In any product liability action, a defendant shall not be liable if the defendant proves that any of the following apply:

. . . .

2. The proximate cause of the incident giving rise to the action was an alteration or modification of the product which was not reasonably foreseeable, made by a person other than the defendant and subsequent to the time the product was first sold by the defendant.

3. The proximate cause of the incident giving rise to the action was a use or consumption of the product which was for a purpose, in a manner or in an activity other than that which was reasonably foreseeable or was contrary to any express and adequate instructions or warnings appearing on or attached to the product or on its original container or wrapping, if the injured person knew or with the exercise of reasonable and diligent care should have known of such instructions or warnings.Ariz. Rev. Stat § 12-683(2), (3) (Supp. 1957–1980).

most troublesome in tort law.[169] The issues of the proximate cause of an injury and the reasonably foreseeable use of a product present substantial questions of law requiring judicial resolution[170] (although some courts have treated the question of foreseeability as involving a question of fact for the jury).[171] Statutes such as Arizona's that contain both terms force courts to perform a traditional analysis of the products liability claim. Thus, defenses based on such statutes probably will be no more robust than those at common law.[172]

iv. Other Alterations That Further Protect the Powerful An Oregon statute creates a rebuttable presumption a product that is manufactured, then sold or leased is not unreasonably dangerous for its intended use.[173] As with Tennessee's compliance-with-governmental-standards statute,[174] this provision tips the scales in favor of manufacturers, sellers, and lessors. The result is that some injured plaintiffs who present otherwise valid complaints will not recover damages because they cannot overcome the presumption. However, the Oregon statute is less offensive than radical statutes of repose because it allows the plaintiff to introduce evidence to rebut the statutory presumption rather than precluding a suit altogether.

A Tennessee statute provides that no liability shall attach against any seller who acquired and sold its product in a sealed container.[175] This conflicts with the majority rule at common law that strict liability applies to "[any]one who vouches for [a manufacturer] by selling the product as his own. . . . [I]t applies to a wholesale dealer and to one at retail."[176] Tennessee has disregarded traditional tort policies by codifying the minority rule in order to insulate the powerful.[177]

---

169. *See* PROSSER, *supra* note 153, at 244 (proximate cause question of the law); *id.* at 250 (foreseeability is the "one issue in the law of torts over which so much controversy has raged"). *See generally* LEON GREEN, JUDGE AND JURY (1930).

170. *See generally* GREEN, *supra* note 169; Leon Green, *Proximate Cause in Texas Negligence Law* (pts. 1–4), 28 TEXAS L. REV. 471, 621, 755 (1950).

171. TASK FORCE LEGAL STUDY, *supra* note 133, at 36. This type of approach leads to greater uncertainty in establishing proper guidelines for evaluation of the foreseeability issue. *Id.*

172. *Id.* at 37–38.

173. ORE. REV. STAT. § 30.901 (1977).

174. TENN. CODE ANN. § 23-3704 (Supp. 5, 1979).

175. *Id.* Although the Tennessee sealed containers exception bars a suit in strict liability, recovery has been allowed against the immediate vendor and installer of a product sold in a sealed container under the contract theory of breach of implied warranty of fitness. Walker v. Decora, Inc., 225 Tenn. 504, 471, S.W.2d 778 (1971). *See also* KY. REV. STAT. ANN. § 411.340 (Baldwin Supp. 1979).

176. PROSSER, *supra* note 153, at 644–65.

177. The sealed container exception is based either on the seller's inability to inspect the goods before sale or the buyer's lack of reliance on the seller's skill. 2A L. FRUMER & M. FRIEDMAN, PRODUCTS LIABILITY § 1903(4)(c), at 5-126 (1980). This reasoning is fallacious, however, because the ability to inspect is not a prerequisite to liability for breach of warranty.

Several states have adopted unique legislative provisions that codify strict liability actions, but permit recovery only against the manufacturer. Such statutes have been adopted in Tennessee,[178] Georgia,[179] and Nebraska.[180] Georgia's statute creates numerous problems:

> The manufacturer of any personal property . . . shall be liable in tort, irrespective of privity, to any natural person who may use, consume, or reasonably be affected by the property . . . because the property when sold by the manufacturer was not merchantable and reasonably suited to the use intended and its condition when sold is the proximate cause of the injuries sustained.[181]

The act protects all sellers except the manufacturer, thus eliminating a large number of defendants (including retailers and wholesalers).[182] It raises further difficulties because the use of a merchantability standard suggests the Uniform Commercial Code test for breach of warranty[183] will be applied rather than the strict tort liability test.[184] In addition, the requirement the product be "reasonably

---

Id. at 5-127. Moreover, the misuse of reliance is "no legitimate part of a requirement for the supplier's strict liability for physical damage caused by his defective product." 2 F. HARPER & F. JAMES, THE LAW OF TORTS 1580–81 (1956). When one sells a defective product that causes injury because it was not fit for the ordinary use for which the product was intended, the sealed container doctrine should not bar recovery. William L. Prosser, *The Implied Warranty of Merchantable Quality,* 27 MINN. L. REV. 117 (1943); *see, e.g.,* Hinderer v. Ryan, 7 Wash. App. 434, 499 P.2d 252 (1972) (proof of reliance unnecessary in action based on breach of implied warranty of merchantability).

178. "No product liability action . . . when based on the doctrine of strict liability in tort shall be commenced or maintained against any seller of a product . . . unless said seller is also a manufacturer of said product . . ." TENN. CODE ANN. § 23-3706(b) (Supp. 5, 1979).

179. GA. CODE ANN. § 105-106(b)(1) (Cumm. Supp. 1980).

180. NEB. REV. STAT. § 25-21, 181 (Cumm. Supp. 1978).

181. GA. CODE ANN. § 105-106(b)(1) (Cumm. Supp. 1980). This has apparently been superceded by the Georgia Supreme Court's adoption of strict liability in Banks v. I.C.I. Ams., 266 Ga. 607 (Ga. 1996).

182. *See* Ellis v. Rich's Inc., 233 Ga. 573, 212 S.E.2d 373 (1975) (product liability suit dismissed because defendant had not manufactured product). *See generally,* E. Hunter Taylor, Jr., *Georgia's New Statutory Liability for Manufacturers: An Inadequate Legislative Response,* 2 GA. L. REV. 538 (1968).

183. *See* U.C.C. § 2-314 (implied warranty of merchantibility); U.C.C. § 2-715 (seller liable for injuries proximately caused by breach of warranty). Arguably, in order for the goods to be "merchantable," the manufacturer must be a merchant. *See* Taylor, *supra* note 182, at 568.

184. However, in Ctr. Chem. Co. v. Parzini, 234 Ga. 868, 218 S.E.2d 580 (1975) the court held the language of the Georgia statute—"not merchantable and reasonably suited for the use intended"—did not incorporate a contract theory of liability. 234 Ga. at 869, 218 S.E.2d at 582, (quoting GA. CODE ANN. § 105-106(b)(1) (Cumm. Supp. 1980). Rather, the statute should be interpreted "in the context of strict liability." *Id.* Under the statute,

suited to the use intended" seems to incorporate the issue of negligence into the strict liability statute.[185] Finally, in applying the Georgia statute, two policy questions must be addressed: whether there was in fact a defect, and whether the defective product was the proximate cause of the injury.[186]

The doctrine of privity (only those in contract with the manufacturer can sue) is one of the original defenses for sellers. Georgia has attempted to resurrect the doctrine of privity by means of an awkward statute:

> [N]o privity is necessary to support an action for tort; but if the tort results from the violation of a duty, itself the consequences of a contract, the right of action is confined to the parties and privies to that contract, except in cases where the party would have a right of action for the injury done independently of the contract . . . .[187]

It is likely many plaintiffs who would be able to sue in tort in other states will be restricted by this provision to a suit in contract. Moreover, this statute further confuses the already clouded distinctions between a suit in tort and one in contract.[188] This vagueness benefits the powerful, who have the assets to press for an interpretation in their favor.

Several states have adopted various forms of the repair doctrine,[189] which excludes evidence of post-accident repairs made to a product by a

---

all a plaintiff need show to recover is that "the manufacturer's product when sold by the manufacturer was defective." *Id. But see Banks*, 266 Ga. 607.

185. GA. CODE ANN. § 105-106(b)(1) (Cumm. Supp. 1980). One of the criteria of a defective product is whether it is reasonably fit for the ordinary purposes for which it is sold and used. *Ctr. Chem.*, 234 Ga. 868, 218 S.E.2d at 582 (1975). Arguably, under the statute the manufacturer need not be aware of the "use intended." Taylor, *supra* note 182, at 569.

186. GA. CODE ANN. § 105-106(b)(1) (Cumm. Supp. 1980).

187. *Id.* § 105-106(a). This provision has been interpreted to mean "[t]he rule of privity in contract actions is . . . a statutory requirement." Ellis v. Rich's Inc., 233 Ga. 573, 577, 212 S.E.2d 373, 376 (1975). However, in actions based on breach of warranty, privity is extended to "any natural person who is in the family or household of his buyer or who is a guest in his home. . . ." *Id.* at 576, 212, S.E.2d at 376 (citing GA. CODE ANN. § 109A-2-318(1979)) (analogue to U.C.C. § 2-318).

188. In Beam v. Omark Indus., Inc., 143 Ga. App. 142, 237 S.E.2d 607 (1977), the court stated that privity was required in a suit founded on a breach of duty arising out of a contract. In other words, to sue in strict tort liability in a suit involving an alleged breach of a duty to warn, "the breach must be shown to have been a duty imposed by law, and not a breach of duty imposed by the contract itself." *Id.* 143 Ga. App. at 146, 237 S.E.2d at 610 (citing GA. CODE ANN. § 105-106(a) (Cumm. Supp.1980)).

189. ARIZ. REV. STAT. ANN § 12-686(2) (supp. 1957-1980). KY. REV. STAT. ANN § 411-330 (Baldwin 1979); NEB. REV. STAT. § 27-407 (Cumm. Supp. 1978).

The repair doctrine provides: "When after an event, measures are taken which, if taken previously, would have made the event less likely to occur, evidence of the subsequent measures is not admissible to prove negligence or culpable conduct in connection with

manufacturer.[190] The Arizona statute bans evidence introduced to show a defect relating to a change in design or method of manufacture or testing of the product subsequent to when the product was first sold by the manufacturer.[191] These statutes make a plaintiff's products liability action proportionately harder to prove. Because there is less economic pressure in the form of potential tort liability to remove defects in existing product lines, there is less incentive for manufacturers to develop safer products,.[192] However, one remedy would be to hold the repair doctrine does not apply in a case resting on strict liability.[193]

---

the event." ARIZ. REV. STAT. ANN § 12-686(2) (supp. 1957-1980). Nebraska allows evidence of subsequent measures for purposes other than proving liability, including showing "feasibility of precautionary measures, if controverted." NEB. REV. STAT. § 27-407 (Cumm. Supp. 1978). In Kentucky, evidence of remedial repairs must be presented first to the court (out of the jury's presence) for an admissibility determination. KY. REV. STAT. ANN § 411-330 (Baldwin 1979).

190. This includes evidence of subsequent installation of safety devices, additional warnings, and changes in the choice of materials or components. Comment, *The Case for the Renovated Repair Rule: Admission of Evidence of Subsequent Repairs Against the Mass Producer in Strict Liability*, 29 AM. U.L. REV. 135, 137 (1979).

191. ARIZ. REV. STAT. ANN § 12-686(2) (supp. 1957-1980). This statute also excludes evidence of subsequent changes in the state of the art. *Id.* § 12-686(1).

192. *See* Comment on *Choice of Law, supra* note 132, at 1130. An important state reform deals with the insurance industry rather than with plaintiffs, defendants, tort law, or the litigation process. For example, Georgia and Missouri have adopted products liability insurance carrier reporting requirements. GA. CODE ANN. § 56.319.1 (Cumm. Supp. 1980); MO. ANN. STAT. § 374-415 (Vernon Supp. 1981). These statutes require each products liability insurer to report annually to the state insurance commissioner regarding the number of products liability claims, the amounts paid in settlement of claims, the amount of premiums received, and the number of policies cancelled. *See, e.g.,* GA. CODE ANN. § 56.319.1 (Cum. Supp. 1980). This reform is based in part on the recognition information about the products liability insurance industry is not generally available. The Task Force found the rise in insurance premiums was not based on empirical data collected by the insurers. Insurance had been priced in a manner that did not generate insurance ratemaking or claims data. Moreover, the Task Force found products liability rates were not controlled by objective standards. TASK FORCE FINAL REPORT, *supra* note 128 at I-22 to I-24. *See also Products Liability Task Force—Interim Report,* 56 MICH. ST. B.J. 410–11 (1977); A better database will result in more reliable pricing of insurance and rate-making procedures. TASK FORCE FINAL REPORT, *supra* note 128, at I-24. Insurance carrier-reporting provisions will have a great impact on future legislative reforms. As more empirical data is collected, state legislatures will be able to remedy the products liability problem with solutions based on concrete evidence rather than the general allegations of manufacturers and insurance carriers. *Id.* at I-21 to I-24.Thus far, this chapter has summarized various state legislative products liability reforms. The following section will discuss the fundamental policies underlying the torts system and will compare these policies to the new state reforms to determine whether the statutes further the goals of tort law.

193. *See* Duchess v. Langston Corp., 769 A. 2d 1131 (Pa. S. Ct., 2001).

2. Comparison of Fundamental Tort Policies with State Legislative Reforms

Legal scholars have discussed in great detail the basic policies and goals of tort law. Dean Green has identified five factors that most influence the determination of legal duties in the torts system: administrative, economic, prophylactic, ethical or moral, and judicial.[194] More recently, Professors Calabresi and Ehrenzweig have argued a fundamental goal of tort law should be to maximize social resources by "shifting the costs of accidents (or accident prevention) to the party to whom it represents the least disutility."[195]

However, the state legislative changes (discussed above) reject these policies. An examination of these "reform" statutes indicates the legislatures were more concerned with protecting powerful manufacturers and sellers from liability than ensuring just and efficient civil reparations.

a. Loss Shifting One of the fundamental policies in tort litigation is the economic impact of the decision on the parties. Judge Calabresi has argued that accident losses should be shifted to the party best able to evaluate them.[196] In most cases, this will be the sellers because they are able to pass accident costs onto the purchasers of their products or to add the costs to the general

---

194. Leon Green, *The Duty Problem in Negligence Cases* (pt. 1), 28 COLUM. L. REV. 1014 (1928) [hereinafter Green pt. 1]; Leon Green, *The Duty Problem in Negligence Cases* (pt. 2), 29 COLUM. L. REV. 255 (1979) [hereinafter Green pt. 2]. Briefly stated, the administrative factor concerns the "workability" of a legal rule or process. Green pt. 1, *supra*, at 1035. If a court or a legislature "is asked to extend its protection to a new interest or against an unusual hazard, it will not do so if its attempt would appear unduly burdensome, expensive or vain." *Id. See also* GUIDO CALABRESI, THE COSTS OF ACCIDENTS 28 (1975) (tertiary goal of accident cost reduction is to reduce costs of administering legal and nonlegal treatment of accidents). The moral or ethical factor is best indicated in legal theory by "liability based on fault." Green pt. 2, *supra*, at 255. The prophylactic factor concerns the actions of courts and legislators to prevent future harms. This is designed "to purify the social stream through the judicial process." *Id.* at 255–56 (citing MacPherson v. Buick Motor Co., 217 N.Y. 382, 111 N.E. 1050 (1916)). The justice factor is reflected in the tendency of courts to apportion "loss where it can be felt the least and can best be borne." *Id.* at 256. Professor Green argues the economic factor transcends the other four factors in that "the larger problems of legal protection and responsibility are not solvable alone by formulas, doctrines, rules, phrases, definitions, or other devices of dialectic." *Id.* at 257.

195. George P. Fletcher, *Fairness and Utility in Tort Theory*, 85 HARV. L. REV. 537, 537 (1972) (citing ALBERT A. EHRENZWEIG, NEGLIGENCE WITHOUT FAULT (1951), *reprinted in* 54. CAL. L. REV. 1422 (1966); CALABRESI, *supra* note 194. Professor Calabresi states the principal purpose of tort law should be to reduce the costs both of accidents and of avoiding accidents. *Id.* at 30. He divides this goal into three subgoals: The "primary" subgoal is to reduce the number and severity of accidents. The "secondary" subgoal is to reduce the societal costs resulting from accidents by shifting their costs to the party best able to bear the loss. The "tertiary" subgoal involves the costs of administering the treatment of accident losses. *Id.* at 30–36.

196. CALABRESI, *supra* note 194, at 39–45, 259–63.

expense of production. Sellers are thus able to effect a "spreading" of accident costs.[197]

State legislative reforms preclude any considerations of this economic analysis because they presume it is better for the loss to rest upon the injured party. For example, the statutes of repose[198] assume accident losses should rest upon the plaintiff after an arbitrary period of time has passed. Similarly, state-of-the-art statutes[199] (which hold the manufacturer only to the standard of the industry at the time the product was first sold), and compliance with governmental standards statutes[200] (which give manufacturers a presumption of safety in their product if they have conformed to a customary or governmental standard), mechanically place the loss upon the shoulders of the consumer or user. These statutes take a narrow view of the loss-shifting policy because they consider only the sellers' losses—specifically, the costs of tort litigation and increased insurance costs. Substantial losses will fall on consumers because manufacturers have little incentive to develop a safer product.[201]

Statutes adopting the presumption the product is not unreasonably dangerous[202] and those allowing recovery only against the manufacturer[203] are

---

197. *Id.* at 51. Arguably consumers can "spread the costs" through private insurance, but the present insurance system provides an inefficient method for achieving total loss spreading. *Id.* at 47–48.

198. COLO. REV. STAT. § 13-21-403(3) (SUPP. 1978); CON. GEN. STAT. § 52-577a(a) (1980); FLA. STAT. ANN. § 95.031(2) (Harrison 1979); GA. CODE ANN. § 105-106(b)(2) (Cum. Supp. 1980); ILL. ANN. STAT. ch. 83, § 22.2(d) (Smith-Hurd Supp. 1966-1979); IND. CODE ANN. § 34-4-20A-5 (Burns Cum. Supp. 1980); NEB. REV. STAT. § 25-224(2) (Cum. Supp. 1978); ORE. REV. STAT. § 30.905 (1977); TENN. CODE ANN. § 23-3703(a) (Supp. 5, 1979); UTAH CODE ANN. § 78-15-3(1) (1977). The Kentucky statute has a provision stating a presumption shall arise that the product is not defective if no injury is caused by the product until after eight years from the date of manufacture or five years from the date of sale to the consumer. KY. REV. STAT. § 411.310 (Baldwin 1979). Although this provision does not consider loss shifting, it technically is not a statute of repose because suit may be brought to rebut the presumption.

199. *See, e.g.,* ARIZ. REV. STAT. ANN. § 12-683(1) (Supp. 1957-1980); IND. CODE. ANN. § 34-4-20A-4(b)(4) (Burns Cum. Supp. 1980); KY. REV. STAT. ANN. § 411.310(2) (Baldwin Supp. 1979); NEB. REV. STAT. § 25-21, 182 (Cum. Supp. 1978); TENN. CODE ANN. § 23-3705(a) (Supp. 5, 1979).

200. *See, e.g.,* TENN. CODE ANN. § 23-3704 (Supp. 5, 1979); UTAH CODE ANN. § 78-15-6(3) (1977). *See also supra* notes 79–87 and accompanying text.

The sealed package statute impliedly considers loss shifting and takes the position (without justification) the loss should rest on the purchaser or user of the product. *See, e.g.,* TENN. CODE ANN. § 23-3706(a) (Supp. 1979).

201. *See, e.g.,* TASK FORCE, Legal Study *supra* note 133, at 103, 110.

202. *See, e.g.,* ORE. REV. STAT. § 30.910 (1977). *Cf.* KY. REV. STAT. ANN. § 411.310 (Baldwin 1979) (presumption product is free from defect arises after eight years from the date of manufacture or five years from the date of sale to the consumer).

203. GA. CODE ANN. § 105-106(b)(2) (Cum. Supp. 1980) (strict liability suit limited to manufacturers); NEB. REV. STAT. § 25-21, 181 (Cum. Supp. 1978) (seller must be the

perhaps the most substantial move away from the principle of loss shifting. The first group reflects the power of the manufacturers' lobby in persuading legislatures to protect their interests.[204] There is no empirical reason a product should be presumed to be *either* dangerous or safe as this is a factual question best left for a case-by-case determination.

Statutes that permit strict liability only against manufacturers insulate both wholesalers and retailers from liability,[205] and function contrary to that theory it would be more efficient to assign liability to the retailer, who may then recover from the wholesaler or manufacturer.[206] An injured plaintiff thus could recover while the more powerful commercial entities develop an appropriate solution among themselves.[207]

In contrast to the other reforms, comparative negligence statutes[208] may result in equitable and efficient loss shifting. By allowing comparative fault to be a factual issue, the jury can apportion a just and efficient award among the parties.[209]

b. Prevention The theory underlying prevention is that accident losses should be placed upon the party who is in the best position to prevent the injury.[210] Statutes of repose[211] ignore the policy of prevention by placing the loss on the plaintiff after an arbitrary period of time has passed even though the plaintiff is often unable to prevent injury from a defective product. (For example, a consumer would be unable to prevent injury from a defective airplane, automobile gas tank, or prescription drug.) Similarly, by holding the manufacturer only to

---

manufacturer in products liability action based on doctrine of strict liability in tort); TENN. CODE ANN. § 23-3706 (Supp. 5, 1979) (seller must be the manufacturer in products liability action based on doctrine of strict liability in tort).

204. *See, e.g.,* Green & Nader, *supra* note 158 at 876 and accompanying text.

205. Ellis v. Rich's Inc., 233 Ga. 573, 212 S.E.2d 373 (1975) (importer and retailer not subject to suit in strict liability under Georgia law as neither was a manufacturer).

206. *See, e.g.,* Cushing v. Rodman, 82 F.2d 864, 870 (D.C. Cir. 1936) (retailer may recover against manufacturer, who may then spread its loss by raising the cost of its product).

207. *Id. See also* CALABRESI, *supra* note 194, at 57 (losses should be placed on those in a position to pass such costs on to purchasers of their products or to factors employed in the production of their products, including labor and capital).

208. CONN. GEN. STAT. § 52-572/(Cum. Supp. 1980); NEB. REV. STAT. § 25-1151 (Cum. Supp. 1978).

209. The Task Force found application of a comparative fault statute may allow recovery in some cases where none might have been possible, and might encourage defendants to settle before trial TASK FORCE LEGAL STUDY, *supra* note 133, at 54–55.

210. *See* Green pt. 2, *supra* note 194, at 255–56. Dean Prosser has stated "the 'prophylactic' factor of preventing future harm has been quite important in the field of torts. . . . Not infrequently one reason for imposing liability is the deliberate purpose of providing that incentive [of preventing future injuries.]" PROSSER, *supra* note 153, at 23.

211. *See supra* notes 125–39 and accompanying text.

the standard of care existing at the time the product was made or sold, state-of-the-art statutes[212] eliminate the manufacturer's incentive to develop new processes or materials that might make the product safer.[213] Prevention is also frustrated by governmental standards statutes[214] because manufacturers obtain statutory protection once they have complied with the pertinent regulations. The point to be remembered is the standard may be too weak to be of value to the victim—and that standard was likely developed by the regulated corporation.

If the prevention policy were followed, new statutes would presume a product to be defective, and the manufacturer would have the burden of proving otherwise. Such statutes would lead to the desired result by providing the greatest incentive for manufacturers (who have the power to do so) to improve their products.[215] Instead, recent statutes make the presumption the product is safe.[216] In some cases, this presumption is so strong the plaintiff will lose the suit even though it would be in the best interests of society to hold the manufacturer liable. For example, the sealed package doctrine[217] ignores the public policy of permitting an action against the local seller in order to save the plaintiff the expense of litigating against the manufacturer in another state or country.

If a seller who has lost to a consumer in a suit then sues a manufacturer, the litigation can be just as effective in preventing the sale of defective products as a suit by a consumer against a manufacturer.[218] In addition, comparative negligence statutes[219] and misuse and alteration statutes[220] support the policy of

---

212. *See supra* notes 161–64 and accompanying text.

213. *See* TASK FORCE LEGAL STUDY, *supra* note 133, at 103–04 (state-of-the-art defense "untenable" as it reduces incentives to improve product safety).

214. *See supra* note 157 and accompanying text.

215. If a manufacturer is made liable for product defects, it will try to prevent the occurrence of such defects. PROSSER, *supra* note 153, at 23.

216. *See, e.g.,* ORE. REV. STAT. § 30.910 (1977) (product not unreasonably dangerous); TENN. CODE ANN. § 23-3707 (Supp. 5, 1979) (compliance with governmental standards); UTAH CODE ANN. § 78-15-6(3) (1977) (compliance with governmental standards).

217. *See supra* notes 175–77, 200, and accompanying text.

218. *See* Cushing v. Rodman, 82 F.2d 864 (D.C. Cir. 1936) (because seller has facilities to determine the soundness or unsoundness of a product, public policy dictates it should be held liable). The preventive value of a suit against the seller is also precluded by statutes that permit strict liability suits only against the manufacturer. *See supra* notes 120–28 and accompanying text; Ellis v. Rich's Inc., 223 Ga. 573, 212 S.E.2d 373 (1975) (injured party could not maintain action for damages against importer, distributor, or retailer of defective product as none was a manufacturer).

219. *See supra* notes 106–14 and accompanying text.

220. ARIZ. REV. STAT. ANN. § 12-683(2), (3) (1956); CONN. GEN. STAT. § 52-572/(1980); GA. CODE ANN. § 105-106(b)(1) (Cum. Supp. 1980); IND. CODE ANN. § 34-4-20A-4(b)(2, (3) (Burns Cum. Supp. 1980); KY. REV. STAT. ANN. § 411.320(2) (Baldwin Supp. 1979); ORE. REV. STAT. § 30.9125 (1977); TENN. CODE ANN. § 23-3708 (Supp. 5, 1979); UTAH CODE ANN. § 78-15-5 (1977).

prevention by allowing juries to weigh the fault of the consumer against the fault of the manufacturer. In some cases, the jury may find the consumer's fault is greater than the seller's.[221]

c. Judge Learned Hand's Theory Judge Hand articulated underlying torts policies in *United States v. Carroll Towing Co.*,[222] in which he stated a defendant's liability depends on whether the burden of prevention by the defendant is less than the probability that injury will occur multiplied by the gravity of the injury.[223] The three most substantial legislative reforms to the products liability system consider only one of these factors: burden on the defendant.

Statutes of repose,[224] state-of-the-art statutes,[225] and governmental standards enactments[226] impliedly weigh only the burden upon the manufacturer of taking adequate precautions. These legislative reforms assume the increase in products liability litigation has resulted in increased products liability insurance costs to manufacturers.[227] Because these statutes cut off a plaintiff's recovery altogether, they do not consider the other two prongs of the *Carroll Towing* test (i.e., the probability of harm and the gravity of the injury).[228] They consider the cost to the seller but not the risk to the consumer.

The presumption-of-a-safe product[229] and the sealed package statutes[230] fail to give any weight to the factors suggested in *Carroll Towing*.[231] By protecting the wholesalers and retailers from strict liability suits, the Georgia[232] and Tennessee statutes[233] do not weigh the risk and damage to the victim. They automatically preclude recovery against the manufacturer even though it might be in the best position to prevent future losses.

d. Precedent Under the concept of precedent, established case law furnishes binding authority for subsequent similar cases.[234] But recent legislative enactments

---

221. *See* Posey v. Clark Equip. Co., 409 F.2d 560 (7th Cir.), *cert. denied*, 396 U.S. 940 (1969) (manufacturer of forklift truck not liable to consumer as danger was obvious).

222. 159 F.2d 169 (2d Cir. 1947).

223. *Id.* at 173. *See generally* PROSSER, *supra* note 153, at 149.

224. *See supra* notes 125–39 and accompanying text.

225. *See* supra notes 161–64 and accompanying text.

226. *See supra* note 157 and accompanying text.

227. *See* Note, *The Utah Liability Limitation of Action: An Unfair Resolution of Competing Concerns*, 1979 UTAH L. REV. 149, 150 (1979).

228. United States v. Carroll Towing Co., 159 F.2d 169, 173 (2d Cir. 1947).

229. *See supra* notes 115–16 and accompanying text.

230. *See supra* notes 117–19 and accompanying text.

231. *Carroll Towing*, 159 F.2d at 173.

232. GA CODE ANN. § 105-106(b)(1) (Cum. Supp. 1980) (only manufacturer is subject to strict liability).

233. TENN. CODE ANN. § 23-3706 (Supp. 5, 1979) (seller must be a manufacturer to be sued in strict liability). *See also* NEB. REV. STAT. § 35-21, 181 (Cum. Supp. 1978) (seller must be a manufacturer to be sued in strict liability).

234. *See* PROSSER, *supra* note 153, at 19.

ignore judicial precedent. For example, statutes of repose[235] have no case authority to support them;[236] they are adopted by the legislatures simply to protect the powerful.

Numerous legislative reforms are contrary to common law precedent. At common law, a manufacturer's adherence to the custom of the industry and compliance with governmental regulations are mere evidentiary factors regarding the issues of due care.[237] However, new statutes have made a manufacturer's adherence to industry custom a complete defense,[238] and have raised a manufacturer's compliance with governmental standards to a rebuttable presumption the product is not unreasonably dangerous.[239] Similarly, statutes that presume a product is safe give the manufacturer an evidentiary benefit without any basis in precedent.[240] The sealed package statutes[241] illustrate a denial of precedent because the common law majority rule does not recognize the sealed package doctrine as a defense.[242] Finally, by their adoption of statutes that allow only the manufacturer to be sued in strict liability,[243] Georgia, Nebraska, and Tennessee ignore the strong precedent that the seller (whether wholesaler, retailer, or manufacturer) should be subject to suit.[244]

However, some statutes are in accord with precedent, misuse and alteration statutes[245] codify the common law.[246] In contrast, the recent comparative negligence statutes[247] have the beneficial effect of changing the rule that a plaintiff's

---

235. *See supra* notes 125–39 and accompanying text.

236. The preamble to Utah's statute of repose states the statute is designed to provide a reasonable time within which products liability actions may be brought against manufacturers while limiting the time to a specific period for which products liability premiums can be calculated. UTAH CODE ANN. § 78-15-2(3) (1977).

237. The T.J. Hooper, 60 F.2d 737, 740 (2d Cir.) *cert. denied*, 287 U.S. 662 (1932) (custom of industry); PROSSER, *supra* note 153, at 203–04 (compliance with governmental statutes and regulations).

238. *See supra* notes 161–64 and accompanying text.

239. *See supra* note 157 and accompanying text.

240. *See supra* notes 115–16 and accompanying text.

241. *See supra* notes 175–77, 200, and accompanying text.

242. PROSSER, *supra* note 153, at 664–65 (4th ed. 1971).

243. GA CODE ANN. § 105-106(b)(1) (1980); NEB. REV. STAT. § 25-21, 181 (Cum. Supp. 1978); TENN. CODE ANN. § 23-3706(b) (Supp.1979).

244. *See* Greenman v. Yuba Power Prod., Inc., 59 Cal. 2d 57, 377 P.2d 897, 27 Cal. Rptr. 697 (1962); RESTATEMENT, *supra* note 12, § 402A (1965). *But see* Peterson v. Lou Bachrodt Chevrolet Co., 61 Ill. 2d 17, 329 N.E.2d 785 (1975) (doctrine of strict liability could not be imposed to hold seller of used automobiles liable in absence of allegations that defects were created by seller or existed when the automobile left the manufacturer's control), *rev'd on other grounds*, 61 Ill. App. 3d 898, 378 N.E.2d 618 (1978), *aff'd and remanded*, 76 Ill. 2d 353, 392 N.E.2D 1 (1979).

245. *See supra* note 167 and accompanying text.

246. *See* TASK FORCE LEGAL STUDY, *supra* note 133, at 35–37.

247. *See supra* notes 106–14 and accompanying text.

contributory negligence is a complete bar to recovery in a products liability suit.[248]

e. Justice and Administration Dean Green stated that justice was one of the fundamental policies underlying tort law.[249] However, none of the recent statutory modifications to the torts system consider this factor, unless the legislative decision to shift the costs of accidents and of products liability insurance from the manufacturer to the consumer (and thereby close the courthouse doors) can be considered just.

Dean Green also suggested problems of administration may be a factor underlying tort law.[250] The only potential administrative problem in products liability cases is the ability of the courts to deal with a threatened flood of litigation.[251] However, careful analysis of the number of cases being filed indicates no such flood exists.[252] Therefore, arguably the new state products liability reforms cannot be justified on the basis of judicial administrative considerations.[253]

The state legislatures have adopted far-reaching acts to protect the powerful. This examination of state legislative enactments indicates a substantial alteration of the judicial function as the new statutes attack the foundation of the civil liability system. In the next few years, more states will likely adopt these far-reaching modifications. For example, ten states have adopted statutes of repose,[254] and it is likely more will follow, because these statutes will probably survive constitutional challenges based on due process and equal protection.[255] The problem with the "reforms" is not that they are unconstitutional, but that they lead to inappropriate results. Their sole function is to insulate the product sellers from suit.

Tort "reform" since about 1980 has been a great victory for corporate interests. They have persuaded state legislatures the losses occasioned in products injuries should rest upon the consumers, and have substantially undermined

---

248. *See* Edwards v. Sears, Roebuck & Co., 512 F.2d 276, 290 (5th Cir. 1975) (damages could be awarded in proportion to defendant's contributory negligence). *But see* Parzini v. Ctr. Chem. Co., 136 Ga. App. 396, 221 S.E.2d 475 (1975) (if plaintiff knew of defect in product and assumed the risk, he is barred from recovery), *on remand from* 234 Ga. 868, 218 S.E.2d 580 (1975).The complete bar theory is viewed by legal writers as inherently unfair to plaintiffs. *See, e.g.*, VICTOR E. SCHWARTZ, COMPARATIVE NEGLIGENCE 207–09 (1974).

249. *See* Green pt. 2, *supra* note 194, at 256; *see also* PROSSER, *supra* note 153, at 23.

250. Green pt. 1, *supra* note 194, at 1035.

251. Leon Green, *Proximate Cause, supra* note 170, at 755; Green pt. 1, *supra* note 194, at 1034–45.

252. The Task Force found there was no certain data indicating the number of products liability claims had increased in the years studied. TASK FORCE FINAL REPORT, *supra* note 128, at I-26.

253. *See* Victor Schwartz, *Proposed Remedies for the American Problem: U.S. Governmental Activity*, 29 MERCER L. REV. 437, 439 (1978); Gingerich, *supra* note 128, at 281 (1978).

254. *See supra* note 125.

255. *See* TASK FORCE LEGAL STUDY, *supra* note 133, at 10–11.

civil liability theory. Traditional civil policies will be of diminished importance in the future. Consumers will lose more cases while progressive decisions that strike a balance with manufacturing interests will likely be superceded in the legislatures. For example, in 2005 Congress passed an act that largely forbids suits against gun manufacturers.[256]

The judicial function of formulating civil policy has changed.[257] The creative strides by the courts over the past 160 years to benefit victims by eliminating privity, discovering implied warranty, and creating strict liability are over. Courts will play a diminished role under the restrictive statutes as their function will be limited by the new statutory provisions. The impact of the legislative modifications to the tort system will be determined by how the courts construe these acts. The powerful have mounted a full-on attack by rewriting justice in the courts and legislatures.

D. POWERFUL INSTITUTES AND ASSOCIATIONS REWRITE THE LAW

Little scholarly attention has been devoted to the role of nongovernmental institutes and associations in shaping products liability law. This section will consider the role of the American Law Institute, the American Trial Lawyers Association, and the Council for Tobacco Research in rewriting justice. The point is that effecting legal change is no longer limited to the courts, legislatures, and agencies as persuasive organizations can also change the law.

1. The American Law Institute (ALI)

The American Law Institute (ALI) is composed of judges, law professors, and practitioners.

The traditional purpose of the ALI is to publish restatements of the common law.[258] The ALI's founders were both critical of the legislative process and

---

256. S. 397, Protection of Lawful Commerce in Arms Act (2005).

257. A court must decide the case in front of it. One way or the other, that decision creates policy. If the legislature does not like it, they can supercede the decision with new legislation.

258. www.ali.org/index.cfm?fuseaction=about.creation.

In recent years, the American Law Institute (ALI) has shifted from producing neutral restatements of the law to being a "law reform think tank":

> This year's substantive program includes a strong cross-section of our law reform agenda. . . . ALI is the leading independent organization in the world dedicated to clarifying and improving the law. History has given us . . . the reputation . . . to contribute . . . to the improved laws . . . globally. . . . I welcome your thoughts . . . about possible law-reform projects.

admiring of the common law.[259] The first director, William Draper Lewis, stated the goal of the ALI was to parse "out of the mass of case authority and legal literature . . . clear statements of the rules of the common law. . . expressed as simply as the character of our complex civilization admits."[260]

Perhaps the clearest manifestation of the ALI's shift to protect powerful sellers is the *Restatement (Third) of Torts: Products Liability*, section 2(b),[261] which is important in two respects. First, it functionally eliminates strict liability from products litigation; second, it requires the plaintiff to show a reasonable alternative design to the alleged defect in the product.[262] The theoretical, economic, and practical problems with section 2(b) have been discussed in several articles.[263] In every respect, section 2(b) is injurious to the consumer and will increase the price of products liability suits by the cost of either an expert witness or the development of a reasonable alternative design.[264] This is estimated to account for an increase of approximately $25,000 or more for each case.

ALI has played a substantial role in reducing justice for consumers over the past several years.[265] This began with the Enterprise Liability Project in 1986, and now section 2(b) in 1997:

The Restatement (Third) of Torts: Products Liability section 2(b) is a wish list for manufacturing America. It returns products liability law to something

---

Letter to Professor Frank J. Vandall from Professor Roberto Cooper Romano, President ALI, Feb. 1, 2010 (available from Professor Vandall).

259. *See* Frank Vandall, *The Restatement (Third) of Torts: Products Liability, Section 2(b): The Reasonable Alternative Design Requirement*, 61 TENN. L. REV. 1407, 1408 (1994).

260. Marshall S. Shapo, *In Search of the Law of Products Liability: The ALI Restatement Project*, 48 VAND. L. REV. 631, 633 (1955).

261. *See* RESTATEMENT (THIRD) OF TORTS § 2(b) (1998).

262. *See id.* (discussing criteria for design defect).

263. *See* Frank J. Vandall, *An Examination of the Duty Issue in Health Care Litigation: Should HMOs Be Liable in Tort for "Medical Necessity" Decisions?*, 71 TEMP. L. REV. 293, 318 (1998) [hereinafter Vandall, *Duty Issue*] (indicating rigid requirements imposed upon consumer in 2(b) are not supported by relevant case law); Frank J. Vandall, *Constricting a Roof Before the Foundation is Prepared: The Restatement (Third) of Torts: Products Liability Section 2(b) Design Defect*, 30 U. MICH. J.L. REFORM 261, 269–70 (1997) [hereinafter Vandall, *Design Defect*] (noting traditional strict liability principles were ignored in drafting Section 2(b)); Frank J. Vandall, *The Restatement (Third) of Torts: Products Liability Section 2(b): The Reasonable Alternative Design Requirement*, 61 TENN. L. REV. 1407, 1423 (1994) [hereinafter Vandall, *Reasonable Alternative Design*] (arguing Section 2(b) contravenes traditional principles of strict liability law).

264. *See* RESTATEMENT (THIRD) OF TORTS § 2(b) (1998) (indicating that in order to prevail in a strict liability lawsuit, the plaintiff must offer evidence of an alternative reasonable design).

265. *See* Vandall, *Design Defect*, *supra* note 263, at 261 (describing Section 2(b) of *Restatement (Third) of Torts* as a "wish list" for manufacturing America).

more restrictive than negligence. What is new from the Reporters is that their proposal is written on a clean sheet of paper. Messy and awkward concepts such as precedent, policy, and case accuracy have been brushed aside for the purpose of tort reform. There has been almost no attempt to evaluate strict liability precedent or the policies underlying previous cases and the Restatement (Second) section 402A. Section 2b has been drafted with little consideration of the policies underlying section 402A or the cases favoring the consumer decided over the last thirty years. The Restatement (Third) of Torts: Products Liability implies that legal analysis is farcical. Avoiding legal analysis is certain to cause section 2(b) to lose convincing power among those searching for solutions to tough cases involving injuries caused by defective products.[266]

Something was missing from the drafters' presentation of the proposed *Restatement (Third) of Torts: Products Liability* section 2(b) at the University of Michigan Symposium—the foundation.[267] The presentation was comparable to deciding the size of the roof to put on a completed building. It presumed a foundation had been laid, but it was not. To lay a foundation for a Restatement, there must be a discussion and critique of the policies underlying contemporary products liability law. But the scholars at the Ann Arbor conference simply assumed current products liability law (as expressed in cases and in the *Restatement (Second) of Torts* section 402A needed to be replaced because of the underlying flaws in the policies (the foundation) on which it rests. This proposition was not self-evident. Before old law and old policies are replaced with the new, their flaws (if any) must first be debated. This fundamental discussion was omitted. In its place there is a new building—the *Restatement (Third) of Torts: Products Liability*— that is not needed. It is as though the Reporters decided that an evaluation of fundamental policies would be too messy and time-consuming, so they just skipped to step two, drafting a radically new definition of design defect. As a result, they failed in their attempt to produce a Restatement.[268] The resulting product insulates the powerful sellers from design defect suits (strict liability).

Section 2(b) of the Restatement does not represent progress. First, it neither relies on nor furthers traditional products liability policies; second, it does not accurately reflect the practice of courts today; and finally, it does not benefit consumers. It solely benefits sellers.

a. The Tripartite Structure of Section 2: Magic Boxes

i. The Structure of Section 2 The purpose underlying section 2 of the *Restatement (Third) of Torts: Products Liability* to protect the powerful sellers is nowhere stated.

---

266. Vandall, *Design Defect, supra* note 263 at 261. *See also* the Appendix, which makes it clear the ALI designed the attack on the common law and solicited powerful corporations for funding.

267. Vandall, *Design Defect, supra* note 263 at 261.

268. *Id.* at 266.

Instead, it is hidden in complex language. Section 2 of the *Restatement*[269] divides all products cases into three categories: warning defect,[270] manufacturing defect,[271] and design defect.[272] A warning defect exists if the warning on the product is inadequate.[273] A manufacturing defect arises when a product differs from the other products on the assembly line (e.g., a screw in chicken soup).[274] By contrast, products containing design defects are precisely as the seller intended (the Ford Pinto).[275] The product with a design defect is the same as every other product on the assembly line.[276]

The Restatement Reporters developed separate subsections of section 2 to limit strict liability's application to manufacturing defects.[277] They placed strict liability on the ice floe that is section 2(a) and set it adrift.[278] In the process, they drafted section 2(b) that creates requirements more restrictive than negligence. To prove a design defect under section 2(b), a plaintiff must show "radical negligence."[279] This standard is "radical negligence" because the plaintiffs must

---

269. *Id.* at 266.

270. *See id.* at 266, § 2(c). According to section 2(c), a product is defective because of inadequate instructions or warnings when the foreseeable risks of harm posed by the product could have been reduced or avoided by the provision of reasonable instructions or warnings by the seller or other distributor, or a predecessor in the commercial chain of-distribution, and the omission of the instructions or warnings renders the product not reasonably safe. *Id.*

271. *See id.* at 266, § 2(a). According to section 2(a), a product contains a manufacturing defect when the product departs from its intended design even though all possible care was exercised in the preparation and marketing of the product. *Id.*

272. *See id.* at 266, § 2(b). According to section 2(b), a product is defective in design when the foreseeable risks of harm posed by the product could have been reduced or avoided by the adoption of a reasonable alternative design by the seller or other distributor, or a predecessor in the commercial chain of distribution, and the omission of the alternative design renders the product not reasonably safe. *Id.*

273. *See id.* at 266, § 2 cmt. h (explaining "sellers down the chain are liable if the instructions and warnings provided by predecessors in the chain are inadequate").

274. *See id.* at 266, § 2 cmt. b.

275. *See id.* at 266, § 2 cmt. c ("[A] product asserted to have a defective design meets the manufacturer's specifications but raises the question whether the specifications them-selves create unreasonable risk."). The Ford Pinto's gas tank tended to catch fire when the small car was hit from behind at about thirty mph.

276. *See* Vandall, *Design Defect, supra* note 263, at 266.

277. *See* RESTATEMENT (THIRD) OF TORTS: Products Liability § 2(a) (Tentative Draft No. 2, 1995) § 2 cmt. a.

278. *See id.* § 2 (applying strict liability only to manufacturing defects). Manufacturing defects are rare.

279. At least one jurisdiction has rejected the reasonable alternative design require-ment in negligence cases. *See* Rahmig v. Mosley Mach. Co., 412 N.W.2d 56 (Neb. 1987). The Restatement Reporters are pushing for an approach that will encourage the produc-tion of more defective products, while the ALI president is urging that at least one product

prove more than negligence: they must demonstrate a reasonable alternative design (RAD) was available at the time the product was sold. This high hurdle protects the sellers.

The broad language of section 2(b) may have subsumed "old fashioned" negligence.[280] Early drafts of section 2(b) strongly implied the cause of action for traditional negligence had been eliminated—that only section 2(b) was available as a cause of action for defective design.[281] At the 1996 University of Michigan symposium, Professor James Henderson was asked from the floor whether an amendment to make certain traditional negligence remained available outside section 2 would be considered later in the year.[282] Professor Henderson stated this amendment would not be considered at the May meeting of the ALI.[283]

ii. Section 2: The Practice Plaintiffs harmed by defective products must fit their claims within one of section 2's three magic boxes: manufacturing defect, design defect, or warning defect.

Separating defective products that belong in the manufacturing defect box from those that belong in the design defect box is challenging. In *Pouncey v. Ford Motor Co.*,[284] the plaintiff was working under the hood of his car with the motor running when a blade spun off the car's radiator fan and hit him in the head.[285] An examination of the fan blade disclosed an excessive number of nonmetallic impurities in the steel, known as inclusions.[286] Arguably, the blade had a manufacturing defect because it contained more inclusions than normally found in the type of steel used to make the blade.[287] Alternatively, the inclusions could be

---

(airplanes) should be safer. When accepting the White House Commission on Aviation Safety and Security Final Report, President Bill Clinton said: "We will also change the way we inspect older aircraft, to include an examination of wiring and hydraulic systems, all to ensure that every plane carrying passengers, regardless of its age, is as safe as it can be." *CNN Special Event* (CNN television broadcast, Feb. 12, 1997), available at LEXIS, News Library, CNN File.

280. "Old fashioned" negligence places the burden on the plaintiff of proving an absence of due care, but does not require proof that a reasonable alternative design was available as a condition precedent to suit.

281. *See* RESTATEMENT (THIRD) OF TORTS: Products Liability (Tentative Draft No. 1, 1994) at 30. ("The rules in this Section exclusively define the bases of tort liability for harms caused by product defects. . . . .").

282. *See* Frank J. Vandall, Remarks at the Colloquy on Products Liability: Comprehensive Discussions on the *Restatement (Third) of Torts*: Products Liability 112 (Mar. 22, 1996) (transcript on file with the *University of Michigan Journal of Law Reform*).

283. *See* James A. Henderson, Remarks at the Colloquy on Products Liability: Comprehensive Discussions on the *Restatement (Third) of Torts*: Products Liability 112 (Mar. 22, 1996) (transcript on file with the *University of Michigan Journal of Law Reform*).

284. 464 F.2d 957 (5th Cir. 1972).

285. *See id.* at 958.

286. *See id.* Inclusions weaken the metal. *See id.*

287. *See id.*

considered a design defect because Ford had used cheap metal in the fan blades, thereby causing the large number of inclusions in the metal.[288]

Harley-Davidson Motor Co. v. Wisniewski[289] also shows the difficulty in trying to categorize product defects as either design or manufacture. As the plaintiff rode his Harley-Davidson motorcycle around a curve, the clamp holding the throttle to the handle bar disconnected. The throttle slid off the handlebar, resulting in the plaintiff being injured.[290] The clamp disconnected because on the assembly line, a screw on it had been cross-threaded.[291] Does this situation involve a manufacturing or a design defect? It would be a manufacturing defect if the assembly line robot malfunctioned and cross-threaded the screw on the "C" clamp. On the other hand, it would be a design defect if the robot was programmed so that every motorcycle leaving the assembly line had a similar problem with its throttle.[292]

The issue of whether a product has a manufacturing or design defect is important because if it is a section 2(a) manufacturing defect, the plaintiff can sue in strict liability. If, however, it is a section 2(b) design defect, the plaintiff has to show "radical negligence."[293] As this is hard to prove, it favors the sellers.

Section 2's effectiveness hinges on the notion that it will be easy to distinguish between manufacturing and design defects. This belief reflects only a superficial analysis. As shown in the *Pouncey* and *Harley-Davidson* cases, applying the magic boxes to actual cases will be challenging. At worst, it will divert the court from the fundamental issue of whether the seller should be liable for the defective product.

iii. The Draft Lacks an Analysis of the Traditional Policies Underlying Strict Liability Geoffrey Hazard, director of the ALI, justified modifying the Restatement in the Foreword to the Tentative Draft, stating "the Restatement Second of Torts has become out of date."[294] Hazard or the Reporters must prove and support this bald conclusion, especially because the opposite conclusion is more accurate. More than three thousand cases have cited section 402A[295] with no court saying it reflects out-of-date policies or needs to be rethought.[296]

---

288. *See id.* at 961.

289. 437 A.2d 700 (Md. Ct. Spec. App. 1981).

290. *See id.* at 702.

291. *See id.* at 703.

292. *See id.* at 703–04.

293. *See* Vandall, *Design Defect, supra* note 263, at 266. In practice, a radical negligence standard will discourage many plaintiffs from bringing close cases.

294. RESTATEMENT (Tentative Draft No. 1), *supra* note 281, at xiii.

295. *See* James A. Henderson, Jr. & Aaron D. Twerski, *A Proposed Revision of Section 402A of the Restatement (Second) of Torts*, 77 CORNELL L. REV. 1512, 1512 n.1 (1992).

296. Perhaps the only exceptions are cases involving prescription drugs, which some courts feel fall within comment k's exception for "unavoidably unsafe." *See, e.g.,* Brown v. Superior Ct., 751 P.2d 470, 475–77 (Cal. 1988).

Furthermore, no article or case states decisions resting on section 402A have reached the wrong results. With no analysis of the validity of the policies underlying strict liability that have been accepted since 1942, the Reporters began instead with a clean sheet of paper.[297]

The traditional strict liability policies have been set out as the foundation to section 402A in comment c, which states:

> The justification for the strict liability has been said to be that the seller, by marketing his product for use and consumption, has undertaken and assumed a special responsibility toward any member of the consuming public who may be injured by it; that the public has the right to and does expect, in the case of products which it needs and for which it is forced to rely upon the seller, that reputable sellers will stand behind their goods; that public policy demands that the burden of accidental injuries caused by products intended for consumption be placed upon those who market them, and be treated as a cost of production against which liability insurance can be obtained; and that the consumer of such products is entitled to the maximum of protection at the hands of someone, and the proper persons to afford it are those who market the products.[298]

These policies have significantly influenced and remain the foundation in the forty-four states that have adopted some form of strict liability.[299] In reading the *Restatement (Third)*,[300] one does not see evidence the Reporters have challenged, debated, weighed, or evaluated these policies. Because law serves as a concrete statement of public policy, these policies must be debated for the new provision to succeed. Perhaps the drafters assumed the courts would adopt the new provision because it was a product of the highly respected ALI and clearly favored the powerful.

iv. Section 6(c) Design Defects in Drugs: A Tabula Rasa The pharmaceutical manufacturers are among the most powerful sellers in the country. The *Restatement (Third)* treats them as privileged. The proposed *Restatement (Third)* distinguishes between prescription drugs and all other products. Section 6(c) of the proposed *Restatement (Third)* provides:

> A prescription drug or medical device is not reasonably safe due to defective design when the foreseeable risks of harm posed by the drug or medical device are sufficiently great in relation to its foreseeable therapeutic benefits so that no reasonable health care provider, knowing of such foreseeable risks

---

297. *Cf.* Vandall, *Design Defect, supra* note 263, at 269.

298. RESTATEMENT (SECOND) OF TORTS § 402A cmt. c (1956).

299. *See* Vargo, *supra* note 9, at 553.

300. *See* RESTATEMENT, Tentative Draft No. 2, *supra* note 277.

and therapeutic benefits, would prescribe the drug or medical device for any class of patients.[301]

This proposal ignores the well-developed common law policies regarding products liability:[302] (1) the consumer lacks sophistication with regard to drugs,[303] (2) the loss should be placed on the manufacturer,[304] (3) the seller can spread the loss,[305] and (4) the seller is the cheapest cost avoider.[306]

The distinction between mechanical products covered by section 2(b) and prescription drugs covered by section 6(c) is artificial and arbitrary. The drug industry is not monolithic, and not all drugs and medical devices are worthy of blanket protection.[307] Some drugs save lives (such as blood pressure medicine and those that prevent infection), but others predominantly cause damage, such as thalidomide,[308] chloromycetin,[309] DES,[310] MER/29,[311] and Oraflex.[312] Indeed,

---

301. *Id.* § 6(c).

302. *See* Shanks v. Upjohn Co., 835 P.2d 1189 (Alaska 1992). The *Shanks* court found that consistent with the purposes underlying strict liability, manufacturers should be deterred from marketing certain products, and the cost of the defense of strict products liability litigation and any resulting judgments should be borne by the manufacturer who is able to spread the cost through insurance and higher prices for its products. *Id.* at 1196.

303. *See, e.g., id.* at 1194–95.

304. *See id.* at 1196.

305. *See id. See also* Sindell v. Abbott Lab., 607 P.2d 924, 936 (Cal. 1980).

306. *See Sindell,* 607 P.2d at 936 ("These considerations are particularly significant where medication is involved, for the consumer is virtually helpless to protect himself from serious, sometimes permanent, sometimes fatal, injuries caused by deleterious drugs.").

307. *See* Grundberg v. Upjohn Co., 813 P.2d 89, 100 (Utah 1991) (Stewart, J., dissenting) (asserting "decongestants, expectorants, deodorants, hair growth stimulants, skin moisturizers, and cough and cold remedies, for example, [would] have the same immunity as rabies or polio vaccines [and] medications essential in the treatment of cancer, heart disease, or AIDS" and finding "no basis for according drugs used to treat comparatively minor ailments a blanket immunity from strict liability if they are unreasonably dangerous to those who use them" (footnote omitted)).

308. *See, e.g.,* United States v. Bogus, 43 F.3d 82, 89 (3rd Cir. 1994) (describing birth defects during the 1960s caused by thalidomide).

309. *See, e.g.,* Stevens v. Parke, Davis & Co., 507 P.2d 653, 655 & n.2 (Cal.1973) (stating chloromycetin "has a history of causing aplastic anemia in certain patients" and that many members of the medical profession consider it to be a dangerous drug, if not "the single most dangerous antibiotic on the market at the time of [the plaintiff's] treatment").

310. *See, e.g.,* Toole v. Richardson-Merrell, Inc., 60 Cal Rptr. 398, 413 (Ct. App. 1967) (discussing eye opacities or cataracts as potential side effects of using MER/29).

311. *See Sindell,* 607 P.2d at 925 (noting DES could cause "cancerous vaginal and cervical growths" in daughters exposed to the drug during their mother's pregnancy).

312. *See, e.g.,* Washington Post Co. v. U.S. Dep't of Justice, 863 F.2d 96, 99 (D.C. Cir. 1988) (describing the many dangerous possible effects, including death, of taking Oraflex).

several Oraflex consumers had been killed in Europe before manufacturers introduced the drug in the United States.[313] The Dalkon Shield, a medical device, caused deaths and serious injuries resulting in $2 billion in damages.[314]

The Reporters should have weighed a handful of important drug design cases: *Brown v. Superior Court*,[315] *Kearl v. Lederle Laboratories*,[316] *Toner v. Lederle Laboratories*,[317] *Grundberg v. Upjohn Co.*,[318] and *Shanks v. Upjohn Co.*[319] All these cases articulate important concerns that deserve consideration. But the Reporters never address the policies of *Kearl*, *Toner*, *Grundberg*, and *Shanks*.[320] Instead, they ignore those policies and virtually grant immunity to all drug and medical device manufacturers for defective design claims.[321] Because of these foundational

---

An estimated fifty deaths occurred as a result of Oraflex being on the U.S. market for four months. *See* Teresa Moran Schwartz, *Prescription Products and the Proposed Restatement (Third)*, 61 TENN. L. REV. 1357, 1396–97 (1994).

313. *See The Miracle Drug That Became a Nightmare for Eli Lilly*, BUS. WK., Apr. 30, 1984, at 104. Eli Lilly obtained the FDA's approval to market Oraflex, although it had not revealed "extensive evidence of adverse reactions and deaths related to the drug overseas." Schwartz, *supra* note 312, at 1396.

314. *See* Malcolm Gladwell, *To Alan Morrison, Justice Falls Short in Robins Case*, WASH. POST, Sept. 19, 1989, at C1.

315. 751 P.2d 470 (Cal. 1988). The Court wrote "there is an important distinction between prescription drugs and other products such as construction machinery, a lawnmower, or perfume. . . . In the latter cases, the product is used to make work easier or to provide pleasure. . . . Moreover, unlike other important medical products (wheelchairs, for example), harm to some users from prescription drugs is unavoidable." *Id.* at 478 (citations omitted).

316. 218 Cal. Rptr. 453 (Cal. Ct. App. 1985). "[W]e are uncomfortable with the rather routine and mechanical fashion by which many appellate courts have concluded that certain products, particularly drugs, are entitled to such special treatment." *Id.* at 463.

317. 732 P.2d 297 (Idaho 1987). As it did in *Kearl*, the *Toner* court rejected the routine analysis other courts have followed when granting drugs the comment k exemption. "Courts must decide the applicability of comment k case-by-case. . . ." *Id.* at 309.

318. 813 P.2d 89 (Utah 1991). "We do not agree, however, with the Brown court's apparent attempt to use the plain language of comment k as the vehicle for exempting all prescription drugs from strict liability rather than relying on the policies underlying that comment." *Id.* at 95.

319. 835 P.2d 1189 (Alaska 1992). "[W]e find it speculative at best that restricting strict liability design defect claims against prescription drug manufacturers will serve the public interest by enhancing the availability and affordability of prescription drugs." *Id.* at 1195.

320. *Cf.* RESTATEMENT, Tentative Draft No. 2, *supra* note 277, § 8 reporters' note cmt. f (outlining the rationale behind section 8(c) without ever mentioning any of these cases).

321. *See* RESTATEMENT, Tentative Draft No.1, *supra* note 281, § 4. The Reporters stated: "Given the very demanding standard that must be met before a case of defective design of a prescription drug or a medical device can be established, liability is likely to be imposed only under unusual circumstances." *Id.* § 4 cmt. f.

omissions, section 6(c) is void of precedent.[322] Courts will not accept section 6(c) until the Reporters evaluate the cases and policies and draft a proposal that restates the law. This provision is a clear example of the privileged treatment afforded the powerful drug manufacturers by the ALI.

An example of judicial treatment of section 6(c) occurs in the Nebraska Supreme Court decision in *Freeman v. Hoffman-LaRouche, Inc.* Mrs. Freeman took Accutane to treat chronic acne. As a result, she developed "multiple health problems," including ulcerative colitis and optic nerve head drusen. When Mrs. Freeman argued for strict liability, the defendant proposed the new section 6(c), but the Nebraska Supreme Court rejected it, reasoning: "[T]here is no support in the case law . . . the majority of courts apply some form of risk-utility balancing—Thus, Section 6(c) does not restate the law and instead seeks to formulate new law with no precedential support. [T]he reasonable physician standard . . . will never allow liability."[323] As of 2009, section 6(c) has been a complete failure.[324]

v. The Restatement (Third) *of Torts: Products Liability Section 2(b) Does Not Reflect the Law* In order to protect the powerful, the Restatement ignores existing law. The *Restatement (Third)*: Products Liability section 2(b) is not an accurate representation of the law[325]—and therefore is simply not a Restatement as we know it. The case law cited by the Reporters fails to support the section 2(b) design defect provision in key ways. First, with regard to risk-utility balancing, the Reporters state: "An overwhelming majority of . . . jurisdictions rely on risk-utility balancing," which the Reporters construe to mean negligence.[326] However, the cases cited by the Reporters do not support risk-utility balancing as a subset of negligence.[327] The judges in the majority of those cases believed they were

---

322. *Cf.* Schwartz, *supra* note 312, at 1378 ("[T]he standards for pharmaceutical design claims depart dramatically from the status quo."); Angela C. Rushton, Comment, *Design Defects under the Restatement (Third) of Torts: A Reassessment of Strict Liability and the Goals of a Financial Approach,* 45 EMORY L.J. 389, 424 (1996) (asserting the "Tentative Draft approach to prescription drugs is a new position that differs substantially from any case law").

323. Freeman v. Hoffman-LaRoche, Inc., 260 Neb. 552, 618 N.W.2d 827 (Neb. S. Ct, 2000).

324. As of December 2009, no cases have been found suggesting sec. 6(c) has been adopted.

325. *See* Howard C. Klemme, *Comments to the Reporters and Selected Members of the Consultative Group, Restatement of Torts (Third): Products Liability,* 61 TENN L. REV. 1173, 1175 (1994) (asserting Tentative Draft No. 1 is "demonstrably defective" and that it requires "a more thoughtful, thorough analysis" of the relevant case holdings); Vargo, *supra* note 9, at 536–37 (arguing that although the Reporters "have expressed strong views on policy," their viewpoint "is not determinative of what the law is").

326. REINSTATEMENT, Tentative Draft No. 1, *supra* note 281, § 2 reporters' note cmt. c.

327. *See id.*; Vandall, *Constricting a Roof . . ., supra* note 263, at 273.

applying strict liability.[328] Indeed, one authority suggests a majority of jurisdictions use a consumer expectations test, not a risk-utility balancing.[329]

Second, the Reporters cite case law in twelve jurisdictions as proof the reasonable alternative design (RAD) should be a requirement,[330] but a majority of jurisdictions that have considered the question decided to the contrary.[331] In fact, contrary holdings govern a total of fourteen jurisdictions. Some hold a RAD is simply one of many factors to consider in the risk-utility analysis;[332] others shift the burden to the defendant manufacturer to prove the product was not defective,[333] and others do not require the plaintiff to present a RAD.[334] Professor John Vargo's two-and-a-half year study of all the case law found only three

---

328. *See id.*

329. *See* Ronald F. Bank & Margaret O'Connor, *Restating the Restatement (Second) § 402A—Design Defect,* 72 ORE. L. REV. 411, 413–14 (1993). *But see* Vargo, *supra* note 9, at 539 (stating ten states use the consumer expectations test).

330. *See* RESTATEMENT, Tentative Draft No. 2, *supra* note 277, § 2 reporters' note cmt. c.

331. *See* Frank J. Vandall, *The Restatement (Third) of Torts: Products Liability § 2(b): The Reasonable Alternative Design Requirement,* 61 TENN. L. REV. 1407, 1413–18 (1994) (reviewing case law of Colorado, Kentucky, Nevada, New Hampshire, and Texas that states reasonable alternative design is one of several factors to consider in determining if a design is defective).In 1994, it was argued the cases cited by Professors Henderson and Twerski did not support their conclusion that the majority of states require proof of a reasonable alternative design to go to the jury on design defect. *Id.* at 1408, footnote 8. In 2009, Henderson and Twerski published an apology and admited they had been overenthusiastic:

[W]e would like to critique [our earlier] article (. . . we identify shortcomings in the earlier effort) . . . In writing the instant Article (2009), we have debated between us whether "consensus" was the right word choice for the earlier piece. Certainly we intended then . . . to convey the message that our courts overwhelmingly embrace a risk-utility/ reasonable-alternative design approach to determine whether the plaintiff should reach the jury with a claim of defective design. . . . [S]uch proof is not always necessary.

Aaron D. Twerski & James A. Henderson, *Manufacturers Liability for Defective Product Designs: The Triumph of Risk-Utility,* 74 BROOK. L. REV. 1062, 1072 (2009).

332. Five jurisdictions consider a reasonable alternative design merely a factor in the design defect analysis. *See* Shipp v. Gen. Motors Corp., 750 F.2d 418, 421, & n.2 (5th Cir. 1985) (applying Texas law); Camacho v. Hondo Motor Co., 741 P.2d 1240, 1247 (Colo. 1987), *cert. dismissed,* 485 U.S. 901 (1988); Nichols v. Union Underwear Co., 602 S.W.2d 429, 434 (Ky. 1980); McCourt v. J.C. Penney Co., 734 P.2d 696, 698 (Nev. 1987); Thibault v. Sears, Roebuck & Co., 395 A.2d 843, 846 (N.H. 1978).

333. Three jurisdictions shift the burden to the defendant to prove the product was not defective. *See* Caterpillar Tractor Co. v. Beck, 593 P.2d 871, 885 (Alaska 1979); Barker v. Lull Eng'g Co., 573 P.2d 443, 455 (Cal. 1978); Ontai v. Straub Clinic & Hosp. Inc., 659 P.2d 734, 739 (Haw. 1983); Masaki v. Gen. Motors Corp., 780 P.2d 566, 579 (Haw. 1989).

334. Six jurisdictions do not require the plaintiff to present a reasonable alternative design. *See* Karns v. Emerson Elec. Co., 817 F.2d 1452, 1457 (10th Cir. 1987) (applying Arkansas law); Ogg v. City of Springfield, 458 N.E.2d 1331, 1338–39 (Ill. App. Ct. 1984); Kallio v. Ford Motor Co., 407 N.W.2d 92, 96–97 (Minn. 1987); Couch v. Mine Safety

jurisdictions support section 2(b)'s requirement that a plaintiff must present evidence of a RAD.[335] In his 450-page study, Professor Vargo examined the cases of every state, concluding only the common law of Alabama, Maine, and Michigan support the Reporters.[336] Another five jurisdictions have adopted the RAD requirement by statute.[337] A total of eight jurisdictions hardly constitutes a majority.

Third, the cases do not draw distinctions between manufacturing defects and design defects (as the Reporters argued).[338] *Cronin v. J.B.E. Olson Corp.*,[339] an important California case, stated the distinction is not tenable,[340] and *Barker v. Lull*[341] expressly refused to draw this demarcation.[342] Fourth, the jurisdictions split evenly on whether a seller should be charged with knowledge at the time of sale versus at the time of trial.[343]

b. The *Restatement (Third)* Section 2(b) Design Defect Should Be Rejected A few states will probably adopt section 2(b). Perhaps three—Alabama[344], Maine,[345] and Michigan[346]—already follow its principal via common law.[347] Forty-four

---

Appliances Co., 728 P.2d 585, 588 (Wash. 1986); Sumnicht v. Toyota Motor Sales, U.S.A., Inc., 360 N.W.2d, 16–17 (Wis. 1984).

335. *See* Vargo, *supra* note 9, at 536.

336. *See id.*

337. *See id.* at 537. Illinois, Louisiana, Mississippi, Ohio. and Texas have enacted statutes imposing the alternative design requirement. *See* 7 ILL. COMP. STAT. 5/2-2104 (West 1995); LA. REV. STAT. ANN. § 9:2800.59 (West 1991); MISS. CODE ANN. § 11-1-63 (1996); OHIO REV. CODE ANN. § 2307.75 (Anderson 1995); TEX. CIV. PROC. & REM. CODE ANN. § 82.005 (West 1986).

338. *See infra* Cronin v. J.B.E. Olson Corp., 501 P.2d 1153 (Cal. 1972) and Baker v. AC&S Inc., 729 A.2d 1140 (Pa. 1998).

339. 501 P.2d 1153, 1163 (Cal. 1972) (affirming verdict that a defective hasp allowed bread trays to slam forward in a truck).

340. *See id.* at 1163 (refusing to distinguish between manufacturing and design defects "to avoid providing . . . a battleground for clever counsel").

341. 573 P.2d 443 (Cal. 1978).

342. *See id.* at 451–52.

343. *See* Vandall, *Design Defect, supra* note 263, at 179–82 (arguing the Reporters have changed strict liability theory into negligence theory by opting for the date-of-sale standard). In Dart v. Wiebe Mfg. Inc., 709 P.2d 876 (Ariz. 1985), the court adopted the time-of-trial approach. *Id.* at 881. Indeed, the Reporters cite four jurisdictions for the theory the manufacturer is charged with knowledge at the time of trial: Hawaii, Massachusetts, Pennsylvania, and Washington. *See* RESTATEMENT, Tentative Draft No. 1, *supra* note 24, § 2 cmt. I *Cf. See also* Ellen Wertheimer, *Unknowable Dangers and the Death of Strict Liability: The Empire Strikes Back*, 60 U. CIN. L. REV. 1183, 1203 & n.71 (1992) (stating "[i]f knowledge of the product's danger is not imputed to the manufacturer, strict products liability becomes a negligence doctrine").

344. *See* Beech v. Outbound Marine Corp., 584 So. 2d 447, 450 (Ala. 1991).

345. *See* St. Germain v. Husqvarna Corp., 544 A.2d 1283, 1285 (Me. 1988).

346. *See* Prentis v. Yale Mfg. Co., 365 N.W.2d 176, 185–86 (Mich. 1984).

347. *See* Vargo, *supra* note 9, at 536.

states have adopted some form of strict liability;[348] only through policy analysis can they be persuaded they were wrong. The Georgia Supreme Court used the Tentative Draft of the *Restatement (Third)* to help define a risk-utility balancing test,[349] although it rejected making the existence of a RAD as a requirement for a design defect claim.[350] In *Denny v. Ford Motor Co.*,[351] the New York Court of Appeals demonstrated a different perspective on products liability. The plaintiff's Ford Bronco II had rolled over when she slammed on her brakes to avoid hitting a deer. The plaintiff brought suit based both on strict liability and breach of implied warranty of merchantability.[352] Applying the risk-utility test, the court upheld the jury's finding the plaintiff could not recover under strict liability because the product was not defective.[353] However, the *Denny* court upheld the trial court's finding *for* the plaintiff on the breach of implied warranty of merchantability,[354] applying the consumer expectations test.[355] In other words, the court concluded there was no liability for design defect because the Bronco II was suitably designed for use as an off-road vehicle, but still found liability under breach of implied warranty of merchantability because although it was marketed as a conventional passenger vehicle, it did not meet consumer expectations for such a vehicle.[356] *Denny* indicates that some courts, provided the opportunity to adopt section 2(b) of the Tentative Draft, will instead reject it and continue to follow their own common law, as happened when Kansas considered section 2(b) but rejected it in favor of their own precedent.[357]

The Supreme Court of New Mexico has also rejected the Reporters' approach in draft section 2(b). In *Brooks v. Beech Aircraft Corp.*,[358] the plaintiff sued the aircraft manufacturer for the wrongful death of her husband,[359] who died flying a plane produced by Beech Aircraft. The plane was not designed or sold with a shoulder harness. The plaintiff claimed the lack of a harness enhanced her

---

348. *See id.* at 553.

349. *See* Bank v. ICI Ams., Inc., 450 S.E.2d 671, 674 (Ga. 1994) ("[W]e see no reason to conclude definitively that the two theories merge in design defect cases.").

350. *See id.* at 674–75.

351. 662 N.E.2d 730 (N.Y. 1995), *reh'g denied*, 664 N.E.2d 1261 N.Y. 1996.

352. *See id.* at 733.

353. *See id.* at 735.

354. *See id.* at 739.

355. *See id.* at 736. The court said the test for implied warranty is whether the product is merchantable and that consumer expectations are a factor of merchantability. *See id.*

356. *See id.* at 733.

357. Delany v. Deere & Co., 999 P.2d 930 (Kan S.Ct., 2000), citing Professor Vandall with approval.

358. 902 P.2d 54 (N.M. 1995).

359. *See id.* at 55.

husband's injury, causing his death.[360] Alleging a design defect, she sued in negligence and strict liability. After reviewing the policies behind strict liability,[361] the court held a plaintiff can bring a design defect claim in negligence and strict liability, and may prove design defect without showing the manufacturer did not meet industry standards or government regulations.[362] The court rejected the Restatement's position that only negligence principles—and not strict liability—apply to design defects.[363]

i. Under the Restatement (Third), *Fewer Suits Will Be Brought* What impact will section 2 have on suits by injured consumers? Many suits for design defect based on radical negligence will be lost because negligence is inherently harder to prove than strict liability.[364] In addition, the courts will likely interpret the RAD concept as a condition precedent to suit or as a requirement for liability.[365] As a result, plaintiffs will not bring small suits or will see their suits dismissed at the pretrial stage. For example, assume the cost of an expert or model to prove a RAD[366] would be $35,000, and the expected verdict is $60,000. If courts apply section 2(b) in that jurisdiction, the prospective plaintiff is not likely to bring suit. Whatever the proof of RAD might cost, this new expense will dramatically affect the plaintiff's attorney's decision regarding bringing suit. The plaintiffs in small cases will not be able to afford the cost of producing evidence of a RAD, either in the form of a prototype or as qualified expert testimony. (On the other hand, plaintiffs will continue to bring suits with expected large verdicts because the outcome will justify the expenditure necessary for the proof of an

---

360. *See id.* No government regulation or industry custom required the installation of shoulder harnesses at the time the defendant manufactured the aircraft. *See id.*

361. *See id.* at 57–58.

362. *See id.* at 55.

363. *See id.* at 62–63. The court stated:

In most instances a manufacturer is aware of the risks posed by any given design and of the availability of an alternative design. . . . [W]e disagree with the premise that fairness requires the rejection of strict liability in design cases. . . .

. . . [W]e believe that it is logical and consistent to take the same approach to design defects as to manufacturing flaws. *Id.* at 63.

364. *See* Cronin v. J.B.E. Olson Corp., 501 P.2d 1153, 1162 (Cal. 1972) (noting "the very purpose of our pioneering efforts in [strict liability] was to relieve the plaintiff from problems of proof inherent in pursuing negligence").

365. This result would mimic Florida, where the plaintiff in a medical malpractice action must attach a certification that a medical doctor is willing to testify the defendant medical doctor was negligent. Without this memorandum, Florida courts dismiss the case. *See* Bill Wagner, Remarks at the Colloquy on Product Liability: Comprehensive Discussions on the *Restatement (Third) of Torts: Products Liability*, 137–38 (Mar. 22, 1996) (transcript on file with the *University of Michigan Journal of Law Reform*).

366. *See* REINSTATEMENT, Tentative Draft No. 2, *supra* note 277, § 2 cmt. e (describing how either a prototype or qualified expert testimony would suffice for plaintiff to establish a prima facie case).

alternative design.)[367] Language in the Restatement suggests the drafters sought precisely this result: the elimination of smaller suits.[368]

ii. Institutionalizing Needless Ambiguity Vagueness is a great argument for the powerful. One of the foundational goals of the *Restatement (Third)* is stated to be clarity.[369] An examination of section 2, however, reveals the second line of section 1(b) uses the vague term "foreseeable."[370] By retaining the concept of foreseeable risk, the reporters have guaranteed ambiguity under section 2(b). This ambiguity results in part from proximate cause, the most challenging and ambiguous concept in tort law, which also rests on the concept of foreseeability.[371] Foreseeability is an open-ended, discretionary decision made by judges and juries. Indeed, even the Reporters became confused over this concept: In the Preliminary Draft, they argued it was not foreseeable that a person would stand on the back of a chair with horizontal bars.[372] But soon thereafter in the Council Draft, they reversed themselves and found that standing on the back of a ladder-back chair was indeed foreseeable.[373]

To better achieve their goal of clarity, the Reporters ought to eliminate the concept of foreseeability—remove it and erase it from the draft. They need to recognize that weighing factors alone suffices as a workable test. Because balancing is already an inherent part of section 2(b), the addition of foreseeability is overkill.[374] Clarifying an ambiguous provision through litigation takes time and is expensive. This favors the powerful.

The treatment of design defect in the *Restatement (Third)* is a political statement favoring the sellers. Section 2(b) is not a restatement of the law and does

---

367. *See* Vandall, *Design Defect, supra* note 263, at 190.

368. *Cf.* RESTATEMENT, Tentative Draft No. 2, *supra* note 277, § 2 cmt. c (stating the requirement of a reasonable alternative design "imposes an important practical constraint in design defect cases. . . . [Seller] liability is not justified unless that added safety [provided by plaintiff's alternative design] would have prevented or reduced the plaintiff's harm").

369. *See* RESTATEMENT (THIRD) OF TORTS: Products Liability (Preliminary Draft No. 1, 1993), at 3; *see also* RESTATEMENT, Tentative Draft No. 2, *supra* note 277, § 2 cmt. c (stating the "confusion brought about by these various definitions [of 'state of the art'] is unfortunate").

370. RESTATEMENT, Tentative Draft No. 2, *supra* note 277, § 2(b).

371. *Compare In re* Arbitration Between Polemis and Furness, Withy & Co., 3 K.B. 560 (1921) (holding defendants liable for all "direct" harms associated with its act), *with* Palsgraf v. Long Island R.R. Co., 162 N.E. 99 (N.Y. 1928) (finding defendant liable only to foreseeably endangered plaintiffs). For additional discussion, *see* FRANK VANDALL & ELLEN WERTHEIMER, TORTS, CASES, MATERIALS, PROBLEMS (first edition, 1997).

372. *See* RESTATEMENT, Preliminary Draft No.1, *supra* note 369, § 101 cmt. l.

373. *See* RESTATEMENT (THIRD) OF TORTS: Products Liability § 101 cmt. p (Council Draft No. 1, 1993).

374. *See id.;* Vandall, *Design Defect, supra* note 263, at 279. Indeed, Professor Oscar Gray suggests the real problem with insurability is not clarity of the law, but rather changes in it. *See* Oscar S. Gray, *Reflection on the Historical Context of Section 402A*, 10 TOURO L. REV. 75, 78 (1993).

not rest on an evaluation of cases and policies. It exists merely because it garnered sufficient votes before the ALI.

The ALI can adopt whatever proposal it wants. What needs to be made clear is that section 2(b) does not rest on case law or historic policy. It is therefore merely opinion, entitled to no more respect than any other opinion. The ALI has changed, and so, apparently, has its mission. The ALI's mission is no longer to restate the law, but rather to issue pro-manufacturer political documents that protect the powerful.[375] Although Congress was unsuccessful in changing products liability law in 1996[376] to reduce consumer rights,[377] the ALI has succeeded in doing so.

Until an appropriate foundation is laid, jurisdictions will reject section 2(b) of the *Restatement (Third)*. There are three reasons for this lack of acceptance: (1) the draft fails to address the policies that underlie traditional strict liability, (2) it is a woefully inadequate representation of the existing case law, and (3) it clearly favors sellers by eliminating strict liability and adopting a radical new theory with little attempt to balance the interests of the consumers.

c. An Examination of the Cases That Have Considered Reasonable Alternative Design Since Promulgation of the *Restatement (Third)* Section 2(b) The following is an analysis of cases that have considered the term "reasonable alternative design" over the eight-year period from 1994 to 2002.[378] The first draft of section 2(b) of the *Restatement (Third)* was published in 1994; the American Law Institute promulgated the final version in 1997. The cases over the eight-year span are a rejection of the ALI's attempt to protect the powerful. Only one state (Iowa) has adopted radical negligence.

i. States Rejecting the Restatement (Third)*'s Reasonable Alternative Design Requirement*

(A) CALIFORNIA Language in *Arena v. Owens Corning*[379] suggests a claimant in California may choose among three tests for design defect: (1) consumer

---

375. *Cf.* 64 A.L.I. PROC. 69 (1987) (remarks of Professor Walter H. Beckham, Jr.); Bill Wagner, *Reviewing the Restatement*, TRIAL, Nov. 1995, at 46.

376. *See* Common Sense Product Liability Reform Act of 1996, H.R. 956, 104th Cong. (1996).

377. *See* President's Letter to Congressional Leaders on Product Liability Legislation, 32 WEEKLY COMP. PRES. DOC. 514 (Mar. 16, 1996).

378. The LEXIS search of "reasonable alternative design" was conducted on October 1, 2002. The search covers the period between 1994 (the date of the first draft of the *Restatement (Third) of Torts:* Products Liability section 2(b)) and October 1, 2002.

In 2009, the Reporters for the *Restatement* published an article admitting a "reasonable alternative design" was not followed by a majority of jurisdictions and that they "overstated" the situation in 1998. Aaron D. Twerski & James A. Hrnderson, Jr., *Manufacturer's Liability for Defective Product Designs: The Triumph of Risk-Utility*, 74 BROOK. L. REV. 1061, 1072 (2009).

379. 63 Cal. App. 4th 1178 (Ct. App. 1998).

expectation test, (2) risk-utility, and (3) "failure to warn of known or knowable inherent dangers in the product."[380] Accordingly, this asbestos exposure case was tried under the "consumer expectation theory pursuant to plaintiff's express election."[381] The California Court of Appeals noted, "Whether or not the defendant is able to design the product in a different way is irrelevant, as the Supreme Court neither requires nor allows proof of the existence of a better design under the consumer expectation test."[382] The court concluded, "Although the proposed draft of the Restatement (Third) of Torts: Products Liability, rejects the consumer expectations test as an independent theory, our Supreme Court declined an invitation to overrule the test, and established it as an independent and alternative test for a product defect."[383]

(B) MISSOURI In *Rodriguez v. Suzuki Motor Corp.*,[384] the plaintiff was injured while driving her Suzuki Samurai. The defendant unsuccessfully argued for adoption of the reasonable alternative design test of the *Restatement (Third)* "as the substantive law of Missouri."[385] The court noted, "[T]he elements of a cause of action for design defect under the *Restatement (Third)* are markedly different from those under the *Restatement (Second)*."[386] The court further declared, "Any further consideration of risk-utility was effectively foreclosed by the enactment [of] . . . Missouri's 1987 tort reform act, which, inter alia, codified section 402A of the *Restatement (Second) of Torts*."[387] Finally, the Supreme Court of Missouri "declined the invitation to adopt the reasonable alternative design theory."[388]

In *Leonard v. Bunton Co.*,[389] the plaintiff was injured in an attempt to clean a walk-behind lawnmower.[390] The court rejected the defendant's motion for summary judgment, stating "Missouri has adopted § 402A of the Restatement (Second) of Torts as its rule of strict liability."[391] It noted, "[The] consumer expectation test has been embraced by some Missouri courts and rejected by others. . . . 'Unless a court can affirmatively say as a matter of law that the design

---

380. *Id.* at 1185.
381. *Id.*
382. *Id.* at 1187 (citing Soule v. Gen. Motors Corp., 882 P.2d 298, 308 (Cal. 1994)).
383. *Id.* at 1185–86 (citations omitted).
384. 996 S.W.2d 47 (Mo. 1999).
385. *Id.* at 64.
386. *Id.* at 65.
387. *Id.*
388. *Id.*
389. 925 F. Supp. 637 (E.D. Mo. 1997).
390. *Id.* at 639–40.
391. *Id.* at 641 (citations omitted).

renders a product unreasonably dangerous, the question is generally one for the jury.'"[392] The court did not mention the *Restatement (Third)*.[393]

(c) MARYLAND In *Nemir v. Mitsubishi Motors Sales*,[394] the plaintiff suffered injuries when the seat belt of a 1991 Dodge Stealth failed.[395] The court granted Mitsubishi's motion for summary judgment.[396] Rather than adopting the new *Restatement (Third)*, the court chose to adhere to Maryland precedent[397] and the *Restatement (Second)*, stating, "For a seller to be liable under § 402A, the product must be both in a 'defective condition' and 'unreasonably dangerous' at the time that it is placed on the market by the seller."[398] The opinion did not mention section 2(b) of the *Restatement (Third)*.[399]

(d) PENNSYLVANIA In *Weiner v. American Honda Motor Co.*,[400] the plaintiff was injured during a single-car accident when a canister of nitrous oxide slid forward from the back of his 1992 Acura Integra hatchback and pinned him.[401] The court concluded as a matter of law that the design of the Acura was not unreasonably dangerous.[402] Declaring that claims of design defect in Pennsylvania are governed by the *Restatement (Second) of Torts* section 402A,[403] the court cited section 402A in its entirety[404] and did not mention the *Restatement (Third)*.[405] The Pennsylvania Supreme Court held:

> [T]he question of whether a product is "unreasonably dangerous" is a question of law to be decided by the trial court, the resolution of which depends upon considerations of social policy, . . . including weighing factors such as "the gravity of the danger posed by the challenged design; the likelihood that such danger would occur; the mechanical feasibility of a safer design; and the adverse consequences to the product and to the consumer that would result from a safer design."[406]

---

392. *Id.* at 642 (quoting Pree v. Brunswick Corp., 983 F.2d 863, 866 (8th Cir. 1993) (citing Nesselrode v. Executive Beechcraft, Inc., 70 S.W.2d 371, 378 (Mo. 1986))).

393. *See id.* at 637–45.

394. 60 F. Supp. 2d 660 (E.D. Mich. 1999) *aff'd in part, rev'd in part, per curium,* No. 99-1907, 2001 WL 223775 (6th Cir. Mar. 2, 2001).

395. *Id.* at 663.

396. *Id.* at 677.

397. Although the suit was filed in Michigan, Maryland law applied. *Id.* at 673.

398. *Id.* (quoting Phipps v. Gen. Motors Corp., 363 A.2d 955 (Md. 1976)).

399. *See id.* at 660–79.

400. 718 A.2d 305 (Pa. Super Ct. 1998).

401. *Id.* at 306.

402. *Id.* at 310.

403. *Id.* at 307.

404. *Id.* at 307 n.3 (citing RESTATEMENT (SECOND) OF TORTS § 402A (1965)).

405. *Id.* at 305–11.

406. *Id.* at 308 (quoting Riley v. Warren Mfg., Inc., 688 A.2d 221, 225 (Pa. Super. Ct. 1997)).

In *Riley v. Warren Manufacturing, Inc.*,[407] a young child received serious injuries after placing his hand into the moving parts of a feed trailer.[408] Defendant manufacturer won a directed verdict because "the benefits of the trailer were clear, no feasible alternatives were shown to exist, the trailer was not defective, and there was no evidence that a risk of injury existed for intended users using the machine for its intended use."[409] The court stated, "In products liability cases, § 402A of the *Restatement (Second) of Torts* has been adopted as the law of this Commonwealth."[410] The court did not mention the *Restatement (Third)*.[411]

ii. States Holding Reasonable Alternative Design as One of Several Factors to Consider in Determining Whether a Product Design is Defective

(A) COLORADO In *Barton v. Adams Rental, Inc.*,[412] the plaintiff was injured while working with an electric sewer auger.[413] The evidence given at trial was insufficient for the jury to determine that the product was defective under Colorado's risk-utility analysis.[414] Although the case did not turn upon a reasonable alternative design, the court followed *Annentrout v. FMC Corp.*[415] by saying a "feasible design alternative may be a factor in the risk-benefit analysis."[416] The court did not mention the *Restatement (Third)*.[417]

(B) NEW YORK In *Garnsey v. Morbank Industries, Inc.*,[418] the plaintiff was injured when he stuck his hand into a wood chipper in the course of his employment.[419] The plaintiff made out a prima facie case by proposing five safer designs for the wood chipper.[420] The court stated, "Design defect claims in New York are determined using a risk/utility analysis."[421] Further, "In order to make out a prima facie case of strict product liability for design defects, the plaintiff must show that the product 'was not reasonably safe and that the defective design was a substantial factor in causing [the] plaintiff's injury.'"[422] Finally, the court noted, "The issue of whether a product is unreasonably dangerous is generally one for

---

407. 688 A.2d 221 (Pa. Super. Ct. 1997).

408. *Id.* at 223.

409. *Id.* at 230.

410. *Id.* at 324 (citing Webb v. Zern, 220 A.2d 853 (Pa. 1966)).

411. *See id.* at 221–30.

412. 938 P.2d 532 (Colo. 1997).

413. *Id.* at 534.

414. *Id.* at 537, 540.

415. 842 P.2d 175 (Colo. 1992).

416. *Barton,* 938 P.2d at 537 n.7 (citing Armentrout v. FMC Corp., 842 P.2d 175 (Colo. 1992)).

417. *See id.* at 532–40.

418. 971 F. Supp. 668 (N.D.N.Y. 1997).

419. *Id.* at 670.

420. *Id.*

421. *Id.* at 671.

422. *Id.* (quoting Parsons v. Honeywell, Inc., 929 F.2d 901, 905 (2d. Cir. 1991)).

the jury to decide, taking into account such factors as alternative designs, their costs, and the usefulness of the product."[423]

In *Urena v. Biro Manufacturing Co.*,[424] the plaintiff was injured while using a meat-cutting machine.[425] Denying the defendants' motion for summary judgment, the court stated, "Alternative design evidence is only one piece of the equation which a jury may take into account in determining whether the risk outweighed the utility of the product."[426]

In *Tompkins v. R.J. Reynolds Tobacco Co.*,[427] the plaintiff allegedly died of lung cancer from smoking Camel cigarettes.[428] The court granted summary judgment to the defense on the basis the "plaintiffs failed to meet their burden pertaining to evidence of a *feasible*, alternative design."[429] However, the court suggested an alternative design is merely one of several factors to consider. The court cited the following seven factors from *Denny v. Ford Motor Co.*[430] to consider in the "utility/risk balancing test":

> (1) the utility of the product to the public as a whole; (2) the utility of the product to the individual user; (3) the likelihood that the product will cause injury; (4) the availability of a safer design; (5) the potential for designing and manufacturing the product so that it is safer but remains functional and reasonably priced; (6) the degree of awareness of the product's potential danger that can be reasonably attributed to the plaintiff; and (7) the manufacturer's ability to spread the cost of any safety related design changes.[431]

(c) OREGON In *McCathern v. Toyota Motor Corp.*,[432] the plaintiff was injured during the rollover of her 1994 Toyota 4Runner.[433] The Oregon Court of Appeals affirmed a jury verdict in favor of the plaintiff,[434] stating, "Oregon is one of roughly a dozen jurisdictions that adhere to the consumer expectation test as the standard for determining strict products liability in manufacturing and design defect cases."[435] The consumer expectation test "was derived from Comment *i* of

---

423. *Id.* (citing Urena v. Biro Mfg. Co., 114 F.3d 359, 364 (2d Cir. 1997)).
424. 114 F.3d 359 (2d Cir. 1997).
425. *Id.* at 361.
426. *Id.* at 365.
427. 92 F. Supp. 2d 70 (N.D.N.Y. 2000).
428. *Id.* at 73.
429. *Id.* at 85.
430. *See supra* notes 350–55 and accompanying text.
431. *Tompkins*, 92 F. Supp. 2d at 84 (citing Denny v. Ford Motor Co., 87 N.Y.2d 248, 257 (N.Y. 1995)).
432. 985 P.2d 804 (Or. Ct. App. 1999).
433. *Id.* at 807.
434. *Id.* at 827.
435. *Id.* at 809.

section 402A of the *Restatement (Second) of Torts* (1965)."[436] The court then bifurcated the consumer expectation test into (1) a representational approach, and (2) a consumer risk-utility approach.[437] The court reasoned that proof of a reasonable alternative design is essential to the risk-utility approach, but immaterial to the representational approach.[438] This ensures an Oregon plaintiff is able to make out a prima facie case of design defect without presenting a RAD.

iii. States Favorably Mentioning the Reasonable Alternative Design Requirement
Several courts discuss RAD favorably.

(A) GEORGIA In *Jones v. NordicTrack, Inc.*[439] the plaintiff was injured when she fell against her stationary indoor ski exerciser and severed two veins in her thigh.[440] The issue presented was whether a product has to be in use at the time of the injury for a defendant to be held liable for defective design. The court held in the negative,[441] citing *Banks v. I.C.I.* for the proposition

> [t]he heart of a design defect case is the reasonableness of selecting from among alternative product designs and adopting the safest feasible one. . . . Consequently, the appropriate analysis does not depend on the use of the product, as that may be narrowly or broadly defined, but rather includes the consideration of whether the defendant failed to adopt a reasonable alternative design which would have reduced the foreseeable risks of harm presented by the product.[442]

The court did not discuss section 2(b) of the *Restatement (Third)*.

(B) NEW JERSEY In *Green v. General Motors Corp.*,[443] the plaintiff was injured when the rear roof of his T-Top Camaro collapsed.[444] The court required the plaintiff to propose a RAD.[445] The plaintiff met this burden by having his expert testify as to two alternative designs for the rear roof of a T-Top Camaro.[446] The court stated "in determining whether the Camaro was defective, a jury must

---

436. *Id.*

437. *Id.* at 810.

438. *Id.* at 811.

439. 274 Ga. 115, 550 S.E.2d 101 (2001).

440. *Id.* 274 Ga. at 116, 550 S.E.2d at 102.

441. *Id.* at 116–18.

442. *Id.* at 118. (citing RESTATEMENT (THIRD) OF TORTS: Products Liability § 2(b) (1998)). But in two other Georgia cases, the court cites to *Banks* in adopting the risk-utility test and refusing to adopt a specific list of factors. Ogletree v. Navistar Int'l Transp. Corp., 269 Ga. 443, 444–46, 500 S.E.2d 570, 570–72 (1998); Bryant v. Hoffmann-LaRoche, Inc., 262 Ga. App. 401, 406, 408, 585 S.E.2d 723, 728, 730 (2003) (discussing design defect in regard to a drug).

443. 709 A.2d 205 (N.J. Super. Ct. App. Div. 1998).

444. *Id.* at 207.

445. *Id.* at 213.

446. *Id.* at 213–14.

determine the risks and alternatives that should have been known to a reasonable manufacturer, and then assess whether the manufacturer discharged its duty to provide a 'reasonably fit, suitable and safe' vehicle."[447] The court continued by noting "the jury employs a risk-utility analysis" to determine whether the manufacturer discharged this duty.[448] The court then indicated that although the classical statement of the risk-utility analysis as enumerated in *Cepeda v. Cumberland Engineering Co.*[449] involves seven factors, "the prevalent view is that, unless one or more of the other factors might be relevant in a particular case, the issue upon which most claims will turn is the proof by the plaintiff of a 'reasonable alternative design.'"[450] The court cited the *Restatement (Third)* for this proposition.[451]

In *Lewis v. American Cyanamid Co.*,[452] the plaintiff was burned when an indoor pesticide fogger exploded in the kitchen.[453] The court ruled in favor of the plaintiff by affirming the reversal of the defendant's judgment notwithstanding the verdict (JNOV).[454] The court cited comment f of section 2 of the *Restatement (Third)*, which states, "'To establish a prima facie case of defect, the plaintiff must prove the availability of a technologically feasible and practical alternative design that would have reduced or prevented the plaintiff's harm.'"[455] The plaintiff was able to meet this burden.[456]

In *Smith v. Keller Ladder Co.*,[457] the plaintiff was injured while using an extension ladder manufactured by the defendant.[458] The plaintiff failed to establish a reasonably feasible alternative design for the ladder.[459] The court held the defendant's JNOV motion was properly granted,[460] citing New Jersey precedent for the proposition that

[u]nless there is some basis for a jury to find that the risks involved in a product's use outweigh its utility even though there is no reasonably feasible alternative design, a plaintiff in a design-defect case is required to show the

---

447. *Id.* at 210 (citing Suter v. San Angelo Foundry Mach. Co., 81 N.J. 150, 169 (N.J. 1979)).

448. *Id.* (citing Jurado v. W. Gear Works, 131 N.J. 375, 385 (N.J. 1993)).

449. 386 A.2d 816 (N.J. 1978).

450. Green v. Gen. Motors Corp., 709 A.2d 205, 210 (N.J. Super. Ct. App. Div. 1998).

451. *Id.*

452. 715 A.2d 967 (N.J. 1998).

453. *Id.* at 970–71.

454. *Id.* at 971–72.

455. *Id.* at 975 (quoting RESTATEMENT (THIRD) OF TORTS: Products Liability § 2 cmt. f (proposed final draft)).

456. *Id.*

457. 645 A.2d 1269 (N.J. Super Ct. App. Div. 1994).

458. *Id.* at 1270

459. *Id.*

460. *Id.*

existence of a "safe and reasonably feasible alternative to [the] defendant's product."[461]

(c) MICHIGAN In *Hollister v. Dayton Hudson Corp.*,[462] the plaintiff suffered extensive burn injuries when her blouse caught fire after coming in contact with a kitchen stove.[463] The court granted the defendant's motion for summary judgment on the design defect issue,[464] stating, "Although Michigan has not adopted the Proposed Final Draft of the *Restatement (Third) of Torts: Product Liability* § 2 (April 1, 1997), the Michigan risk-utility test is consistent with the principles of section 2(b)."[465] Michigan considers its risk-utility test to be a pure negligence test.[466] "Under Michigan's risk-utility test, a plaintiff does not establish a prima facie case of product design defect if evidence of a reasonable alternative design, available and practicable at the time of distribution of defendant's product, is not produced."[467] The Michigan six-part risk-utility test requires the plaintiff to show:

> (1) that the severity of her injury was foreseeable by the manufacturer; (2) that the likelihood of occurrence of her injury was foreseeable by the manufacturer at the time of distribution of the product; (3) that there was a reasonable alternative design available; (4) that the available reasonable alternative design was practicable; (5) that the available and practicable reasonable alternative design would have reduced the foreseeable risk of harm posed by defendant's product; and (6) that omission of the available and practicable reasonable alternative design rendered defendant's product not reasonably safe.[468]

iv. States Incorporating the Restatement's Reasonable Alternative Design Requirement into Their Statutes This section demonstrates lobbies representing the powerful have substantial persuasive power.

(A) LOUISIANA In *Lawrence v. General Motors Corp.*,[469] the plaintiff was injured when her used-1987 Pontiac Bonneville suddenly accelerated into a tree.[470]

---

461. *Id.* at 1271 (quoting Macri v. Ames McDonough Co., 512 A.2d 548, 551 9 N.J. Super. Ct. App. Div. (1986)).
462. 5 F. Supp. 2d 530 (E.D. Mich. 1998) *aff'd in part*, 201 F.3d 731 (6th Cir. 2000).
463. *Id.* at 535.
464. *Id.* at 536.
465. *Id.* at 533.
466. *Id.* at 531 (citing Prentis v. Yale Mfg. Co., 365 N.W.2d 176 (Mich. 1984)).
467. *Id.* at 534 (citing Owens v. Allis Chalmers Corp., 326 N.W.2d 372 (Mich. 1982)).
468. *Id.* at 535.
469. 73 F.3d 587, 590 (5th Cir. 1996).
470. *Id.* at 588.

The court held for the defendant manufacturer, citing Louisiana's codification of the RAD requirement:[471]

> A product is unreasonably dangerous in design, if, at the time the product left its manufacturer's control: (1) [t]here existed an alternative design for the product that was capable of preventing the claimant's damage; and (2) the likelihood that the product's design would cause the claimant's damage and the gravity of that damage outweighed the burden on the manufacturer of adopting such alternative design and the adverse effect, if any . . . on the utility of the product. . . .[472]

Under this statute, the plaintiff's evidence was insufficient as a matter of law to support a finding of design defect.[473]

(B) TEXAS Texas has codified the RAD requirement in section 82.005(a) of the *Texas Civil Practice and Remedies Code,* which states: "[The] burden is on the claimant to prove by a preponderance of the evidence that: (1) there was a safer alternative design; and (2) the defect was a producing cause of the personal injury, property damage, or death for which the claimant seeks recovery."[474] Despite this clear statutory language, subsequent case law has been less than uniform.

In *Smith v. Aqua-Flow,*[475] the plaintiff family sued the defendant manufacturer after six-year-old Stephanie Smith drowned when her hair became entangled in their spa's plastic intake cover.[476] Although the Smith's expert proposed an alternative design (i.e., an automatic shutoff valve), the court held the Smiths failed to make out their prima facie case because they did not show that design was both technologically and economically feasible.[477] The court attempted to reconcile the *Restatement (Second)* with the *Restatement (Third)* because "Texas has adopted the *Restatement (Second) of Torts* section 402A."[478] Ultimately, however, although the court did not explicitly cite the *Restatement (Third)*, it required the plaintiff to prove a RAD .[479] The court finally cited *American Tobacco Co. v. Grinnell*[480] for the proposition "[i]f no evidence is offered that a safer design existed, the product is not unreasonably dangerous as a matter of law."[481]

---

471. *Id.* at 590.
472. LA. REV. STAT ANN. § 2800.56 (West 1995).
473. *Lawrence,* 73 F.3d at 590.
474. TEX. CIV. PRAC. & REM. CODE ANN. § 82.005(a) (Vernon 1997).
475. 23 S.W.2d 473 (Tex. App. 2000).
476. *Id.* at 475.
477. *Id.* at 478.
478. *Id.* at 476.
479. *Id.* at 478; *see supra* text accompanying note 202.
480. 951 S.W.2d 420, 433 (Tex. 1997).
481. *Smith,* 23 S.W.3d at 477.

In *Uniroyal Goodrich Tire Co. v. Martinez*,[482] the plaintiff was injured when a 16-inch Goodrich tire exploded that he was mounting on a 16.5-inch rim.[483] The court affirmed a jury verdict in favor of the plaintiff.[484] In a footnote, the court noted that "[a]lthough not applicable to the present case, the Texas Legislature has recently codified the 'reasonably safe alternative' requirement."[485] The court was ambiguous in its analysis, stating:

> While there is language in Turner suggesting that whether a safer alternative design exists is merely one of the factors to be weighed by the jury, we made clear in Caterpillar that a safer alternative is a prerequisite to a finding of design defect. Our approach in Caterpillar is reflected in the new Restatement.[486]

However, the court later said, "We agree with the new Restatement that warnings and safer alternative designs are factors, among others, for the jury to consider in determining whether the product as designed is reasonably safe."[487] Although the court frequently cited to the *Restatement (Third)*, it did not clarify whether the RAD requirement is merely one factor or the primary factor to consider in a design defect case.

In *Hayles v. General Motors Corp.*,[488] a federal district court case, the plaintiff was injured in a single-car accident.[489] She alleged a defect in the air bag and seat belt systems of her 1995 Chevrolet Silverado were responsible for her injuries.[490] The court stated, "Texas has adopted the strict products liability standard set forth in section 402A of the *Restatement (Second) of Torts*."[491] The plaintiff did not present an expert witness.[492] General Motors's motion for summary judgment was granted because the plaintiff "failed to raise a genuine disputed issue of material fact that her vehicle sustained the type of impact necessary to deploy the air bag."[493] The court did not mention the *Restatement (Third)* or the requirement of a reasonable alternative design.

---

482. 977 S.W.2d 328 (Tex. 1998).

483. *Id.* at 331–32.

484. *Id.* at 331.

485. *Id.* at 335 n.3 (referring to TEX. CIV. PRAC. & REM. CODE ANN. § 82.005 (Vernon 1997)).

486. *Id.* at 335 n.4 (citations omitted)

487. *Id.* at 337.

488. 82 F. Supp. 2d 650 (S.D. Tex. 1999).

489. *Id.* at 651.

490. *Id.* at 651–52.

491. *Id.* at 654.

492. *Id.* at 656.

493. *Id.* at 657.

The Fifth Circuit Court of Appeals clarified the law in *Smith v. Louisville Ladder Co*[494] in which the plaintiff was injured from falling off a ladder.[495] The Fifth Circuit reversed the jury verdict in favor of the plaintiff because the plaintiff had failed to show the existence of a safer alternative design.[496] The court cited the Texas statute as being on point and requiring proof of a RAD.[497]

(c) MISSISSIPPI *Watkins v. Telsmith, Inc.*[498] dealt with the requirements of *Daubert*.[499] In dicta, the court noted a Mississippi products liability statute that defines a RAD as "'a design that would have to a reasonable probability prevented the harm without impairing the utility, usefulness, practicality or desirability of the product to users or consumers.'"[500]

As the appendix to this section makes clear,[501] the American Law Institute has been striving to insulate sellers in general and the tobacco industry in particular.[502] *The Restatement (Third)*, section 2 reads like a wish list for manufacturing America as it immunizes tobacco manufacturers from liability.[503] The Supreme Court of Iowa has recently made this bias abundantly clear. In *Wright v. Brook Group Ltd.*,[504] where the defendant was a tobacco manufacturer, the court adopted sections 1 and 2 of the *Restatement (Third)* thus foreclosing the possibility the manufacturer of the most dangerous product—tobacco—can be held liable for design defect.[505] The court noted that under this standard, consumers cannot recover unless they can prove a RAD exists that would have reduced or avoided the foreseeable risk of harm.[506] Because there is no RAD for tobacco, the seller won.

This exemplifies the need for an accurate Restatement of design defect law: one that does not insulate tobacco from liability and that accurately reflects the developments in legal theory over the last 160 years. A new *Restatement (Third) of Torts*: Design Defect should rest on the over-three thousand cases decided under the *Restatement (Second)* section 402A. It should be a true restatement of

---

494. 237 F.3d 515 (5th Cir. 2001).

495. *Id.* at 517–18.

496. *Id.* at 523.

497. *Id.* at 518; *see supra* text accompanying note 202.

498. 121 F.3d 984 (5th Cir. 1997).

499. *Id.* at 985.

500. *Id.* at 993 (quoting MISS. CODE ANN. § 11-1-63(f)(ii)).

501. *See infra* Appendix.

502. See *id.*

503. Frank J. Vandall, *Constructing a Roof Before the Foundation is Prepared: The Restatement (Third) of Torts: Products Liability Section 2(b) Design Defect*, 30 U. MICH. J.L. REFORM 261, 261 (1997).

504. 652 N.W.2d 159 (Iowa 2002).

505. *Id.* at 169, 178–83 ("Under the principles set forth in the Products Restatement [Third] adopted today. . . . a plaintiff may not recover from a cigarette manufacturer. . . .").

506. *Id.*

existing case law, not a battle plan for manufacturing America.[507] The ALI should not permit the new Restatement to insulate the manufacturers of the most dangerous products on the market or to shift from strict liability to radical negligence without a careful consideration of the foundational policies. As of January 2010, the ALI has not engaged in an analysis of fundamental policies that underlie products liability law .

d. You Won, Now Let Us Reduce the Amount of Your Recovery: Apportionment In May 1999, the American Law Institute (ALI) adopted the provisions of the *Restatement (Third) of Torts:* Apportionment of Liability. At first blush, apportionment appears to be an arcane and academic subject, but upon closer analysis it becomes clear the *Restatement (Third):* Apportionment affects the substance of numerous civil damage suits, especially those involving two or more defendants, whether they are sued as parties or whether they are solvent or bankrupt. Two points are important in regard to the *Restatement (Third):* Apportionment. First, this is a technical subject with substantial policy implications. Second, the *Restatement (Third):* Apportionment is a veiled attempt by the ALI Reporters to accomplish tort reform judicially because such reform could not be accomplished legislatively in all states. Each adoption of several liability benefits the manufacturers and sellers at the expense of the victim. Pennsylvania law has been selected for comparison with the *Restatement (Third):* Apportionment because it is a large industrial and technological state with traditional rules for joint and several liability and apportionment.[508] The critique of the *Restatement (Third):* Apportionment begins with an evaluation of the history of joint and several liability.

i. History of Joint and Several Liability Apportionment is a study of joint and several liability, contributory negligence, comparative fault, and contribution. This section will provide a brief historical background of the first two of these components of apportionment and analyze their development in Pennsylvania.

Joint and several liability is the concept that the victim can recover all of his or her damages from one of several defendants. It originated over three hundred years ago in the English report of *Sir John Heydon's Case,*[509] resting on the theory

---

507. The language of the solicitation letter from Geoffrey Hazard, Director of the American Law Institute, made clear that tort reform to assist manufacturers, insurers, and tobacco was the goal of the ALI. *See infra* Appendix.

508. Joint and several liability was cast aside by the Pennysylvania legislature in Act. 2002-57 sec. 2. This was reversed by Deweese v. Weaver, 880 A.2d 54 (Pa. Cmwealth. 2005). The current Pennsylvania code reads: "The plaintiff may recover the full amount of the allowed recovery from any defendant . . . " 42 PA. C.S.A. § 7102.

509. 77 Eng. Rep. 1150 (K.B. 1613). Sir John Heydon brought a trespass of battery action against three defendants. The court found that when "the jury find[s] for the plaintiff.., the jurors cannot assess several damages against the defendants because all is one trespass." *Id.* at 1151. "Several liability" means that each defendant is liable in proportion to his or her fault.

of concerted action.[510] In 1916, joint liability was expanded to include defendants who caused an indivisible injury to the plaintiff.[511] The rationale for allowing a victim to recover for injuries from one tortfeasor was based upon practicality— the Virginia Supreme Court found no basis for separating the amount caused by one actor from that caused by another. In adopting this rationale, other courts wanted to make certain there was a source of recovery for the plaintiff[512] when the tortfeasor was negligent and had caused the injury in fact. By 1980, almost all states had adopted the concept of joint liability.[513]

Pennsylvania's tort law regarding joint liability and comparative fault has paralleled the development in other states and in England. Over a century ago, joint and several liability among multiple defendants was recognized in *Borough of Carlisle v. Brisbane*[514] and *Gallagher v. Kemmerer*,[515] each holding that injury caused concurrently by two or more persons permits the plaintiff to take action against them either jointly or severally.[516] Three years after the *Brisbane* decision

---

510. Concerted action requires that "there was a common purpose, with mutual aid in carrying it out; in short, there was a joint enterprise, so that 'all coming to do an unlawful act, and of one party, the act of one is the act of all of the same party being present.'" W. Page Keeton et al, Prosser and Keeton on the Law of Torts § 46, at 323 n.3 (5th ed. 1984) (citing *Sir John Heydon's Case*). For an early view of concerted action in Pennsylvania, see Bard v. Yohn, 26 Pa. 482 (1856), which held joint liability was not present where there was no concerted action.

511. *See* Carolina, Clinchfield & Ohio Ry. Co. v. Hill, 89 S.E. 902 (Va. 1916). The plaintiff brought suit based on damage to his property caused by the railway's construction of a railroad and the contributing harm by Yellow Poplar Lumber Company, which was engaged in removing large numbers of trees from the area and floating them downstream past the plaintiff's property. *See id.* at 902–03. The Supreme Court of Virginia found it was impossible to separate the damages (if any) caused by the two defendants. *See id.* at 903.

512. *See* Keeton et al., *supra* note 510, § 47, at 327 n.25, Prosser and Keeton state the result of refusing to permit joinder is that "in . . . separate suits it is open to each defendant to prove that the other was solely responsible, or responsible for the greater part of the damage," a situation that can lead to a minimal recovery for plaintiff or no recovery at all. *Id.*

513. *See* Richard W. Wright, *Allocating Liability Among Multiple Responsible Causes: A Principled Defense of Joint and Several Liability for Actual Harm and Risk Exposure*, 21 U.C. Davis L. Rev. 1141, 1164–65, 1185 (1988).

514. 6 A. 372, 372 (Pa. 1886). The plaintiff in this case suffered a broken leg when the sleigh in which he was a passenger turned over due to poor street conditions. *See id.* at 372.

515. 22 A. 970, 971 (Pa. 1891) (holding unless the "negligence of two persons is joint and concurrent, each is liable for his own negligence only"). The action was brought in trespass to recover for damages to the plaintiff's land due to a deposit of mine waste accumulated through runoff from the defendants' separate mining operations. *See id.* at 970.

516. *Brisbane*, 6 A. at 373; *Gallagher*, 22 A. at 971; *see also* O'Malley v. Philadelphia Rapid Transit Co., 93 A. 1014 (Pa. 1915); Leidig v. Bucher, 74 Pa. 65 (1873). The *Brisbane*

in 1889, the Pennsylvania Supreme Court held the plaintiff had the option of proceeding against a single joint tortfeasor for recovery of the entire judgment.[517] However, once the judgment was satisfied (by settlement or otherwise), the plaintiff was barred from pursuing a claim against any other joint tortfeasor.[518]

More recent cases continue to embrace the doctrine of joint and several liability in Pennsylvania.[519] *Voyles v. Corwin*[520] identified the factors that should be

---

court also held that where the plaintiff contributed to his injury, no recovery was available because of contributory negligence. 22 A. at 373.

517. *See* Seither v. Philadelphia Traction Co., 17 A. 338 (Pa. 1889) (holding that once a judgment was obtained, the plaintiff had the option of pursuing any joint tortfeasor for the full amount); *see also* Baker v. AC&S Inc., 729 A.2d 1140, 1146 (Pa. 1998) (citing Glomb v. Glomb, 530 A.2d 1362, 1365 (Pa. Super. Ct.1987)), which held "[i]mposition of joint and several liability enables the injured party to satisfy an entire judgment against any one tortfeasor, even if the wrongdoing of that tortfeasor contributed only a small part of the harm inflicted"; Halsband v. Union Nat. Bank of Pittsburgh, 465 A.2d 1014, 1018 (Pa. 1983); Jones v. Harrisburg Polyclinic Hosp., 437 A.2d 1134, 1141 (Pa. 1981) (holding a plaintiff is not required to sue all joint tortfeasors jointly, but rather may choose to sue a particular joint tortfeasor for the full amount); Smith v. Philadelphia Transp. Co., 173 F.2d 721, 724 n.2 (3d Cir. 1949) (holding a full recovery may be had against any one of several joint tortfeasors).

518. *See Seither*, 17 A. at 338. The plaintiff in this case was riding as a passenger in a railcar owned by People's Passenger Railway Company that was struck by a car owned by the defendant, Philadelphia Traction Company. *See id.* Plaintiff sued both companies. When it settled with People's and executed a release in its favor, it was barred from also seeking recovery against Philadelphia Traction as People's had satisfied the claim in full. *See id.*; *see also* Thompson v. Fox, 192 A. 107, 109 (Pa. 1937) (holding a release of one joint tortfeasor releases all joint tortfeasors as there can be only one satisfaction "either as payment of a judgment recovered or consideration for a release executed by him").

519. *See* Little v. Dresser Indus., Inc. 599 F.2d 1274, 1277–78 (3d Cir. 1979) (citing *Gallagher* as establishing joint liability in Pennsylvania and holding the incidents leading to plaintiff's injury were separated by an expanse of time; therefore, joint tortfeasor status was not created); Kendrick v. Piper Aircraft Corp., 265 F.2d 482, 485 (3d Cir. 1959) (holding an accident can be caused by the negligence of two or more parties); Carpini v. Pittsburgh & Weirton Bus Co., 216 F.2d 404, 407 (3d Cir. 1954) (citing Pennsylvania law and holding there can be more than one legal responsible cause for a given injury); Pennine Resources, Inc. v. Dorwart Andrew & Co., 639 F. Supp. 1071, 1075 (E.D. Pa. 1986) (holding the evidence of the case could establish the defendants were joint tortfeasors); Panichella v. Pennsylvania, 150 F. Supp. 79, 81 (W.D. Pa. 1957) (holding there was "no concert of action, common design or duty, joint enterprise or other relationship" between the defendants that would make them joint tortfeasors); *Baker*, 729 A.2d at 1146 (citing Kovalesky v. Giant Rug Market, 618 A.2d 1044 (Pa. Super. Ct. 1993)); Koller v. Pennsylvania R.R. Co., 40 A.2d 89, 90 (Pa. 1944) (holding one is a joint tortfeasor where there is a community of fault causing injury).

520. 441 A.2d 381 (Pa. Super. Ct. 1982).

considered in determining joint tortfeasor status.[521] In *Capone v. Donovan*,[522] a Pennsylvania court applied joint and several liability to a case where two defendants caused an indivisible injury.[523] In *Capone*, the plaintiff suffered a broken arm that was improperly diagnosed and set by three separate doctors.[524] The court held "[i]f two or more causes combine to produce a single harm which is incapable of being divided on a logical, reasonable, or practical basis," then apportionment would be "arbitrary," and the actors should be held to be joint tortfeasors, each liable for the entire injury.[525] Joint liability thus benefits the victim by allowing recovery of damages from one defendant when the other lacks insurance or is bankrupt.

Until 1910, contributory negligence (in any degree) functioned as an absolute bar to suit.[526] The impact of contributory negligence was weakened with the widespread adoption of comparative fault.[527] The purpose of comparative fault is to eliminate the plaintiff's negligence as a complete bar; instead, a jury may reduce the recovery in proportion to the plaintiff's negligence.[528] At present, only five states allow contributory negligence to function as a complete bar to the plaintiff's recovery.[529] The result of comparative fault has been that a plaintiff who is partially at fault is able to recover a proportionate share of damages from a defendant who was at fault only to a small degree. Conversely, a joint tortfeasor

---

521. The court recognized as factors that had to be considered in determining whether defendants were joint tortfeasors (1) "the existence of a common or like duty"; (2) evidence supporting an action against all defendants; (3) whether the injury was indivisible in nature; (4) "identity of the facts as to time, place or result"; and (5) "responsibility of the defendants for the same [injury]." *Id.* at 383 (citing WILLIAM PROSSER, LAW OF TORTS 46 n.2 (4th ed. 1971)).

522. 480 A.2d 1249 (Pa. Super. Ct. 1984).

523. *Id.* at 1251; *see also* Rabatin v. Columbus Lines, Inc., 790 F.2d 22, 26 (3d Cir. 1986) (holding actors may be joint tortfeasors where their acts combined to produce a single indivisible result).

524. *Capone*, 480 A.2d at 1250.

525. *Id.* at 1251. The court held further that a release executed in favor of one defendant did not release the other two, but merely reduced any potential recovery against them by the amount received in settlement. *See id.* at 1251–52.

526. *See* KEETON ET AL., *supra* note 510, § 67, at 471. In 1910, Mississippi became the first state to adopt a comparative negligence statute, followed shortly by Georgia. *See id.* By the mid-1960s, only seven states had comparative negligence statutes in force. *See id.* But by the early 1980s, more than forty states had comparative negligence statutes or analogous judicially created doctrines. *See id.*

527. *See id.* at 472.

528. *See id.*

529. Only Alabama, Maryland, North Carolina, Virginia, and the District of Columbia still consider contributory negligence to be a complete bar to recovery. *See* RESTATEMENT (THIRD) OF TORTS: Apportionment of Liability § 7 cmt. a, at 99 (Proposed Final Draft (Revised), 1999).

who is at fault and has caused the injury may have to pay more than its share of liability.[530] Comparative fault thus benefits victims by allowing recovery of some of their damages from one of several defendants.

Pennsylvania began realizing the importance of apportionment in 1951 when it enacted the Pennsylvania Contribution Among Tortfeasors Act (PaCATA),[531] modeled after the Uniform Contribution Among Tortfeasors Act,[532] which advocated allocating joint tortfeasor liability comparatively. Pennsylvania initially chose instead to adopt a pro rata theory of comparative fault, which provided the total liability would be equally apportioned among joint tortfeasors.[533] Pennsylvania later adopted by statute in 1976 the concept of comparative fault,[534] but followed the modified form of comparative fault, meaning the plaintiff can recover as long as his or her fault is not greater than the defendant's fault.[535] Moreover, where there are multiple joint tortfeasors, Pennsylvania follows the theory of aggregation in comparative fault, which measures the plaintiff's liability against the aggregate liability of all joint tortfeasors to determine whether the plaintiff can recover.[536] Therefore, as long as the plaintiff's liability is less than the total aggregate liability of all joint tortfeasors, the plaintiff can recover a proportionate share of damages from one or all of the joint tortfeasors.[537]

ii. Analysis of the ALI's Proposal to Eliminate Joint and Several Liability The impetus for "reform" in the law of apportionment was provided by a Florida

---

530. Prosser and Keeton state "[t]he rule of joint liability favors plaintiffs, since the aggregate wealth of the defendants stands behind the judgment, without regard to the proportionate responsibility of the defendants individually for the loss." KEETON ET AL., *supra* note 510, § 67, at 475.

531. Pennsylvania Contribution Among Tortfeasors Act, 1951 Pa. Laws 1130 (codified at 42 PA. CONS. STAT. ANN. § 8321 (West 1998)).

532. 12 U.L.A. 57-59 (1975).

533. *See* R. Michael Lindsey, *Compensation, Fairness, and the Costs of Accidents—Should Pennsylvania's Legislature Modify or Abrogate the Rule of Joint and Several Liability Among Concurrently Negligent Tortfeasors?*, 91 DICK. L. REV. 947 (1987), which stated that in 1943, a bill proposing comparative fault was introduced in the Pennsylvania General Assembly, but failed. *Id.* at 956 n.48 (citing H.B. 604, 135 Gen. Assembly, 1942 Sess., I Pa. Leg. J. 725 (1943)); *see also* Arthur R. Harris, Note, *Comparative Negligence in Pennsylvania?*, 17 TEMP. L.Q. 276 (1943).

534. Comparative Negligence Act of 1976, 1976 Pa. Laws 855 (codified at 42 PA. CONS. STAT. ANN. § 7102 (West 1998)). This act modified Pennsylvania law as to joint tortfeasors and apportionment of damages.

535. *See, e.g.*, Elder v. Orluck, 515 A.2d 517 (Pa. 1986).

536. In *Elder*, fault was apportioned to the plaintiff at twenty-five percent, defendant Orluck at sixty percent, and defendant Harrisville at fifteen percent. 515 A.2d at 518. Defendant Harrisville argued that because its liability was less than that of the plaintiff, it was not required to pay damages. *See id.* The Pennsylvania Supreme Court held otherwise. *See id.* at 525.

537. *Id.*

case, *Walt Disney World v. Wood*.[538] In *Disney World*, a woman was injured at the "Grand Prix" automobile racing attraction when her fiancé's "race car" bumped into hers.[539] She sued Disney World and was found to be 14 percent at fault while her then-husband was found to be eighty-five percent at fault, with Disney World's fault set at only 1 percent.[540] Because of the doctrine of spousal immunity, the plaintiff's husband could not be required to pay the judgment, so Disney World (under joint liability) was held liable for 86 percent of the damages (approximately $75,000) when it was only 1 percent at fault.[541]

In response to *Disney World* and similar cases, the ALI has initiated a massive fundamental change in the law of joint and several liability and apportionment by adopting the *Restatement (Third)*: Apportionment. The goal of this project appears to be preventing a corporate defendant who is slightly at fault from being held liable for a large portion of the damages,[542] thus protecting the powerful from paying more than their share. It reverses 380 years of history.

The ALI's reversal of joint and several liability and apportionment is an extreme overreaction to the rare fact pattern of *Disney World*.[543] The main theme

---

538. 515 So.2d 198 (Fla. 1987).

539. *Id.* at 199.

540. *See* Walt Disney World Co. v. Wood, 489 So.2d 61, 62 (Fla. Dist. Ct. App. 1986). Presumably the jury found Disney liable based on negligent design of the bumper car ride.

541. Florida "imposes joint and several liability for economic damages on any independent tortfeasor whose comparative responsibility is greater than the plaintiff's." *See* RESTATEMENT (THIRD) OF TORTS: Apportionment of Liability § 28E cmt. b, at 349 (Proposed Final Draft (Revised), 1999); *see also* AMERICAN LAW INSTUTE, REPORTER'S STUDY: ENTERPRISE RESPONSIBILITY FOR PERSONAL INJURY, VOL. II: APPROACHES TO LEGAL AND INSTITUTIONAL CHANGE 151 n.28 (1991); June F. Entman, *The Nonparty Tortfeasor*, 23 MEM. ST. U.L. REV. 105, 106 (1992).

542. This is inferred from the text of the *Restatement (Third):* Apportionment based on an assessment of who is benefited (defendants) and who is harmed (plaintiffs) in almost every section. *See also* the Appendix.

543. No mention has been made that the injury would not have occurred if Disney World had carefully designed the dangerous amusement park ride. Further, holding Disney World liable for eighty-six percent of the plaintiff's damages can be justified on the basis of Judge Calabresi's theory that Disney World is the "cheapest cost avoider." Guido Calabresi & Jon T. Hischoff, *Toward a Test for Strict Liability in Torts*, 81 YALE L.J. 1055, 1073 (1972) (discussing the history of assumption of risk and stating the emphasis should not be on "whether the defendant had the 'right' to impose the risk on the plaintiff" but on "knowledge and appreciation of the risk and availability of alternatives" that could easily serve to "absolve the defendants only in those situations where . . . the cost-benefit analysis was better left to the plaintiff") (citations omitted). Here, Disney can evaluate the risk created by bumper cars and do something about it. The plaintiff does not realize the risk and can do little to alter it.

of the *Restatement (Third)*: Apportionment is that anything is better than joint and several liability. The corporation must be insulated from excessive liability.

The Reporters describe their proposal:

> The Institute takes no position on whether joint and several liability, several liability, or some combination of the two should be adopted for independent tortfeasors who cause an indivisible injury. As noted in § 20, Comment a, there is currently no majority rule on this question, although joint and several liability has been substantially modified in most jurisdictions both as a result of the adoption of comparative fault and tort reform during the 1980s and 1990s. Nevertheless, five different versions of joint and several, several, and combination of the two are presented in the five separate and independent tracks that follow this section. These five tracks are mutually exclusive, although modifications (or combinations of some) of them are possible.[544]

The Reporters admit there is little case authority for each track except joint and several liability (Track A), which is followed by sixteen states, including Pennsylvania.[545]

The Reporters seem to have adopted their novel "track" approach to avoid weighing and evaluating the large number of cases that have applied joint and several liability theory over the past 380 years. The Reporters' method is first to present the basic rule of joint and several liability in section 28A (Track A): "If the independent . . . conduct of two or more persons is a legal cause of an indivisible injury, each person is jointly and severally liable . . . ."[546] Then they present four separate and unique tracks they imply are equal to (or better than) joint and several liability. Track B is presented in section 28B: "If two or more persons' independent tortious conduct is the legal cause of an indivisible injury, each defendant . . . is severally liable . . . ."[547] This is the opposite of Track A and a complete rejection of joint and several liability. Track C is introduced in section 28C: "If the independent tortious conduct of two or more persons is a legal cause of an indivisible injury, each person is jointly and severally liable . . . subject to

---

544. *See* RESTATEMENT, *supra* note 541, at § 27, cmt. a, at 203.

545. *See id.* at § 28A reporters' note cmt. a, at 211. "B" track: "Fourteen states have abolished (or virtually abolished) joint and several liability for multiple tortfeasors whose independent actions results in an indivisible injury to plaintiff. . . . In most jurisdictions, however, the abolition of joint and several liability was the result of tort legislation in the latter part of the 1980s. . . ." *Id.* § 28B reporters' note cmt. b, at 225. "C" track: "a few jurisdictions." *Id.* § 27 cmt. a, at 204. "D" track: "The 'D' series reflects legislation in approximately a dozen states. . . ." *Id.* at 205. "E" track: "The 'E' series reflects legislation in about a half dozen states. . . ."

Id. at 180.

546. RESTATEMENT (THIRD) OF TORTS: Apportionment of Liability § 28A, at 206 (Proposed Final Draft (Revised), 1999).

547. *Id.* § 28B, at 221.

the reallocation provision of [a later section]."[548] Track C allows the plaintiff's recovery to be reduced merely because the judgment cannot be collected from an insolvent defendant. Track D is introduced in section 28D: "If the . . . conduct of two or more persons is a legal cause of an indivisible injury, each defendant who is assigned a percentage of comparative responsibility equal to . . . the legal threshold is jointly and severally liable, and each defendant who is assigned a percentage . . . below the legal threshold is . . . severally liable."[549] Section 28D introduces a mathematical concept, the threshold, which serves to reduce the plaintiff's recovery in certain cases. Track E is presented in section 28E: "If the . . . conduct of two or more persons is a legal cause of an indivisible injury, each defendant is jointly and severally liable for . . . economic damages . . . and . . . is severally liable for the comparative share . . . of the remaining non-economic damages . . . ."[550] Track E divides the plaintiff's damages into economic losses and pain and suffering, with different standards of recovery for each.

The implied conclusion is that any of these new and complicated approaches to indivisible injury is better than joint and several liability— in other words, it is better for the individual victims to carry their own losses than the defendants who were at fault. The Reporters' radical approach allows them to criticize joint and several liability without acknowledging over three hundred years of common law or debating the underlying policies. Unfortunately, it also allows the ALI to grant its imprimatur to a work that is not a new Restatement but rather a critique of joint and several liability without policy analysis and without the labor required of a new Restatement. In contrast to this approach, the law and policies of each of the important sections of the *Restatement (Third)*: Apportionment will be compared with the corresponding law of Pennsylvania to demonstrate that much of the *Restatement (Third)*: Apportionment contradicts the historical law of Pennsylvania, disregards the policies underlying joint and several liability, and violates economic theory.

The first part, which is an examination of the ALI's proposals as compared with Pennsylvania law, will make clear the *Restatement (Third)*: Apportionment is biased tort "reform," designed to benefit two powerful clients: sellers and the insurance industry. If adopted, *the Restatement (Third)*: Apportionment would constitute a radical reversal of fundamental Pennsylvania law and history, the representative jurisdiction for this section. The second part will analyze the apportionment provisions in terms of two tracks proposed by the Reporters.

iii. Analysis of the Potential Impact of the Restatement (Third): *Apportionment on the Pennsylvania Law of Joint and Several Liability* Section 27 of the *Restatement (Third)*: Apportionment begins the critique of joint and several liability by refusing to take a position on whether joint and several liability should apply, instead

---

548. *Id.* § 28C, at 245–46.
549. *Id.* § 28D, at 300–01.
550. *Id.* § 28E, at 337.

looking to each jurisdiction for a determination of the issue:[551] "if the independent tortious conduct of two or more persons is a legal cause of an indivisible injury, whether those persons are jointly and severally . . . or severally liable is determined by the law of the applicable jurisdiction."[552] By failing to adopt the majority view (joint liability), section 27 harms victims because it means in many situations they will be unable to recover their full damages (or even any damages at all) because the tortfeasors who caused the injury will not be held jointly and severally liable.

The Reporters suggest, without discussion, there are five different approaches or "tracks" to the question of joint liability. Over one-third of the 479 pages of the *Restatement (Third)*: Apportionment are devoted to these replacements for joint and several liability.[553] The new Restatement has three major problems. First, it suggests the five tracks are interchangeable. Second, it is not a restatement of the law. Third, it functions solely to benefit sellers.

By presenting the five tracks without ranking and evaluating each, the Reporters imply that one track can serve as well as another. In fact, each track is dramatically different, and all except the first are clear rejections of Pennsylvania apportionment law, which is that if two or more tortfeasors cause an indivisible injury, they will be held jointly and severally liable.[554]

In addition to the inequality of the tracks, the Restatement is not what it purports to be. The traditional role of the ALI was to restate the common law, but this five-track proposal is not a restatement. With the exception of Track A (joint liability), the *Restatement (Third)*: Apportionment is merely a catalogue of the tort "reform" accomplished in the past nineteen years, all of which benefit the powerful. What is missing from the *Restatement (Third)*: Apportionment is a restatement of the cases—the common law.

The implication of the five-track proposal is that the law of Pennsylvania needs to be changed, but the Reporters' argument for this point is missing. In contrast to the new Restatement, the Pennsylvania law of joint and several liability rests on the policies that the injured victim should have a source for recovery and that wrongdoers should be deterred. It builds on the concept that those who cause injury and are at fault should be liable to the plaintiff for damages. As will be shown, the new *Restatement (Third)*: Apportionment rejects these foundational policies of Pennsylvania law.

(A) TRACK A Section 28A presents what the Reporters call Track A. It provides that tortfeasors who cause indivisible injury to the plaintiff may be held jointly

---

551. *Id.* § 27, at 203. The Comment asserts "there is currently no majority rule on this question," and that both comparative fault and tort reform are largely responsible for substantial modifications of joint and several liability in most jurisdictions. *Id.* cmt. a.

552. *Id.*

553. *See generally* RESTATEMENT, *supra* note 541.

554. *See* KEETON ET AL., *supra* note 510, § 52, at 347.

and severally liable:[555] "a plaintiff may sue any of those [independent tortfeasors] who are jointly and severally liable and recover all damages" from any one of those defendants.[556] From a victim's perspective, Track A is the best to use in seeking recovery because the plaintiff does not bear the risk of a decreased recovery if one tortfeasor is judgment proof, immune, or outside the jurisdiction. Unlike Track A, the other four tracks reduce the plaintiff's recovery through various novel and sometimes radical devices, all to benefit the powerful.

Section 29A contributes only a procedural rule providing that in cases of indivisible injury, the question of allocation among defendants, other parties, and settlers is submitted to the jury:[557] "if one defendant and at least one other party . . . may be found responsible . . . for plaintiff's indivisible injury, each of the parties . . . is submitted to the factfinder for assignment of a percentage of comparative responsibility."[558] However, approximately 92 percent of cases are settled and thus never go to the jury;[559] therefore, section 29A will not be helpful in the majority of cases.

(B) TRACK B: SEVERAL LIABILITY Section 28B introduces Track B and provides "[i]f two or more persons' . . . conduct is the . . . cause of an indivisible injury, each defendant . . . is severally liable."[560] This track is a complete rejection of the Pennsylvania law of joint and several liability that follows the traditional rule of joint and several liability in assigning full responsibility to each defendant.[561] Under Track B, the plaintiff can recover from each defendant only in proportion to each defendant's fault.[562] This obviously favors sellers.

---

555. RESTATEMENT, *supra* note 541, § 28A, at 207. Track A is based on pure joint and several liability and "results in the imposition of joint and several liability on all tortfeasors who are the legal cause of an indivisible injury." *Id.*

556. *Id.* As an example of an indivisible result, Prosser and Keeton describe a collision between two automobiles that injures a third person. KEETON ET AL., *supra* note 510, § 52, at 347 (citations omitted).

557. RESTATEMENT, *supra* note 541, § 29A, at 214.

558. *Id.* Section 29A of the *Restatement (Third):* Apportionment favors the consumer in part because damages are allocated only among parties to the exclusion of nonparties. *Id.*

559. *See, e.g.,* Marc Galanter, *Reading the Landscape of Disputes: What We Know (And Think We Know) and Don't Know About Our Allegedly Contentious and Litigious Society,* 31 UCLA L. REV. 4, 28 (1983).

560. RESTATEMENT, *supra* note 541, § 28B, at 221. The Comment notes that for this section to become applicable, "defendants must not have a relationship or connection that would justify imposition of liability pursuant to §§ 23, 24, or 25." *Id.* § 28B cmt. c, at 222.

561. *See supra* notes 531–37 and accompanying text.

562. RESTATEMENT (THIRD) OF TORTS: Apportionment of Liability § 28B, cmt. d, at 197 (Proposed Final Draft, 1998). In this earlier draft, the Reporters observed the rationale behind imposing several liability is to "limit the liability of any tortfeasor to the plaintiff's damages." *Id.* It was noted further this change shifts the "obligation to join additional parties . . . from the defendant to the plaintiff." *Id.*

Several distinguished economists disagree with the *Restatement (Third):* Apportionment and conclude economic efficiency is better served by a rule of joint and several liability than by one of several liability only.[563] For example, Professors Kornhauser and Revesz stated that negligence rules are efficient under joint and several liability as long as the standard of care for each of the actors is set at the socially optimal level, but negligence rules are not efficient in the absence of joint and several liability.[564] Professors Theodore Eisenberg, Henry Mark, and Stuart Schwab also conclude joint and several liability is more efficient:

> The basic law and economics model suggests that joint and several liability is more efficient than several-only liability. By ensuring that each actor faces the full social costs of its actions, joint and several liability induces optimal behavior. The [economic] models reach less determinate outcomes when insolvency . . . and settlements are considered. But no model shows that several liability is generally more efficient. The [economic] models suggest then, that one should skeptically view empirical claims that several liability is more efficient than joint liability. This is particularly so when there are no studies that can cleanly separate the effects of joint and several liability reforms from other factors.[565]

In addition to providing for several liability only, section 28B permits the fact finder to assign responsibility not only to all parties, settling tortfeasors, and immune persons, but also to other identified persons for whom there is sufficient evidence introduced at trial to permit the fact finder to determine the person's tortious conduct was a legal cause of the indivisible injury.[566] This enables the fact finder to assign responsibility reflecting the percentage share of the plaintiff's damages for which each tortfeasor is liable.

The Reporters define a *person* as someone who is not a party to the suit and who has not entered into a settlement with the plaintiff, but who is alleged by one or more parties to have caused in fact the plaintiff's injury.[567] This formulation creates a legal quagmire for the injured victim. It is possible to have both a

---

563. Lewis A. Kornhauser & Richard L. Revesz, *Sharing Damages Among Multiple Tortfeasors,* 98 YALE L.J. 831, 834 (1989). Because joint and several liability is a "unitary share rule," it produces efficient outcomes. *Id.* at 851. Several liability, on the other hand, is a "fractional share rule and, in general, is not efficient." *Id.*

564. *Id.* at 870.

565. Theodore Eisenberg & Stuart Schwab, *Analysis of Proposed Pennsylvania Civil Justice Reforms and Projected Economic Impact of Such Reforms* (June 7, 1999) (unpublished manuscript, on file with the author).

566. RESTATEMENT (THIRD) OF TORTS: Apportionment of Liability § 28B cmt. c, at 196–97.

567. RESTATEMENT (THIRD) OF TORTS: Apportionment of Liability § 29D cmt. c, at 317 (Proposed Final Draft (Revised), 1999).

pure several liability rule and a rule that does not permit the fact finder to assign comparative responsibility to nonparties.[568] Track B rejects this harmonization and permits an allocation of responsibility to nonparties. Under section 28B, the risk of not joining a party or being unable to join a party is borne by the plaintiff.[569] Section 28B is best explained by looking at comment (d) of the 1998 Proposed Final Draft providing the section's rationale: "the obligation to join additional parties and have their liability determined by the fact finder is shifted from the defendant to the plaintiff."[570] However, there is a continuing debate over what should happen when someone has caused injury to the plaintiff, but is not joined in the suit because that person is unidentified or judgment proof, and therefore is not a party.[571] Section 28B answers that question by allowing an allocation of responsibility to the nonparty.[572] The problem for victims is that this will reduce their recovery, and in some cases may entirely eliminate it.

In the American civil justice system, all roads lead to the courthouse. The trial and the various rules and procedures for it have developed over hundreds of years. The purpose of these historic rules and procedures is to accomplish justice and provide fair treatment to each party.[573] One of the foundations of the trial system is that only properly joined parties can influence and affect the victim's recovery.[574] For example, an unknown person who drives in front of another driver, causing her to swerve into oncoming traffic, resulting in injury to the

---

568. The Reporters made this point. *See* Restatement (Third) of Torts: Apportionment of Liability § 28B cmt. d, at 197 (Proposed Final Draft, 1998). The import of pure several liability is to place the risk on the defendant of insolvent persons who are not joined rather than on the plaintiff.

569. *Id.* § 28B cmt. d, at 198. Additionally, the Reporters note the decision to apportion responsibility to nonparties is "[c]onsistent with the large majority of jurisdictions with either pure several liability or a hybrid system that submit nonparties to the factfinder for an apportionment of responsibility." *Id.*

570. *Id.* § 28B cmt. d, at 197. This Comment was deleted from the 1999 Revised Draft.

571. *See* Keeton et al., *supra* note 510, § 67, at 475–76 n.64. Prosser and Keeton identify the wide range of solutions individual jurisdictions have created to handle the problem. *Id.*

572. Restatement (Third) of Torts: Apportionment of Liability § 28B cmt. b, at 196. This notion was perpetuated in the 1999 revision. *See* Restatement (Third) of Torts: Apportionment of Liability 28B cmt. a, at 222 (Proposed Final Draft (Revised), 1999); *id.* § 29B, at 228. An exception to section 28B is that an individual who has intentionally caused an injury is still held jointly and severally liable by means of section 22. *See id.* § 28B cmt. c, at 222. Whether the tortfeasor has met the intentional tort standard is measured by the tortfeasor's "intent" as defined in section 8A of the *Restatement (Second) of Torts. See id.*

573. Fed. R. Evid. 102.

574. *See generally id.; see generally also* Fed. R. Civ. P., Rule 17 (a).

passenger, cannot affect the passenger's recovery against the driver. The tort "reform" statutes of the 1980s change this result.[575]

The rule that "only parties" may affect the allocation of damages provides a predictable and efficient laboratory in which to apply the procedural and evidentiary rules that lead to justice. The Reporters, in contrast, allow persons (including immune persons such as an employer, a spouse, or the state) to be considered by the jury in apportionment to reduce the plaintiff's recovery, even though they have not been joined as parties.[576] The result will be chaos.

By allowing liability to be apportioned to nonparties, the Restatement approach reduces the plaintiff's recovery because the plaintiff cannot recover from a nonparty. The more the nonparty is at fault, the less the plaintiff recovers. The solution to the patent injustice of section 28B is to eliminate the concept that the fault of nonparties can be considered to reduce the victim's recovery.

Section 28B is contrary to Pennsylvania law because Pennsylvania case law has uniformly rejected the theories underlying the Reporters' track system. In *Ball v. Johns-Manville Corp.*,[577] the court stated, "We are aware of no principle of Pennsylvania law that allows a jury to make a finding of liability against a party who has not been sued,"[578] and the court in *Gross v. Johns-Manville Corp.*[579] refused to instruct the jury to apportion damages among settling and non-settling defendants because this would destroy the policy favoring settlement. If settling parties are put before the jury, it would decrease the incentive for settlement.[580]

Pennsylvania statutory law also clearly rejects the theory that responsibility can be assigned to nonparties. In *Kemper National P & C Cos. v. Smith*,[581] the Pennsylvania Superior Court held that although other jurisdictions "permit[ted] the apportionment of liability among all tortfeasors, even those not made parties," Pennsylvania's statute was not as permissive.[582] Additionally, the court chose not to extend apportionment of liability to nonparties because to do so

---

575. The Reporters noted "[f]ourteen states have abolished joint and several liability for multiple tortfeasors whose independent actions result in an indivisible injury to plaintiff." RESTATEMENT (THIRD) OF TORTS: Apportionment of Liability § 27B, at 193 (Proposed Final Draft, 1998).

576. *Id.* § 28B at 198–99. It was the Reporters' position in the 1998 draft that "at a minimum" responsibility should be apportioned to "all parties and settling tortfeasors, including those against whom the plaintiff may not recover pursuant to § 2 of this Restatement." *Id.* § 28B cmt. c, at 196.

577. 625 A.2d 650 (Pa. Super. Ct. 1993).

578. *Id.* at 659–60.

579. 600 A.2d 558 (Pa. Super. Ct. 1991).

580. *See id.* at 565.

581. 615 A.2d 372 (Pa. Super. Ct. 1992).

582. *Id.* at 380.

would "disrupt the legislative scheme."[583] Moreover, the court reasoned "[i]f a new theory of recovery is to be recognized in Pennsylvania, it should come from either our Supreme Court or the legislature."[584]

As noted above, the essential purpose of a Restatement is to restate the common law.[585] There has occasionally been a small amount of prospective content in a Restatement, but it has heretofore been clearly presented as non-law. An example is the gesture requirement for assault. The Reporters for the *Restatement (Second) of Torts* stated that a person who reasonably suffers great fear, even in the absence of a gesture, should be able to recover for an assault.[586] However, the *Restatement (Second)* makes it crystal clear this is not supported by case law.[587]

If the Reporters had wanted to restate the law, they would have said the application of joint and several liability for indivisible injury is the dominant rule.[588] Additionally, they would have presented the four other approaches (tracks) as statutory alternatives used in a minority of jurisdictions.[589] This would have made clear that much of their document was aimed at placing the loss on the victim and not at serving as a Restatement. The document mainfests the Reporters have not compared, critiqued, evaluated, and synthesized the law of apportionment as has been done in earlier Restatements.[590]

The track system contained in the *Restatement (Third)*: Apportionment is a presentation by the Reporters of defense and insurance policy. How this has occurred is important to an understanding of the *Restatement (Third)*: Apportionment. During the 1980s, the myth of a litigation crisis was created and widely disseminated.[591] This myth provided the opportunity for the insurance

---

583. *Id.*

584. *Id. See also* 42 Pa. Cons. Stat. § 7102.

585. *See* Frank J. Vandall, *The Restatement (Third) of Torts, Products Liability, Section 2(b): Design Defect,* 68 TEMP. L. REV. 167, 196 (1995); *see also* Marshall S. Shapo, *In Search of the Law of Products Liability: The ALI Restatement Project,* 48 VAND. L. REV. 631, 633 (1995).

586. *See* RESTATEMENT (SECOND) OF TORTS § 27 (1965).

587. *See* PROSSER, *supra* note 153, at 39 n.12.

588. *See* RESTATEMENT (THIRD) OF TORTS: Apportionment of Liability § 27B, at 203 (Proposed Final Draft (Revised), 1999). The Reporters state that joint and several liability is the rule in fifteen states (including Alabama, Arkansas, Delaware, Illinois, Idaho, Maine, Maryland, Massachusetts, North Carolina, Pennsylvania, Rhode Island, South Carolina, South Dakota, Virginia, and West Virginia) as well as the District of Columbia. *Id.* § 28B reporters' note cmt. b, at 225–27.

589. *See id.* at 178–80 (presenting the alternative approaches to joint and several liability, including Tracks A, B, C, and D).

590. *See* RESTATEMENT (THIRD) OF TORTS: Apportionment of Liability § 1, at 1–20; § 28E, at 337–48; § 50, at 453–79.

591. *See* Marc S. Galanter, *The Day After the Litigation Explosion,* 46 MD. L. REV. 3 (1996); Marc S. Galanter, *News from Nowhere: The Debased Debate on Civil Justice,* 71 DENV. U. L. REV. 77 (1993). *See* the Appendix.

industry to lobby state legislatures for civil law changes that restricted the victims' opportunities to recover.[592] A popular approach for limiting consumer suits was modification of the rules of apportionment by means of state legislation.[593] The Reporters label these insurance-driven legislative intrusions into the common law as tracks.

This pro-insurance and corporate defense document has emerged from the ALI because of the recent expansion of the organization's purview to include statutory as well as common law.[594] Its main goal is to insulate powerful manufacturers and sellers from excess liability. The apparent purpose of the tracks is to mask the fact the Reporters are opposed to joint and several liability, [595] whereas a true Restatement would adopt the dominant position, which is joint and several liability.[596] Therefore, the debate over the future of the *Restatement (Third)*: Apportionment becomes one of policy: which tracks make more sense— those protecting victims or those protecting tortfeasors? The legislature and courts of each state will have to examine the precedent and policy of their jurisdictions to answer that question. When a provision of the *Restatement (Third)*: Apportionment is argued before a court, the first question from the bench should be, "Why should the loss be shifted from the powerful to the innocent victim?"

The solution is for the ALI to return to a Restatement of the common law and to ignore the state statutes. This would result in a Restatement document that resembles joint and several liability, as followed in Pennsylvania.[597] The tracks could be treated in one short comment as interesting variations among the states.

The courts in evaluating the *Restatement (Third)*: Apportionment must realize that, except for joint liability, there are no predominant rules in the document.[598] The courts should acknowledge there never was a litigation crisis and that the state apportionment statutes adopted during the 1980s were a creation of the

---

592. The Reporters state: "joint and several liability . . . gained wide acceptance before the tort reform legislation of the mid and late 1980s." *Id.* at 250.

593. *See id.* at 193.

594. *See generally* Vandall, *supra* note 585.

595. In the Foreword, the Director refers to the *Restatement (Third):* Apportionment as "a major work of original scholarship." RESTATEMENT (THIRD) OF TORTS: Apportionment of Liability at xiii (Proposed Final Draft (Revised), 1999). Does "original work" mean it is an opinion piece and not a restatement of the law? If so, the title should be changed to "Apportionment Study" or "Apportionment Reform."

596. *See* RESTATEMENT (THIRD) OF TORTS: Apportionment of Liability § 27A reporters note cmt. a, at 183 (Proposed Final Draft, 1998).

597. *See supra* notes 531–37 and accompanying text.

598. *See* RESTATEMENT (THIRD) OF TORTS: Apportionment of Liability § 27A & cmts., at 178–80, 183(Proposed Final Draft, 1998).

insurance industry.[599] Accordingly, the courts should look instead to their pre-1980 precedent (which embraces joint and several liability) as reflected in the law of Pennsylvania.

In order to have a Restatement, there must be a substantial body of decisions to restate. In the area of apportionment, the Reporters admit there is no meaningful volume of case law on the subject.[600] In its present form, the *Restatement (Third): Apportionment* is a choppy and poorly organized law review article, not a Restatement. Because the track concept has little support in the case law, the Restatement, if taken at face value, will cause misunderstanding rather than helping to clarify this important and complex field. It will provide fuel for the powerful who seek to increase profits by decreasing the bottom line.

Overturning six hundred years of civil law because of a minor injury at Disney World is an extreme reaction to a rare problem. In that case, the defendant was both negligent and a cause-in-fact of the injury. The radical "tort-reform" nature and pro-corporate bias of the *Restatement (Third): Apportionment* makes clear the ALI should return to its original purpose of restating the law.

2. The Council for Tobacco Research

The most outstanding example of private institutes and councils that actively strive to mislead Congress and the public is the Council for Tobacco Research (CTR). It was created by Phillip Morris Tobacco Company in 1954 and originally known as the Tobacco Industry Research Committee (TIRC).[601] Its original stated purpose was "to find out whether smoking was dangerous and if so, 'the next job tackled will be to determine how to eliminate the danger from tobacco.'"[602]

These goals soon shifted to developing and disseminating misleading information to doctors, Congress, and the public:

> The Tobacco Industry Research Committee immediately ran a full-page promotion in more than 400 newspapers aimed at an estimated 43 million Americans . . . entitled "A Frank Statement to Cigarette Smokers." . . . In this advertisement, the participating tobacco companies recognized their "special

---

599. *See* RESTATEMENT (THIRD) OF TORTS: Apportionment of Liability § 27 cmt. a, at 203 (Proposed Final Draft (Revised), 1999) (explaining alternative versions of joint and several liability are offered because of the advent of comparative fault and the tort reform of the 1980s and 1990s).

600. *See id.* (stating there is no majority rule on the issue of apportionment for independent tortfeasors causing an individual injury).

601. *See Impropaganda Review; A Rogues Gallery of Industry Front Groups and Anti-Environmental Think Tanks*, CENTER FOR MEDIA AND DEMOCRACY, July 30, 2003. *See also Tobacco Industry Hires Top Cancer Scientist to Head its Research*, http://www.sourcewatch. org/index.php?title=Council_for_Tobacco_Research, notes 1 and 3.

602. *Tobacco Industry Hires Top Cancer Scientist to Head its Research*, http://www. sourcewatch.org/index.php?title=Council_for_Tobacco_Research#_note-0, note 1.

responsibility" to the public, and promised to learn the facts about smoking and health. The participating tobacco companies promised to sponsor independent research. . . . The participating tobacco companies also promised to cooperate closely with public health officials. . . .

After thus beginning to lull the public into a false sense of security concerning smoking and health, the Tobacco Industry Research Committee continued to act as a front for tobacco industry interests. Despite the initial public statements and posturing, and the repeated assertions that they were committed to full disclosure and vitally concerned, the TIRC did not make the public health a primary concern. . . . In fact, there was a coordinated, industry-wide strategy designed actively to mislead and confuse the public about the true dangers associated with smoking cigarettes. Rather than work for the good of the public health, as it had promised, and sponsor independent research, the tobacco companies and consultants, acting through the tobacco trade association, refuted, undermined, and neutralized information coming from the scientific and medical community.[603]

In 1964 the TIRC was renamed the CTR.[604] In 1988, Judge H. Lee Sarokin described the CTR as "nothing but a hoax created for public relations purposes with no intention of seeking the truth or publishing it."[605] While purporting to study whether smoking causes cancer, CTR chose instead to provide grants to study areas that would not cast a shadow upon tobacco. "Instead (of smoking and cancer), the CTR funded studies of cell biology, developmental biology, genetics, immunology, neuroscience, pharmacology and virology."[606]

The key to understanding the work of the CTR is an eighteen-page pamphlet TIRC published in 1954. This was filled with half-truths intended to mislead the public about the dangers of smoking: "[T]the evidence is still inconclusive; something other than smoking may be responsible; statistical evidence can't be trusted; the issue is too complicated, even for scientists; more research is necessary; tests on animals don't apply to humans."[607] The public relations firm for tobacco

603. *A Frank Statement to Cigarette Smokers*, http://www.sourcewatch.org/index.php?title=The_Frank_Statement.

See also: http://www.sourcewatch.org/index.php?title=Council_for_Tobacco_Research#_note-0

604. *Impropaganda Review*, *supra* note 601. http://www.sourcewatch.org/index.php?title=Council_for_Tobacco_Research, note 1.

605. http://www.sourcewatch.org/index.php?title=Council_for_Tobacco_Research#_note-1. *See also* Fred Panzer, *The Roper Proposal*, May 1, 1972.

http://www.sourcewatch.org/index.php?title=Council_for_Tobacco_Research,note 2.

606. *See* http://www.sourcewatch.org/index.php?title=Council_for_Tobacco_Research#_note-1

607. Hill & Knowlton PR Memorandum, May 3, 1954, *available at* http://www.sourcewatch.org/index.php?title=Council_for_Tobacco_Research#_note-1, note 4.

boasted that "205,000 copies of the booklet were printed. It was sent to 176,800 doctors, members of Congress, and 15,000 members of the press. [It] resulted in favorable publicity in '"hundreds of papers and radio stations throughout the country.'"[608]

CTR conducted its lobbying efforts through the Tobacco Institute: "which would eventually have a budget of about $20 million, and a staff of 120 and would be acknowledged . . . as one of the most powerful lobbies in the country."[609] The devious work of the CTR and Tobacco Institute in "refuting, undermining and neutralizing" science and policy did not halt until they were sued (along with the tobacco manufacturers) by the state attorney generals. As part of the $206 billion settlement with the states, the tobacco companies agreed in 1999 to disband the CTR.[610]

3. The American Association for Justice

The American Association for Justice (formerly ATLA) is an association of over 65,000 trial lawyers whose purpose is to educate their members.[611] Most of their members are plaintiffs'[612] attorneys, but some are from the defense bar.[613] The Association also works to influence Congress in adopting legislation that will benefit the judicial process.[614] Their educational outreach has been described as follows:

> Jameson indicates that ATLA's "oldest and most important function" is to make it "possible for plaintiff's attorneys to share insights gained from experience and research in the area, and to enable members pursing similar actions to pool resources."[615] (Jameson also indicates that ATLA has always been involved in lobbying as well as in litigation.)
>
> Some of the specific private goods provided to members are[616] subscriptions to two publications, access to a database including deposits from members of documents and case information about 5,000 subject areas, use

---

608. *Id.* http://www.sourcewatch

609. *See* .org/index.php?title=Council_for_Tobacco_Research#_note-1 ("Although CTR and the Tobacco Institute were formally separate, the two groups were complimentary.")

610. *See id.* ("The Council for Tobacco Research and the Tobacco Institute both quietly closed their doors in 1999, disbanding as part of the historic settlement between U.S. state attorney generals and the tobacco industry.")

611. Paul H. Rubin & Martin J. Bailey, *The Role of Lawyers in Changing the Law*, 23 J. LEGAL STUD 807, 815–16 (1994).

612. *Id.* 814–15 (1994). *See also* American Association for Justice Mission and History, *available at* http://www.justice.org/cps/rde/xchg/justice/hs.xsl/418.htm.

613. *Id.*

614. *Id.*

615. *Id.* at 816. *Citing* Rita Jameson, ATLA, TRIAL, July 1980, at 56.

616. *Id.*

of an expert database, legal writing and research services, an "Answer Line" providing cases and citation service, opportunities to attend seminars, discounts and books and tapes, and opportunities to join litigation groups. These last are "voluntary networks of ATLA members sharing an interest in particular types of cases."[617] These groups share case information.[618]

Katherine Sowle provides more detail:

> The Association of Trial Lawyers of America ("ATLA"), for example, provides a research and information service, the ATLA Exchange, a repository of data on thousands of cases tried by ATLA members. In addition, ATLA offers an expert witness database, a planned deposition bank, and a brief and memorandum writing service. ATLA has facilitated formation of thirty-three litigation groups for exchanging information. Many of the litigation groups specialize in individual products or product areas. ATLA offers educational programs involving both skills training and substantive law training. These programs have included presentations on proof of damages, trial advocacy, products liability, and toxic torts. The *ATLA Advocate* includes a "Networking" section for ATLA members seeking information on specific types of cases.[619]

The Association engages in extensive lobbying:

> It is all but impossible to get a firm handle on the amount of money flowing from trial lawyers into Washington, but according to Legal Times, contributions by the ATLA Political Action Committee (PAC) and law firm PACs was $3.4 million in the 1987–88 election cycle. For 1989–90, the figure will probably come closer to $4.5 million.[620]

The chief distinction between the American Law Institute (ALI) (discussed in Section A) and the American Association for Justice is that the ALI's procorporate work in drafting section 2 of the *Restatement (Third) of Products Liability* was secret and deceptive. The Restatement's purpose is to restate the law. The ALI nowhere states that its purpose is to protect corporations such as insurance and tobacco. In contrast, the work of the American Association for Justice in strengthening the judicial process and educating trial lawyers is obvious and transparent.

---

617. *Id.*

618. *Id.*

619. Katherine Dix Sowle, *Toward a Synthesis of Products Liability Principles: Schwartz's Model and the Cost-Minimization Alternative,* 46 U. MIAMI L. REV. 1 (1991), at 39–41 (footnotes omitted). As quoted in Rubin & Bailey, *supra* note 611.

620. R.S. England, *Congress and the Ambulance Chasers,* 23 AMERICAN SPECTATOR 18 (Sept. 1990).

Two economists, Paul H. Rubin and Martin J. Bailey, were impressed to discover that lawyers work to expand the law and that the American Association for Justice is, therefore, a primary vehicle for this growth:

> There are two broad theories of the effect of litigation on legal change. One is that judges are responsible for the legal change. In this view, the law tracks the preference (conscious or unconscious) of judges. The alternative view is that litigants drive the law; this is the import of the evolutionary models of legal change. In this article we propose a variant of the second view: the law is driven by the preferences of attorneys, not of litigants or of judges (although both parties have a place in our story). This view contrasts with the William Landes and Richard Posner hypothesis that the law tracks economic efficiency. Our basic argument is that the law will come to favor the more concentrated class of parties with an interest in the law.[621]

More specifically, they argue:

> That the structure of products liability law can best be understood by examining the ability of different classes of litigants to organize and seek their goals by litigating to change precedents. The major group with an interest in changing tort law is tort lawyers. This point is also made by Christopher Curran in his discussion of comparative negligence. Tort law has been influenced by the ability of plaintiffs' attorneys to organize and by the interest of lawyers in the future value of precedents. This is our basic hypothesis: *The shape of modern product liability law is due to the interests of tort lawyers.*[622]

Professors Rubin and Martin departs from the author on the question of lawyer influence, as they argue the developing law will favor lawyers. They conclude:

> The major implication is this: *In general, the common law will come to favor organized interest groups, just as does statute law. For those bodies of law where there are no other organized parties with strong interests in the form of the law, then the law should come to favor the interests of lawyers.*[623]

The theme of this book is different, arguing that since about 1980, reform of products law favors the powerful, generally corporations. But perhaps we have broad ground for agreement, as powerful lawyers are hired by powerful corporations to change the law in their favor. Lawyers work to change the law—and the most effective lawyers are those employed by powerful corporations.

---

621. Rubin & Bailey, *supra* note 611.
622. *Id.* at 808.
623. *Id.* at 625.

APPENDIX A

The following materials are from Clifford A. Rieders and Nicholas F. Lorenzo, Jr., *Pennsylvania Trial Lawyers Publication—The Barrister.*[624]

On Nov. 20, 1991, Roswell B. Perkins, President of the American Law Institute, wrote to me and other members of the consultative group, indicating that Geoffrey Hazard had prepared a "perspective" for fund-raising purposes which was sent to donors who might be interested in the Enterprise Liability Project. Illustrative letters to foundations were also enclosed . . . and to the RJR–Nabisco Foundation.

The Solicitation letter stated, in relevant part:

Over the last 25 years liability for injuries resulting from services and products has greatly expanded in scope, cost, direct impact, and influence on activities of professionals and businesses. This is true of tort liability for personal injuries generally. It is true particularly with respect to the practice of medicine, the provision of health care by hospitals, medical clinics and other providers, and the development, manufacture and sale of health care products such as vaccines and drugs. The exposure to risk and losses from liability in these activities directly affects myriad decisions whether to continue such activities, and how those activities are pursued if undertaken.

. . .

A secondary consequence of these risks and losses is escalation of liability insurances rates, a phenomenon also well recognized with respect to the activities of health care services and providers. On the other side of the ledger is the fact that the availability of compensation for losses from such injuries is unsystematic and often fortuitous. In many instances liability is imposed even where there is coverage through "first person" insurance. In other instances there may be no private insurance against injuries and only a weak "safety net" by way of public health services. The present tort liability system provides large compensation to a small number of victims, but entails very high transaction costs, notably litigation costs and fees. Page 3, letter to the Robert Wood Johnson Foundation, September 12, 1986.

It is clear the intended purpose of the Enterprises Liability Project and the subsequent *Restatement (Third): Products Liability* was to restrict tort law based upon a hunch that compensation to victims was bad for manufacturers and raises insurance costs.

---

624. Pennsylvania Trial Lawyers Publication No. 189-1999, Reprinted in the BARRISTER 236.

Witness the language in the letter to [the foundation funded by a major tobacco manufacturer] RJR–Nabisco Foundation:

> Over the last 25 years liability for injuries resulting from services and products has greatly expanded in scope, cost, direct impact, and influence on activities of professionals and businesses. The exposure to risk and losses from liability in these activities directly affects myriad decisions whether to continue such activities, and how those activities are pursued if undertaken.
>
> A secondary consequence of these risks and losses is escalation of liability insurances rates, a phenomenon also well recognized. In many situations liability insurance coverage has been drastically reduced or becomes simply unavailable. These developments constitute an immediate deterrent to pursuing activities that entail tort liability risk. It is common knowledge that many businesses presently have had to close or radically restrict their operations on this account.
>
> On the other side of the ledger is the fact that the availability of compensation for losses from such injuries is unsystematic and often fortuitous. In many instances liability is imposed even where there is coverage through "first person" insurance. It appears that most injured persons have some kind of insurance available to them, health or accident insurance or liability insurance proceeds. There is little legal or financial coordination of such coverages, and many injured persons discover that they have quite inadequate provision for medical care for injuries. . . . Present tort liability law provides large compensation to a small number of victims, but entails very high transaction costs, notably litigation costs and fees.
>
> Thus, the present situation in personal injury law—it cannot be called a "system"— is such that there is both [a] chilling risk of tort liability for enterprises, on one hand, and, on the other hand, chilling fear on the part of individuals that there will be inadequate compensation for real and serious losses. (Letter to Mr. John L. Bacon, December 10, 1987).

5. CORPORATIONS WRITE THE LAW

The unique theme of this chapter will be to argue that civil justice no longer rests on historic foundations such as fairness and impartiality, but has shifted to power and influence. To understand the law surrounding products today, it is necessary to study factual reality, not philosophy or history. Examples used to make points will be actual cases, enacted legislation, and battles within agencies. The theme is that in those areas where corporations have an interest (always true with products), corporations determine the law. This point will be illustrated with three socially important examples: tobacco litigation, gun suits, and SUV rollover standards.

In the previous chapters we saw the rapid expansion in strict liability in the courts followed in time by constrictions in both substantive and procedural law dealing with products. This chapter will demonstrate the historical embrace of the powerful continues today in judicial, legislative, and agency decisions dealing with products, making clear the impact of power on the law (of products) extends from 1980 to the present.

Lobbying is the conduit of power from the corporations to government. In his 2008 campaign for the presidency, Barack Obama promised to remove special interests (lobbies) from government.[1] He strongly implied they were the enemy of good government.[2]

Lobbying is defined as:

[T]he practice of trying to persuade legislators to propose, pass, or defeat legislation or to change existing law. A lobbyist may work for a group, organization, or industry, and presents information on legislative proposals to support his or her clients' interests.[3]

Lobbies have never been held in high regard:

Winding in and out through the long, devious basement passage, crawling through the corridors, trailing its slimy length from gallery to committee

---

1. Barack Obama, Remarks of Senator Barack Obama: A Change We Can Believe In (Nov. 3, 2007) (*available at* http://www.barackobama.com/2007/11/03/remarks_of_senator_barack_obam_30.php); Helene Cooper & Jeff Zeleny, *Obama's Transition Team Limits Lobbyists' Role*, N.Y. TIMES, Nov. 12, 2008, at A19.

2. Remarks of Senator Barack Obama, *supra* note 1 ("I don't take a dime of their money, and when I am President, they won't find a job in my White House.").

3. U.S. Senate, Definition of Lobbyist, www.Senate.gov (follow references hyperlink) (last visited Nov. 22, 2009).

room, at last it lies stretched at full length on the floor of Congress—this dazzling reptile, this huge, scaly serpent of the lobby.[4]

The core function of a lobbyist is to provide information to members of Congress.[5] Lobbyists may draft model legislation, answer questions on complex subjects, or explain how a proposed bill might affect the lobbyists' clients.[6]

Insight into the work of lobbies is provided by examining who they represent. The twenty industries with the highest lobbying expenditures in 1998–2009 included: pharmaceuticals and health products, insurance, electric utilities, business associations, education, oil and gas, real estate, hospitals, health professionals, air transport, automotive, defense, and aerospace.[7] In 2008, lobbies spent a combined $3.24 billion to educate and influence Congress, and $2.5 billion in 2009.[8] *Fortune* magazine reported in 2001 that the National Rifle Association had replaced the AARP as "the group with the most clout in the capital."[9]

In 1998 the Violence Policy Center reported:

Although the National Rifle Association (NRA) insists it represents only firearm consumers, the organization has joined with the gun industry to lobby for legislation to severely restrict the rights of consumers killed or injured by defective firearms and ammunition. The NRA and the gun industry are major backers of Congressional efforts to restrict consumer rights in product liability suits.[10]

---

4. U.S. Senate, *Lobbyists*, http://www.senate.gov/legislative/common/briefing/Byrd_History_Lobbying.htm (last visited Nov. 22, 2009).

5. Neil K. Komesar, *Injuries and Institutions: Tort Reform, Tort Theory, and Beyond*, 65 N.Y.U.L. Rev. 23, 31 (1990).

6. *See, e.g.*, Dori Apollonio et al., *Access and Lobbying: Looking Beyond the Corruption Paradigm*, 36 Hastings Const. L.Q. 13, 29–30 (Fall 2008); Thomas M. Susman, *Private Ethics, Public Conduct: An Essay on Ethical Lobbying, Campaign Contributions, Reciprocity, and the Public Good*, 19 Stan. L. & Pol'y Rev. 10, 11–12 (2008); Tom LoBianco, *Lobbyists Help Dems Draft Climate Change Bill*, Wash. Times, May 4, 2009, http://www.washingtontimes.com/news/2009/may/04/green-lobby-guides-democrats-on-climate-bill/.

7. Center for Responsive Politics, *Top Industries—Lobbying in 1998–2009*, http://www.opensecrets.org/lobby/top.php?indexType=i (Oct. 20, 2009); *see also* Jeffrey H. Birnbaum, *Fat & Happy in D.C.*, Fortune, May 28, 2001, at 94 (listing results from Power 25 Survey, *Fortune's* list of the capital's most powerful lobbyists).

8. Center for Responsive Politics, *Tobacco Lobbying Spent $67.3 Million in 1998* (and at least $19 million each and every year during 1998–2009). *Id.* at *Tobacco Industry Profile 1998*, http://www.opensecrets.org/lobby/indusclient.php?year=1998&lname=A02&id=.

9. Birnbaum, *supra* note 7.

10. Violence Policy Center, *The National Rifle Association and the Gun Industry are Working Hand in Hand to Limit Consumers' Rights*, http://www.vpc.org/fact_sht/nraindus.htm (1998).

From 1998–2009, the top-named clients for lobbying efforts included: the U.S. Chamber of Commerce, the American Hospital Association, the Pharmaceutical Research & Manufacturers of America, Exxon-Mobil, Verizon, and General Motors.[11] Clearly most major industries fund lobbying in Washington. This presence proved especially beneficial to the airline industry in September 2001: it was poised and therefore able to persuade Congress (in a mere eleven days) to pass an act that insulated the airlines from suits by persons who were killed or injured by the terrorist airplane crashes.[12]

The lobbying activities before state legislatures reflect those in Washington. Almost every major financial interest seeks to lobby state lawmakers. Georgia is a good example. The following players were in the top ten for spending on lobbying in 2009: Savannah Chamber of Commerce, University System of Georgia, Georgia Beverage Association, AT&T, Georgia Power Co., Georgian Trial Lawyers Association, and the Coca-Cola Company.[13] The amount spent to lobby the Georgia lawmakers was substantial; during the first three months of the 2009 legislative session, lobbyists spent $908,746.00 on gifts and meals.[14]

However, the amounts spent on lobbying in Washington during the first half of 2009 were down:

> In a year when Washington's influence industry should be thriving, with epic battles over health care and energy legislation, lobbying in many sectors is in marked decline as defense contractors, real estate firms and other companies pull back in a down economy.
>
> Overall spending on lobbying has leveled off for the first time in a decade, according to disclosure data filed with Congress. Lobbying revenue for many of the city's most powerful advocacy firms, . . . plunged 10 percent or more in the first half of the year.
>
> . . .
>
> Lobbying insiders say factors other than the economy are driving the numbers down. Trade groups and private corporations, for example, are increasingly pouring resources into television ads, grass-roots organization and other advocacy efforts not counted under the narrow definition of lobbying required for House and Senate disclosure forms.[15]

---

11. Center for Responsive Politics, Top Spenders Lobby 1998–2009, http://www. opensecrets.org/lobby/top.php?showYear=a&indexType=s (Oct. 26, 2009).

12. Anthony J. Sebok, *What's Law Got to Do With It? Designing Compensation Schemes in the Shadow of the Tort System*, 53 DePaul L. Rev. 501, 501 (2003).

13. James Salzer, Cameron McWhirter, & John Perry, *Despite Recession, Lobbyists Still Have Plenty to Spend*, Atl. J.- Const., Apr. 19, 2009, at 3b.

14. *Id.*

15. Dan Eggen, *Lobbyists Take an Examination Hit*, Atl. J.- Const. Sept. 6, 2009, at A16.

Contrary to popular wisdom, lobbyists at the federal level may not cross certain lines. Under the Lobbying Disclosure Act (LDA), lobbyists are (with limited exceptions) prohibited from providing gifts, meals, travel (including private jet transportation), bribes, and illegal gratuities.[16] However, lobbies in Georgia are not so limited.[17]

The common theory of lobbies is that they are poisonous vipers crushing opponents and maiming the weak as they slither about.[18] Reality is different: lobbies are an inherent part of government, like the mortar between bricks or oil in an automobile engine. Lobbies are an integral part of the legislative and administrative lawmaking process. They are the conduit of power: they communicate the wishes of interest groups to the lawmakers.

The following are three contemporary examples of how corporations make the law.

A. TOBACCO LITIGATION

Tobacco is an excellent example of powerful corporations writing the law. Because of the power of tobacco manufacturers, the tobacco industry had not paid a penny for the millions of deaths caused from the mid-1950s until 1998. Cigarette-induced death and illness is one of the most important and costly health problems facing American society. Each year smoking kills approximately four hundred thousand persons.[19] This yearly death toll exceeds the total number

---

16. Lobbying Disclosure Act of 1995, 2 U.S.C. § 1601 (2007) (requiring lobbyists to register and file disclosure reports at least six times a year); 18 U.S.C. § 201 (2009) (criminalizing bribery and illegal gratuities); Honest Leadership and Open Government Act of 2007, Pub. L. No. 110-81, 121 Stat. 735-776 (amending parts of LDA and increasing disclosure requirements and prohibitions on gift giving). President Obama has taken steps to reduce the influence of lobbying even more. *See supra* notes 1 and 2 and accompanying text; Michelle Austein Brooks, *Obama Administration Imposes Tough Lobbying Restrictions*, America.gov, Feb. 23, 2009, http://www.america.gov/st/usg-english/2009/February/2009 0223152245hmnietsua0.8490259.html&distid=ucs.

17. *See* Ethics in Government Act, GA. CODE ANN. § 21-5-1 et seq. (1981). The EiGA provides lobbyists must (1) register with the State Ethics Commission; (2) file disclosure reports listing all expenditures (gifts, meals, entertainment, lodging, equipment, advertising, travel, and postage) made on behalf of or for the benefit of a public officer (but not prohibiting them); and (3) follow certain post-employment restrictions. *Id.* Additionally, an executive order in 2003 prohibits most gifts to state employees. However, the policy is "widely" disregarded and contains one broad exception. James Salazar & Cameron McWhirter, *Georgia's Gift Ban has Wide Loophole*, ATL. J.- CONST., Feb. 8, 2009.

18. *See supra* note 4 and accompanying text.

19. *Hearing before H. Subcomm. on Health and the Environment of the Comm. on Energy and Commerce*, 99th Cong. 4 (1986) [hereinafter *Health & Environment*]. Compare with "Experts say smoking kills nearly 400,000 people in the United States each year. . . ." *Men*

of Americans killed in World War I, the Korean War, and Vietnam.[20] In comparison to other critical addictive health problems, heroin and cocaine each year claim an estimated combined total of only ten thousand persons.[21] Studies also show cigarettes are the leading cause of death from cancer in women.[22]

At present nonsmokers pay a large portion of the health and welfare costs of smoking-caused cancer through higher taxes and health insurance premiums.[23]

Who Smoke May Cut Lives Short by 18 Years, Atl. J.- Const., May 13, 1990, at A14. In contrast, Elizabeth Whelan stated that smoking causes 350,000 deaths per year. Elizabeth Whelan, A Smoking Gun: How the Tobacco Industry Gets Away with Murder 10 (1984). [There is little to suggest these numbers are less true today.]

20. Atl. J.- Const., Feb. 21, 1987, at A8.

21. *America's AIDS Cases Pass 100,000, Double the Number of 18 Months Ago*, Atl. J.- Const., Aug. 15, 1989, at A37. *Health Consequences of Smoking: Nicotine Addiction: Hearing before H. Subcomm. on Health and the Environment of the Comm. on Energy and Commerce*, 100th Cong. 23 (1988) [hereinafter *Nicotine Addiction*].

22. "A dramatic 44 percent increase in lung cancer deaths among women since 1979 is fueling a steady rise in the country's deadliest form of cancer, federal health researchers [CDC] reported Thursday. Health experts say the trend is a direct result of women's smoking habits . . . [T]he bad news is that lung cancer is now the leading cause of cancer death in women. It has eclipsed breast cancer, and it is getting worse." Atl. J.- Const., July 28, 1989, at A1. "[T]hose who smoke two packs are seven times as likely to suffer a heart attack as those who have never smoked." Atl. J.- Const., Jan. 25, 1990, at A1.

23. When smokers contract cancer, their medical expenses are often paid for by their health insurance. The nonsmoker's rates are therefore higher because of the cancer expenses of the smoker. If smokers lack health insurance, they will seek to obtain treatment at a public hospital. The costs of this treatment are borne, in large part, by society in general.

The thought behind the absolute liability proposal is that because cigarettes are unique and not necessities, and cigarette-caused cancer is identifiable, the market system would work more efficiently if the cost of smoking-caused cancer were borne as much as possible by the cigarette manufacturers and smokers.

Elizabeth M. Whelan argues: "How can the economic burden of tobacco be shifted to where it belongs—on the backs of smokers and tobacco producers? One frequently proposed solution is a 'health tax' on cigarettes, with proceeds used to fund social welfare programs which pay for public medical costs of smoking." Whelan, *supra* note 19, at 151. Of course, it is highly unlikely Congress would pass such an act; therefore, the absolute liability proposal rests upon creative decision making by the courts.

Arguably the expenses of the state for testing cancer were settled in the 1998 agreement (MSA) between tobacco companies and the states. This asks for further analysis.

Several scholars argue, however: "Although nonsmokers subsidize smokers' medical care and group life insurance, smokers subsidize nonsmokers' pension and nursing home payments. On balance, smokers probably pay their way at the current level of excise taxes on cigarettes. . . ." Manning et al. *The Taxes of Sin: Do Smokers Pay Their Way?*, 1989 J.A.M.A. 1604.

In reply, cigarette excise taxes go into the general fund and do not help to reduce nonsmokers' health insurance costs, nor do they pay for treatment for smokers with cancer.

The cigarette advertising industry spent approximately $250,000 per hour, every hour, day and night for product promotion in 1988.[24] People begin to smoke at age twelve and become hooked[25] as cigarette smoking is as addictive as heroin.[26] Young people try cigarettes, become addicts, and die in their prime from cancer. With this addiction of children resulting in death to men and women at the peak of their productive lives, the time has come to examine how the legal system deals with the continuing power of the tobacco corporations and the resulting carnage. Over the past roughly fifty years, there have been three waves of tobacco litigation.

1. The 1960s and the *Green v. American Tobacco Co.* Case[27]

In the mid-1950s, a series of cases were brought against the tobacco manufacturers, but the plaintiffs lost.[28] The reasoning varied, but is perhaps best summarized in the vague and twisted 1958 decision in *Green v. American Tobacco Co.* Cigarettes were held to be not-defective and not warranted to be safe.[29] By the

---

The excise taxes do not encourage cigarette manufacturers to market a safer cigarette or to spend funds on research to cure cancer. Finally, as excise taxes are not earmarked for cancer caused by smoking, they do not depict the true costs of smoking.

24. *Health & Environment, supra* note 19, at 2; Cipollone v. Liggett Group, Inc., 683 F.Supp. 1487, 1497 (D.N.J. 1988) ($2.3 billion divided by 8,760 hours = approximately $250,000 per hour).

25. "About 26 percent of people between ages 12 and 17 try smoking. . . . Those who smoke are lighting up their first cigarette at the average age of 12." ATL. J.- CONST., May 17, 1990, at A8.

26. "Surgeon General C. Everett Koop announced unequivocally today that cigarettes and other tobacco products are addictive like heroin and cocaine. . . ." ATL. J.-CONST., May 16, 1988, at A3.

27. 391 F.2d 97 (5th Cir. 1968), *rev'd,* 409 F.2d 1166 (5th Cir. 1969) (en banc).

28. Approximately 100 to 150 cases were brought against the cigarette manufacturers in 1953 and 1954. *See* Lawrence A. Schemmel, *Cigarette Litigation and Products Liability: Did Someone Win the War or Have the Battle Lines Just Been Drawn?,* 14 MISS. C.L. REV. 657, 665 (1994). Of these cases, only ten went any significant distance into trial. Four were voluntarily dismissed, three resulted in jury verdicts for the manufacturers, and three ended in summary judgment for the manufacturer. *See id.* at 665–66.

29. The suit was filed in 1958. *See* Green v. Am. Tobacco Co., 391 F.2d _97, 99–101 (5th Cir 1968), rev'd 409 F.2d 1166 (Fifth Cir. 1969) (en banc) (finding the consumer was entitled to rely on implied assurances that cigarettes were wholesome and fit for the purpose intended, and that the manufacturer could be held absolutely liable for a consumer's death from cancer cause by smoking cigarettes). The U.S. Fifth Circuit overruled en banc its previous decision and instead embraced the dissent in its first *Green* decision. *See* Green v. Am. Tobacco Co., 409 F.2d 1166 (5th Cir. 1969) (en banc), *cert. denied,* 397 U.S. 911 (1970) The dissent in that case stated:

In substance, my position is that the majority has failed to recognize the uniqueness of the situation resented. We are not dealing with an obvious, harmful, foreign body in a product. Neither do we have an exploding or breaking bottle case wherein the defect

conclusion of the 1950s, it was clear the cigarette manufacturers had won the day.

2. The *Cipollone v. Liggett Group, Inc.* Case[30]

The second wave of suits against the cigarette manufacturers began on August 1, 1983, when Rose Cipollone (who had smoked for a large portion of her sixty years) filed suit against three major cigarette manufacturers.[31] *The Cipollone v. Liggett Group, Inc.* case extended over nine years and now occupies the pages of thirteen federal cases.[32] It went to the U.S. Supreme Court twice[33] and finally led to a decision essentially holding the state causes of action against cigarette manufacturers based on failure to warn of the risks of smoking were preempted by the federal cigarette acts.[34]

It has been estimated the plaintiff's attorneys in *Cipollone* spent approximately $6 million prosecuting the case.[35] But after an apparent plaintiff's victory before the Supreme Court, the plaintiff's attorney voluntarily dismissed it.[36] The speculation was the plaintiff's law firm had decided that because no money had been

---

is so obvious that it warrants no discussion. Instead, we have a product (cigarettes) that is in no way defective. They are exactly like all others of the particular brand and virtually the same as all other brands on the market. . . . "If a man buys whiskey and drinks too much of it and gets some liver trouble as a result I do not think the manufacturer is liable unless (1) the manufacturer tells the customer the whiskey will not hurt him or (2) the whiskey is adulterated."

Green, 391 F.2d at 110 (Simpson, J., dissenting) (quoting Pritchard v. Liggett & Myers Tobacco Co., 295 F.2d 292, 302 (3d Cir. 1961) (Goodrich, J., concurring)).

30. 505 U.S. 504 (1992).

31. *See* Cipollone v. Liggett Group. Inc., 593 F.Supp. 1146 (D.N.J. 1984), *modified,* 789 F.2d 181 (3d Cir. 1986). The final decision came down in 1992. *See* Cipollone v. Liggett Group. Inc., 505 U.S. 504 (1992).

32. See Frank J. Vandall, *Reallocating the Costs of Smoking: The Application of Absolute Liability to Cigarette Manufacturers,* 52 Ohio St. L.J. 405, 407 & n.14 (1991).

33. *See* Cipollone v. Liggett Group. Inc., 499 U.S. 935 (1991), *aff'd in part, rev'd in part,* 505 U.S. 504 (1992).

34. *See Cipollone,* 505 U.S. at 524. In *Cipollone,* the Supreme Court found the 1969 Cigarette Labeling Act preempted Cipollone's failure-to-warn claim "insofar as claims . . . require a showing that respondents' post-1969 advertising or promotions should have included additional, or more clearly stated warnings." *Id.*

35. The attorneys for the plaintiff spent more than $5 million for their time and over $1 million in out-of-pocket expenses. *See* Henry J. Reske, *Cigarette Suit Dropped,* A.B.A. J., Feb. 1993, at 30.

36. *See* Raymond E. Gangarosa et al., *Suits by Public Hospitals to Recover Expenditures for the Treatment of Disease, Injury and Disability Caused by Tobacco and Alcohol,* 22 Fordham Urb. L.J. 81, 130 (1994). Despite the Supreme Court's finding that numerous causes of action were not preempted, the case was voluntarily withdrawn. *See id.*

made and $6 million had gone out, it was time to drop the Cipollone litigation.[37] Between 1984 and 1992, Rose Cipollone had died, and her husband took up the gauntlet. Her husband remarried and then also passed away. In the final stages, the *Cipollone* case was prosecuted but then dropped by her son.[38]

The message of *Cipollone* is the cigarette manufacturers' primary strategy is to spend the plaintiffs' attorneys to death.[39] The cigarette manufacturers had adopted the theory of General Patton that rather than spending their money, they would force the plaintiff to spend all of his.[40] This "scorched earth" theory was victorious in the second wave of lawsuits.

Indeed, cigarette manufacturers have continued to spend hundreds of millions of dollars each year to defend cigarette suits.[41] The message from the *Cipollone* case was clear: plaintiffs' attorneys should not bring cigarette cases because they will spend millions of dollars litigating only to lose. By the end of the *Cipollone* cases, cigarette manufacturers had still not paid one penny to an individual who had been injured by tobacco smoke.[42]

3. The *Castano v. American Tobacco Co.* Case[43]

The third wave of cigarette litigation was ushered in with *Castano v. American Tobacco Co.*, a class-action suit filed in a Louisiana federal district court in 1994.[44] The foundation of the *Castano* suit was the claim cigarette manufacturers had defrauded consumers by failing to tell them tobacco smoke was injurious to people's health and smoking was addictive.[45] The district court certified

---

37. *See* Reske, *supra* note 35. *See also* Thomas C. Bigosinski, Note, *Constitutional Law—Premption and Products Liability—Federal Cigarette Labeling and Advertising Act Held Not to Preempt State Common Law Damage Actions*—Cipollone v. Liggett Group, Inc., 112 S. Ct. 2608 (1992), 23 SETON HALL L. REV. 1791, 1838 (1993).

38. *See Cipollone,* 505 U.S. at 509.

39. The wealthy cigarette manufacturers can afford to defend aggressively. Tobacco company profits have risen from $2.3 billion in 1981 to an estimated $7.8 billion in 1997. *See* Julia Malone & Mike Williams, *The Tobacco Battle—Fate of National Deal, Other Suits Uncertain,* ATL. J.- CONST., Aug. 26, 1997, at F8.

40. One tobacco industry lawyer summarized their strategy: "To paraphrase General Patton, the way we won those cases was not by spending all of [R.J.] Reynolds' money, but by making that other son-of-a bitch spend all of his." William E. Townsley & Dale K. Hanks, *The Trial Court's Responsibility to Make Cigarette Disease Litigation Affordable and Fair,* 25 CAL. W. L. REV. 275, 278 (1988).

41. For just the *Cipollone* cases alone, the Liggett Group spent more than $75 million. *See* Elizabeth Gleick, *Tobacco Blues,* TIME, Mar. 11, 1996, at 54–55.

42. *See* Christopher John Farley, *Cough Up That Cash,* TIME, Mar. 6, 1995, at 47.

43. 870 F.Supp. 1425 (E.D. La. 1994) (denying preemption of claim).

44. *See id.*

45. *See id.* at 1430 (listing various other claims, including "fraud and deceit, negligent misrepresentation, intentional infliction of emotional distress, violation of consumer protection statutes, breach of express warranty, breach of implied warranty, negligence, strict

the class,[46] but the defendant appealed the certification. The federal court of appeals determined certification of the class action was inappropriate for the following reasons: the class action was not superior to individual actions; the district court erred in certifying immature torts; and the complexity of the choice-of-law inquiry made individual adjudication superior to class treatment.[47]

The *Castano* case signaled the death of cigarette class actions—and it certainly presented a strong criticism of the class action theory in similar cases.[48] The court quoted Judge Posner: "One jury . . . will hold the fate of an entire industry in the palm of its hand. . . . That kind of thing can happen. . . . But need not be tolerated . . ."[49] Yet this rejection of the class is strange considering cigarette-cancer cases seem to be designed for class-action litigation: there are a large number of very similar suits that if tried as a single class action, would reduce

---

liability, redhibition, and equitable relief"). The court noted: "Plaintiffs' claims are based on their contention that defendants intentionally failed to disclose, and in fact concealed, knowledge that *nicotine* is addictive and that defendants manipulate nicotine levels in their cigarettes for the purpose of addicting consumers to their products and sustaining that addiction." *Id.*

46. The plaintiffs proposed to define the class as:

(a) All nicotine dependent persons in the United States, its territories and possessions and the Commonwealth of Puerto Rico who have purchased and smoked cigarettes manufactured by the Tobacco Companies; (b) the estates, representatives, and administrators of these nicotine dependent cigarette smokers; and, (c) the spouses, children, relatives and "significant others" of these nicotine dependent cigarette smokers as their heirs or survivors.

Castano v. American Tobacco Co., 160 F.R.D. 544, 549 (E.D. La. 1995) (footnote omitted), *rev'd*, 84 F.3d 734 (5th Cir. 1996). The district court certified the proposed class "only in regard to the liability issues of fraud, breach of warranty (express or implied), intentional tort, negligence, strict liability and consumer protection and punitive damages issues." *Id.* at 560.

47. *See Castano*, 84 F.3d at 747–50. The Fifth Circuit Court of Appeals noted:

What the district court failed to consider, and what no court can determine at this time, is the very real possibility that the judicial crisis may fail to materialize. The plaintiffs' claims are based on a new theory of liability and the existence of new evidence. Until plaintiffs decide to file individual claims, a court cannot, from the existence of injury, presume that all or even any plaintiffs will pursue legal remedies. Nor can a court make a superiority determination based on such speculation.

Id. at 747–49 (footnotes and internal citations omitted). The court of appeals also noted certification of immature torts consumes more judicial resources tan certification will save. *See id.* at 749. On the issue of competing state laws, the court stated: "[W]hile the task may not be impossible, its complexity certainly makes individual trials a more attractive alternative and renders class treatment not superior." *Id.* at 750. The court of appeals ultimately held the class complaint should be dismissed. *See id.* at 752.

48. *See infra* note 101 and accompanying text.

49. *Castano*, 84 F.3d at 748.

the amount of time spent by attorneys and the courts. The Fifth Circuit, however, did not see it that way. As a result, numerous suits that were bound together in *Castano* have now been brought individually in various states.

4. Why the Early Cigarette Trials Were Lost

In spite of the serious problems plaintiffs had in the appellate courts, several cases progressed to the jury stage,[50] but the plaintiffs lost the cases. Some have speculated juries felt the plaintiffs knew cigarettes were injurious and could have stopped smoking if they had wished.[51] The juries evidently rejected the argument that smoking is as addictive as heroin.[52]

Instead the juries adopted the theory of assumption of risk: the consumers knew the risk, and voluntarily began to continued to smoke.[53] Numerous tobacco cases also failed because the plaintiffs could not prove that smoking in fact caused the cancer. For example, Melvin Belli brought the first cigarette suit to go before a jury. It returned a verdict against the plaintiff, finding the death of the smoker could have been caused by a large number of serious illnesses from which the plaintiff was suffering, only one of which was lung cancer.[54]

At the end of 1991, the victims injured by cigarettes were in a very difficult position. By that time, all of their cases had been lost, the appellate courts were unsympathetic to their plight, and juries seemed to be sending a message that people may smoke if they want, but would not be able to recover damages from cigarette manufacturers for the illnesses caused by their volitional activity. As of 1998, the tobacco manufacturers had still never paid a cent for cancer caused by smoking.

---

50. *See* Vandall, *supra* note 32, at 429 (noting the first cigarette case to be tried in the 1980s, Galbraith v. R.J. Reynolds Tobacco Co., No. C 144147 (Cal. Super. Ct. Nov. 20, 1985), ended in a jury verdict for the defendant). *See also* Schemmel, *supra* note 36, at 665–66.

51. In *Cipollone*, the jury believed Rose Cipollone's volitional smoking should have barred any recovery. *See* Cipollone v. Liggett Group, Inc., 893 F.2d 541, 554 (3d Cir. 1990), *aff'd in part, rev'd in part*, 505 U.S. 504 (1992).

52. One commentator wrote that "cigarette smokers behave remarkably like heroin addicts. . . [and] cigarette smoking is an addiction." EDWARD M. BRECHER, LICIT AND ILLICIT DRUGS 226–27 (1972).

53. *See* Bruce A. Levin, *The Liability of Tobacco Companies—Should Their Ashes Be Kicked?* 29 ARIZ. L. REV. 195, 222–23 (1987).

54. *See* Galbraith v. R.J. Reynolds Tobacco Co., No. C 144147 (Cal. Super. Ct. Nov. 20, 1985).The favorite tactic of the cigarette manufacturer is to provide the jury with so many other potential causes of the injured party's injury that they feel compelled to return with a verdict in favor of the defendant. *See* Vandall, *supra* note 36, at 428–29.

5. The Theory and the Visionaries That Won the War

The theory that won the tobacco war was developed by a core of visionaries working from different perspectives: Richard Daynard, Mike Lewis, Michael Moore, Susan Nial, Ray Gangarosa, Brian Willis, and Frank J. Vandall. The earthshaking concept Gangarosa, Willis, and Vandall developed is that states should be able to sue to recover the costs of treating disease and illness caused by cigarette smoking. They argued the defenses used against individual smokers should not apply to the states.[55]

In 1985, Richard Daynard began thinking about a subrogation suit against tobacco manufacturers.[56] Over a period of several years, Daynard held a conference for state attorneys general to discuss state suits brought against the tobacco companies.

One of the heroes of the tobacco war is Mike Lewis, an attorney from Clarksdale, Mississippi.[57] When Lewis's part-time bookkeeper died from cancer caused by smoking, Lewis wanted to bring an individual suit against the tobacco manufacturers, but believed it would be defeated because of the assumption-of-risk defense.[58] Estimating the state had spent about $1 million in caring for his secretary's cancer, he suggested to his friend and law school classmate, Mississippi Attorney General Michael Moore, that the state (rather than the individual) should sue the tobacco manufacturers.[59]

Moore, running with Lewis's idea, decided to file a suit on behalf of the State of Mississippi against tobacco manufacturers.[60] (Perhaps he had read an article written by Professor Frank Vandall in 1991 that argued the state could sue for damages caused by smoking.)[61] The complaint in the Mississippi case was drafted by the firm of Ness, Motley, Loadholt, Richardson & Poole of Charleston, South Carolina.[62] Apparently Moore thought a firm specializing in asbestos litigation would have the necessary expertise.

---

55. Raymond Gangarosa, Brian Willis, and Frank Vandall, wrote: "The public hospital is the preferred plaintiff because it bears the costs of treating disease and illness caused by alcohol and tobacco, but experiences no economic benefit . . ." Gangarosa et al., *supra* note 36, at 85 n.19 (In the state's suits against the tobacco manufacturers, the states sued for the losses suffered by the public hospitals). Brian Willis had been one of the author's students at Emory and was working at the CDC.

56. *See* Telephone Conversation with Richard Daynard, Professor, Northeastern Law School, in Atlanta, Ga. (Nov. 26, 1997) [hereinafter Telephone Conversation with Richard Daynard].

57. *See Clarkdale's Mike Lewis: Father of the Tobacco Suits*, 4 Miss L. Wk., Oct. 19–25, 1997, at 1.

58. *See id.*

59. *See id.*

60. *See id.*

61. Vandall, *supra* note 32.

62. *See* Telephone Conversation with Richard Daynard, *supra* note 56.

At that point, however, there was a serious flaw in the theory of the case.[63] Because the suit by the state rested on the theory of subrogation, it would still be subject to the blockbuster defenses available against individual smokers: assumption of risk and cause-in-fact.[64] The cigarette manufacturers could easily defeat the state's subrogation claim by arguing the smokers knew smoking caused cancer and had assumed that risk.[65] The manufacturers could also perhaps force the state to prove the cancer was caused by smoking.

Susan Nial, a partner at Ness, Motley, asked Richard Daynard if he knew of any strategy to avoid these defenses.[66] Daynard replied he had recently been told by Dr. Ray Gangarosa that the states could bring their own suit—a direct action for the states' own losses—that would not be subject to the defenses of assumption of risk and cause-in-fact.[67]

Susan Nial understood the importance of Gangarosa's and Willis's theory (although she had never heard of them by name). In 1993, she drafted the claim as a direct action by the state rather than one resting on subrogation.[68] She based the claim on unjust enrichment, as suggested by Richard Daynard.[69] Ms. Nial spent long hours in the library perfecting the theory with Dick Scruggs and Steve Bozeman of Pascagoula, Mississippi.[70] She remembers many discussions with Richard Daynard and several law professors who were used to test the theory.[71] People said "she must be out of her mind" to sue the cigarette manufacturers. Ms. Nial reflects "they laughed when I sat down at the piano, but cheered when I played Chopin."[72] However, while others laughed at Ms. Nial's endeavor, Ronald Motley, a senior partner in the firm, supported and encouraged her.[73] In the end, state attorney general Michael Moore filed the complaint on behalf of the State of Mississippi, which was soon joined by forty other states, eventually

---

63. See id.

64. See id. Subrogation is clear in a car crash case. You are injured in a car crash. Your insurance company pays your damages and becomes subrogated to your claim for damages against the other driver. But the insurance company "steps into your shoes" and is also subject to the defenses against you, such as, assumption of risk or contributory negligence.

65. See id.

66. See id.

67. See id.

68. See id.

69. See id. Ms. Nial remembers Dick Scruggs made a substantial contribution to the unjust enrichment theory. See Telephone Conversation with Susan Nial, Partner, Law Firm of Ness, Motley, Loadholt, Richardson & Poole, in Atlanta, Ga. (Dec. 1, 1997) [hereinafter Telephone Conversation with Susan Nial].

70. See Telephone Conversation with Susan Nial, supra note 69.

71. See id.

72. Id.

73. See id.

leading to a proposed $368.5 billion settlement in June 1997.[74] This was finally negotiated to a $206 billion settlement, the largest civil litigation (tort) settlement in history.

After 1993, Moore spoke at several conferences Daynard presented at Northeastern University School of Law for state attorneys generals.[75] Moore's suit was later challenged by the governor of Mississippi, who brought a separate suit to prevent the attorney general from suing.[76] Despite the governor's efforts, Moore persisted and has since recovered $3.2 billion against the cigarette manufacturers for the State of Mississippi.[77]

Shortly after Moore filed his suit in Mississippi, Florida also filed suit against the cigarette manufacturers to recover the Medicaid costs expended by the state.[78] Florida's suit was based on a new Florida statute that had been drafted and enacted in secret.[79] The statute does not specifically mention cigarette manufacturers,[80] but merely says the state should be able to recover for the cost of Medicaid against those responsible for the expenditures.[81] Much to the surprise of the tobacco lobbyists,[82] the statute passed the Florida legislature.

---

74. *See* Jim Yardley, *Mississippi Wins Billions in Tobacco Deal,* ATL. J.-CONST., July 4, 1997, at A1.

75. *See* Telephone Conversation with Richard Daynard, *supra* note 56.

76. Governor Fordice asserted the attorney general needed the governor's approval before filing suit. *See Cigarette Companies See Mississippi Suit's Dismissal,* WALL ST. J., Feb. 21, 1996, at B9.

77. Attorney General Moore settled his state's suit against the tobacco companies for a reported $3.6 billion. *See* Judy Holland, *Tobacco Evidence Fills 2 Warehouses,* TIMES UNION (Albany, N.Y.), Sept. 21, 1997, at A2.

78. *See* Stephen Gillers, *Florida Backs Out on a Deal,* N.Y. TIMES, Oct. 10, 1997, at A1.

79. Governor Chiles of Florida said the bill had to be sneaked through the legislature because of "the strength of the special interests when you're trying to do something up here." Bill Moss, *Chiles Signs Anti-Tobacco Measure,* ST. PETERSBURG TIMES, May 27, 1994, at A1.

80. The Medicaid Third-Party Liability Act expressly eliminates the key defenses available to cigarette manufacturers: "Principles of common law and equity as to . . . comparative negligence, assumption of risk, and all other affirmative defenses normally available to a liable third party, are to be abrogated to the extent necessary to ensure full recovery by Medicaid from third-party resources. . . ." 1994 Fla. Laws ch. 251.

81. *See id.* The law had the effect of undercutting the traditional defense of tobacco companies that the fault should rest on the smoker. *See* Barry Meier, *Tobacco, Implant Settlements Offered Florida Gets $11.3 Billion, Public Health Concessions,* DETROIT FREE PRESS, Aug. 26, 1997, at A1. *See also* Linda Kleindienst & John Kennedy, *Law Declares Medicaid War on Tobacco,* ORLANDO SENTINEL, May 27, 1994, at C1.

82. *See* Kleindienst & Kennedy, *supra* note 81. Tobacco representatives had vowed to fight the legislation in court. *See* Mary Ellen Klas, *Tobacco Industry Vows to Fight New Liability Law,* PALM BEACH POST, May 27, 1994 at A10 (reporting two potential constitutional challenges that the tobacco industry might mount—the stripping of "traditional defenses" and a potential equal protection rights violation).

Similar to Mississippi, the governor of Florida challenged the suit. Again, despite the governor's efforts, the state litigation was also successful, resulting in a $11.3 billion settlement against the tobacco manufacturers.[83]

As an interesting footnote, there was a debate in Florida as to whether the $11.3 billion would be used by the state to educate children about the dangers of smoking or to help defray the costs of treating patients with tobacco-related injuries.[84] In addition, as part of the Florida settlement, all the cigarette billboards were removed and cigarette manufacturers were forced to stop recruiting children to become smokers.[85]

Since the filing of the Mississippi suit by Attorney General Moore, over forty states filed suits to recover their Medicare expenses against the cigarette manufacturers.[86] Interestingly, two tobacco-growing states, Georgia and South Carolina, also filed suit against the cigarette manufacturers.[87] However, this should not be a surprise, considering the injury and damage caused by cigarettes far exceed the value of the employment and income cigarettes bring to the states.[88]

The theory of Dr. Ray Gangarosa, Brian Willis, and Frank Vandall that Ms. Nial used as the foundation of the Mississippi case is that states could bring suits to recover the costs they expended in treating people who have suffered

---

83. The tobacco industry agreed to pay Florida $11.3 billion over a period of 25 years to settle its case with the state. *See Up to Speed, The Week's Top Stories, That Settles That,* ATL. J.-CONST., Aug. 31, 1997, at C2 [hereinafter *Up to Speed*].

84. *See Campaign for Tobacco-Free Kids Statement on Florida Tobacco Companies Suit,* U.S. NEWSWIRE, Aug. 25, 1997.

85. *See Tobacco Firms to Pay Fla. Billions,* BALTIMORE MORNING SUN, Aug. 26, 1997, at A1. Part of the settlement says tobacco companies will spend $200 million over the next two years to help dissuade children from smoking. *See id.*

86. These other state suits are premised on the same theory—that states can recover for expenses caused by tobacco products. The damages to the state were the expense of treating smokers who had contracted cancer. Moore filed his suit in 1994, and since then more than four out of every five states have followed suit. *See* Yardley, *supra* note 74, at A1.

87. *See* Foon Rhee, *Florida Gets $11.3 Billion from Tobacco; N.C. Waiting,* CHARLOTTE OBSERVER, Aug. 26, 1997, at A1. Georgia became the 41st state to file suit for recovery of public expenses due to tobacco. *See id.*

88. *See id.* Congress is also looking to implement a plan to wean tobacco growers from that crop and teach them to harvest other crops. *See id.* In Georgia, tobacco represents only 9.5% of the state's total agricultural production, valued at $200 million per year. *See* Editorial, *One Time Buy-Out of Tobacco Land Is Fair,* ATL. J.-CONST., Sept. 4, 1997, at A14. Smoking costs the nation more than $52 billion annually in health care and lost productivity. *See* Louis W. Sullivan, *Smoking Ailment Costing Nation $52 Billion,* ATL. J.-CONST., Feb. 21, 1990, at A7. *See also* Vandall, *supra* note 32, at 421 (noting the costs of tobacco outweigh the benefits by more than $17 billion).

tobacco-related injuries.[89] As a medical doctor, Gangarosa along with Willis espoused their theory in a paper they submitted to *Science* and the *Journal of the American Medical Association.* However, those publications did not understand the importance of the legal argument and did not publish the paper. Dr. Gangarosa then presented his direct action theory in 1992 to Richard Daynard at Northeastern University School of Law.[90]

Earlier in 1989, Ray Gangarosa and Brian Willis had asked the author to translate their technical and scientific theory into legal terminology and to co-author the article containing the theory of cigarette manufacturers' liability.[91]

89. *See* Gangarosa et al., *supra* note 36, at 85 (suggesting "an examination of the medical, social, historical, economic, and legal factors dictates that a cause of action against alcohol and tobacco manufacturers should be available to public hospitals to recover their expenditures for the uncompensated medical treatment that is necessitated by alcohol and tobacco abuse").

90. *See* Discussion with Ray Gangarosa in Atlanta, Ga. (Nov. 21, 1997).

91. *See* Gangarosa et al., *supra* note 36, at 81.In February 2002, Brian Willis sent the author an email asking for a clarification of the Southwestern Law Review Article:

Frank,

As we discussed last spring, I would like to have the Southwestern University School Law Review print a letter clarifying several issues in the article The Legal Theory and the Visionaries that Led to the Proposed $368.5 Billion Tobacco Settlement, which was published in 1998.

The basic point of clarification that is needed is that I developed the legal theory that Dr. Ray Gangarosa shared with Richard Daynard, which, according to the article on page 481, "Ms. Nial used in the Mississippi case" brought by the Mississippi Attorney General Mike Moore.

By way of background, Dr. Gangarosa contacted me in 1989 and asked me to help him write an article outlining a case for public hospitals to sue tobacco companies for the cost of treating uninsured patients who have tobacco-related illness. During the next year, while in law school and later while working at CDC, I researched this issue from the legal perspective while Ray continued to address the epidemiologic issues in the article. I soon realized that public hospitals would not be good plaintiffs due to the cost of litigation. However, I determined that states would be in a better position to sue tobacco companies because they were in a better position than hundreds of public hospitals to undertake the litigation and there was a cause of action under existing state laws to recover the cost of damages states incurred repairing damage to public property from private companies. A case I found, for example, the state recovered the cost of repairing a bridged that was damaged by a barge.

Dr. Gangarosa and I also discussed the economic issue of externalities in regard to this possible lawsuit. Further legal research revealed that no one had published anything that suggested the theory that states should be able to recover the costs incurred under Medicare or Medicaid, or by public hospitals caring for uninsured patients, for treating patients with tobacco-related illness.

According to the Southwestern University School Law Review article, on pages 481-482, "[a]s a medical doctor, Gangarosa espoused his theory in a paper that he

The author argued the states and public hospitals had been injured, and that their suits would skirt the defenses of assumption of risk and cause-in-fact.[92] The article was published by the *Fordham Journal of Urban Law.*[93]

6. The Tobacco Settlement

a. **Components of the Settlement** The suits brought by the forty states were preliminarily settled in June 1997, after a great deal of speculation as to whether the states would win anything.[94] As mentioned in the previous section, the amount of the settlement was $206 billion,[95] which will be paid to the states over a period of twenty-five years.[96]

In addition to the monetary payout, the settlement stipulates the cigarette manufacturers will eliminate both billboard and print advertisements and cease using caricatures, such as Joe Camel, that are aimed at attracting child smokers.[97] The settlement also stipulates the cigarette manufacturers will cease

---

submitted to Science and the Journal of the American Medical Association (JAMA). Please note that, as you correctly state, as a medical doctor and epidemiologist, Dr. Gangarosa contributed the medical and epidemiological evidence of the tobacco-related illness suffered by smokers. However, Dr. Gangarosa, as a medical doctor, did not develop the legal theory on which the proposed lawsuit was based. As the lawyer working with Dr. Gangarosa on the article I developed the legal theory and co-authored both of the articles submitted to Science and JAMA.

Again, on page 482 the Southwestern University School Law Review article states that, after Science and JAMA rejected the articles "Dr. Gangarosa then presented his direct action theory in 1992 to Richard Daynard at Northeastern University School of Law," and in the following paragraph it is stated that "In 1989, Ray Gangarosa and Brian Willis hired [asked] me to translate a technical, scientific theory into legal terminology and to co-author the article containing the theory of cigarette manufacturers' liability."

Dr. Gangarosa and I submitted our article to Science and JAMA in, respectively, I believe, 1991 and 1992. It was after the rejection from JAMA in 1992, after Gangarosa decided not to revise the article and resubmit it to another journal that I spoke with you regarding collaborating on the revising the article. You suggested that the article should be revised to a law review format and submitted to various law reviews. After this point, you had the lead on re-writing the article and submitting to the various law review journals.

92. *See id.* at 125–35.

93. *See id.*

94. The reason for this speculation was the tobacco companies had never paid a single penny to a plaintiff in any suit. *See* Vandall, *supra* note 32.

95. *See* Barry Meier, *Tobacco Lawyers' Papers Are Made Public*, N.Y. Times, Aug. 7, 1997, at A18.

96. *See* Barnaby J. Feder, *No Clear Outlook from Tobacco Settlement*, N.Y. Times, Aug. 3, 1997, at § 3, at 6.

97. *See* Chris Burritt, *Tobacco Deal: Companies Accept Penalties, Restrictions*, Atl. J.-Const., June 21, 1997, at A1.

recruiting children as consumers—and carries a penalty to be assessed against the manufacturers if they do not reduce the number of children smoking cigarettes.[98]

b. Post-Settlement That the tobacco industry has tremendous support in Congress is evidenced by the $50 billion tax credit for the tobacco manufacturers a Republican member of Congress (apparently either Newt Gingrich or Trent Lott) inserted into a bill.[99] The function of the tax credit was to offset the tax burden on the cigarette manufacturers to ease the pain of the settlement.[100] If the settlement was in the interest of the American people, it is not clear why the cigarette manufacturers should receive a tax credit—except to honor the power of the cigarette manufacturers.

The tobacco wars over the last fifty years are an excellent example of raw power at work. The tobacco manufacturers were able to mislead and control the courts from 1958 until 1996. The result was total victory for tobacco. The settlement only occurred because the tobacco interests met something more powerful: the states united in one suit. Nevertheless, the tobacco manufacturers were so confident they could control the results in individual suits by victims that these were carved out of the settlement, and continue, one by one, as of February 2010.[101]

The initial proposed settlement would have required Congressional approval because it included changes to the Federal Food, Drug, and Cosmetic Act.[102] This failed to pass. Therefore, the major cigarette companies continued negotiations with the states. In November 1998, forty-six states signed a contractual agreement, the Master Settlement Agreement (MSA), with the tobacco manufacturers for $206 billion.[103] Four states settled their tobacco cases separately from the MSA states.[104]

---

98. *See* Barry Meier, *New Negotiations Reported on Tobacco Pact,* N.Y. TIMES, Sept. 10, 1997, at A14. If the number of young people who smoke does not fall below certain goals over the next decade, the tobacco companies will have to pay up to $2 billion in fines per year. *See id.*

99. The credit was tucked away in tax-cut legislation. Many legislators claimed it was so well hidden, they had no idea it was there. *See* Editorial, *Another Gasp by Tobacco,* N.Y. TIMES, Aug. 19, 1997, at A22.

100. *See id.* In September 1997, the Senate voted 95 to 3 to kill the $50 billion credit. Newt Gingrich, feeling pressure from the public, urged the House of Representatives to kill the credit as well. *See* Editorial, *Tobacco Break Withers in Daylight,* ATL. J.-CONST., Sept.16, 1997, at A8.

101. For example, in Philip Morris v. Williams, 2007 WL 505781 (U.S.), the Oregon jury awarded a life-long smoker $1 million in compensatory damages and $79.5 million in punitive damages based on fraud.

102. http://assets.openCRS.com/rpts/RL32619-2004/203PDF.

103. *Id.*

104. *Id.*

7. A Solution to the Power Tobacco Exercises Over the Legal System

This section makes clear that because of problems with the present causes of action, substantial costs of smoking rest upon the nonsmoker as well as the smoker. It argues for a reversal of this subsidy, shifting the costs to the cigarette manufacturer and the smoker by means of a different cause of action: absolute liability.

The most important suit by individuals against cigarette manufacturers, *Cipollone v. Liggett Group,* demonstrates the need for absolute liability as a cause of action.[105]

Mr. and Mrs. Cipollone filed a complaint against several cigarette manufacturers in the federal district court on August 1, 1983[106] seeking damages resulting from Mrs. Cipollone's lung cancer. The promise of the *Cipollone* case (and several others)[107] was that the cigarette manufacturers would be taken to trial and required to pay for the damages caused by smoking. Indeed, the greater promise was that a wave of cigarette suits would arise and compel a shift in the allocation of cigarette losses.[108]

The reality of the *Cipollone* cases is more like a ripple on a pond. After twelve *Cipollone* decisions, almost seven years of litigating, and plaintiffs' expenditure of perhaps $6 million, the cigarette manufacturers could still boast they had not paid a cent to a cancer plaintiff.[109] The Cipollone case demonstrates the courts

---

105. Cipollone v. Liggett Group, Inc., 893 F.2d 541, 548–51 (3d Cir. 1990).

106. *Id.* at 552.

107. As of October 1985, at least 240 cigarette- and tobacco-related cases had been filed. Note, *Plaintiff Conduct as a Defense to Claims Against Cigarette Manufacturers,* 4 HARV. L. REV. 809 n.l. (1986). In June 1988, following the $400,000 *Cipollone* verdict, Atlanta attorney Guerry Thornton said, "I expect to see 300 to 500 new suits filed because of this." ATL. J.-CONST., June 19, 1988, at C7.

108. *See* Marc Z. Edell, *Cigarette Litigation: The Second Wave,* 22 TORT & INS. L.J. 90, 92 (1987).

> Why then . . . has there been a new wave of cigarette litigation sweeping the country? One of the primary reasons is the substantial changes in the law of strict liability, comparative negligence, state of the art, and other theories of liability. Another major factor is the approach taken by plaintiffs' counsel in the prosecution of large, sophisticated toxic-tort litigation. No longer do we find sole practitioners trying these cases, but rather larger firms with the financial, technical, and manpower resources necessary to go the distance. Groups of law firms have joined together to litigate these cases collectively.

> *Id.*

109. The court of appeals referred to their being ten *Cipollone* opinions plus the one in January equalings eleven. *Cipollone,* 893 F.2d at 564. The January decision was stayed to allow the New Jersey Supreme Court to interpret the New Jersey Products Liability Act. Cipollone v. Liggett Group, Inc., No. 88-5732 (3d Cir. Stay Granted 3/2/90).

"[Marc Z.] Edell [a New Jersey attorney who has argued much of the *Cipollone* case] says his firm has spent about $600,000 in out-of-pocket expenses and racked up about

are far from making a clear and coherent statement of cigarette manufacturers' liability. No cause of action has emerged that will enable smokers to recover their damages and shift the losses from the public to the smokers and cigarette manufacturers. Winning a cigarette case is far from certain. The settlement discussed above was between the states and the tobacco manufacturers; it provided nothing for individuals who have suffered and died or their families.

More litigation and greater complexity in cigarette cases was guaranteed when the federal court of appeals held in the *Cipollone* case that the Cigarette Labeling and Advertising Act of 1965 "preempts those state law damage actions relating to smoking and health that challenge either the adequacy of the warning on cigarette packages or the propriety of a party's actions with respect to the advertising and promotion of cigarettes . . . ."[110] On remand, the district court interpreted the appellate decision as "preempting the plaintiff's failure to warn, express warranty, fraudulent misrepresentation, and conspiracy to defraud claims to the extent that they sought to challenge the defendants' advertising, promotional, and public relations activities after January 1, 1966."[111] As a result of these decisions, a cause of action for failure to warn might exist for someone who began to smoke before 1965, but be barred for those who began thereafter. This was a huge victory for the powerful cigarette manufacturers as it seemed people who began to smoke after 1965 would have no suit based on failure to warn.

The *Cipollone* line of cases clearly demonstrates the need for a simpler and more efficient cause of action in dealing with cigarette cancer. The following proposal responds to this need by arguing for the adoption of absolute liability for cancer caused by smoking. The goal of the proposal is to reallocate the loss from smokers, nonsmokers, and their families and insurers to the cigarette manufacturers. The victims should be able to recover their economic losses from the tobacco manufacturers. Smoking should be a closed system.

$2 million in billable time in the *Cipollone* litigation." *Rust, Smoke Alarms,* CAL. LAW 22, 25 (Oct. 1987). This statement is three years old, however.

"The tobacco industry proudly points to the fact that it has never paid a single dollar to a plaintiff for a smoking-related illness. . . ." Note, *Liability of Cigarette Manufacturers for Smoking Induced Illness and Deaths,* 18 RUTGERS L.J. 165 (1986) (quoting from the PHILA. INQUIRER, Dec. 1, 1985, at A1).

110. *Cipollone,* 893 F.2d at 552.

111. *Id.* at 552–53. Other courts have reached the same result. *See* Rovsdon v. R.J. Reynolds Tobacco Co., 849 F.2d 230 (6th Cir. 1988), *aff'g* 623 F.Supp. 1189 (E.D. Tenn. 1985); Palmer v. Liggett Group, 825 F.2d 620 (1st Cir. 1987), *rev'g* F. Supp. 1171 (D. Mass. 1986); Stephen v. Am. Brands, 825 F. 2d 312 (11th Cir. 1987) (per curiam); Semowich v. R.J. Reynolds Tobacco Co., 1988 WL 86, 313 (N.D.N.Y. 1988). *But cf.* Forster v. R.J. Reynolds Tobacco Co., 423 N.W.2d 691, 700–01 (Minn. Ct. App. 1988) (no preemption found absent express statement from Congress).

a. The History, Policy, and Economics of Absolute Liability as Applied to Cigarette Manufacturers Under the historical theory of absolute liability, an injurer is liable if it causes damage.[112] There is no defense except the absence of causation.[113] In one of the earliest recorded torts cases (1466), the defendant was held liable on the basis of absolute liability:

> [I]f a man does a thing he is bound to do it in such a manner that by his deed no injury or damage is inflicted upon others . . . . [I]f a man commits an assault upon me and I cannot avoid him, if he wants to beat me, and I lift my stick in self-defense in order to prevent him, and there is a man in back of me, and I injure him in lifting my stick, in that case he would have an action against me. . . .[114]

Absolute liability is different from strict liability. In both strict liability related to land (referred to as abnormally dangerous activities by the American Law Institute), and strict liability in regard to products, there is a balancing of costs and benefits. For both of these forms of strict liability, defenses are available such as proximate cause and assumption of risk.[115] For absolute liability, however, the only defense is cause-in-fact.

This book proposes that cigarette manufacturers should be held liable on the basis of absolute liability: if a cigarette manufacturer causes injury to a smoker, it is liable. The remainder of this part will be devoted to considering why a cigarette manufacturer should be held absolutely liable for smoking-caused cancer from historical, social policy, and economic views.

i. A Historical View of Absolute Liability Civil liability began with absolute liability. To suggest cigarette manufacturers should be held absolutely liable is merely a return to the foundation of civil liability. The basis of primordial law was absolute liability resting upon causation:

> [If at] your request I accompany you when you are about your own affairs: my enemies fall upon and kill me, you must pay for my death. You take me to see a wild beast show or that interesting spectacle, a mad man; beast or mad man kills me; you must pay. You hang up your sword; someone else knocks it down so that it cuts me; you must pay. In some of these cases can you honestly swear that you did nothing that helped to bring about death or wound.[116]

---

112. *See* Wex S. Malone, *Ruminations on the Role of Fault in the History of the Common Law of Torts*, 31 LA. L. REV. 1, 3 (1970).

113. *Id.*

114. Anonymous, Y.B. IV, Edw. 4, Fol. 7, pl. 18 (1466).

115. *See* W. PAGE KEETON ET AL., PROSSER AND KEETON ON THE LAW OF TORTS § 710–12 (5th ed. 1984).

116. Malone, *supra* note 112, at 1.

Prior to about 1800, liability was absolute: "The imposition of virtual no-fault liability in both Trespass and Trespass on the Case in England continuously throughout the middle ages and, in fact, up until the nineteenth century . . . . reflected the ethical, social and economic needs of the times . . . ."[117]

Within the last forty years, absolute liability has been applied to abnormally dangerous activities such as blasting. In 1969, the New York Court of Appeals in *Spano v. Perini Corp.* stated:

> The concept of absolute liability in blasting cases is hardly a novel one. The overwhelming majority of American jurisdictions have adopted such a rule. . . . Indeed, this court itself, several years ago, noted that a change in our law would conform to the more widely (indeed almost universal) approved doctrine that a blaster is absolutely liable for any damages he causes, with or without trespass.[118]

If absolute liability should apply to blasting because of the certain and unpreventable damages, it should apply even more to the manufacturing of cigarettes considering the four hundred thousand smoking-caused deaths per year. As concluded in *Spano:* "The question . . . was . . . *who* should bear the cost of any resulting damage . . . ."[119] With cigarette-caused cancer, the question is also who should bear the loss: smokers, families, nonsmokers, and society in general—or the cigarette manufacturers?

The tobacco manufacturers should be subject to absolute liability in order to pay their own way.[120] The impact of the preemption, assumption of risk, and cause-in-fact defenses in cigarette litigation is that the smoker is often going to lose, in part because of inadequate financial resources to bring suit.[121]

Since 1849 there have been numerous legal developments (comparable to the absolute liability being proposed) that make it easier for an injured person to win in tort: strict liability, res ipsa loquitur, negligence per se, and the deterioration of immunities.[122] Absolute liability, which does not require the plaintiff to prove negligence, is based on the theory the loss should rest upon the seller.[123] Absolute liability appears designed for cigarette victims.

---

117. *Id.* at 24.

118. Spano v. Perini, 250 N.E.2d 31, 33 (N.Y. 1969).

119. *Id.* at 34.

120. The price of the product should represent not merely labor and materials, but also the damages caused by the product.

121. *See* Townsley & Hanks, *The Trial Court's Responsibility to Make Cigarette Disease Litigation Affordable and Fair*, 25 CAL. W. L. REV. 275, 276–77 (1988).

122. *See* FRANK VANDALL, STRICT LIABILITY: LEGAL AND ECONOMIC ANALYSIS 6–12 (1989).

123. *See* Greenman v. Yuba Power Prods., Inc., 377 P.2d 897 (Cal. 1963).

The concepts of res ipsa loquitur[124] and negligence per se[125] reflect the underpinnings of absolute liability and have furthered an expansion of liability.[126] Professor Gregory argued:

> For years there have been some American precedents openly embracing the doctrine of [absolute liability] as part of our common law. But most of our state courts have been more cautious; and if they have achieved what seems like absolute liability, they have done it under some category of negligence. As indicated above, *res ipsa loquitur* was their normal recourse, in such instances.[127]

The theory of negligence per se is that if a person violates a regulation or an ordinance (state or federal), the court may consider this evidence of negligence.[128] In truth, it is unlikely a cigarette manufacturer will be found in violation of a statute for the simple reason that the statutes have been drafted expressly to protect the cigarette manufacturer.[129]

With the expansion in tort liability over the last 160 years aimed at making it easier for an injured person to sue and recover, the insulation of the tobacco industry is an anomaly.[130] Absolute liability is a means of finally ending this insulation.

ii. The Reasons for Applying Absolute Liability to Tobacco Manufacturers The reasons that have been embraced for the application of strict liability to product sellers also support the extension of absolute liability to cigarette manufacturers.

---

124. KEETON ET AL., *supra* note 115, at 242–62.

125. *Id.* at 229–31.

126. *See* Frank Vandall, *Applying Strict Liability to Pharmacists*, 18 U. TOL. L. REV. 1, 16–18 (1986).

127. Charles O. Gregory, *Trespass to Negligence to Absolute Liability*, 37 VA. L. REV. 359, 383 (1951).

128. *See* KEETON ET AL., *supra* note 115, at 229–31.

129. The Federal Food, Drug and Cosmetics Act, *infra* note 193, and the Consumer Product Safety Act, *infra* note 196, both exclude tobacco products from their coverage. New Jersey, 15 PSLR 670, section 3(a)(2) and California, Civil Code, section 1714.45(a)(1), passed legislation that protects the cigarette manufacturers.

In early 2009, President Obama gave some power to the FDA to regulate tobacco. *See,* Family Smoking, *infra*, note 178.

130. In contrast, the veil protecting the manufacturers of alcohol from suit has been pierced. Summary judgment for the beer manufacturer was reversed in Hon v. Stroh Brewery Co., 835 F.2d 510 (3d Cir. 1987), where the plaintiff allegedly developed pancreatitis from beer consumption. Again the court in Brune v. Brown Forman Corp., 758 S.W.2d 827 (Tex. App. 1988), reversed a summary judgment in favor of the manufacturer. The issue was whether the manufacturer of tequila had a duty to warn a college student who allegedly died as a result of drinking tequila shooters of the dangers of drinking straight shots of Pepe Lopez Tequila.

These reasons run the full spectrum from reallocating the loss and the protection of health through superior knowledge and economic considerations.

(A) REALLOCATING THE LOSS The reasoning behind reallocating the loss is that the cigarette manufacturer is in a better position than the smoker (and society in general) to bear the damages caused by smoking. In 1944, Justice Traynor in *Escola v. Coca Cola* stated in his concurring opinion that liability in products cases should rest upon absolute liability. He reasoned: "[T]he risk of injury can be insured by the manufacturer and distributed among the public as a cost of doing business. It is to the public interest to discourage the marketing of products having defects that are a menace to the public."[131] In *Greenman v. Yuba Power Products, Inc.*, the California Supreme Court adopted the reasoning and holding that had been foreshadowed in *Escola*, concluding: "The purpose of such liability is to insure that the cost of injuries resulting from defective products are borne by the manufacturers that put such products on the market rather than by the injured persons who are powerless to protect themselves."[132] This reasoning goes back at least to the 1913 case of *Mazetti v. Armour*: "The obligation of the manufacturer should . . . rest . . . upon 'the demands of social justice.' . . . Our holding is that . . . a manufacturer of food products under modern conditions impliedly warrants his goods . . . ."[133]

The impact of absolute liability upon cigarette manufacturers is they will raise the price of their goods to cover losses. This will have the beneficial effect of forcing the price of the product to increase and reflect the damage it causes.[134] As there will be many large cancer "claims" under absolute liability to which all cigarette manufacturers will be subject, the impact upon cigarette manufacturers will be clear. It is unlikely one manufacturer will have a competitive

---

131. Escola v. Coca Cola Bottling Co., 150 P.2d 436, 440–44 (Cal. 1944) (Traynor, J., concurring).

132. Greenman v. Yuba Power Prods., Inc., 377 P.2d 897, 901 (Cal. 1963).

133. Mazetti v. Armour & Co., 135 P. 633, 636 (Wash. 1913).

134. There may be a possibility that shifting all of these cancer losses to the cigarette manufacturers will force them into bankruptcy. If the cigarette manufacturers went bankrupt, large portions of the losses might then be shifted back upon the nonsmokers, smokers, and the public in general. There are several replies to this. First, there is no data on how much loss the cigarette manufacturers could absorb before being forced into bankruptcy. Judging from the billions of dollars per year they spend on promotions, their capacity to absorb losses may be enormous. Second, products liability suits are surgically precise, not bludgeons. In the Pinto gas tank case, the Pinto was removed from the market. Ford has continued to prosper, however. Indeed, the "father of the Pinto," Lee Iacocca, seems to be doing quite well. Finally, a "golden goose" approach would likely be employed by the bankruptcy court. A separate trust would be created by the court and funded by the cigarette manufacturers. The level of funding would guarantee fair payments to injured smokers but would not kill the "golden goose," the cigarette manufacturers. *See* ATL. J.-CONST., June 26, 1990, at E1.

advantage over another under absolute liability. Smokers will have few choices: pay the new, higher price or quit.[135] The reallocation of losses to cigarette manufacturers will have two benefits: (1) prices will rise and some people will stop smoking, and (2) fewer cigarettes will be sold.[136]

(B) HEALTH PROTECTION A fundamental reason for applying absolute liability to cigarette manufacturers is to protect life and health.[137] The theory is that if the manufacturer is subject to absolute liability, it will exercise a high degree of care to avoid liability. Critics might respond by saying a cigarette will always be lethal. However, society does not know the extent to which a cigarette can be made safe. We may have seen the light of a safer cigarette in the palladium example.[138] Perhaps it will be possible for the cigarette manufacturers to develop a cigarette that does not cause cancer or a form of nicotine that is not addicting.[139] At present, society simply does not know how safe a cigarette might become. If it is accurate to state that holding manufacturers liable has made numerous products safer (such as automobiles,[140] airplanes,[141] and vaporizers[142]), it makes sense absolute liability will also encourage manufacturers to develop safer cigarettes.

---

135. Certainly, rather than pay the higher prices, some smokers may grow their own tobacco and roll their own cigarettes.

136. Compare:

The available clinical and research data suggest that the demand for cocaine is relatively elastic among the great majority of consumers who are occasional or recreational users. . . . Price increases will reduce the quantity demanded, while price decreases should have the opposite effect. On the other hand. . . . addicts represent inelastic demand. Addicts are less likely than nonaddicts to be responsive, to changes in price in setting their demand for cocaine.

A. Morgan Cloud, *Cocaine, Demand and Addiction: A Study of the Possible Convergence of Rational Theory and National Policy,* 42 VAND. L. REV. 725, 762–63 (1989).

137. The application of absolute liability to cigarette manufacturers will force them to invest in research for a safer cigarette. It may also encourage them to seek a "cure" for cigarette-induced cancer. If a "cure" were discovered that was cheap and effective, the cigarette manufacturers could greatly reduce the number of cancer-related damage suits. This discovery would, of course, be of great value to all of society.

138. The "safer" palladium cigarette would reduce the risk of lung cancer by eight to seventeen percent. Cipollone v. Liggett Group, Inc., 683 F. Supp. 1487, 1493 (D.N.J. 1988).

139. Current studies suggest nicotine is the addictive substance in tobacco., SURGEON GENERAL OF THE PUBLIC HEALTH SERVICE, U.S. DEP'T OF HEALTH, EDUC. & WELFARE, THE HEALTH CONSEQUENCES OF SMOKING: CANCER V at i (1982) [hereinafter REPORT OF THE SURGEON GENERAL].

140. *See* Turner v. Gen. Motors Corp., 514 S.W.2d 497 (Tex. Civ. App. 1974).

141. *See* McGee v. Cessna Aircraft Co., 147 Cal. Rptr. 694 (Cal. Ct. App. 1978).

142. *See* McCormack v. Hankscraft Co., 154 N.W.2d 488 (Minn. 1967).

(c) SUPERIOR KNOWLEDGE The third reason for holding a cigarette manufacturer absolutely liable is that it is an expert in regard to cigarettes. The courts have indicated that because of their superior knowledge, it is more appropriate to hold the manufacturers liable than the consumer.[143] This is especially true in regard to cigarettes. The average smoker is often not well educated or at the top of the income ladder[144] (although certainly there are numerous exceptions).[145] The new teen smoker is not likely to realize cigarettes are as addictive as heroin[146] or kill "more than the combined death tolls from alcohol, illegal drugs, traffic accidents, suicide, and homicide . . . ."[147] He or she is not likely to appreciate that each year cigarettes kill more than the total combined American battle deaths in World War II and Vietnam[148] or that smoking causes cancer of the lungs, larynx, oral cavity, and esophagus as well as heart disease.[149] Although these smokers may have heard of "coffin nails,"[150] they may not realize the truth of the statement as they have never seen someone die slowly from emphysema. Since 1950, perhaps twenty-four million Americans have died from smoking- caused cancer and related illnesses.[151] Absolute liability allows society to treat the cigarette manufacturer as an expert in such things. Held to this level of knowledge, the cigarette manufacturer will take appropriate action in regard to safety in order to reduce the price of the product. In contrast, the addicted smoker is not in a position to make a rational choice.[152]

(d) THE CHEAPEST COST AVOIDER Judge Calabresi has developed a unique test for strict liability. His goal is to reduce the amount spent on the entire legal system because of "a desire to accomplish better primary accident

---

143. *See* Borel v. Fibreboard Paper Prods., 493 F.2d 1076 (5th Cir. 1973), *cert. denied*, 419 U.S. 869 (1974).

144. "[B]lacks, teenage girls and people with a high school education or less continue to pick up the habit. . . .

[T]he national Centers for Disease Control (CDC) said about 1.5 million Americans—mostly white, well-educated adults—kick the habit each year, but at least a million others—predominantly teenagers and women with less than a college education—join the ranks of smokers. . . . The researchers said smoking habits have changed . . . from a widespread practice among all segments of American society to an addiction of poorly educated and low-income people. . . ." ATL. J.- CONST., Jan. 6, 1989, at A3.

145. It is rumored both President Obama and Justice Thomas smoke.

146. REPORT OF THE SURGEON GENERAL, *supra* note 139, at iv–v.

147. ATL. J.- CONST., Feb. 21, 1987, at A8.

148. *Id.*

149. *Health & Environment, supra* note 19, at 338–40.

150. *See* R. MILES, COFFIN NAILS AND CORPORATE STRATEGIES 30–53 (1982).

151. 400,000 deaths per year times 60 years equals 24 million.

152. *See* REPORT OF THE SURGEON GENERAL, *supra* note 139, at i.

cost reduction."[153] To reach this goal, he proposes a test that goes beyond both negligence and traditional strict liability:

> The strict liability test we suggest does not require that a government institution make such a cost-benefit analysis. It requires of such an institution only a decision as to which of the parties to the accident *is in the best position to make the cost-benefit analysis between accident costs and accident avoidance costs and to act on that decision once it is made.* The question for the court reduces to a search for the cheapest cost avoider.[154]

If we ask who is the cheapest cost avoider as between the smoker and the cigarette manufacturer, the answer will always be the manufacturer. It has the assets, experience, knowledge, and ability to compile data, conduct experiments, test, and make changes in the product.

(E) ECONOMIC ANALYSIS In terms of economic efficiency, it would seem that if we are going to permit smoking, its impact should be isolated to those directly involved. We should create a closed system in which the costs of smoking are born solely by cigarette manufacturers and smokers. The costs of smoking should be internalized, and the price of cigarettes should reflect all the damages they cause.[155] Absolute liability would go far toward accomplishing this.

Today, the problem is that the costs of smoking are paid by nonsmokers as well as smokers.[156] This occurs in two ways. First, if smokers have insurance,

---

153. Guido Calabresi & Jon T. Hirschoff, *Toward a Test for Strict Liability in Torts*, 81 YALE L.J. 1055 (1972).

154. *Id.* at 1060.

155. *See* Steven Shavell, *Strict Liability Versus Negligence*, 9. J. LEGAL STUD. 1 (1980): A. POLINSKY, AN INTRODUCTION TO LAW AND ECONOMICS 98 (1983).On the other hand, cigarettes contain all of the elements necessary to be banned by the Consumer Product Safety Commission. *See* 15 U.S.C. §§ 2051, 2056, 2057, 2058, 2061, 2064 (1990). Of course, the CPSC expressly lacks jurisdiction over tobacco products. *See supra* note 142.Three wheel all-terrain vehicles were recently banned. See United States v. Polaris Indus., No. 87-3525 (D.D.C. Dec. 30, 1987) (1987 WL 33507).

156. In terms of health insurance contracts, arguably nonsmokers have no basis to complain. They knew the price of the insurance when they purchased it, and cannot now object because part of that price includes the coverage of smokers' cancer. However, in terms of efficiency, both Shavell and Polinsky argue the price of a product should reflect the damages it causes. Spreading the losses to nonsmokers masks the true cost of smoking. *See supra* note 155.

Another reply to the contract argument is that placing the loss on the cigarette manufacturers has a strong deterrence function. *See* Escola v. Coca Cola Bottling Co., 150 P.2d 436 (Cal. 1944). The manufacturers will then seek the means to reduce damages.

Of course, some of the benefits from the taxes on tobacco products accrue to nonsmokers. *See* Manning et al., *supra* note 23, at 1604; WHELAN, *supra* note 19, at 150.

they recover their medical expenses from their insurance carriers.[157] These expenses are in turn spread among the other smoking and nonsmoking policy holders.[158] The result is that through increased health insurance premiums, non-smokers bear much of the costs for the smoker's "freedom" to smoke. A closed system could be accomplished by forcing cigarette manufacturers to pay for most smoking-caused damages through a suit based on absolute liability. The manufacturer would, in turn, pass on the costs by raising prices. As the system would then be closed, nonsmokers would no longer shoulder the costs of smoking. Because of the higher prices, fewer would begin to smoke or continue to do so.

Second, if smokers lack insurance or exhaust it and other assets, they will turn to welfare.[159] The costs of smoking are then spread among both the smoking and nonsmoking public. Economically this is disadvantageous because it conceals the real costs of smoking from both the smoker and the public. That is, cigarettes are inexpensive because the manufacturers do not have to pay for the damages they cause, these costs are covertly spread among the nonsmoking public. As cigarettes are a discrete product that are neither necessities nor building blocks (such as steel), it would make more sense to place the loss on the manufacturers and allow the price of cigarettes to rise so as to reflect their actual costs. As discussed earlier in this chapter, this was the core concept in the tobacco settlement of 1998: reimburse the states for funds they had expended to treat tobacco victims. However, as previously noted the settlement did nothing for individual smokers and their families.

Some argue that because of heavy taxes on tobacco, cigarettes pay their own way.[160] However, these taxes flow into a general fund and are not designated for smokers' injuries.[161] These funds are not available to injured smokers who do not make welfare claims and do not affect smokers' insurance claims. By not being set aside for smokers' health care expenses, these sales taxes help to conceal the true costs of smoking. They make tobacco appear to be just another product.

---

157. Examples of such insurance would be Blue Cross/Blue Shield and health maintenance organizations.

158. Expenses for cigarette cancer are treated like other payments and spread among all of the policy holders. See WHELAN, *supra* note 19, at 150.

159. *Id.*

160. "Although nonsmokers subsidize smoker's medical care and group life insurance, smokers subsidize non-smokers pensions and nursing home payments. On balance, smokers probably pay their way at the current level of excise taxes on cigarettes." Manning et al., *supra* note 23, at 1604.

161. "[T]he amount of revenue obtained from these taxes [state and federal excise taxes on cigarettes] is woefully inadequate to cover the cost of smoking. If cigarette smoking provides any economic 'benefit' to the general population, it does so by reducing Social Security payouts to smokers who die prematurely." WHELAN, *supra* note 19, at 150.

(F) OTHER CONSIDERATIONS Cigarettes are addictive! The 1988 Surgeon General's report stated:

Careful examination of the data makes it clear that cigarettes and other forms of tobacco are addicting. An extensive body of research has shown that nicotine is the drug in tobacco that causes addiction. Moreover, the processes that determine tobacco addiction are similar to those that determine addiction to drugs such as heroin and cocaine.[162]

What this means is that children who try smoking even for a short time will likely become addicted.[163]

In addition, cigarette smoking has little social benefit.[164] When courts talk about strict liability and negligence, they often say that liability depends on

---

162. REPORT OF THE SURGEON GENERAL, *supra* note 139, at iii.

"Most smokers want to quit, but the task can be so daunting that surprisingly few try, fewer succeed, and even fewer seek any help to stop. . . .

During the 1980s about 17.3 million have tried to quit for at least a day each year, but only 1.3 million stay off for a year or more. Of those, about 40 percent relapse in two to 10 years, and half of those never try to quit again."

ATL. J.- CONST., July 25, 1989, at C1.

Schwartz argues that cigarettes are not addictive: "[A]llegedly addictive substances such as tobacco and alcohol do not generate physical withdrawal costs that are so high as to overcome the will of an ordinary person to discontinue use when she comes to believe that the costs f consuming exceed the benefits." Alan Schwartz, *Views of Addiction and the Duty to Warn*, 75 VA. L. REV. 509, 521–22 (1989).

163. *See* Koop, *supra* note 26.

164. An argument is sometimes made that cigarettes have substantial social utility because the cigarette manufacturers donate millions to the arts and academic research as well as provide jobs. However, an early *Cipollone* case put that line of reasoning to rest: Evidence of the benefits of cigarette production to the tobacco industry, the Internal Revenue Service, stockholders and employees, and to society at large was irrelevant and inadmissible in an action to recover from a cigarette manufacturer for the death from cancer of a consumer who smoked. Under a risk-utility analysis, the risk to the consumer could not be measured against the benefit to society as a test of a product's defectiveness. To be admissible, the evidence must show the benefit to the individual consumer outweighed the risks.

Cipollone v. Liggett Group, 644 F. Supp. 283, 290 (D.N.J. 1986).

To admit into evidence all of the jobs created by the activity and the donations made by the sellers would suggest that selling cocaine is a socially beneficial activity.

Smokers would likely argue there is psychological satisfaction in smoking, and that it is a response to peer group pressure. If smoking were not so lethal, this argument might have some merit. Peer group pressure is an acceptable reason for trying a hula hoop or trying to water ski. It is not an acceptable reason for playing Russian roulette with a friend.

whether the costs of avoiding the activity exceed its benefit. For example, Judge Learned Hand in *Carroll Towing* stated:

> [T]he owners duty . . . to provide against resulting injuries is a function of three variables: (1) the probability that she will break away; (2) the gravity of the resulting injury, if she does; (3) the burden of adequate precautions. . . . [I]f the probability be called P; the injury L; and the burden B; liability depends upon whether B is less than L multiplied by P; i.e., whether B is less than PL.[165]

Similarly the 1978 case of *Barker v. Lull* concludes:

> We hold that a trial judge may properly instruct the jury that a product is defective in design . . . if the plaintiff proves that the product's design proximately caused his injury and the defendant fails to prove . . . that on balance the benefits of the challenged design outweigh the risk of danger inherent in such design.[166]

Benefit is often a challenging question in cases involving defective automobiles,[167] airplanes,[168] and forklifts[169] because the social benefit of the product is substantial. This is an easy question to answer for cigarettes, however, because they have no beneficial use. The myth is that smoking is relaxing and helps the smoker to concentrate.[170] Actually, smoking merely relieves the tension produced by the nicotine addiction.[171] If the smoker did not smoke, he or she would not be addicted to nicotine, would not be tense, and would not need a cigarette to relax. For those who argue that smoking keeps them slim, research shows it only keeps off five to ten pounds on the average.[172] There are safer ways to lose weight.

---

165. United States v. Carroll Towing Co., 159 F.2d 169, 173 (2d Cir. 1947).

166. Barker v. Lull Eng'g Co., 574 P.2d 443, 455–56 (Cal. 1978).

167. *See* Turner v. Gen. Motors Corp., 514 S.W.2d 497 (Tex. Ct. App. 1974).

168. *See* McGee v. Cessna Aircraft Co., 147 Cal. Rptr. 694 (Cal. Ct. App. 1978).

169. *See Barker*, 574 P.2d at 455–56.

170. "Beyond the physical addiction, there is the social-psychological dependence on the smoking habit. For many smokers, the behavior modification needed to stop smoking presents more of a barrier than the physical addiction. (For example, many people who give up smoking 'don't know what to do' with their hands.)" WHELAN, *supra* note 19, at 2.

171. *See* REPORT OF THE SURGEON GENERAL, *supra* note 139, at iv. Peer pressure and psychological addiction cannot be dismissed of course. "A substantial part of the 'enjoyment' [from smoking] that . . . occurs comes from releasing the 'tension' caused by the gnawing, cigarette induced desire." A. A. White, *Strict Liability of Cigarette Manufacturers and Assumption of Risk*, 29 LA. L. REV. 589, 596 (1969).

172. "Smokers on average weigh five to 10 pounds less than non-smokers." ATL. J.- CONST., Apr. 6, 1989 at A10.

Whelan concluded in 1984 that the costs of smoking exceed the benefits by over $17 billion:

> According to 1978 estimates, smoking accounts for nearly 8 percent of all direct health care costs and over 11 percent of the total direct and indirect cost of disease in the United States. . . .
>
> . . . [C]igarette-related diseases are responsible for more than $11 billion per year in medical expenses and $36 billion in lost productivity. . . .
>
> These figures do not take into account the indirect impact on families, employers, friends, community, etc., or the multiplier effects of lost incomes.[173]

Whelan suggests cigarettes may contribute only $29.2 billion to the economy annually: "[T]otal domestic sales are over $20 billion per year. . . . Exports bring in another $2.2 billion per year. Federal, state and municipal revenues from excise and sales taxes on tobacco products amounted to over $7 billion in 1981."[174] Whelan admits: "No economists has ever attempted a comprehensive and complete assessment of tobacco's effect on the U.S. economy, including both the costs related to tobacco-induced disease and its contribution to the Gross National Product. . . ."[175]

Help in dealing with the cigarette problem is unlikely to come from Congress, as most legislation has worked to insulate and protect the powerful cigarette manufacturers. This is also likely to be true in the future. Under the Food, Drug, and Cosmetics Act, a drug is defined as: "(B) articles intended for use in the diagnosis, cure, mitigation, treatment, or prevention of disease in man . . .; (C) articles (other than food) intended to affect the structure or any function of the body of man. . . ."[176] Under this definition, it is clear cigarettes are strong drugs (for example, they adversely affect the oral cavity, lungs, heart, and kidneys). We would therefore expect cigarettes to be regulated by the Food and Drug Administration (FDA). This is a faulty assumption, however. A court rejected the regulation of cigarettes as "drugs" under the Food, Drug, and Cosmetics Act, reflecting the court's response to tobacco power:

> The court granted summary judgment against an anti-smoking group's effort to force the F.D.A. to regulate cigarettes. The court agreed with the Commissioner's view that the statutory definition included "only those cigarettes for which therapeutic claims have been made," emphasizing that "[t]he 'intent' element of the definition of drug, when applied to cigarettes, has always been construed as that of the vendor."[177]

---

173. *See* WHELAN, *supra* note 19, at 146–47.

174. *Id.* at 149.

175. *Id.*

176. 21 U.S.C. § 321 (2008).

177. Action on Smoking & Health v. Califano, Food Drug Cosm. L. Rep. (CCH) ¶ 38.219 (D.D.C. 1979).

Clearly, the court could have easily gone the other way. In June 2009, President Obama signed a bill allowing the FDA to regulate tobacco.[178]

The Consumer Product Safety Commission (CPSC) was implemented to protect the consumer from injurious products.[179] However, the Consumer Product Safety Act carefully excludes tobacco (the most dangerous product) from the province of the agency: "The term 'consumer product' . . . does not include—(B) tobacco and tobacco products."[180] Thus, tobacco products are insulated from CPSC review.

In Congress, we have seen the meticulous steps taken to avoid protecting the consumer from the hazards of cigarette smoking.[181] No meaningful legislation that encroaches upon tobacco manufacturing or sales is likely to come out of Congress. Professor Macey provides an explanation:

> According to the so-called interest group or economic theory of legislation, market forces provide strong incentives for politicians to enact laws that serve private rather than public interests, and hence statutes are supplied by lawmakers to the political groups or coalitions that outbid competing groups.[182]

---

178. In June 2009, President Obama signed the bill putting tobacco products under FDA regulation. Family Smoking Prevention and Tobacco Control Act, Pub. L. No. 111-31, H.R. 1256, 111th Cong. (2009) (to be codified in several sections of 21 U.S.C. 301).

FDA regulation of tobacco creates a risk, however. If the Supreme Court applies preemption to the FDA tobacco regulations, that could trump state and federal damage suits.

179. *See* Consumer Product Safety Act, 15 U.S.C. § 2051(a)(3) (1990).

180. 15 U.S.C. § 2052(a)(1).

181. *See* WHELAN, *supra* note 19, at 106–08. The pressure from cigarette manufacturers is often not subtle: "Tobacco companies hav/e contributed more than $1 million to Sen. Jesse Helm's political campaigns and built a museum in his honor." ATL. J.-CONST., July 2, 1990, at A4.

"The tobacco industry is forging new, behind-the-scenes relationships in its effort to fight smoking bans and excise taxes and polish its image.

The $35 billion-a-year industry has aligned itself with organized labor and black. Hispanic and women's groups whose civil rights rhetoric and appeals for social justice have a special resonance in American life.

Cash and public relations know-how are being lavished on these allies. Tobacco money may buy anything from scholarships and entertainment to printing and legal services."

ATL. J.-CONST., May 23, 1988, at C1.

182. Jonathan R. Macey, *Promoting Public-Regarding Legislation Through Statutory Interpretation: An Interest Group Model*, 86 COLUM. L. REV. 223, 224 (1986) (citations omitted): *see also* RICHARD POSNER, THE FEDERAL COURTS 271 (1985); Mark Green & Ralph Nader, *Economic Regulation vs. Competition: Uncle Sam the Monopoly Man*, 82 YALE L.J. 871, 876 (1973).

An example of this is the Cigarette Labeling and Advertising Act of 1965.[183] Today, as modified that Act provides that each pack of cigarettes and each advertisement for cigarettes must contain one of four warnings. One reason the cigarette-label warnings have largely failed is because of the effective advertising and marketing by cigarette manufacturers. These four sterile warnings have been undermined by cigarette overpromotion. In *Stevens v. Parke, Davis & Co.*,[184] the drug manufacturer provided a warning on the label of the risks of Chloromycetin, an antibiotic. However, Parke-Davis then engaged in an elaborate advertising campaign, led by their "detail men," to persuade medical doctors that the warnings were too severe and should be disregarded. The court held the injured patient could recover from Parke-Davis because the advertising and overpromotion by Parke-Davis significantly watered down the warnings. *Stevens* supports the argument the cigarette warnings have been undermined by clever and continuous advertising and marketing.[185] The point is that the bland and vague federally required cigarette warnings are eclipsed by inviting and enticing cigarette promotions.[186]

iii. Absolute Liability for Damages from Smoking The proposal has four parts.[187] First, the liability of the cigarette manufacturer is absolute. Second, the plaintiff who has regularly smoked at least one pack of cigarettes per day for at least fifteen years has a presumption that his or her cancer was caused by smoking. Third, the damage recovery is limited to four types of cancer: lung, larynx, oral cavity, and esophagus (but including the cancer resulting from the spread of the original cancer). The plaintiff must submit a statement from a physician (oncologist) that the victim has contracted one of the four types of cancer and that it was probably caused by smoking. Fourth, damages under the proposal are restricted to medical expenses and lost wages; punitive damages are not available, and there is a $200,000 cap on pain and suffering.

One of the most important aspects of the absolute liability cause of action is that it does not depend upon advertising, promotion, or warnings by the cigarette manufacturer; therefore, it will not be affected by the *Cipollone* preemption decision.[188] Further, as absolute liability has as its foundational policy the reallocation of losses from smokers, nonsmokers, and the general public to the

---

183. 15 U.S.C. § 1333–36 (2009).

184. 507 P.2d 653 (Cal. 1973).

185. *See supra* note 184.

186. This point has been somewhat weakened since the 1996 tobacco settlement, which called for a reduction in advertising to children. But advertising is not the sole problem. Cigarettes have always been viewed as the key to maturity and independence. Regardless of ads, children have always sought cigarettes.

187. Perhaps the first article to mention a no-fault scheme for cigarette caused cancer was Garner's. Donald W. Garner, *Cigarettes and Welfare Reform*, 26 EMORY L.J. 269, 314–15 (1977).

188. *See* Cipollone v. Liggett Group, Inc., 789 F.2d 181 (3d Cir. 1986).

cigarette manufacturers, defenses such as assumption of risk, contributory negligence, and misuse will not apply.

Later cases would be settled, but the proposal would function as follows in the first few. John sues XYZ (cigarette manufacturer) for one or more of the four cancers caused by smoking. The judge adopts the absolute liability cause of action and sends John's case to the jury. The only issues for the jury are cause-in-fact and damages as the only defense is cause-in-fact. Because John proves he smoked a brand of cigarette manufactured by XYZ for over fifteen years, and an oncologist testifies John's lung cancer was probably caused by smoking, John receives a presumption that XYZ caused his cancer. This presumption shifts the burden of proof to XYZ[189] However, this does not mean that all cases will go to the jury, or that the jury verdict will always be for the plaintiff.[190] For example, the judge might find after XYZ presents evidence that there is insufficient evidence that one of the four types of cancer is indeed present.[191] In *Galbraith v. R.J. Reynolds Tobacco Co.*, the plaintiff lost before the jury because cause-in-fact was not proved.[192] (The jury reported that they wanted to find for the plaintiff, but felt the attorney had not proved the case.) By contrast, if the jury agrees John has made his case, they may award all reasonable medical expenses (past and future), lost wages, and pain and suffering up to $200,000. After several trials, tobacco manufacturers would begin to settle these cases.

As a matter of fairness, John cannot recover punitive damages. To recover punitive damages, some form of willfulness must be shown by the defendant.[193] Absolute liability rests upon loss reallocation and other social policies;[194] it does not inquire whether the cigarette manufacturer's conduct was willful. John's recovery of pain and suffering would therefore be limited to a maximum of $200,000.[195]

---

189. *See infra* notes 225–41 and accompanying text.

190. *See infra* notes 225–41 and accompanying text.

191. *See id.*

192. *See* Galbraith v. R.J. Reynolds Tobacco Co., No. 144417 (Cal. Super. Ct., Santa Barbara Co., Dec. 23, 1985).

193. *See* Fischer v. Johns-Manville Corp., 512 A.2d 466 (N.J. 1986). However, to encourage attorneys to bring the first suit in each jurisdiction, the judge may want to allow the recovery of punitive damages if willfulness can be shown.

194. *See supra* notes 136–50.

195. *See* Jeffrey O'Connell & Keith Carpenter, *Payment for Pain and Suffering Through History*, 50 Ins. Couns. J. 411 (1983): William Zelemyer, *Damages for Pain and Suffering*, 6 Syracuse L. Rev. 27 (1955).

Compare with medical malpractice actions: Cal Civ. Code § 3333.2(b) (West Supp. 1989) places a $250,000 limit on recoveries for pain and suffering. The statute was held to be constitutional in Fein v. Permanente Med. Group, 695 P.2d 665 (Cal. 1985). In Illinois, Ill. Rev. Stat. ch. 70, § 101 placed a $500,000 limit on total recovery, but this act was struck down as violative of the Constitution in Wright v. Central DuPage Hosp. Assoc., 347

This cap on pain and suffering and the elimination of punitive damages is a matter of balancing several considerations. The goal is not to bankrupt the cigarette manufacturers—merely force them to pay for the damages caused by their products. However, experience with the *Cipollone* case teaches that the first case to bring the absolute liability proposal will likely be long, expensive, and hard-fought. Therefore, to encourage suit and to compensate the attorneys, punitive damages (if willfulness is shown) and full pain and suffering should be recoverable for the first case brought in each jurisdiction. Plaintiffs in the second and later suits where absolute liability has been adopted will not be able to recover punitive damages and will have a cap of $200,000 on pain and suffering (unless the tobacco seller raises technical defenses).

Because the cause of action is absolute liability, no defenses such as assumption of risk,[196] contributory negligence,[197] or misuse[198] are available. The policy is to create a closed system where the manufacturers pay the costs of smoking. Defenses would furnish the cigarette manufacturers with a means for shifting the loss back to smokers and their insurers, which ultimately means nonsmokers.

During the determination of whether smoking caused the plaintiff's cancer, the judge must be alert that the cigarette manufacturer will attempt to win through superior financial strength.[199] This will be a serious issue both during discovery and trial. The first rule of the Federal Rules of Civil Procedure provides: "These rules . . . shall be construed to secure a just, speedy, and inexpensive determination of every action."[200] This means judges are bound to use every technique at their disposal to make certain the trial is affordable to the plaintiff. To insure an economical trial, the judge may be required to limit the scope of discovery or the number of witnesses at trial.[201]

N.E.2d 736 (Ill. 1976). The National Childhood Vaccination Injury Act of 1986 caps pain and suffering at $250,000. This involves children with perhaps full lives to live, not persons often in the last third of their lives, 42 U.S.C. § 300aa-15(a)(1)(4) (2007).

196. KEETON ET AL., *supra* note 115, at 711–12.

197. *Id.*

198. *Id.*

199. Cigarette manufacturers have grossly inflated the costs of suits:

By resisting all discovery . . . thus requiring a court hearing and order, . . . by getting confidentiality orders attached to the discovery materials . . . by taking exceedingly lengthy oral depositions . . . and by gathering . . . every scrap of paper ever generated about a plaintiff . . . by taking endless depositions of plaintiffs, expert witnesses, . . . by naming multiple experts of their own, . . . [a]nd . . . by taking dozens . . . of oral depositions all across the country . . . in the final days before trial.

Townsley & Hanks, *supra* note 121, at 277.

200. FED. R. CIV. P. 1.

201. *See* Townsley & Hanks, *supra* note 121, at 279–84.

iv. The Policies Supporting a Modification to Cause-in-Fact Until recently, the keystone to tort liability was cause-in-fact. To recover civil damages, a plaintiff had to prove those damages were caused in fact by the act of the defendant. There are two generally accepted tests for cause-in-fact: (1) the "but for" test, and (2) the "substantial factor" test. The "but for" test is applied by asking whether the injury would not have occurred "but for" the defendant's conduct.[202] If the injury would have occurred in spite of the defendant's act, the defendant was not a cause-in-fact of the injury and there is no liability. Second, the "substantial factor" test asks whether the defendant's conduct was a "substantial factor" in bringing about the injury.[203] It admits there may be numerous causes of the injury and asks merely: was this one a "substantial factor"? If the answer is negative, there can be no liability.

Dean Leon Green shed light on the inquiry by arguing cause-in-fact is a matter of science.[204] Green's test is: did defendant's conduct have something to do with the plaintiff's injury as a matter of science? In most cases, cause-in-fact is straightforward and creates no problems. For example, in a fist fight, it may be clear defendant broke the plaintiff's nose, or in a car crash, that defendant's careless driving caused the crash and the plaintiff's broken leg. Applying Green's test to cancer, the question would be: as a matter of science, did cigarette smoking have something to do with the cancer?

The courts have not shied away from tough cases in which it was not clear the defendant was a cause-in-fact of the plaintiff's injury. These challenging cases are a mixture of fact and policy. The best-known cause-in-fact case is *Summers v. Tice*,[205] which involved three hunters. The two defendants negligently fired their shotguns in the direction of the plaintiff, with one pellet hitting him in the eye. From the facts, the pellet could have been fired from the rifle of either defendant. Faced with the prospect of letting both escape liability because the plaintiff could not prove which one was the cause-in-fact of his injury, the court held the plaintiff could recover the whole amount from either defendant:

> When we consider the relative position of the parties and the results that would flow if plaintiff was required to pin the injury on one of the defendants only, a requirement that the burden of proof on that subject be shifted to defendants becomes manifest. They are both wrongdoers . . . . They brought about a situation where the negligence of one of them injured the plaintiff, hence it should rest with them each to absolve himself if he can. The injured party has been placed by defendants in the unfair position of pointing to

---

202. KEETON ET AL., *supra* note 115, at 265–68.

203. *Id.*

204. *See* Leon Green, *The Casual Relation Issue in Negligence Law*, 60 MICH. L. Rev. 543 (1962).

205. 199 P.2d 1 (Cal. 1948).

which defendant caused the harm. If one can escape the other may also and plaintiff is remediless . . . .

[T]he same reasons of policy and justice shift the burden to each of the defendants to absolve himself if he can . . . .[206]

More recently, the diethylstilbestrol (DES) cases have forced the courts to be as far-reaching in regard to cause-in-fact as the problems created by the technology that produced the injury. In *Sindell v. Abbott Laboratories*,[207] the best-known DES case, the plaintiff's mother took DES to prevent a miscarriage while the plaintiff was *in utero*. The plaintiff, now an adult, developed vaginal cancer. The plaintiff could not prove who manufactured the particular DES her mother had consumed. The court was faced with the choice of creating law or dismissing the case. The court held that, if the plaintiff joined the manufacturers of a substantial share of the DES produced, she could recover from them in proportion to the share of the DES market represented by the defendants. The court reasoned:

> In our contemporary complex industrialized society, advances in science and technology create fungible goods which may harm consumers and which cannot be traced to any specific producer. The response of the courts can be either to adhere rigidly to prior doctrine, denying recovery to those injured by such products, or to fashion remedies to meet these changing needs. . . .
>
> From a broader policy standpoint, defendants are better able to bear the cost of injury . . . "[T]he risk of injury can be insured by the manufacturer and distributed among the public as a cost of doing business."[208]

In time, the *Sindell* case was followed by *Collins v. Eli Lilly Co.*,[209] a Wisconsin case. The facts are similar in that the plaintiff developed vaginal cancer because her mother took DES (while the plaintiff was *in utero*) and the plaintiff could not prove who manufactured the particular DES. However, the Wisconsin Supreme Court rejected the *Sindell* rule in holding the plaintiff need only show her mother consumed the same form of DES (color of pill, shape) as manufactured by a single defendant. Further, rather than recovering only a percentage of her damages as provided in *Sindell*, she could recover all of her damages (except punitives) from the DES manufacturer. The court reasoned:

> Practical considerations favor permitting the plaintiff to proceed . . . against one defendant. One alternative would be to require the plaintiff, as in *Sindell*, to join as defendants "a substantial share" of the producers . . . . Another

---

206. *Id.* at 4–5.

207. 607 P.2d 924 (Cal. 1980).For a more recent treatment of the DES, market share issue, see Hymowitz v. Eli Lilly, 539 N.E.2d 1069 (N.Y. 1989).

208. Sindell, 607 P.2d at 936.

209. 342 N.W.2d 37 (Wis. 1984).

alternative would be to require the defendant to join a "reasonable number" of possibly liable defendants . . . . [E]ither alternative would waste judicial resources by requiring an initial determination of whether the plaintiff has joined a sufficient number of defendants.

Thus, the plaintiff need commence suit against only one [DES] defendant . . . .[210]

Summers, Sindell, and *Collins* make clear that in contemporary cases involving the outer limits of science, policy is an important part of cause-in-fact, and the court must be as creative as demanded by the facts of the case and the needs of justice. But where is this creativity with regard to the tobacco cases? Virtually everyone agrees cigarette smoking causes cancer.[211] The Surgeon General on behalf of the U.S. government has unequivocally said: "Cigarette smoking is the major cause of cancer mortality in the United States."[212] In 1964, the Surgeon General's Report stated: "Cigarette smoking is casually related to lung cancer in men . . . . The data for women . . . point in the same direction."[213] More recent studies indicate: "Women's risk of lung cancer has increased by a factor of four since the early 1960s, when smoking became more popular among women. In 1986, lung cancer overtook breast cancer as the leading cause of cancer deaths among women."[214]

Where then is the disagreement in regard to cause-in-fact and cigarette smoking? It emerges as a function of our court system. Presently, plaintiffs

---

210. *Id.* at 50. *See also Hymowitz,* 539 N.E.2d at 1076–78.

211. *See* WHELAN, *supra* note 19, at 83–87.

Smokers are *10 times* more likely to die from lung cancer than nonsmokers. Very heavy smokers (two packs or more per day) are up to *25 times* more likely to die of lung cancer.

. . . .

Cigarette smoking has been established as a significant cause of cancer of the larynx, oral cavity, esophagus and bladder, and is significantly associated with cancer of the pancreas and kidney.

Id. at 11.

Compare "American Tobacco Co. . . . is sticking to the hard-line position . . . that lung cancer has not been significantly linked to cigarette smoking." ATL. J.- CONST., Jan 6, 1988, at D1, *with* "EPA scientists, will conclude that smoking is responsible for more than 3,000 cases of lung cancer among non-smokers every year." ATL. J.- CONST., May 9, 1990, at A1, *and* "Dr. Stanton A. Glantz of the University of California at San Francisco estimated that passive smoke killed 50,000 Americans a year, two-thirds of whom died of heart disease," N.Y. TIMES, May 29, 1990, at C1.

212. SURGEON GENERAL'S REPORT, *supra* note 139.

213. ADVISORY COMMITTEE TO THE SURGEON GENERAL OF THE PUBLIC HEALTH SERVICE, U.S. DEP'T OF HEALTH, EDUC. & WELFARE, SMOKING AND HEALTH 31 (1964) [hereinafter SMOKING AND HEALTH].

214. ATL. J.-CONST., Jan. 25, 1990, at A1.

(or their survivors) have the burden of showing that "but for" smoking the defendant's brand of cigarettes, they would not have been injured. At trial, one of the cigarette manufacturers' chief defenses is "other cause."[215] That is, the manufacturer is free to prove the cause-in-fact of the plaintiff's cancer may have been polluted air, a garden pesticide, asbestos dust breathed at work, or a hereditary tendency to develop cancer.[216] The issue is whether smoking cigarettes was a cause-in-fact of this plaintiff's particular cancer. The plaintiff must prove that it was.

A presumption is needed to ensure that in most cases, the plaintiff's case will reach the jury if not settled before trial.[217] *Summers, Sindell,* and *Collins* support the proposed adoption of a presumption of cause-in-fact in suits by individuals against cigarette manufacturers. As discussed earlier in this chapter, a presumption arises that smoking caused the victim's cancer, with the case going to the jury if the plaintiff smoked regularly for fifteen years or more, claims one of the four types of cancer, and a medical doctor specializing in oncology affirms the cancer was likely caused by smoking.

The first cigarette case to be tried in the 1980s, *Galbraith v. R.J. Reynolds Tobacco Co.,*[218] highlighted a fundamental cause-in-fact problem: people who smoke often have other illnesses that may also have been a cause-in-fact of death. The position of the cigarette manufacturers is that they should be liable only if the plaintiff's death would not have occurred "but for" smoking their brand.[219] In *Galbraith,* the jury returned a verdict for the cigarette manufacturer.

The *Galbraith,* trial has obscured the reality of cause-in-fact: every injury always has several causes. Over fifty years ago, Dean Leon Green stated: "There may be and usually are several factors contributing to a plaintiff's hurt, but it is not required that a defendant's negligence be the only cause of the hurt. It is enough that the defendant's negligence is a material factor in the result."[220] In the cigarette cases, cause-in-fact has become a cause célèbre and every "other

---

215. *See* Townsley & Hanks, *supra* note 121, at 286–91.

216. *Id.*

217. Townsley & Hanks argue "Judicial notice should be taken that cigarette smoking can and does cause lung cancer," *Id.* at 285.

Rosenberg argues "courts determine causation under a proportionality rule, which would hold manufacturers of toxic agents liable for the proportion of total injuries attributable to their products." David Rosenberg, *The Causal Connection in Mass Exposure Cases: A "Public Law" Vision of the Tort System,* 97 HARV. L. REV. 851, 851 (1984).

218. *See* Townsley & Hanks, *supra* note 121, at 296–98.

219. *Id.* at 286–91.

220. Leon Green, *Proximate Cause in Texas Negligence Law,* 28 TEX. L. REV. 471, 475 (1950).

cause" is put forth as a defense by the manufacturer. For example, two cigarette plaintiffs' attorneys argue:

The Big-6 [cigarette manufacturers] contend the "other potential causes" defense in a lung cancer case justifies discovery of the victim's lifetime stress experiences, all personality traits, all genetic factors, all environmental exposures during the victim's lifetime, as well as discovering everything ever taken into his body.

This discovery strategy (if allowed by the trial court . . .) enables a cigarette manufacturer to scrutinize every minute of a person's life . . . . They claim this defense confers the right to scrutinize every school record from kindergarten through graduate school; every medical record ever made, whether with hospitals, mental institutions, physicians, pharmacists, insurance companies, or employers. . . . [T]his defense would allow the [cigarette manufacturer] to interrogate everyone the smoker ever knew . . . .[221]

Proving cause-in-fact in the usual cigarette case is therefore unnecessarily expensive. This plays into a key tactic in the cigarette trials, which has been to force plaintiffs' attorneys to spend large amounts of money to prove their cases (for example, estimates in *Cipollone*[222] range from $1.2 million to $6 million). The defendants forced this expenditure by extensive use of the discovery and trial process as well as appeals:

The . . . cigarette manufacturers, in defending cigarette disease claims, have adopted strategies to undermine the civil justice system by making the litigation unaffordable . . . .

The reality for most cigarette disease victims and their families is that they cannot find a lawyer to handle their cases . . .

How can this be? . . . [T]he reason why is simple: they [plaintiff's attorneys] cannot afford to. The cigarette manufacturers, through a national team of lawyers, have adopted a uniform strategy of defense designed to ensure that few lawyers can afford to take on a cigarette case . . . .

[A] tobacco industry lawyer . . . [stated]: "To paraphrase General Patton, the way we won those cases was not by spending all of [R.J.] Reynolds' money, but by making that other son-of-a-bitch spend all of his."[223]

Clearly the "spend them to death" tactic by the powerful cigarette manufacturers has been effective. One cigarette manufacturer's attorney stated: "[T]he aggressive posture we have taken regarding depositions and discovery in general continues to make these cases extremely burdensome and expensive for

---

221. Townsley & Hanks, *supra* note 121, at 287.
222. *See* ATL. J.-CONST., June 25, 1988, at A10.
223. Townsley & Hanks, *supra* note 121, at 275–78 (footnote omitted).

plaintiffs' lawyers, particularly sole practitioners."[224] The use of the civil litigation system raises the question whether cigarette manufacturers should be permitted to win merely because of their financial strength and adroit manipulation of the legal system. This manipulation manifests the power of the tobacco sellers and the complicity of the courts.

v. The Cause-in-Fact Proposal The cause-in-fact proposal is as follows: people who prove they have smoked at least one pack of cigarettes a day for fifteen or more years and submit an oncologist's statement that their cancer was probably caused by smoking will receive a presumption that smoking caused the cancer.[225] People will only be able to recover economic damages resulting from four types of cancer: lung,[226] larynx,[227] oral cavity,[228] and esophagus.[229]

The effect of giving the smoker a presumption in regard to cause-in-fact is to shift the burden of proof on this issue to the cigarette manufacturer.[230] Of course, the impact of the presumption is that in some cases, the smoker will recover for a cancer whose actual cause is unknown. This is accepted and clearly desirable as compared with the present harsh result where a smoker may be unable to recover for tobacco-caused cancer. That is, under the absolute liability proposal, the risk of failing to prove causation will now rest on the tobacco manufacturer rather than the smoker.

This approach to cause-in-fact resembles the administrative procedures used in black lung cases. For coal miners, a rebuttable presumption is used to determine black lung benefits:

> When the coal mine worker is disabled by pneumoconis, the mine operator is required to pay certain disability benefits. Proof that the individual coal

---

224. Townsley & Hanks, *supra* note 121, at 278.

225. One pack a day for fifteen years as the standard for establishing smoking-caused cancer was selected because that is a benchmark employed in cancer research, and it is also relatively easy to prove. *See Advertising of Tobacco Products: Hearings Before the H. Subcomm. on Health and the Environment of the Comm. on Energy and Commerce*, 99th Cong. 99-167 (1986). *See* Smoking and Health, *supra* note 213, at 100, 106. *See* U.S. Dep't of Health, Educ. & Welfare, The Health Consequences of Smoking: A Public Health Service Review, 34, 135–38 (1967) [hereinafter Health Consequences].

There is a rise of about 50 percent in the mortality ration for those who had smoked 15–35 years, with a further rise for those smoking longer than 35 years." Smoking and Health, *supra* note 213, at 90.

However, a study of Canadian Pensioners found: "For cigarette smokers as compared to nonsmokers, overall mortality ratios were elevated after 5 years of smoking at any time in their life and remained elevated as long as they continued to smoke cigarettes." Health Consequences, *supra*, at 11.

226. *See* Smoking and Health, *supra* note 213, at 102–12. *See* Health Consequences, *supra* note 225, at 33–37.

227. *Id.*

228. *Id.*

229. *Id.*

230. *See* Edward W. Cleary, McCormick on Evidence 968 (3d ed. 1984).

miner's pneumoconis was caused by working in the coal mine is accomplished by the use of a rebuttable presumption. After ten years in the mines, the miner's black lung or his death from a respiratory disease is presumed to be caused by such employment, and the burden shifts to the operator to rebut the presumption.[231]

The cause-in-fact portion of the absolute liability proposal is also similar to the provisions of the National Childhood Vaccine Injury Act of 1986.[232] Under the Act, people prove cause-in-fact if they suffer from an injury listed in the Act and the onset of the injury is within a set period of time after the vaccination.[233] The recovery rests on no-fault liability and is made from a trust fund supported by a tax on vaccines.[234]

Lung, larynx, oral cavity, and esophagus cancers were selected for compensation because they are the most common forms of smoking-caused cancer,[235] although there is substantial evidence heart,[236] stomach,[237] and liver disease[238] (as well as other illnesses)[239] are also caused by smoking.[240] One-pack-a-day was selected as the threshold because it is simple to identify and relatively easy to prove. Researchers tend to use one-pack-a-day as the pivot point for cancer caused by smoking.[241] Fifteen years of smoking was elected as the minimum because that is, in general, when the four compensable cancers begin to appear.[242] Of course, if the plaintiff smokes for fewer than fifteen years or smokes less than a pack each day, there is no recovery under the proposal (in that case, the plaintiff would be left with a traditional suit). Under the absolute liability proposal, the smoker can only recover for one or more of the four cancers because the cigarette manufacturer is subject to absolute liability. Plaintiffs who suffer from some other cancer must bring a traditional suit.

---

231. Garner, *supra* note 187, at 315 (citations omitted).

232. 42 U.S.C. § 300aa-1 to -34 (2007).

It would be efficient for Congress to develop a compensation program for smokers that resembles the National Childhood Vaccine Injury Act of 1986. However, due to the virtual control of Congress by the cigarette manufacturers, this will not likely occur. *See supra* note 198 and accompanying text.

233. § 300aa-11(c)(1).

234. Omnibus Budget Reconciliation Act of 1987, 26 U.S.C.S. § 9510 (A) (Law. Co-op. Supp. 1988).

235. *See supra* notes 228–41 and accompanying text.

236. *See* SMOKING AND HEALTH, *supra* note 213, at 102, 105, 108.

237. *See id.*

238. *See id.*

239. *See id.*

240. *See id.*

241. *See supra* note 246.

242. *See id..*

One question will likely arise under the proposal: who pays if the plaintiff has smoked numerous brands of cigarettes during the fifteen-year period? To answer this, we must consider the underlying policies of placing the loss upon the cigarette manufacturer.[243] There are several approaches. First, in order to recover, plaintiffs could file a claim against all of the manufacturers who produced the brands they smoked. The manufacturers would be treated as joint tortfeasors, each one liable for the whole amount.[244] Plaintiffs could then elect against which to enforce the judgment.[245]

Second, plaintiffs could file a suit against the manufacturer whose brand they smoked over 50 percent of the time.[246] The manufacturer could, of course, join other cigarette manufacturers.[247]

Third, smokers or their representatives could sue and recover from a cigarette manufacturer whose brand was smoked enough to be a "substantial factor" in the smoker's cancer.[248] Fourth, plaintiffs would be required to join in their action the cigarette manufacturers who, when added together, had produced a substantial share of the cigarettes plaintiffs smoked.[249]

A critique of these solutions is that a cigarette manufacturer will be obligated to pay damages because the plaintiff smoked the defendant's brand only some of the time during the fifteen years prior to contracting cancer. The response is that the loss should rest on the manufacturer rather than the victim. With a large number of claims each year, it is likely each manufacturer will pay its fair share over time. For example, the judge in the *Collins* DES case stated:

> Each defendant contributed to the *risk* of injury to the public and, consequently, the risk of injury to individual plaintiffs such as Therese Collins. Thus each defendant shares, in some measure, a degree of culpability in producing or marketing . . . . [T]he drug company is in a better position to absorb the cost of the injury. The drug company can either insure itself against liability, absorb the damage award, or pass the cost along to the consuming public as a cost of doing business.[250]

---

243. *See supra* notes 128–75.

244. *See* KEETON ET AL., *supra* note 115, at 324–30. *See* Rosenberg, *supra* note 217. Numerous jurisdictions have rejected joint liability and now lean toward several liability: each defendant is liable in proportion to his or her fault.

245. *See* KEETON AT AL., *supra* note 115, at 330–32.

246. Fifty percent was selected because it is easy to prove. Smokers would know which brand they smoke most of the time or fifty percent of the time. However, under this requirement, if they smoked three different brands equally, they could not sue under absolute liability.

247. *See* Sindell v. Abbott Laboratories, 607 P.2d 924 (Cal. 1980).

248. *See* KEETON ET AL., *supra* note 115, at 267–68.

249. *See Sindell*, 607 P.2d 924, *and* Rosenberg, *supra* note 217.

250. Collins v. Eli Lilly Co., 342 N.W.2d 37, 49 (Wis. 1984) (citations omitted).

Under the absolute liability proposal, a person with cancer who has smoked for at least fifteen years is able to recover lost wages, medical expenses, and up to $200,000 for pain and suffering. Preemption by the Cigarette Labeling and Advertising Act would not be a defense; indeed, the only defense is that cigarette smoke did not cause cancer of the lung, larynx, oral cavity, or esophagus. To assist plaintiffs in recovering, they are given a strong presumption that smoking did in fact cause the cancer. A goal of the proposal is to reallocate the costs of smoking from nonsmokers to the cigarette manufacturers. If there is a resulting reallocation of resources in the cigarette industry, this is to be preferred to the present imbalance where much of the loss is borne by nonsmokers and insurance companies. The clear message from years of cigarette litigation is that a fundamental change is needed, one that places the loss on the cigarette manufacturer: absolute liability. This would be a shift in power from the tobacco manufacturers to the victims. It is needed because the courts have historically favored the tobacco manufacturers over the victims.

B. GUN POLICY

Gun policy is the schizophrenia of American society. Even while thousands of people are being shot each month, gun advocates call for expanded gun ownership. This section will examine the carnage of eighteen thousand violent shootings per year, the Congressional immunization of the powerful gun manufacturers, and the Supreme Court's payback with its decision supporting the Second Amendment. Gun worship and expanded gun sales clearly manifest the powerful at work.

The truth is that bringing a gun into the home for self-protection is often a costly and lethal mistake. The powerful gun proponents have created a delusional culture:

> A hundred years from now, historians and social scientists will look back on our own crazed obsession with guns and wonder why the madness lasted so long. They'll shake their heads over a time in which a church or nursing home or community center could suddenly fall prey to a gunman armed with a determination to murder indiscriminately.
>
> Yes, these mass shootings are a form of madness, but what's even more insane is our passive reaction. We shrug our shoulders.
>
> . . .
>
> We fume over an inept regulatory system that allows peanut butter to be infected by salmonella. We demand that politicians take back undeserved bonuses and clean up our food supply.
>
> But the proliferation of weapons of war on our streets and in our homes? The indulgence of a gun culture that insists average Americans should own

assault rifles? The complicity with a gun industry that supplies Mexican drug cartels? Who cares?

. . .

If these attacks were the work of foreign-born terrorists—say, al-Qaeda— the White House would be swamped with protests, President Barack Obama's poll numbers would be in free fall and Republicans would be readying to retake the Oval Office. But attacks by Americans on fellow Americans are met with public indifference and official cowardice.

Though gun sales have soared since Obama's election, apparently spurred by fear of tougher gun laws, Democrats cower before the National Rifle Association. Recently, Attorney General Eric Holder backed away from a suggestion that the ban on assault weapons might be reinstated.

. . .

My father, a hunter, wouldn't understand a culture in which it is harder for me to purchase over-the-counter sinus medication than to buy a firearm at a gun show. I don't understand it either. It's more than a little crazy.[251]

Snipings, mass murders by disgruntled employees, children shooting children, and a vast number of spousal murders are everyday news across the country. In the numerous lawsuits brought by individual victims and over thirty cities, it has been argued gun manufacturers and sellers have an important role to play in designing guns to be safer and in closely monitoring gun sales. The courts are weighing these issues, but have dismissed most individual and city suits for various reasons. With congressional passage of immunity for gun manufacturers, several remaining issues need to be examined. Part 1 examines the collapse of the gun suits in the state courts. Part 2 evaluates the gun violence epidemic. Part 3 considers critical gun control policies, and Part 4 weighs the judicial construction of the Second Amendment.

1. Suits Against the Gun Manufacturers Have Foundered in the State Courts

In *Merrill v. Navegar*, the California Court of Appeals held that Navegar, the manufacturer of an automatic weapon known as the TEC-9, should be held liable to the surviving families of eight victims murdered by an irate law firm client.[252] The novel basis of the suit was that Navegar negligently marketed the TEC-9 to people who were likely to use it for criminal purposes.[253] The court cited Bureau of Alcohol, Tobacco, and Firearms (BATF) data that found "due to its

---

251. Cynthia Tucker, Op-Ed, *Shootings are Insane, But So is Response*, ATL. J.-CONST., Apr. 12, 2009, at A14.

252. Merrill v. Navegar, Inc., 89 Cal. Rptr. 2d 146 (Cal. Ct. App. 1999), *rev'd*, 28 P.3d 116 (Cal. 2001).

253. *See id.* at 155.

unsurpassed firepower, concealability, and low price," the TEC-9 was a favorite among violent criminals.[254] The BATF report stated the TEC models are used in one out of every five crimes involving gun violence.[255] Thus *Merrill* had been heralded as a forward-looking decision for gun responsibility.[256] But in August 2001, the California Supreme Court reversed it on the basis the negligence action against Navegar fell within California Code Section 1714.4: "(a) In a products liability action, no firearm shall be deemed defective in design on the basis that the benefits of the product do not outweigh the risk of injury posed by its potential to cause serious injury, damage, or death when discharged."[257] The court ruled Section 1714.4 applied to a case sounding in negligent marketing:

> [M]ost of the evidentiary matters relevant to applying the risk/benefit test in strict liability cases "are similar to the issues typically presented in a negligent design case." . . . This similarity is not surprising, because to say that a product was "negligently designed" is to say it "was defective, for purposes of establishing liability under a theory of negligence." . . . This similarity also is not accidental; over the years, we have incorporated a number of negligence principles into the strict liability doctrine, including *Baker's* risk/benefit test. . . .

> [T]his [negligent marketing] is a products liability action based on negligence, which asserts that the TEC-9/DC9 was defective in design because the risks of making it available to the general public outweighed the benefits of that conduct, and that defendants knew or should have known this fact. Plaintiffs may not avoid this conclusion, or the legislative policy section 1714.4 reflects, simply by declining to use the word "defect" or "defective."[258]

The second important suit against the gun manufacturers to meet a roadblock was the New York case, *Hamilton v. Accu-Tek*.[259] The foundation of *Hamilton*

---

254. *Id.*

255. *Id.*

256. *See* Frank J. Vandall, *Economic and Causation Issues in City Suits Against Gun Manufacturers*, 27 Pepp. L. Rev. 719, 727 (2000).

257. Merrill v. Navegar, Inc., 28 P.3d 116, 134 (Cal. 2001). Section 1714.4 has since been repealed: "The primary effects of Chapter 913 are to repeal Section 1714.4 and to amend . . . its provisions to the design, distribution, and marketing of firearms and ammunition."

John Fowler, *Will a Repeal of Gun Manufacturer Immunity from Civil Suits Untie the Hands of the Judiciary?*, 34 McGeorge L. Rev. 339, 348 (2003).

258. *Merrill*, 28 P.3d at 125–26.

259. Hamilton v. Accu-Tek, 62 F.Supp.2d 802 (E.D.N.Y. 1999), *vacated*, Hamilton v. Beretta U.S.A. Corp., 264 F.3d 21 (2d Cir. 2001).

is the theory that in the southern states, the gun manufacturers created a negligent oversaturation of guns.[260] As a result, guns were purchased and transported to New York and Chicago (where they are banned), and there sold on the black market.[261] The plaintiffs claimed "the manufacturers' indiscriminate marketing and distribution practices generated an underground market in handguns, providing youths and violent criminals with easy access to the instruments they have used with lethal effect."[262] The key to this suit was that the manufacturers of handguns foresaw these saturation sales and encouraged them.[263] The jury found in favor of the victims and against the gun manufacturers.[264] The plaintiffs claimed, on a certified question, that:

> [T]he jury could reasonably have concluded that in considering all the circumstances—industry knowledge of widespread trafficking in new handguns, heavy movement of guns from 'weak law' to 'strong law' states and risks associated with criminals' easy access to these dangerous instruments— defendants were negligent in failing to take appropriate steps to reduce the risk of their products' being sold to persons with a propensity to misuse them.[265]

However, this federal district court holding in *Hamilton* for the plaintiffs has been undermined by the New York Court of Appeals.[266] On a certified question from the federal district court, the appellate court killed the suit by holding that under New York law, no duty extended from the gun manufacturers to the shooting victims because the connection was "remote."[267] The court reasoned:

> The pool of possible plaintiffs is very large—potentially, any of the thousands of victims of gun violence. Further, the connection between defendants, the criminal wrongdoers and plaintiffs is remote, running through several links in a chain consisting of at least the manufacturer, the federally licensed distributor or wholesaler, and the first retailer. The chain most often includes numerous subsequent legal purchasers or even a thief. Such broad liability, potentially encompassing all gunshot crime victims, should not be imposed without a more tangible showing that the defendants were a direct link in the causal chain that resulted in the plaintiffs' injuries, and that the

---

260. *Id.* at 835.
261. *Id.* at 808–09.
262. *Id.* at 808.
263. *Id.* at 827.
264. *Id.*
265. *Id.*
266. Hamilton v. Beretta U.S.A. Corp., 750 N.E.2d 1055 (N.Y. 2001).
267. *Id.* at 1062.

defendants were realistically in a position to prevent the wrongs. Giving plaintiffs' evidence the benefit of every favorable inference, they have not shown that the gun used to harm plaintiff Fox came from a source amendable to the exercise of any duty of care that plaintiffs would impose upon defendant manufacturers.[268]

Regardless of their complex reasoning, the California and New York decisions both protect the powerful gun sellers and abandon the shooting victims.

The third important challenge to the firearms industry is the more than thirty suits by various cities including New Orleans, Atlanta, and Chicago.[269] Their goal was to recover the expenses paid by the cities in dealing with gun violence.[270] However, these suits have also foundered, with their being dismissed on appeal for various reasons. Part of the Atlanta suit was dismissed because strict liability was held not available to the city; the New Orleans case was dismissed because "it improperly intruded on the state's exclusive power to regulate the firearms industry."[271] The Cincinnati suit was thrown out because it "is an improper

---

268. *Id.* at 1061–62.

269. *See New York City Sues Gun Industry*, U.S. NEWSWIRE, June 20, 2000:
"In October 1998, the Legal Action Project filed for the City of New Orleans the first lawsuit ever brought by a governmental entity against the gun industry. Since that time, cities and counties across the nation, including Atlanta, Boston, Chicago, Los Angeles and Philadelphia, have launched a legal attack on the gun industry to hold it accountable for designing and distributing guns with no regard for public health and safety. The Legal Action Project represents 25 out of the 32 cities and counties that have filed suit so far." *Id. See also* Bill Rankin, *Ruling Jump-Starts Atlanta's Gun Lawsuit*, ATL. J.-CONST., Feb. 17, 2001, at A1 (reporting the Georgia Supreme Court ruled the suit against gun manufacturers was prematurely dismissed); Dan Horn & Spencer Hunt, *City's Firearms Lawsuit Revived; Supreme Court of Ohio Agrees to Hear Case*, CINCINNATI ENQUIRER, Jan. 18, 2001 (reporting the Ohio Supreme Court will hear the city's case previously dismissed by the lower courts).

270. For example, the Chicago suit is asking for over 433 million dollars in damage for primary and secondary costs associated with gun violence, including the costs of extra police, medical costs, and welfare expenditures for surviving families. *See* Fox Butterfield, *Chicago is Suing Over Guns from Suburbs*, N.Y. TIMES, Nov. 13, 1998, at A4. *See also* Roberto Suro, *Suits Against Guns Use Tobacco Model*, TIMES-PICAYUNE, Dec. 24, 1998, at A1 (stating the New Orleans suit seeks recovery for the city's costs of "police protection, emergency services, facilities and services, as well as lost tax revenues due to the gun manufacturers' products and actions").

271. Richmond Eustis, *Gun Makers: Halt City Suit Until Georgia High Court Rules*, FULTON COUNTY DAILY REP., Aug. 10, 2001 at 1. Ed Anderson, *Appeal Draws Fire from Foster; Gunmakers Not Liable for Violence*, TIMES-PICAYUNE, Aug. 2, 2001, at 1. The U.S. Supreme Court has refused to review the dismissal of the New Orleans suit by the Louisiana Supreme Court. Alan Sayre, *High Court Finishes Off N.O. Gun Suit*, ADVOCATE (Baton Rouge, La.), Oct. 10, 2001, at 1B.

attempt to have [the] Court substitute its judgment for that of the legislature." Strict liability and negligent design as well as public nuisance and fraud claims against the gun manufacturers have all been rejected.[272] The judicial victories by the gun manufacturers, in suits both by individuals and the cities, suggest the courts prefer the powerful gun manufacturers to the innocent victims. No suit has held the huge number of guns did not cause substantial damage to individuals and cities or that the gun manufacturers were powerless to act.

2. The United States is Facing a Gun Violence Epidemic

The United States experiences a large number of injuries and deaths from firearms on a continuing basis.[273] Over thirteen thousand adults and children died from gun-related deaths in 1992.[274] More Americans were murdered with firearms in 1993 through 1994 than were killed in eight-and-half years of combat in Vietnam.[275] The total of handgun deaths in 1992 (13,220) "exceeds the combined total of Great Britain, Sweden, Switzerland, Japan, Australia, and Canada by nearly 13,000 deaths."[276] Professor Zimring found an epidemic of gun violence among youths aged ten to seventeen.[277] The violence is not uniformly distributed

---

272. 27 Products Safety & Liab. Rep. (BNA) 1003 (Oct. 15, 1999). Because the injury to the city of Bridgeport was indirect, the Connecticut Supreme Court found in favor of the gun manufacturers, ATL. J.-CONST., Oct. 2, 2001, at A9.

273. *See generally* Alan Clendenning, *Security Didn't Deter Gunfight Two Students Hospitalized*, ATL. J.-CONST., Sept. 27, 2000, at A4 (reporting on a gunfight in a New Orleans middle school between two students); *4 Teens Shot in 2d Seattle Weekend Attack*, ATL. J.-CONST., Sept. 25, 2000, at A4 ("An assailant opened fire on a car carrying young people as it stopped at a ride light in Seattle, critically wounding three of them."); Sheila Edmundson & Ruma Banerji, *Disgruntled Worker Shoots 2, Turns Gun on Himself*, THE COMMERCIAL APPEAL (Memphis, Tenn.), June 29, 2000, at DS1 ("It's kind of a situation that . . . was a wakeup call. . . . It can happen anywhere. It's not just limited to big cities."); Melody McDonald, *Lubbock Man Killed Accidentally; Friend Mistakes 9mm Weapon for a BB gun*, FORT WORTH STAR–TELEGRAM, June 26, 2000, at M2 (reporting on two men "wrestling around the living room when they both ran for what they believed was the BB pistol on the mantel"); Lyda Longa, *Boy Finds Gun, Kills 5-Year-Old Brother*, ATL. J.-CONST., June 21, 1999, at 1A ("Minutes before the shooting, Roshon, his brother, and three other youngsters had been playing with water pistols when they found a loaded .380 semiautomatic handgun in a box stuffed with garbage."); Bill Montgomery, *Road Rage: Needless Deaths*, ATL. J.-CONST., May 13, 2000 at A1 (reporting on a recent death resulting from a confrontation between two drivers, one of whom had a gun).

274. *See* Alana Bassin, *Why Packing a Pistol Perpetuates Patriarchy*, 8 HASTINGS WOMEN'S L.J. 351, 354 and n.33 (1997) (citing HANDGUN CONTROL INC., FIREARM FACTS (Jan. 1995)).

275. *Id.* at 354.

276. *Id.*

277. Franklin E. Zimring, *Kids, Guns, and Homicide: Policy Notes on an Age-Specific Epidemic*, 59 LAW & CONTEMP. PROBS. 25, 26 (1996) ("This essay is a brief examination of three dimensions of the juvenile firearms use epidemic of the period since 1985.").

across society as a higher proportion of black males die than white males as a result of gun violence.[278]

Federal gun immunity legislation also ignores the substantial risk of people being shot by noncriminals.[279] The assumption is that the risk of gun violence comes solely from criminals,[280] but a substantial percentage of homicides are committed by noncriminals;[281] for example, spouses and friends are a common target of gun violence.[282] In many cases the shooter had no

---

278. See Mary E. Becker, The Politics of Women's Wrongs and the Bill of "Rights": A Bicentennial Perspective, 59 U. CHI. L. REV. 453, 502 (1992) (citing the U.S. Department of Justice Crime Statistics for the proposition "[t]he number one cause of death for African-American males between the ages of fifteen and twenty-four is murder"). Census Bureau statistics bear this out as well. In 1996, black males died at a rate of 50.6 per 100,000 due to firearms; white males died at a rate of only 19 per 100,000. BUREAU OF CENSUS, U.S. DEP'T OF COMMERCE, DEATH AND DEATH RATES FOR INJURY BY FIREARMS BY RACE AND SEX: 1980–1996, 109, tbl. 151 (1999). Further, a 1989 Public Heath Report stated that an analysis of firearm deaths in California determined "firearms were the number one cause of death for black men ages 25 to 34 years and black women aged 15 to 24 years." U.S. DEP'T OF HEALTH & HUMAN SERVICES; PUBLIC HEALTH REPORTS, 104:111-120, at 4 (1989).

279. See, e.g., Katherine Kaufer Christoffel, Toward Reducing Pediatric Injuries from Firearms: Charting a Legislative and Regulatory Course, 88 PEDIATRICS 294, 300 (1991) (arguing "most shootings are not committed by felons . . . but are acts of passion that are committed using a handgun that is owned for home protection); David Kairys, A Carnage in the Name of Freedom, PHILADELPHIA INQUIRER, Sept. 12, 1988, at A15 ("That gun in the closet to protect against burglars will most likely be used to shoot a spouse in a moment of rage. . . .") See Protection of Lawful Commerce in Arms Act, Pub. L. No. 92, 119 Stat. 2095 (2005).

280. See, e.g., Randy E. Barnett & Don B. Kates, Under Fire: The New Consensus on the Second Amendment, 45 EMORY L.J. 1139, 1245 (1996) ("The homicide data collected over the past thirty-five years have consistently shown that 70—80% of those charged with murder had prior adult records, with an average adult criminal career of six or more years, including four major felony arrests."); Phillip J. Cook et al., Regulating Gun Markets, 86 J. CRIM. L. & CRIMINOLOGY 59, 63 (1995) ("An effective transfer-regulating scheme that prevents guns from going to dangerous people would be nearly as successful as a much more intrusive scheme targeted at current gun owners. Each new cohort of violent criminals must obtain guns somewhere.").

281. See infra notes 282–83. However, Don B. Kates suggested in a private conversation with the author that there are no shootings by persons without criminal records. Chicago, Fall 2002. See also D.B. Kates & D.D. Polsby, The Myth of the "Virgin Killer": Law-Abiding Persons Who Kill in Fit of Rage (Nov. 2000) (paper presented at the American Society of Criminology Annual Meeting, San Francisco).

282. A firearm in the home is forty-three times more likely to injure a member of the household (whether a homicide, suicide, or unintentional shooting) than to injure an intruder. See Arthur L. Kellerman & Donald T. Reay, Protection or Peril? An Analysis of Firearm-Related Deaths in the Home, 314 NEW ENG. J. MED. 1557, 1559 (1986). Further it is estimated 150,000 cases of domestic violence involve firearms, and that in these cases "death was twelve times as likely to occur." Bassin, supra note 274, at 356.

criminal record.[283] Typical cases involve one spouse shooting another, or friends who are shot while "playing" with a firearm.[284] Children are also often victims of gun violence,[285] with a common fact pattern involving a young child finding a gun in his or a family member's home and using it to shoot a playmate or a sibling.[286]

The facts indicate it is very dangerous to everyone in the family to have a gun in the home. Dr. Arthur Kellerman found a person in a household with a gun is forty-three times more likely to be shot than an intruder.[287] Even if the high percentage of suicides is removed from this statistic, a person with a gun (or a member of her family) is much more likely to be shot than an intruder.[288] In short, a gun owner is more at risk of being shot than someone who does not own a gun.[289]

Because of the gun violence epidemic, the nature of secondary education is changing. In responding to concerns about gun violence, public schools are spending millions of dollars to insure no guns enter the schools.[290] Public schools

---

283. *See* Nicholas Dixon, *Why We Should Ban Handguns in the United States*, 12 St. Louis U. Pub. L. Rev. 243, 265–66 (1993) ("Gun control measures that are targeted solely at those with criminal records fail to protect us from the most likely source of handgun murder: ordinary citizens."); *see also Handgun Crime Control: Hearings before the Subcomm. on Crime of the Comm. on the Judiciary*, 94th Cong. 1774 (1975) (statement of Dee Helfgott, Coordinator, Coalition for Handgun Control of Southern California, Inc.).

"Most murders (seventy-three percent) are committed impulsively by previously law abiding citizens during arguments with family members or acquaintances. . . . A readily available gun is what turns an assault into a murder. The handgun, often kept in the home for self-defense, is six times as likely to be used against a family member as it is to be used against an intruder." *Id.*

284. *See supra* notes 282–83.

285. *See supra* note 273 and *infra* note 286.

286. Lyda Longa, *Boy Finds Gun, Kills 5-Year-Old Brother*, Atl. J.-Const., June 21, 1999, at A1 ("Minutes before the shooting, Roshon, his brother, and three other youngsters had been playing with water pistols when they found a loaded .380 semiautomatic handgun in a box stuffed with garbage.").

287. *See* Kellerman & Reay, *supra* note 282, at 1559. But Professor Kleck argues that if attacked, an armed individual will fare better than an unarmed one:

Gary Kleck's analysis of 1979-85 national data in Point Blank shows the following comparative rates of injury: only 12.1-17.4% of gun-armed victims resisting robbery or assault were injured; 24.7-27.3% of victims who submitted were nevertheless injured; 40.1-48.9% of those who screamed were injured, as were 24.7-30.7% of those who tried to reason with or threaten the attacker, and 25.5-34.9% of those who resisted.

Barnett & Kates, *supra* note 280, at 1259 n.478.

288. Kellerman & Reay, *supra* note 282.

289. *Id.*

290. Judy Mann, *Unheeded Warnings, Tragic Endings*, Wash. Post, Mar. 9, 2001, at C9 ("The sad truth is that no one can predict which troubled kid is going to start shooting up his school. Millions of dollars have been spent in the last couple of years on safe-school

have erected fences, purchased metal detectors, hired full-time guards, required children to purchase and carry see-through book bags, and conducted extensive locker searches.[291] Many schools now have zero tolerance for weapons.[292]

The problem is that even if the schools themselves become safe from firearm violence, the risk of children being shot will remain: the shooting gallery will simply shift from inside to outside the school.[293] Children may still be shot while off school property: on the street, in their home, or at a friend's home.[294]

---

projects, including one in San Diego County, where the latest carnage occurred, and no clear pattern has emerged.").

291. *See* David C. Anderson, *Curriculum, Culture and Community: The Challenge of School Violence*, 24 CRIME & JUST. 317, 334 (1998) (noting that may schools use "hard security measures" to counteract gun violence including searching lockers, closing the school during lunch, use of security officers who routinely searched students, use of drug sniffing dogs, metal detectors, and use of closed circuit television.). Anderson argues that more innovative approaches through curriculum, the administration, and the community have had success. *Id. See* David Hall, *Shootings Spotlight School Safety Proposal Seeks to Put Officers in All Michigan Schools*, SOUTH BEND TRIBUNE, May 3, 1999, at B6.

> The school shooting in Littleton, Colo., has prompted one Michigan legislator to propose police officers be posted in public schools. . . . He also suggested that one way to deal with annual costs of the program would be to handle them jointly between the schools and the police department.

Id. Ellen O'Brien, *Deadly Acts Put Focus on Need for Prevention: Colorado School Killings/The Threat of Violence*, BOSTON GLOBE, Apr. 21, 1999, at A30 (discussing, in part, the use of both stationary and handheld metal detectors in Boston schools); Mary Ellen Moore, *School Security Chiefs Deal with Guns*, PATRIOT LEDGER (Quincy, Mass.), Apr. 27, 1996, at 34 ("School security staffs have become an integral part of public school systems, . . . and are often represented at faculty meetings, PTA meetings and sporting events.").

292. *See* Paul M. Bogos, *Expelled. No Excuses. No Exceptions.—Michigan's Zero-Tolerance Policy in Response to School Violence: M.C.L.A. Section 380.1311*, 74 U. DET. MERCY. L. REV. 357, 374–76, n.118 (1997). Under Michigan's program, a student found possessing a weapon on school grounds is permanently expelled from all schools in the state and no alternative educational program is provided. *Id.* at 359. The zero tolerance standard has created its own set of problems, however, because the application of the standard can lead to ridiculous results. In 1995, a twelve-year old boy was expelled for *turning in* a gun brought to school by *another* student. *See Zero Tolerance Proves to Be a Little Ridiculous in Knawha*, CHARLESTON GAZETTE & DAILY MAILING, Dec. 8, 1995, at A4.

293. This is especially true in areas where the school is part of an already unsafe neighborhood. *See* Anderson, *supra* note 291, at 326–27 (based on a "re-analysis of the Safe School Study data," it was determined that "neighborhood social conditions [is] . . . an important predictor of disorder within schools, along with school size and resources, organization of instruction, and school climate and discipline.").

294. *See* Thomas J. Walsh, *The Limits and Possibilities of Gun Control*, 23 CAP. U. L. REV. 639, 641 (1994) (recounting incidents of youth gun violence and victimization, including the injury of a seven-year-old boy who was in his home when he was wounded by a stray

What can be done? First, gun dealers can be asked to exercise more care to make certain guns do not reach children. Gun manufacturers can also be asked to design guns that cannot be operated by children.[295]

3. An Analysis of Gun Control and Liability

This section will evaluate the foundational issues surrounding gun control and liability. Clear answers to these concerns were needed before sweeping congressional immunity was granted to the powerful gun manufacturers.

a. Self-Protection Many issues surrounding the use of firearms for self-protection are unresolved. Scott Jacobs argues the costs of gun violence and death exceeds the benefit of gun ownership.

> In contrast with the 500,000 violent crimes and 15,377 firearms related homicides committed in the United States during 1992, only 308 cases were classified as justifiable homicide by a private citizen using a firearm in self defense against a felonious perpetrator. . . . the statistics do not account for those instances where the defending citizen was injured or killed while attempting armed self defense.[296]

Arguably the possession of a gun in the home presents a risk to every member of the family.[297] Dr. Arthur Kellerman found that when there is a gun there, it is more likely someone in the home (a father, mother, one of the children, or a guest) will be shot than an intruder.[298] Newspaper accounts of shootings in the home tell the story: a spouse comes home unexpectedly at night and is shot and

---

bullet from a gunfight in the street, a child killed on the way to the zoo, and a young man killed when "some young men across the street from his house opened fire").

295. A basic reason for tort liability is to ask the defendant to exercise reasonable care. Perhaps a gun manufacturer could design a child-proof handgun.

296. Scott Jacobs, Note, *Toward a More Reasonable Approach to Gun Control: Canada as a Model*, 15 N.Y.L. Sch. J. Int'l & Comp. L. 315, 336 (1995) (citing Federal Bureau of Investigation, U.S. Dep't of Justice, Uniform Crime Reports for the United States 1992, tbl. 2.16 (1994)).

In contrast David Kopel and Christopher Little argue "there is copious evidence that a significant number of crimes are deterred every year by gun wielding Americans. . . . Studies of prison inmates confirm that criminals are deterred when they believe that their potential victims are armed." Davis B. Kopel & Christopher C. Little, *Communitarians, Neorepublicans, and Guns: Assessing the Case for Firearms Prohibition*, 56 Md. L. Rev. 438, 504–06 (1997).

297. *See supra* notes 282–83 and accompanying text.

298. Kellerman & Reay, *supra* note 282. *See also* Anthony Spangler, *62-Year-Old Accidentally Shoots Himself, Grandson*, Fort Worth Star-Telegram, Sept. 11, 2000, at 3M (where a man accidentally shot himself and his 11-year-old grandson when the gun discharged during cleaning).

killed;[299] family members get into an argument and one is shot;[300] a child finds a gun and shoots his mother, father, sibling, or a playmate;[301] or a young child is injured while playing with a gun. Women especially are at risk when there is a gun in the house.[302] The substantial risk to the members of the gun owners' family must therefore be weighed against the very slight risk of dying at the hands of an armed intruder.[303]

---

299. *See*, e.g., *Woods Cross Man Shoots Pregnant Wife by Accident*, DESERET NEWS (Salt Lake City, Utah), Mar. 1, 2001, at B3 (where a man shot his pregnant wife believing she was an intruder).

300. *See*, e.g., Sarah Antonacci, *Police Say Man Killed Wife, Turned Gun On Self; Couple from Buffalo Were Married 11 Years*, STATE J.-REG. (Springfield, Ill.), Sept. 12, 2000, at 1 (where an argument over their impending separation apparently led a man to kill his wife and then turn the gun on himself).

301. *See*, e.g., *Gun Play: Game of Life and Death*, ATL. J.-CONST., Nov. 15, 1999, at A8 (where a twelve-year-old boy fatally fired his mother's gun at his friend's back, believing the gun was unloaded).

302. *See*, e.g., Beth Warren, *Police Probing Case of Girl, 4, Killed by Gun*, ATL. J.-CONST., Aug. 23, 2000, at JJ1 (where a four-year-old girl spotted her aunt's gun on a shelf, bounced on the bed high enough to reach it, and fatally shot herself).

. . . . . *See*, e.g., Max B. Baker, *Crimes Against Women Targeted*, FORT WORTH STAR-TELEGRAM, Jan. 12, 2001, at M1 (recounting an incident in which a man came home to find his wife in the kitchen with another man, shooting her six times in a moment of "sudden passion"); Christopher Goffard, *Household Conflict Ends in Shootings*, ST. PETERSBURG TIMES, Apr. 3, 1999, at 1 (where a man came into the kitchen and shot his wife and niece after a history of domestic conflicts); Ryan Frank, *Cooper Mountain Man Indicted in Wife's Killing*, OREGONIAN, Nov. 15, 2000, at B2 (where a man shot his wife in the kitchen of their home the morning after the couple decided she should move out); John Marzulli et al., *S.I. Cop Kills Wife, Self*, DAILY NEWS (New York, NY), Oct. 21, 1998, at 3 (where a police officer shot his wife then himself in the kitchen of their home).

303. Dixon, *supra* note 283, at 277–78 (1993).

> Taking handguns from law-abiding citizens does not deprive them of many methods of self-defense. They still have the option of escaping or calling for help, using weapons other than handguns, using their bare hands, reasoning with the criminal, or simply not resisting. . . . It is possible that in some cases a victim would be able to avoid theft, injury, or even death had she been armed with a handgun. This "cost" of my proposal needs to be weighed against the likely negative results of the defensive use of handguns described above: unnecessary and excessive use of handguns in self-defense; and the deaths shown by Kellerman and Reay to result from the abuse of handguns in the home.

Id. See also id. at 282.

> Whatever protection would be lost by disarming the small number of women who currently own handguns is outweighed by the reduction in all violence against women that would be affected by a handgun ban, which would take one of the most potent weapons out of the hands of many potential assaulters.

Id.

b. Enforce Existing Gun Laws Gun advocates suggest that rather than make more laws limiting the ownership and sale of guns, the federal government should enforce existing laws.[304] They argue penalties should be stiffened for criminals who commit crimes with guns.[305] For example, the National Rifle Association (NRA) advocates Project Exile, where every convicted felon apprehended with a gun, or committing a crime with a gun, will go to prison for five years.[306]

The assumption is that guns sales and ownership is heavily regulated,[307] but in fact there are few meaningful gun regulations.[308] This was shown quite clearly in the New York suit, *Hamilton v. Accu-Tek*,[309] in which the oversaturation of guns in the South led to their being transported to places they were banned to be sold on the black market.[310] If guns had been tightly regulated, they would not

---

304. Wayne LaPierre, *2000 NRA Annual Meeting of Members* (May 20, 2000), *available at* http://www.narhq.org/transcripts/wlpam.shtml ("If the issue is making our streets safer from gun crime, prosecution is the answer. If the issue is making our kids safer from gun accidents, education issue is making our schools safer, then parenting and mentoring is the answer."). *See also* Charlton Heston, *Truth and Consequences* (Apr. 16, 1999), *available at* http://www.nrahq.org/transcripts/yale.asp

> [T]he Clinton Administration is not prosecuting violations of federal gun law. In fact, they reversed the Bush Administration's policy of prosecuting felons with guns. Instead, with plea bargains, a wink and a nod, they've been letting armed felons off the hook. From 1992 to 1998, prosecutions have been cut almost in half. . . . Passing laws is what keeps politicians' careers alive. Enforcing laws is what keeps you alive. But nobody's getting arrested, nobody's going to jail, it's all a giant scam. It's not real life. It's a big lie.

305. Bob Dart & Scott S. Greengerger, *High Noon for Gun Control Fight: Mother's Day March Spotlights Safety Issue, and Politicians Rush to Offer Solutions, Court Votes*, ATL. J.-CONST., May 13, 2000, at A1 ("In general, [Governor, now former President] Bush argues that the best gun control policy is to enforce existing laws and stiffen penalties for criminals who commit crimes with guns.").

306. Heston, *supra* note 304:

> Project Exile simply enforces existing federal law. Project Exile means every convicted felon caught with a gun, no matter what he's doing, will go to prison for five years. No parole, no early releases, no discussion, period. . . . Project Exile, in its first year in Richmond, cut gun homicides by 62 percent. And as you'd expect, related gun crimes like robbery, rape and assault also plummeted. That means hundreds of people in Richmond today are alive and intact who, without Project Exile, would be dead or bleeding. For years the NRA has demanded that Project Exile be deployed nationwide.

307. *See* Brady Bill, 18 U.S.C. § 922 (2000); Merrill v. Navegar, 28 P.3d 116 (Cal. 2001).

308. Brady Bill, 18 U.S.C. § 922 (2000).

309. 62. F.Supp.2d 802 (E.D.N.Y. 1999).

310. The plaintiffs claimed "the manufacturers' indiscriminate marketing and distribution practices generated an underground market in handguns, providing youths and

have been sold beyond the saturation point in the South and would not have made their way into the hands of violent criminals in New York and Chicago.[311] As noted above, *Hamilton* was won in the trial court but lost on appeal.[312] (However, New York City did not give up: in 2006, it conducted a sting operation in Georgia against gun shops that sold to straw men. They recorded the sales by gun shops that violated federal law and prevented them from continuing, causing numerous Georgia gun shops to close their doors.)[313]

Existing gun regulations leave gaps large enough to permit 7.5 million gun sales per year.[314] For example, the teen shooters at Columbine High School obtained their guns from parents, friends, or gun shows.[315] None of the teens had meaningful criminal records and obtaining guns was effortless.[316]

There are only a few substantive limitations on the sale of guns: one was the now-lapsed ban on automatic weapons,[317] and another is the ban on sales of guns to known criminals.[318] Guns may be freely sold and traded at gun fairs without

---

violent criminals with easy access to the instruments they have used with lethal effect." *Id.* at 808.

311. Suggestions for regulation included:

(1) requiring distributors to sell only to stocking gun dealers, i.e., retailers who stock guns for sale from legitimate retail outlets, (2) prohibiting sales at gun shows, where widespread unrecorded and unsupervised sales to nonresponsible persons were said to take place, and (3) analyzing trace requests to locate retailers who disproportionately serve as crime gun sources, and cutting off distributors who do business with them.

Id. at 831.

312. Hamilton v. Beretta U.S.A. Corp., 750 N.E. 2d 1055, 1061–62 (N.Y. Ct. App. 2001).

313. Press Release, New York City Law Dept., Gun Dealer Adventure Outdoors Defaults in Prominent Gun Case (June 2, 2008) *available at* media@law.NYC.gov.

314. *See* Andrew D. Herz, *Gun Crazy: Constitutional False Consciousness and Dereliction of Dialogic Responsibility*, 75 B.U. L. Rev. 57, 59 n.4 (1995).

315. Butterfield, *supra* note 270.

316. *See* Gary Harmon, *Pain of Columbine Still Lives*, Cox News Service, Apr. 15, 2000 (statement of Dr. Bob Sammons, a Grand Junction psychiatrist). "The Columbine killers had criminal records, but their lawbreaking wasn't of the frequency or extremity that would suggest the destruction they actually caused." *Id. See also* Butterfield, *supra* note 270.

317. 18 U.S.C. § 922(d) (2000) ("It shall be unlawful for any licensed importer, licensed manufacturer, license dealer, or licensed collector to sell or deliver–(4) to any person any destructive device, machinegun . . . short-barreled shotgun, or short-barreled rifle, except as specifically authorized by the Secretary consistent with public safety and necessity.").

318. 18 U.S.C. § 922(d) (2000):

It shall be unlawful for any person to sell or otherwise dispose of any firearm or ammunition to any person knowing or having reasonable cause to believe that such person— (1) is under indictment for, or has been convicted in any court of, a crime punishable by imprisonment for a term exceeding one year; (2) is a fugitive from justice; (3) is an unlawful user of or addicted to any controlled substance. . . .

criminal background checks being done.[319] The mistaken belief fueled by gun advocates and the powerful gun manufacturers is that Americans have only criminals to fear and that citizens are safe in their homes as long as they have a gun.[320] The reality is average citizens are much more at risk from their spouses, friends, and children with guns than they are from criminals.[321]

The Brady Bill was passed for the purpose of reducing gun sales to criminals and certain other classes of people.[322] It does not prevent the sale or purchase of guns by law-abiding citizens.[323] Instead, the Brady Bill merely provides for a short waiting period[324] and a prohibition against purchases by criminals;[325] it also requires background checks to see if the purchaser has a criminal record.[326] Recent studies suggest the Brady Bill has been effective in prohibiting the

---

319. Brady Campaign, Brady Background Checks–Gun Show Loophole Brady Campaign to Prevent Gun Violence, http://www.bradycampaign.org/legislation/backgroundchecks/gunshowloophole (last visited Sept. 19, 2009). A bill to close the loophole has been introduced in both the House and Senate. Gun Show Background Check Act of 2009, S. 843, 111th Cong. (2009); H.R. 2324.

320. For a strong rebuttal argument, *see* Kairys, *supra* note 279, at 4: "The more handguns there are, the more people see them as necessary for self-defense. Their spread is very much an epidemic, carried by fear rather than a virus. It is an unusual epidemic in that the cause is widely seen as the cure, as fear breeds more fear and guns create demand for more guns. . . ."

See also Dixon, *supra* note 283, at 275: "[I]t is in response to the proliferation of handguns that an increasing number of people believe they need to buy a handgun for self-defense. . . . [W]hile some potential criminals may be deterred by a heavily-armed citizenry, others will arm themselves with more and more powerful firearms in order to outgun resisters. Trading gunfire or playing chicken with increasingly heavily-armed criminals is a tenuous basis for the defense of society."

321. *See* Kellerman & Reay, *supra* note 282, at 1559:

Guns kept in King County homes were involved in the deaths of friends or acquaintances 12 times as often as in those of strangers. Even after the exclusion of firearm-related suicides, guns kept at home were involved in the death of a member of the household 18 times more often than in the death of a stranger. . . .

Id.

322. 18 U.S.C. § 922 (2000).

323. Id.

324. 18 U.S.C. § 922(c) (2000).

325. 18 U.S.C. § 922(d) (2000):

It shall be unlawful for any person to sell or otherwise dispose of any firearm or ammunition to any person knowing or having reasonable cause to believe that such person- (1) is under indictment for, or has been convicted in any court of, a crime punishable by imprisonment for a term exceeding one year; (2) is a fugitive from justice; (3) is an unlawful user of or addicted to any controlled substance. . . .

Id.

326. 18 U.S.C. §922(s)(2) (2000).

purchase of guns by approximately five hundred thousand criminals.[327] But it did not prevent the Columbine and the District of Columbia sniper shooters from obtaining the guns they needed. Thus, it authorizes and supports the continuing saturation of the country with guns.

c. **Personal Responsibility** Gun proponents suggest the key to gun policy is personal responsibility.[328] Their position is that only the shooter should be held liable, not the gun dealer or manufacturer.[329] The obvious problem with this argument is that it sets up a straw man, someone with no assets.[330] Almost all criminals are judgment proof.[331] If they are not before the shooting, they are afterward because any assets they have are used to pay their attorneys.[332] Young children and teen shooters are judgment proof because they have no assets to start with.[333] Indeed, if we assume the value of a life today to be approximately

---

327. President Bill Clinton, Speech at Democratic National Convention (Aug. 14, 2000) ("We put 100,000 new police officers in every street, virtually, in every community throughout these United States. We stopped the manufacture of 19 specific kinds of assault weapons, and we have prevented a half-million felons, fugitives and domestic abusers from buying guns, because of the Brady bill.").

328. *See* Heston, *supra* note 304 ("If you say guns create carnage, I would answer that you know better. Declining morals, disintegrating families, vacillating political leadership, an eroding criminal justice system and social morals that blur right and wrong are to blame—certainly more than any legally owned firearm.").

329. *Id.* ("When . . . gunmakers are responsible for criminals' acts . . . something is wrong."). *See also* NRA-ILA Research & Information Division, *"Junk Lawsuits" Against Gun Manufacturers, available at:* http://nraila.org/research/19990825-LawsuitPreemption-001.shtml (last visited July 13, 2000) ("In all these suits the plaintiffs seek to wipe out centuries-old tort law principle. . . . Defendants can't be held liable for injuries that occur only because a properly operating product is criminally or negligently misused.").

330. The straw man insulates the manufacturer from liability: if the manufacturer is not held liable and the perpetrator is judgment-proof, no one bears the responsibility for the harm caused by the firearm. *See* Kairys, *supra* note 279, at 7–8 ("This structure, which the manufacturers have created, also provides them with a deceptive deniability: they can claim that they have no responsibility for whatever occurs after they sell to the wholesalers, which hides their lack of even minimal safeguards or concern for the public or costs to the cities.").

331. Phillip J. Cook & James A. Leitzel, *Perversity, Futility, Jeopardy: An Economic Analysis of the Attack on Gun Control*, 59 LAW & CONTEMP. PROBS. 96 (Winter 1996) (arguing a system of ex post liability poses difficult problems with collecting a judgment equal to the amount of injury to the victim).

332. Although imprisonment may be an alternate form of a fine, there is no guarantee such punishment will be a sufficient deterrent to the perpetrator in the heat of passion. *See id.* at 96–97.

333. *Id.* at 105 ("[M]ost youthful criminals, even those who sell drugs occasionally, have small incomes."). The situation is further complicated because youths may behave irrationally, choosing to risk the punishment even when it is contrary to their best interests.

$1 million, practically all shooters are judgment proof.[334] Congressional immunity for firearms sellers argues this million dollar loss must remain on the shoulders of the innocent victim and their families, and that the gun industry must be insulated from responsibility. In 2005, Congress passed the "Protection of Lawful Commerce in Arms Act" that immunizes gun manufacturers from liability whenever the shooter was involved in a crime.[335]

d. Economic Impact The argument for gun ownership as a means of self-defense needs to be evaluated in terms of microeconomic theory.[336] The benefits from gun ownership must exceed the costs of such ownership to be economically efficient. The more than fifteen thousand deaths each year and the directly related losses strongly suggest the costs of gun ownership substantially exceed its benefits. The suits brought by the cities and shooting victims argue the costs of gun violence should be shifted to the gun manufacturers. The expenses being paid by the cities and the taxpayers are enormous: "[the] medical costs of treating the gunshot injuries received during 1994, in the United States, was $2.3 billion."[337] In view of the substantial risks to the homeowner and the family when there is a gun in the home, the alleged benefits of firearm ownership for self-defense are overstated. If there are approximately fifteen thousand firearm homicides each year (costs),[338] and keeping a gun in the home prevents only 308 deaths from attackers (benefits),[339] and if we assume each life is worth $1 million,[340] the costs of gun violence ($15 billion) exceed the benefits ($308 million) by more than $14 billion each year.[341] Immunity leaves this loss on the victim and society. The powerful gun manufacturers win again.

---

334. *Id.* at 98 (citing W. KIP VISCUSI, *Strategic and Ethical Issues in the Valuation of Life*, STRATEGY AND CHOICE 380 (1992) (estimating the value of a life to be between $1 million and $10 million)).

335. Protection of Lawful Commerce in Arms Act, Pub. L. No. 92, 119 Stat. 2095 (2005).

336. *See* Louis Kaplow & Steven Shavell, *Accuracy in the Assessment of Damages*, 39 J. L. & ECON. 191, 192 (1996); A. Mitchell Polinsky & Steven Shavell, *Should Liability be Based on the Harm to the Victim or the Gain to the Injurer?*, 10 J. L. ECON. & ORG. 427, 428 (1994) (tort and contract claims are based on harm to the injured party). Laurence Tribe argues guns are appropriate for self-defense. *See* LAURENCE H. TRIBE, AMERICAN CONSTITUTIONAL LAW 901–02 n.221 (2000); Laurence H. Tribe & Akhil Reed Amar, *Well-Regulated Militias, and More*, N.Y. TIMES, Oct. 28, 1999, at A31.

337. Merrill v. Navegar, 89 Cal.Rptr.2d 146, 169–70 (Cal. Ct. App. 1999), *rev'd*, Merrill v. Navegar, 28 P.3d 116 (Cal. 2001).

338. Jacobs, *supra* note 296.

339. *Id.*

340. Cook & Lietzel, *supra* note 331.

341. This calculation omits the $2.3 billion costs of treating gunshot victims, the costs of increased police and gunfire cleanups, the gun-flight from the cities, and the cost of the fear of being shot. On the benefits side, it omits the benefit of feeling secure in the home because of a gun, the thrill of hunting, and the sport of shooting tin cans and paper

4. Immunity Legislation for Firearms Sellers

Section 2 of the Immunity Bill provides: "The Congress finds the following: (1) Citizens have a right, protected by the Second Amendment to the United States Constitution, to keep and bear arms."[342]

The Second Amendment states "A well-regulated militia, being necessary to the security of a free state, the right of the people to keep and bear arms, shall not be infringed."[343] This section will provide an overview of Second Amendment case law, and demonstrate there is little basis for firearms sellers being immunized from civil suits by the Second Amendment.

A detailed study of the history of the Second Amendment was recently provided by the Fifth Circuit Court of Appeals. In *United States v. Emerson*, decided in October 2001, the majority carefully examined the text of the Second Amendment and the history surrounding its development:

> [T]he amendment achieves its central purpose by assuring that the federal government may not disarm individual citizens without some unusually strong justification consistent with the authority of the states to organize their own militias. That assurance in turn is provided through recognizing a right (admittedly of uncertain scope) on the part of individuals to possess and use firearms in the defense of themselves and their homes.[344]

The court then examined the recognized treatises of the 1800s and concluded "[t]he great Constitutional scholars of the 19th century recognized that the Second Amendment guarantees the right of individual Americans to possess and carry firearms."[345] The narrow holding of the case, however, is that a federal statute is constitutional in authorizing the removal of a pistol from a physician who threatened his former wife.[346]

The leading case law supports the regulation of gun ownership. In *United States v. Miller*,[347] the defendants were arrested for carrying an unregistered sawed-off shotgun.[348] The National Firearms Act of 1934 required the weapon to be registered.[349] Scott Jacobs comments that *Miller*, decided in 1939 by the

---

targets. It also omits the value of gun collecting and assumes that each of the 308 attackers would have killed the gun owner.

342. *See* Protection, *supra* note 335.

343. U.S. Const. amend. II.

344. 270 F.3d 203, 236 (5th Cir. 2001) *cert. denied*, 536 U.S. 907 (2002) (quoting Laurence H. Tribe, 1 American Constitutional Law 902 n.221 (3d ed. 2000)).

345. *Id.* at 255.

346. *Id.* at 261.

347. 307 U.S. 174 (1939).

348. *Id.* at 175.

349. *Id.* (quoting 26 U.S.C. § 1132(d)):

Within sixty days after the . . . effective date of this Act every person possessing a firearm shall register, with the collector of the district in which he resides, the number or

U.S. Supreme Court, stated that federal legislation prohibiting the purchase and sale of sawed-off shotguns was "neither an unconstitutional invasion of the . . . state's authority guaranteed by the Tenth Amendment nor did it infringe upon the right to keep and bear arms as protected by the Second Amendment."[350] Indeed, Jacobs reports the Court held "Congress had the right to determine whether certain firearms would be restricted in the interest of national public safety and whether those weapons were appropriate for militia use."[351]

The question of whether a citizen has a constitutionally protected right to keep a gun in his home was decided in *Heller v. District of Columbia* (2008).[352] Heller, a D.C. policeman, was not permitted to possess a gun in his home because it was prohibited by a District of Columbia ordinance. However, the U.S. Supreme Court threw out the ordinance, with Justice Scalia (writing for the majority of the Court) reasoning the ordinance was in violation of the Second Amendment. Scalia used his famous theory of "original intent" to review documents and statements around the time of the drafting of the Second Amendment to show that a citizen historically had a right to own a gun. Unfortunately, Scalia's narrow approach prevented him from considering the present-day carnage in the homes, streets, and schools from gun violence.

The question since *Heller* is whether the case will be used to strike down all regulations dealing with gun ownership. Has it made a difference? Is the right to own a gun absolute? The answer is no. Professor Adam Winkler of U.C.L.A. has examined federal cases decided since *Heller* and concluded the case has had little impact on gun regulation: "To date, the federal courts have yet to invalidate a single gun control law for violating the Second Amendment right to bear arms, despite scores of cases."[353] Apparently these courts are pushing for a very narrow interpretation of *Heller,* limiting it to its facts.

---

other mark identifying such firearm, together with his name, address, place where such firearm is usually kept, and place of business or employment, and, if such person is other than a natural person, the name and home address of an executive officer thereof. . . .

350. Jacobs, *supra* note 296, at 330. *See also Miller,* 307 U.S. at 177 ("In the absence of any evidence tending to show that possession or use of a 'shotgun having a barrel less than eighteen inches in length' at this time has some reasonable relationship to the preservation or efficiency of a well regulated militia, we cannot say that the Second Amendment guarantees the right to keep and bear such an instrument.").

351. Jacobs, *supra* note 296, at 330.

352. District of Columbia v. Heller, No. 07-290 (U.S. June 26, 2008).

353. Adam Winkler, *Heller's Catch 22,* 56 UCLA L. Rev. 1551 (2009).The Supreme Court has heard argument on whether *District of Columbia v. Heller* will apply to eliminate state gun control statutes. The case argued is *McDonald v. Chicago.* Adam Liptak, "Supreme Court Remains Divided Over Gun Control,"http://www.nytimes.com/2010/03/03/us/03scotus.html

The general rule for products liability is that all those who sell defective products are subject to liability.[354] The Protection of Lawful Commerce in Arms Act reverses that 150-year-old rule for gun manufacturers.[355] It wrongly assumes guns in the home are a good idea and essential to self-defense, and therefore deserving of wide protection.

In evaluating the firearms manufacturers' immunity bill, Congress should have considered the gun violence epidemic, the foundering of gun cases in the state courts, and the Supreme Court's historical interpretations of the Second Amendment. Congress should have permitted the courts to continue to hammer out gun policy over the next several years. Immunization of the gun industry not only is a rejection of 160 years of products liability theory, but flies in the face of concerns over continuing widespread gun violence. The gun industry has an important role to play in reducing gun violence, but they must be encouraged to participate in developing the framework and details of the solution. Now is not the appropriate time for giving immunity to the powerful and manipulative gun industry. However, as this section indicates, the courts and Congress respond to the wishes of that industry.

C. THE SUV ROLLOVER INDEX

One of the themes of the book is that power tends to win in legal disputes. In the early part of the book, we looked at this in the legislatures and the courts; now we will examine whether the thesis also holds before administrative agencies that deal with products. The thesis is that if an agency such as the National Highway Traffic Safety Administration (NHTSA) is faced with an important issue, it will likely decide in favor of the vehicle manufacturers rather than the consumers.

One of the most dangerous vehicles is the Sports Utility Vehicle (SUV) because it has a tendency to roll over when it makes a quick high-speed turn.[356] For example, when a driver of a Bronco II swerves to miss a deer,[357] the SUV has a higher tendency than a car to tip and roll over.[358] This book's thesis is that it would be helpful for the consumer to know whether a certain SUV was relatively stable, somewhat tippy, or quite dangerous and likely to flip. A simple numerical

---

354. *See* KEETON ET AL., *supra* note 115, at 677–724.

355. *See* FRANK J. VANDALL, STRICT LIABILITY 1–16 (1989). Protection of Lawful Commerce in Arms Act, Pub. L. No. 92, 119 Stat. 2095 (2005).

356. Nancy Denny pressed her Bronco II brakes firmly to avoid a deer. Denny v. Ford Motor Co., 662 N.E.2d 730 (N.Y. 1995).

357. *Id.*

358. NHTSA, DEP'T OF TRANSP., 3.4 DOT HS 810 872, BUYING A SAFER CAR 2008 (2007) *available at* http://www.safercar.gov/staticfiles/DOT/safercar/pdf/BASC2008.pdf [hereinafter BUYING].

scale from one to ten would work as an index. Ten would represent the most tippy SUV, such as a Bronco II.[359] Five would represent something in the middle, while one would be for an SUV or car that was quite stable such as a Honda 2000 sports car.[360] This index would provide valuable information and help consumers determine the danger level of their SUVs.

SUVs have been the big moneymakers for the auto industry,[361] so all major manufacturers produce them. Ford made as much as $10,000 profit on each Expedition model during the good old days.[362] In the NHTSA debate over the index, we would expect the powerful manufacturers to oppose the index concept because of lost sales. Consumers would see their potential purchase received a high-risk index number and would walk away from the SUV. (This is quite similar to U.S. News law school rankings. This ranking provides useful information to students, but law schools rail against the rankings as being superficial and misleading.)[363] Further, we can predict the NHTSA would side with the manufacturers and reject the idea of an index even though it would provide the consumer with valuable information and could save lives.

This is what happened in 1987. Senator Timothy E. Wirth argued to NHTSA that the highway safety administration should adopt a "stability factor" for SUVs to be made available to potential consumers.[364] Wirth defined the "stability factor" as:

> one-half of a vehicle's track width divided by the height of the vehicle's center of gravity; or $T/2/H$, where T is track width and H is the center of gravity height that equals or exceeds a specific minimum value.[365]

The basis of Senator Wirth's theory was: "vehicles with the lowest stability values 'rollover more than vehicles with higher measures because they are . . . designed in defiance of the laws of nature.'"[366]

---

359. Denial of Motor Vehicle Defect Petitions, 53 Fed. Reg. 34866 (NHTSA, Dep't of Transp. Sept. 8, 1988) [hereinafter Defect].

360. For the rollovers, the Honda S2000 has the best rating (5 stars), BUYING, supra note 359, at 8.

361. E.g., Nichole Christian, Ford's New Monster, TIME, Mar. 8, 1999, #http://www.time.com/time/magazine/article/0,9171,990378,00.html.

362. E.g., Keith Bradsher, The Nation: Making Tons of Money and Fords, Too, N.Y. TIMES, Feb. 14, 1999, http://www.nytimes.com/1999/02/14/weekinreview/the-nation-making-tons-of-money-and-fords-too.html.

363. Jordan G. Lee, Three Grad Schools Keep Top U.S. News Ranking; Law School Slips to Third, HARV. CRIMSON, Apr. 3, 2006, http://www.thecrimson.com/article.aspx?ref=512406.

364. Denial of Petition for Rulemaking; Vehicle Rollover Resistance, 49 CFR pt. 571, 52 Fed. Reg. 49033 (NHTSA, Dep't of Transp. Dec. 29, 1987) [hereinafter Vehicle Rollover].

365. Id. at 49034.

366. Id.

SUV rollovers cause about ten thousand deaths per year.[367] Because they have been popular for about thirty years, SUVs have caused perhaps three hundred thousand needless deaths and many more serious injuries.[368] Nevertheless, NHTSA rejected Senator Wirth's proposal for a "stability factor" index that would be made available to prospective consumers.[369] This is in spite of NHTSA's own statement that "rollovers account for 44 percent of all light truck deaths . . ."[370]

The following section will examine and critique NHTSA's reasons for rejecting Senator Wirth's proposed "stability factor" index.

1) "[T]he key issue in the agency's evaluation is whether a vehicle's stability factor has been shown to be so intrinsically related to rollover that all vehicles with . . . 'low' stability values should be considered inherently unstable . . ."[371]

Comment: The consumer should have enough data to make an informed choice. A low "stability factor" would be a red flag to a consumer. Manufacturers would have an opportunity to explain to the contrary why their SUV is stable.

2) "The rate of a vehicle's accident involvement . . . is related to the basic design characteristics of the vehicle, which in turn, reflect the function for which it was designed."[372]

Comment: No, SUVs in and of themselves mislead the public. Many have substantial ground clearance so they can be driven off-road as the manufacturer intended. But very few are ever driven off-road.[373] The result is a vehicle with a substantial likelihood to roll over that is almost never used for its intended purpose.[374] Usage reality should be the test, not the "function for which it was designed."

3) NHTSA is unable to agree [that the "stability factor"] "isolates the cause of rollover."

---

367. BUYING, note 358, at 3–4. A high percent of rollovers involve SUVs. *Id.*

368. 10,000 x 30 years = 300,000.

369. Vehicle Rollover, *supra* note 364, at 49035.

370. *Id.*

371. *Id.*

372. *Id.*

373. LAURA MACCLEERY, PUBLIC CITIZEN, SUV'S: THE HIGH COST OF LAX FUEL ECONOMY STANDARDS FOR AMERICAN FAMILIES 13 (2003) *available at* http://www.citizen.org/documents/costs_of_SUV's.pdf ("Despite being marketed to consumers as rugged, go-anywhere vehicles, only 1 to 10 percent of SUV owners use their vehicles for off-road driving or towing.")

374. *Id.* at 7 ("In 2002, SUV and pickup rollover deaths accounted *for 46 percent of the increase in all occupant fatalities and 78 percent of the increase in passenger vehicle rollover fatalities*").

Comment: NHTSA sounds as though the agency is looking for one perfect test for rollover. This search for the Holy Grail has resulted in delay, and delay equals perhaps ten thousand rollover deaths per year.[375] SUVs are complex vehicles, covering a broad spectrum of vehicles ranging from Toyota Highlanders (low and therefore stable) to Ford fifteen- passenger vans (top heavy when full of passengers and therefore quite likely to roll over).[376] A helpful index would be better than nothing when the goal is to save lives.

4) "The agency does not believe that the sample selected for study, comprising three older utility vehicles, . . . is representative of the real-world . . ."[377]

Comment: More test subjects would have improved the study. But everything we know argues that the omitted SUVs (such as the Ford Bronco II, Chevrolet Blazer, and Jeep Cherokee)[378] have a high tendency to roll over.[379] Studies are expensive. Who will fund them? NHTSA should engage in rollover testing, or require it on the part of the manufacturers.[380]

5) "[R]egulating the height and width of a vehicle is not by itself, a reasonable means of addressing the rollover accident problem. . . . [A] vehicle's stability factor is but one factor among many others affecting rollovers."[381]

Comment: NHTSA, what factors do you suggest? What rollover index do you propose? By dragging your feet, you have encouraged the powerful vehicle manufacturers to make millions of dollars—and you have had a part in causing tens of thousands of rollover deaths.[382] Also, Senator Wirth merely asked for information and notice to consumers.[383] Design regulation by NHTSA is unlikely.

6) "More than one-half of the vehicles involved in the roll-over . . . were sliding sideways prior to rolling over."[384]

---

375. BUYING, *supra* note 358, at 3.

376. The Ford 15-passenger van has a poor rollover rating of two stars, BUYING, *supra* note 358, at 19. Highlander gets four stars. *Id.* at 17.

377. Vehicle Rollover, *supra* note 364, at 49036.

378. *Id.*

379. Defect, *supra* note 359, at 34866.

380. About thirty years later, NHTSA tested SUVs for rollovers. BUYING, *supra* note 358, at 2.

381. Vehicle Rollover, *supra* note 364, at 49036 (emphasis added).

382. See a similar delay before the Food and Drug Administration in regard to Chloromycetin. Stevens v. Park, Davis & Co., 507 P.2d 653 (Cal. 1973).

383. Vehicle Rollover, *supra* note 364, at 49033–34.

384. *Id.* at 49036.

Comment: If sliding is critical, it should be incorporated into the rollover index. Perhaps sliding is the first step before the roll, and needs to be further examined.[385]

7) "The adoption of the stability factor requirement could contravene section 103(f)(3) of the National Traffic and Motor Vehicle Safety Act which provides that the Federal motor vehicle safety standards must be reasonable and appropriate for each vehicle type to which they apply, . . . Thus it is not intended that standards will be set which will eliminate . . . small cars or convertibles and sport cars so long as all motor vehicles meet basic minimum standards."[386]

Comment: NHTSA's interpretation of 103(f)(3) is consistent with the theme that power tends to win because vehicle manufacturers hire lobbyists to influence the language of legislation. Section 103(f)(3) allows for numerous interpretations:

- All vehicle types must be safe.
- A rollover index would go far to make SUVs safer.
- 103(f)(3) ties NHTSA's hands so they can do nothing. This was the agency's interpretations.
  - Wide discretion remains, and NHTSA has a great deal of room when it comes to safety.
  - The section does not mention SUVs; therefore, NHTSA can issue rollover indexes for SUVs.

8) "Congress . . . is planning to address the issue of . . . rollover stability . . . of utility vehicles."[387] [Therefore, we will leave the development of an index to Congress.]

Comment: In other sections, the argument was made that the powerful manufacturers have substantial influence over Congress.[388] In the more than twenty years since this statement by NHTSA, Congress has done nothing meaningful to address the problem of SUV rollovers.[389] Rather, Congress has delegated vehicle safety to NHTSA.[390] Therefore, NHTSA is poorly advised in waiting for Congress to do NHTSA's work.

---

385. Modern SUVs (2009) have incorporated vehicle stability control to reduce sliding and therefore rollovers. *See* Buying, *supra* note 358, at 4.

386. Vehicle Rollover, *supra* note 364, at 49037.

387. *Id.* The bracketed comment is the authors.

388. *See supra* Chapter 5 [Parts 2 and 3, discussing tobacco and guns].

389. The problematic star rating system took NHTSA thirty years. *See* Buying, *supra* note 358, at cover page.

390. NHTSA was established as a separate organizational entity in the Department of Transportation in March 1970. It succeeded the National Highway Safety Bureau, which previously had administered traffic and highway safety functions as an organizational

9) "[T]he fatality rates for utility vehicles are much higher than those for other vehicle classes. . . . [U]tility vehicle accidents result in greater numbers of severe injuries and fatalities compared to other vehicle classes."

Comment: This is true. Develop a rollover index for SUVs and give notice to consumers. Vehicle safety is clearly the responsibility of the NHTSA.

At this point it would be helpful if we could examine the NHTSA's arguments in regard to a specific SUV. NHTSA has provided such an example: the famous Suzuki Samurai.[391] NHTSA begins its analysis on whether to regulate the Samurai by agreeing it has a very high tendency to roll over and produce serious injuries: "There are 113 reported rollovers for the Samurai [and its cousin]. These reported rollovers involve 120 injuries and 25 fatalities."[392] NHTSA found the Ford Bronco II, the Chevrolet Blazer, and the Jeep Cherokee also had high tendencies to roll over, but the Samurai was somewhat less tippy.[393] Based on these findings, NHTSA refused to conduct a defect investigation into the rollover propensity of the Samurai.[394]

Instead of the Samurai's design, NHTSA pointed to other factors for causing the rollovers: Young drivers (73 percent were twenty-five or younger); "alcohol usage" (50 percent); driving at night (58 percent); driving on the weekend (55 percent); and driving in California as contrasted with Florida.[395]

Comment: Undoubtedly age, alcohol, and darkness play a role in many vehicle crashes. NHTSA misses the point: the Suzuki Samurai is among a group of five SUVs that have a very high tendency to rollover and cause death and serious injury. NHTSA even admits this.[396]

In rejecting the Samurai's rollover investigation request, NHTSA embraced the rollover index (discussed above) it had rejected only one year earlier:[397]

The Samurai was found to have a static stability factor (ratio of the half track width to center of gravity height) higher than most other [SUVs] when empty.

---

unit of the Federal Highway Administration. Highway Safety Act of 1966, Pub. L. No. 89-563, sec. 1, 80 Stat. 718 (codified as amended at 49 U.S.C. ch. 327) ("The purpose of this chapter is to reduce traffic accidents and deaths and injuries resulting from traffic accidents. Therefore it is necessary - (1) to prescribe motor vehicle safety standards for motor vehicles and motor vehicle equipment in interstate commerce; and (2) to carry out needed safety research and development.").

391. For example, the Samurai was held to be defective for not having seatbelts and an appropriate warning. It did not roll over in the crash. Bowersfield v. Suzuki Motor Corp., 111 F. Supp.2d 612 (E.D.Pa. 2000). Consumers Union won a defamation case where it had said the Samurai was subject to rollover. Suzuki Motor Corp. v. Consumers Union, 330 F.3d 1110 (9th Cir. 2003).

392. Defect, *supra* note 359, at 34866.

393. *Id.*

394. *Id.*

395. *Id.*

396. *Id.*

397. Vehicle Rollover, *supra* note 364, at 49033.

. . . The stability factor has been shown to have a positive statistical relationship to the likelihood of a vehicle rolling over in an accident.[398]

Although NHTSA agrees the Samurai has a high tendency to roll over and take lives, it sets forth unconvincing arguments in order to protect the powerful manufacturers from design change, public criticism, and loss of profits.[399] When the common factors in most cases (age, alcohol, darkness) are stripped away, we are left with a vehicle with a high tendency to flip because of a clear design problem.

After twenty years, NHTSA finally developed a (star) rollover index for SUVs. During this long delay, perhaps two hundred thousand people died in SUV rollovers.[400] In 2007, the agency stated:

> NHTSA rollover . . . ratings measure the chance your vehicle, will roll over if you are involved in a single-vehicle crash. . . . Vehicles with a higher number of stars are less likely to roll over if involved in a single-vehicle crash.
>
> The rollover resistance rating is based on: (1) an at rest laboratory measurement known as the Statistic Stability Factor (SSF) which determines how "top-heavy" a vehicle is, and (2) the results of a driving maneuver that tests whether a vehicle is vulnerable to tipping up on the road in a severe maneuver. . . .
>
> More than 10,000 people die each year in rollover crashes.[401]

There are three substantial problems with the star rollover index as adopted by the NHTSA. First, it took too long (twenty years) for NHTSA to act, during which time hundreds of thousands of people died or were seriously injured. Second, the star ratings are misleading. Stars imply something good, but SUVs are problematic because they tend to roll over more often than cars. The star ratings gloss over this point. Finally, the stars are misleading because the area covered by the three and four stars given to SUVs is too broad. As a consequence, all SUVs have a three- or a four-star rollover rating. Perhaps that is NHTSA's and the manufacturers point: all SUVs are equally safe. Finally, the star rating for rollovers is never fully explained. The severe risk in driving an SUV remains difficult to determine. The much higher risk of death and serious injury from an SUV rollover crash (as compared to a sedan) is not made clear to the consumer.

---

398. Defect, *supra* note 359, at 34867.
399. *See* Suzuki Motor Corp. v. Consumers Union, 330 F.3d 1110 (9th Cir. 2003).
400. *See supra* notes 367–68.
401. Buying, *supra* note 358, at 3.

6. THE APPLICATION OF CONCEPTS TO CONTEMPORARY EXAMPLES

The previous chapters argue that civil justice in areas dealing with products no longer rests on historic foundations such as precedent, fairness, and impartiality, but instead has shifted to power and influence. "Reform" in the law—legislative, judicial, and regulatory—is now driven by financial interests rather than a neutral search for justice. Never has it been less true that we live under the rule of law. Congress, the courts, and agencies make the law, but they are driven by those who have a large financial stake in the outcome.

Specific arguments were made in the preceding five chapters: (1) corporations affect the content of the law; (2) in regard to products liability, "think tanks" are working to insulate corporations from liability; (3) reform in the law today is driven by power and influence, not to make the law better for all; (4) tort "reform" is aimed at insulating the powerful from challenge in the courts, thereby increasing profits; (5) gun suits brought by the victims and the cities were lost because the plaintiffs took aim at those with influence: the gun manufacturers; and (6) SUV rollover indexes for over ten years reflected the interests of the manufacturers more than consumers. Chapter VI takes many of these themes and applies them to other, often more recent examples to demonstrate the degree of influence exerted by those with power.

A. LOBBIES ARE EFFECTIVE

One of the best examples of the power of lobbies is the success of Georgia Power in funding the construction of a new nuclear reactor. Georgia Power lobbied the Georgia legislature and persuaded its members to permit the customers to pay for the construction of a nuclear reactor (prior to completion):

> [A] Republican dominated Legislature with a strong aversion to increasing rates . . . approved a bill allowing Georgia Power to charge customers early for nuclear reactors. . . . Critics . . . point to the company's powerful lobbying effort: businesslike, efficient and devastatingly effective.[1]

---

1. Margaret Newkirk & Aaron Gould Sheinin, *Georgia Power Gets Its Wish as Foes Fume,* Atlanta J.-Const., Mar. 1, 2009, at A1.

The lobbying of the legislature was a road map for success:

> [Georgia Power] pulled its law firm, registered its chief executive as a lobbyist and spent thousands buying lawmakers meals and sports tickets, burnishing its reputation as the most polished lobbying outfit around.
>
> It was a textbook example of how to get one's way at the Capitol, said state Representative Mary Margaret Oliver . . . who opposed the bill.[2]

Sometimes, however, lobbyists do their job too well. The Georgia House Speaker, Glenn Richardson, resigned his post allegedly over the allegation he had an affair with a female lobbyist. The *Atlanta Journal-Constitution* reported:

> Doubts about the affair vanished when Susan Richardson told Atlanta TV station WAGA she had discovered her husband was cheating on her with the lobbyist. . . . The couple ended their 17-year marriage in 2008.[3]

President Obama campaigned on a pledge to keep lobbyists out of government: "When I'm President [lobbyists] won't find a job in my White House."[4] However, just days before being sworn in as President, Obama nominated William J. Lynn III—a former lobbyist for the defense contractor Raytheon—to be the deputy secretary of defense.[5] Obama apparently felt Lynn was the best person for the job. This shows lobbyists are an inherent part of government. They communicate the wishes of the powerful corporations to government, and often serve in the government itself.

Obama vowed "the rule of law will be the touchstone of this presidency."[6] This statement challenges the theme of the book that Congress is persuaded to adopt new laws by lobbyists representing the powerful. It may be true the president and his administration will follow the laws—the "rule of law"—passed by Congress, but the statement glosses over the fact corporations by means of their lobbies had a hand in initially developing the law.

---

2. *Id.* at A15.

3. Alan Judd, *Ethics Panel Did Nil*, Atlanta J.-Const., Dec. 5, 2009, at A10.

4. Interview by Jim Acosta with President Barack Obama, *Obama Administration Following the Bush Model?* CNN. (Dec. 19, 2008), *available at* http://transcripts.cnn.com/TRANSCRIPTS/0812/19/ltm.02.html.

5. *Ex-Lobbyist Gets Defense Post*, Atlanta J.-Const. Jan. 24, 2009, at A6.In her February 7, 2010 speech before the Tea Party Convention held in Nashville, Sarah Palin alleged there were forty former lobbyists in the Obama administration. CNN, Feb. 7, 2010, 9:00 p.m.

6. *Vowing Transparency, Obama OKs Ethics Guidelines*, CNN.com, Jan. 21, 2009, *available at* http://www.cnn.com/2009/POLITICS/01/21/obama.business/index.html.

One indication of who is influencing the president is the record of his visitors. Lobbyists were among the first to meet with him:

[P]rominent lobbyists [and] corporate executives . . . were among the first to score visits with President Barack Obama . . . at the White House, newly released records show.

Among the guests [at the White House]: Bill Gates, Microsoft Cofounder . . . Andrew Stern . . . president of the Service Employees International Union . . . Ed Yingling, chief executive of the American Bankers Association and a registered lobbyist . . . Camden Fine, chief executive of the Independent Community Bankers of America and a Washington lobbyist for the group.[7]

Apparently even a semblance of power is sufficient to allow someone to meet the president and shake his hand. Strangers not on the guest list met with the president in 2009. Here is a summary of this serious breakdown in state security:

This much is known: About 7:15 Tuesday night, a glittering blond, decked out in a red and gold sari, holding the hand of her black-tuxedoed escort, swept past the camera crews and reporters camped out to catch the red-carpet arrivals for the first state dinner given by President Barack Obama.

. . .

The couple [was] Michaele Salahi and her husband, Tareq.[8]

Somehow "the Virginia couple . . . got past layers of experienced, executive-branch security."[9] Perhaps many of the guests at the state dinner were donors and lobbyists, and those assigned to check the guest list were apprehensive they might offend someone with power—and therefore looked the other way.

Sometimes lobbyists go too far and commit crimes. One important example of corrupt lobbying is Jack Abramoff, who was once one of Washington's most powerful Republican lobbyists. Abramoff (in his own words) "happily and arrogantly engaged" in a lavish lifestyle and political corruption, but is now the "butt of jokes, the source of laughs, the title of scandals."[10] In 2006, Abramoff pled

---

7. Sharon Theimer, *Celebrities, Lobbyists on White House Guest Lists*, ATLANTA J.-CONST., Nov. 1, 2009, at A18.

8. *Obama Dinner Crashers Walk Right In*, ATLANTA J.-CONST., Nov. 26, 2009, at A18.

9. Jason Horowitz, Roxanne Roberts, & Michael D. Shear, *Party Crashers Shook Hands with Obama*, ATLANTA J.-CONST., Nov. 28, 2009, at A1.

10. Richard B. Schmitt, *Ex-GOP Lobbyist Abramoff Sentenced to 4 Years in Prison*, L.A. TIMES, Sept. 5, 2008.

The author appreciates the contributions of Anna Diehn to these two paragraphs on criminal acts.

guilty in federal court to fraud, tax evasion, and conspiracy to bribe officials.[11] He was sentenced to four years in prison.[12]

Particularly egregious was Abramoff's Indian Tribe Scandal, in which he secretly pushed for anti-casino legislation while persuading several tribes to pay him huge lobbying fees (totaling $84 million) to promote casinos.[13] At least $4 million of these fees went to Ralph Reed, former executive director of the Christian Coalition, to raise anti-gambling sentiment in the public and in the legislature.[14] Abramoff's goal was to be paid by one tribe to promote its interest in obtaining a casino license while he was also being paid by another tribe (with a casino) to resist additional casinos. Similarly, Reed put pressure on members of Congress to prohibit online gambling while simultaneously receiving proceeds from eLottery, a firm that had hired Abramoff to lobby in favor of online gambling.[15] Abramoff replied to all of this by saying: "I can't imagine there's anything I did that other lobbyists didn't do and aren't doing today."[16]

B. GOVERNMENT REWARDS THE POWERFUL: CORPORATE BAILOUTS

An excellent example of government responding to the needs and wishes of the powerful is the 2008 governmental bailout of the financial institutions, GM, and Chrysler, with the promise of $700 billion in funds. It is apparent "nearly two-thirds of the money released to banks has gone to the nation's eight largest institutions: Citigroup $45 billion; Bank of America $45 billion; JP Morgan Chase $25 billion; Wells Fargo $25 billion; Morgan Stanley $10 billion; Goldman Sachs $10 billion; Bank of New York $3 billion; State Street $2 billion."[17] It is now clear

---

11. *Id.*

12. *Id.*

13. *See* Susan Schmidt, *Insiders Worked Both Sides of Gaming Issue*, WASH. POST, Sept. 26, 2004, at A01, and Susan Schmidt, *Casino Bid Prompted High-Stakes Lobbying*, WASH. POST, Mar. 13, 2005, at A01.

14. Susan Schmidt, *Insiders Worked, supra* note 13.

15. Susan Schmidt & James V. Grimaldi, *How a Lobbyist Stacked the Deck*, WASH. POST, Oct. 16, 2005.

Thomas B. Edsall, *Another Stumble for Ralph Reed's Beleaguered Campaign*, WASH. POST, May 29, 2006. Ralph Reed interned for Abramoff in 1981 on the College Republican National Committee (CRNC), and the two remained close friends. Reed managed to engage in his own list of questionable activities: plagiarism and election-rigging in college; resignation from the Coalition during a fraudulent billing investigation; and work as a campaign leader for Mitch Skandalakis, who was charged in federal court relating to campaign tactics.

Most recently, Reed lost the Republican primary election for lieutenant governor of Georgia.

16. Compiled by Washington Post.com, *Unraveling Abramoff: Key Players in the Investigation of Jack Abramoff*, June 26, 2007, *available at* http://www.washingtonpost.com/wp-dyn/content/custom/2005/12/23/CU2005122300939.html.

17. David Chou & Lori Montgomery, *Bailout Backlog Angers Small Firms*, ATLANTA J.-CONST., Jan. 24, 2009, at B3.

"Rescue loans provided to Chrysler, General Motors Corp. and GMAC, General Motor's auto-financing arm, now total a combined $20.8 billion."[18]

Congress, former President George W. Bush, and President Obama chose to give the rescue money to the huge corporations, not individuals. They decided to bail out the huge corporations rather than let them sink. The reasoning is straightforward: The banks will loan the money to other corporations, small businesses, and people buying homes and cars. But if the stimulus money were given to individual citizens, they might hoard it.[19] This would not produce jobs or growth, and would do little to jump-start the economy.[20]

The bailout proves the point: corporations drive the law. Notably these funds were the direct result of intense corporate lobbying. Representative Scott Garrett (Rep. N.J.) stated: "It's not going to be the most efficient institution that gets the rescue money, . . . It's going to turn out to be whoever has the best lobbyists and the biggest clout."[21]

Lobbying pays even in a crisis:

Wells Fargo, which received $25 billion in federal money, spent $580,000 lobbying the government in the fourth quarter [of 2009] up from $516,000 in the third.

. . .

GM reported spending $3.3 million in the fourth quarter [of 2009] as it pressed for the bailout legislation, a boost from $2.7 million in the previous three months.[22]

Earlier in Chapter V, it was argued that lobbying is a normal facet of government and not to be shunned. Greg Martin, a spokesman for GM, reflected: "Lobbying is the transparent and effective way that GM has its voice heard on critical policy issues that have a significant impact on our business . . ."[23]

---

18. Marcy Gordon, *Firms Increase Lobby Spending*, ATLANTA J.-CONST., Jan. 24, 2009, at B3.

19. *See* Joseph Lawler, *We're All Keynesians Again*, 42 AM. SPECTATOR 52, 52 (2009) (arguing President Obama and his economic team have made John Maynard Keynes "fashionable again"). "Keynes's basic insight is that in recessions pessimistic consumers and businessmen hoard cash and refuse to spend no matter how low interest rates become, rendering monetary policy useless." *Id. See also* Posting of Richard Posner to the Beckner-Posner Blog, The Obama "Stimulus" (Deficit Spending) Plan, http://www.becker-posner-blog.com/archives/2009/01/the_obama_stimu.html (Jan. 11, 2009, 9:19 p.m.) (describing the background of President Obama's stimulus plan).

20. Gordon, *supra* note 18, at B3.

21. *Id.*

22. *Id.*

23. *Id.* Stimulus money has been broadened to include "shovel ready projects" such as roads and money that can be used to keep teachers in their classrooms. Brian Naylor, NPR.org, *Stimulus Bill Gives 'Shovel-Ready' Projects Priority* (Feb. 9, 2009), http://www.npr.org/templates/story/story.php?storyId=100295436; Sam Dillion, *Stimulus-Assisted Schools Still Facing Crippling Cuts*, N.Y. TIMES, Sept. 8, 2009, at A1. *See generally* Recovery.Gov,

C. EXAMPLES OF WEAK REGULATIONS AND AGENCY POLICY
FAVORING THE REGULATED INDUSTRY: PHARMACEUTICALS,
AIRCRAFT, AND SECURITIES

Chapter 5 argued that regulations often fall short of what is needed for public safety because the agency favors the powerful industry over the safety interests of the public. In addition to car safety, three examples are regulation of pharmaceuticals, aircraft, and securities.

1. Pharmaceutical Regulation

Numerous articles have been written about the "revolving door" and the fact regulatory failure is often produced because the agencies lack sufficient personnel and funds.[24] However, even if this argument is accepted, the point being made is different: agencies fail to represent the public because they represent the interests of the powerful—the regulated industry. Rather than present express statements to that effect, the argument will be made via res ipsa loquitur (the thing speaks for itself).

Agency failure begins with the head of the agency and with its initial design. First, the head of a major agency is often a former high-ranking employee in the regulated industry.[25] For example, the head of the department of agriculture is often the former head of a large agro-business.[26] The chief counsel of the FDA under President George W. Bush was the former attorney for large tobacco and

---

http://www.recovery.gov/ (last visited Mar. 11, 2010) (official U.S. government Web site tracking spending under the Recovery Act).

24. *E.g.*, Julie Schmit, *Report: FDA So Underfunded, Consumers Are Put at Risk*, USA TODAY, Dec. 3, 2007, at 6b. *See also infra* note 25.

25. *See* Mindfully.org, The Revolving Door, http://www.mindfully.org/Farm/Green-Revolution-Revolving.htm (last visited Mar. 11, 2010) (listing examples of the revolving door syndrome). Allen Johnson was president of the National Oilseed Processors Association (NOPA) before becoming the Chief Agricultural Negotiator at the Office of the U.S. Trade Representative (USTR). *Id. See* Katherine Q. Seelye, *Bush Is Choosing Industry Insiders to Fill Several Environmental Positions*, N.Y. TIMES, May 12, 2001, at A10 (discussing particular agency nominations by President Bush). For example, Bush nominated Linda J. Fisher—who had previously been the head of Government Affairs at Monsanto—to be deputy administrator of the EPA. *Id.*

26. *See* PHILIP MATTERA, CORPORATE RESEARCH PROJECT OF GOOD JOBS FIRST, USDA INC.: HOW AGRIBUSINESS HAS HIJACKED REGULATORY POLICY AT THE U.S. DEPARTMENT OF AGRICULTURE 10 (2004) (listing examples of appointees to the USDA with past industry ties). For example, former secretary Ann Veneman served on the board of the biotech company Calgene (later taken over by Monsanto) prior to her appointment; her former chief of staff Dale Moore was the executive director for legislative affairs of the National Cattlemen's Beef Association (NCBA). *Id.*

pharmaceutical companies.[27] Second, the power of the agency is often cut off at the roots by Congress. For example, the FDA was for years forbidden to regulate tobacco.[28] The Consumer Product Safety Commission (CPSC) has also never had the power to regulate tobacco—even though it is the most dangerous product.[29] Finally, Congress has prohibited the CDC from keeping statistics on gun violence.[30]

The story of the prescription drug Vioxx (Rofecoxib) shows how the FDA was designed to fail. After going through an accelerated approval process,[31] Vioxx quickly became the leading seller for Merck & Co.[32] Merck's worldwide sales of Vioxx in 2003 totaled $2.5 billion.[33] However, complaints arose early on based on an alleged connection between Vioxx and serious heart problems.[34] Following its usual approach, the FDA negotiated (because they lacked the power to demand) a stronger warning for the drug.[35] This delay consumed more than a year and allowed Merck to reap several additional billion dollars in sales.[36] Finally, after numerous lawsuits were filed, Merck voluntarily pulled Vioxx off the

---

27. *See* Stacey Schultz, *Mr. Outside Moves Inside*, U.S. NEWS & WORLD REP., Mar. 16, 2003, http://health.usnews.com/usnews/health/articles/030324/24fda.htm.Stephanie Mencimer, *Daniel Troy's Poison Pill*, MOTHER JONES, Mar. 7, 2008, http://motherjones. com/politics/2008/03/daniel-troys-poison-pill (same).

28. Family Smoking Prevention and Tobacco Control Act, Pub. L. No. 111-31, 123 Stat. 1776 (2009). *See Obama Signs Bill Putting Tobacco Products Under FDA Oversight*, CNN, June 22, 2009, http://www.cnn.com/2009/POLITICS/06/22/obama.tobacco/index.html; CDC.gov, Smoking & Tobacco Use- Legislation, http://www.cdc.gov/tobacco/data_statistics/by_topic/policy/legislation/index.htm(last visited Mar. 11, 2010).

29. CPSC.gov, FAQ-Jurisdiction, http://www.cpsc.gov/about/faq.html (last visited Mar. 11, 2010).

30. WILLIAM KISTNER, CENTER FOR INVESTIGATIVE REPORTING, FIREARM INJURIES: THE GUN BATTLE OVER SCIENCE (1997), *available at* http://www.pbs.org/wgbh/pages/frontline/shows/ guns/procon/injuries.html (discussing how CDC's budget for pure firearm injury-related research was significantly reduced).

31. Susan Okie, *What Ails the FDA*, 352 NEW ENG. J. MED. 1063, 1063 (2005) (noting "Rofecoxib is among the most swiftly approved drugs to be withdrawn for safety reasons"); John Simons, *Will Merck Survive Vioxx?*, FORTUNE, Nov. 1, 2004, at 90 ("On the cover of its 1999 annual report, Merck boasted that the drug was its 'biggest, fastest, and best launch ever.'").

32. Simons, *supra* note 31, at 90 (describing how Vioxx helped turn Merck around financially, at least initially).

33. Press Release, Merck, Merck Announces Voluntary Worldwide Withdrawal of VIOXX® (Sept. 30, 2004) (http://www.merck.com/newsroom/vioxx/pdf/vioxx_press_release_final.pdf).

34. Henry A. Waxman, *The Lessons of Vioxx—Drug Safety and Sales*, 352 NEW ENG. J. MED. 2576 (2005).

35. Gardiner Harris, *F.D.A. Official Admits "Lapses" on Vioxx*, N.Y. TIMES, Mar. 2, 2005, at A1.

36. *See id.*

market in 2004[37] and eventually settled with the victims for $4.85 billion.[38] The FDA was not the prime mover in getting Vioxx off the market; instead it was the thousands of plaintiffs threatening individual and class action lawsuits. The FDA failed to protect the consumers from the Vioxx scandal because the agency was designed to fail from the start.[39] For example, the FDA's chief counsel, Daniel Troy, had earlier represented tobacco and pharmaceutical companies against the FDA.[40]

2. Aircraft Regulation

In an earlier chapter, it was argued the Federal Aeronautics Administration (FAA) knew of an earlier incident where the cargo doors popped off an airplane, but did little to prevent a reoccurrence.[41] The result was that several hundred people died in a McDonnell Douglas plane crash in France.[42] These deaths occurred because the FAA dragged its feet in failing to ground the planes and ensure cargo door repairs were made effectively. This is demonstrated in the television documentary *The World's Worst Airplane Crash*.[43] The apparent goal of the FAA was to keep the planes flying and to avoid embarrassing McDonnell Douglas.[44]

This type of tragedy was repeated in 2009, when a commuter plane crashed near Buffalo, New York. The accident occurred while the plane was flying in wing-icing conditions. Apparently it stalled due to the ice on its wings; forty-nine people were killed.[45] Almost the same facts had occurred in 1994 in Roselawn, Indiana, when a commuter plane crashed and killed sixty-eight persons because the wings iced. The National Transportation Safety Board (NTSB) made safety

---

37. Press Release, Merck, *supra* note 33.

38. Carrie Johnson, *Merck Agrees to Blanket Settlement on Vioxx*, WASH. POST, Nov. 11, 2007, at D1. "Merck continues to face civil and criminal investigations as well as lawsuits from states seeking to recover Medicare and Medicaid funds they used to purchase Vioxx." *Id. See generally* Merck.com, Newsroom-Vioxx, http://www.merck.com/newsroom/vioxx/ (last visited Mar. 10, 2011).

39. The FDA lacks the power to force drug companies to change labels or conduct testing after a drug has been approved. Harris, *supra* note 35.

40. *See supra* note 27.

41. *Scandals: The Great DC-10 Mystery*, TIME, April 8, 1974, http://www.time.com/time/magazine/article/0,9171,908559-2,00.html.

42. Aviation Safety Network, Accident Description, http://aviation-safety.net/database/record.php?id=19740303-1 (last visited Mar. 5, 2010).

43. "The World's Worst Airplane Crash," March 3, 1974, Thames TV. *See also supra*, note 41.

44. *Scandals: The Great DC-10 Mystery*, *supra* note 42 (finding it was more likely McDonnell Douglas wanted to avoid bad press than keep costs low).

45. David Porter, *DOT Sued Over Pace of Air Safety Improvement*, ATLANTA J.-CONST. Feb. 25, 2009, at A7.

recommendations in 1996 that were apparently never adopted by the FAA.[46] The point is simple: the power of the airplane manufacturers and the airlines has a huge (and intended) impact on FAA safety decisions. Public safety is not their sole concern.

This argument can also be made in regard to the history of nuclear power regulation. The original Atomic Energy Commission (AEC) had two conflicting goals: (1) the promotion of atomic energy, and (2) its regulation.[47] It soon became clear the agency could not fulfill its conflicting responsibilities of ensuring public safety while promoting nuclear power. The victim of this conflict of interest was the public. After much public criticism, the agency was split into two parts: (1) the Energy, Research, and Development Administration to promote the use of nuclear energy; and (2) the Nuclear Regulatory Commission (NRC) to regulate its use.[48]

Automobile safety recalls is another example. While Toyota struggled to identify and repair the problems its cars were having with brakes and sudden acceleration, the *Charlotte Observer* reported the solution might rest on previous lobbying efforts:

[Toyota] has friends and employees in high places. Toyota has friends in high places in Washington, including some of the very people now investigating the Japanese automaker. The company has sought to sow goodwill and win allies with lobbying, . . . and perhaps most important, creating jobs.

Lawmakers on the committees investigating Toyota's massive recall represent states where Toyota has factories—and the well-paying manufacturing jobs they bring. The company's executives include a former employee of the federal agency that is supposed to oversee that automaker.[49]

3. The SEC–Madoff Example

Courts and the legislatures reflect the interests of the powerful. This holds true for regulatory agencies as well. The fact agencies represent the interests of the regulated industry rather than the public is so common that it has earned a

---

46. *Id.* However, the NTSB reported in February 2010 the Buffalo crash was probably caused by the captain's "inappropriate action that led the aircraft to stall." B.D. Wolf, *2009 Buffalo Plane Crash Causes FAA to Rethink Pilot Training*, AIRPORT BUSINESS, Feb. 9, 2010. http://www.airportbusiness.com/web/online/Top-News-Headlines/2009-Buffalo-Plane-Crash-Causes-FAA-to-Rethink-Pilot-Training/1$34202.

47. NRC.gov, Our History, http://www.nrc.gov/about-nrc/history.html (last visited Mar. 6, 2010).

48. NRC.gov, Glossary—Atomic Energy Commission, http://www.nrc.gov/reading-rm/basic-ref/glossary/atomic-energy-commission.html (last visited Mar. 6, 2010).

49. Sharon Theimer, *Toyota's Connections Run Deep in Washington*, THE CHARLOTTE OBSERVER, Feb. 8, 2010, at 1.

name—"agency capture."[50] The most recent and outrageous example of an agency failing to protect the public involves Bernie Madoff. In a Ponzi scheme: "Madoff accepted funds from his investors and stole instead of investing it. He used fresh funds to make payments to other investors."[51] Madoff's fraudulent financial empire was huge: "Madoff's crime cost thousands of victims at least $21 billion in cash losses, part of the $64.8 billion in paper wealth that vanished when his scheme collapsed."[52]

Madoff stole from his friends, nonprofit organizations, and the rich and the famous.[53] It became an honor to have Madoff handle your investments.[54] The SEC should have detected the scheme decades earlier because of Madoff's continuous high return rates and lack of investments. Indeed, beginning in 1992, complaints were made to the SEC.[55] But with regard to a Madoff investigation, the SEC was mired in cement:

> [T]he SEC had received six substantive complaints since 1992–and botched the investigation of every one of them. The SEC's inspector general

---

50. *See* Dion Casey, Note, *Agency Capture: The USDA's Struggle to Pass Food Safety Regulations*, 7 Kan. J.L. & Pub. Pol'y 142, 142 (1998) ("Agency capture occurs when 'through lobbying the regulated firm is able to win the hearts and minds of the regulators'") (citing Ian Ayres & John Braithwaite, Responsive Regulation: Transcending the Deregulation Debate 63 (1992)); Mark C. Niles, *On the Hijacking of Agencies (and Airplanes): The Federal Aviation Administration, "Agency Recapture," and Airline Security*, 10 Am. U. J. Gender Soc. Pol'y & L. 381, 390 (2002) ("Proponents of the theory have generally observed that capture occurs when a regulated entity—like a large corporation, or more likely an association of corporate interests—succeed, through lobbying or other influential devices, in replacing what would otherwise be the public-policy agenda of the agency with its own private and self-serving agenda."); Bradford C. Mank, *Superfund Contractors and Agency Capture*, 2 N.Y.U. Envtl. L.J. 34, 49 (1993) (arguing agency capture should be seen as a "continuum in which the degree of capture ranges from an interest group exercising some influence over an agency's policies to situations where a regulated industry completely captures a regulatory agency").

51. Jennifer Liberto, *SEC Investigation: We Missed Madoff*, CNN Money.com, Sept. 2, 2009, *available at* http://money.CNN.com/2009/09/02/news/economy/Madoff_SEC_investigation/

52. Diana Henriques, *Lapse Helped Scheme, Madoff Told Investigators*, N.Y. Times, Oct. 20, 2009.

53. Keren Blankfeld Schultz & Duncan Greenberg, *Bernie Madoff's Billionaire Victims*, Fortune, Mar. 12, 2009, http://www.forbes.com/2009/03/12/madoff-guilty-plea-business-wall-street-celebrity-victims.html (noting Madoff's victims included Elie Wiesel, Steven Spielberg, and Warren Buffett).

54. *See id.*

55. Diana Henriques *Exhibits Show How SEC Missed on Madoff* Atlanta J.-Const., Nov. 1, 2009, at A13.

found no evidence of any bribery, collusion or deliberate sabotage of those investigations.[56]

How did the SEC miss telltale signs for almost thirty years? The answer is power. Bernie Madoff was the former chair of Nasdaq—a powerful person and "one of the boys."[57] Harry Markopolos, a former securities fraud investigator, warned the SEC that Madoff was running a Ponzi scheme as early as 2000. Markopolos stated: "The SEC is . . . captive to the industry it regulates and is afraid to bring big cases against prominent individuals . . . The agency 'roars like a lion and bites like a flea' . . ."[58]

In fact, Madoff was surprised he was not caught earlier. He later pinpointed the reason:

> The first time, in 2004, he assumed the investigators would check his clearinghouse account. [He was not buying much stock.] He said he was [astonished] that they did not, and theorized that they might have decided against doing so because of his stature in the industry. "I am very proud of the role I played in the industry," he said.[59]

Bernie Madoff was eventually arrested and prosecuted. He is now serving a 150-year prison sentence.[60]

D. PERSUASIVE ORGANIZATIONS

One of the goals of this book is to examine how the law is really made. We look below the surface and ask how the courts, legislatures, and agencies are influenced in making their decisions. In Chapter IV, we examined the ALI, CTR, and AAJ. These organizations do not make law, but they publish papers or lobby to persuade others to do so. The Searle Center on Law Regulations and Economic Growth at Northwestern Law School is another example of such an organization. It holds conferences and promotes papers in order to affect the law. The homepage of the Searle Center states its goal: "We are a non-profit research and educational organization committed to the study of the impact of laws and regulations on economic growth."[61]

---

56. *Id.*

57. *Ponzi Scheme Investors Briefed on Losses, Plans*, ATLANTA J.-CONST. Feb. 21, 2009, at B3.

58. Marcy Gordon, *Madoff Tipster Says SEC "Afraid" to Bring Big Cases*, ATLANTA J.- CONST., Feb. 5, 2009, at B3.

59. Henriques, *supra* note 55, at A13.

60. Diana B. Henriques et al., *Madoff, Apologizing, Is Given 150 Years*, N.Y. TIMES, June 30, 2009, at A1.

61. http://www.law.northwestern.edu/searlecenter/about-us/

Insight as to what this means is reflected in the titles of recent papers published and conferences presented by the Center. All of the papers and conferences argue against suing and regulating corporations; they have subjects such as: Public Nuisance Litigation, Third Party Litigation Financing, Consumer Arbitration, and State Consumer Protection Acts: An Empirical Investigation of Private Litigation.[62] The Center's goal is apparently to produce papers and present programs that will influence legislators and courts when they deal with cases and regulations affecting corporations.

The Searle Center states it was "founded in 2006 with a generous grant from the late Daniel C. Searle."[63] Daniel Searle was the CEO of G.D. Searle & Company from 1966 until 1977, when he was replaced by Donald H. Rumsfeld, former U.S. Secretary of Defense.[64] The G.D. Searle & Company became a wholly owned subsidiary of Monsanto Company.[65] The Searle Company developed a number of well-known products, including Metamucil, Dramamine, the first birth control pill (Enovid), and aspartame (Nutrasweet). In 1985, Monsanto paid $2.7 billion for Searle.[66] However, the Searle Center strives to present balanced conferences. For example, the author was invited to the conference dealing with public nuisance theory, and it appeared scholars were in attendance who represented diverse views on the topic.[67]

But sometimes this attempt at balance by "think tanks" goes the wrong way. In 1997, the author spoke at a conference presented by the University of Kansas's Law and Economics Center. About twenty leading torts scholars were also invited to discuss the new *Restatement (Third) of Torts:* Products Liability. Over one hundred state court judges were guests, as well as the authors of the Restatement, who were there to promote the core of their new product, Section 2(b) of the new Restatement. In his presentation, the author urged the judges to rely on their local law to reject the new Restatement as it was far from setting forth a majority

---

62. http://www.law.northwestern.edu/searlecenter/issues/.

63. http://www.law.northwestern.edu/searlecenter/about-us/.

64. *See* John J. Miller, *Daniel C. Searle, R.I.P,* Nat, Rev. Online, Nov. 8, 2007, *available at* http://article.nationalreview.com/333258/daniel-c-searle-rip/john-j-miller. ("He rose to become its president in 1966, CEO in 1970, and finally chairman of the board in 1977 . . . Searle's most important decision probably involved the hiring of a new CEO who had just left the Ford administration. Donald Rumsfeld strengthened the company and developed a reputation for leadership that made him an attractive choice for a future president who needed a defense secretary.").

See also G.D. Searle & Co. Company History, *available at* http://www.fundinguniverse.com/company-histories/G-D-Searle-amp;-Co-Company-History.html.

65. *Id.*

66. *Id.*

67. The program was titled "Expansion of Liability Under Public Nuisance," and it was held on April 7–8, 2008, at the Searle Center. Information *available at* http://www.law.northwestern.edu/searlecenter/issues/index.cfm?ID=77.

rule on the subject of design defect.[68] That view was later adopted by the Kansas Supreme Court in *Delaney v. Deere & Co.*,[69] although the goal of the Law and Economics Center was to promote Section 2(b), not to have it rejected by the Kansas Supreme Court.

E. CORPORATIONS DICTATE MORALITY

The purpose of this section is to demonstrate how corporations use power to implement their view of morality. In late 2009, professional golfer Tiger Woods was reported to have had numerous affairs. His wife left him and took his two young children. Because of this, global consulting firm Accenture cancelled its endorsement contract with him. This was followed by news that Gillette had stopped advertisements featuring the pro-golfer, and AT&T has said it is reevaluating its relationship with him.[70] Similarly, the New York Giants released Plaxico Burress, a wide receiver, who now "stands to lose millions of dollars in salary" for carrying a concealed weapon in New York and accidentally firing it (he shot himself). The gun was also not licensed in New York. Burress agreed to a two-year prison sentence on the weapons charge.[71]

The Washington Post reported the "National Basketball Association . . . suspended Washington Wizard's guard Gilbert Arenas indefinitely without pay."[72] This action was taken because Arenas brought guns to the Verizon Center, which is located in a "gun free zone" (within one thousand feet of a day care center).[73] A final example involves actor Charlie Sheen. The clothing company Hanes Brands, Inc. severed its ties with the television star after Sheen was arrested on domestic violence charges for allegedly threatening his wife with a knife.

---

68. Frank J. Vandall, *State Judges Should Reject the Reasonable Alternative Design Standard of the Restatement (Third), Products Liability, Section 2(b)*, 8 Kan. J. Law & Public Policy 62–66 (1998).

69. 999 P.2d 930 (Kan. 2000).

70. Kate Stanhope, *Nike Chairman: Tiger Woods' Indiscretions a "Minor Blip,"* Seattle TV Guide, Dec. 15, 2009.

71. *Burress Pleads Guilty to Gun Charge, Faces 2 Years*, Reuters.com, Aug. 20, 2009. *See also* Karen Matthews, *Plaxico Burress Sentenced to 2 Years in Gun Case*, Huffington Post. com, Sept. 22, 2009, *available at* http://www.huffingtonpost.com/2009/09/22/plaxico-burress-sentenced_n_294617.html.

72. Mike Wise, *New Details on Arenas Gun Incident*, Washington Post, Jan. 7, 2010, *available at* http://www.cbsnews.com/stories/2010/01/07/politics/washingtonpost/main6066658.shtmls.com/stories/2010/01/07/politics/washingtonpost/main6066658.shtml.

73. Joseph White, *Official: Wizards Plan to Fine Players Who Took Part in Arenas Gun Antics*, The Canadian Press, *available at* www.google.com/hostednews/canadianpress/article.

To avoid bad publicity, Hanes immediately pulled a series of television commercials featuring Sheen.[74]

American corporations pay cultural icons substantial amounts for a purpose: to support and enhance what the corporation produces, be it underwear, razors, or other products and services. To keep the stars in line, endorsement contracts are awarded. But if the star commits an "immoral act" (as defined by the corporation), the contract is terminated by the corporation to publicly punish the star (and threaten others). Apparently corporations believe Americans will hesitate to buy a product or a service that is tinged by its connection to an immoral act. At the same time, a clear message is conveyed by the corporation to the general population: do not engage in marital infidelity, domestic abuse, or violations of gun laws.

F. PROXIMATE CAUSE V. TORT "REFORM"

The continuing cries for tort "reform" to further protect corporations from civil liability fly in the face of a complex judicial concept known as proximate cause, which has protected corporations from excessive liability for 150 years.[75] The concept of proximate cause is used to sever the chain of liability in negligence cases. In the cases where proximate cause is applied, often the defendant (who is protected by proximate cause) is a corporation whose negligence caused damage to the plaintiff. Let us examine several important and well-known examples.

In 1866, a fire was started by a spark from a train. The fire burned a building owned by the railroad, then spread to and destroyed the plaintiff's building. The court rejected the plaintiff's claim and adopted a proximate cause concept to insulate the railroad from liability. It said that only the owner of the "first building" damaged could recover, not the owner of the second building.[76] The plaintiff therefore lost because damage from the fire was limited to the "first building."

---

74. Dian Bramaged, *Why Did Hanes Stand By Sheen For So Long?*, DEMOCRATIC UNDERGROUND.COM, Jan. 8, 2010, *available at* www.democraticunderground.com/discuss/duboard.php?.

75. *See* Cass R. Sunstein et al., *Assessing Punitive Damages (with Notes on Cognition and Valuation Law)*, 107 YALE L.J. 2071, 2074 (1998) (discussing various reform proposals to overcome erratic, unpredictable, and arbitrary awards); STEPHANIE MENCIMER, BLOCKING THE COURTHOUSE DOOR: HOW THE REPUBLICAN PARTY AND ITS CORPORATE ALLIES ARE TAKING AWAY YOUR RIGHT TO SUE (2006) (identifying Republicans and corporations as the major proponents of tort reform proposals); Newsbatch.com, Tort Reform, http://www.newsbatch.com/tort.htm (last visited Mar. 5, 2010) (summarizing the development of tort reform).

See William L. Prosser, *Comparative Negligence*, 41 CAL. L. REV. 1, 3–4 (1953).

76. Ryan v. New York Central R. R. Co., 35 N.Y. 210, 213 (N.Y. 1866).

This protection of the railroads was further expanded by the New York Court of Appeals in the famous *Palsgraf* case (1928).[77] In *Palsgraf*, a railroad attendant was helping a passenger board a train when the passenger dropped a box filled with fireworks, which exploded. Allegedly the explosion caused a penny scale to fall over and injure Mrs. Palsgraf, the plaintiff. In a long and complex decision, the judge held that only a "foreseeable plaintiff" could recover. Because Mrs. Palsgraf was not a "foreseeable plaintiff" as she was at the other end of the platform, she lost and could not recover for her injuries. Thus, the powerful railroad won the case against a cleaning woman.[78]

More recently, because of negligence on the part of the Consolidated Edison Power Co., the electric power in New York City went out. Because plaintiff's apartment building did not have light, the plaintiff fell on the stairs and was injured. In his suit against the power company for negligence in permitting the electric power to be lost, the court held in favor of Consolidated Edison, reasoning the plaintiff was not in "privity" with the defendant company. Thus, the huge power company was protected from liability by means of a proximate cause concept.[79]

Enright v. Eli Lilly & Co. is a challenging case involving a defective drug (DES),[80] which was a calmative marketed by Eli Lilly for pregnant women. It produced vaginal cancer in the daughters of the women who took the drug. The *Enright* case involved the granddaughter of a woman who took DES, in which the granddaughter alleged her cerebral palsy and other disabilities were caused by DES. The court found for the large drug manufacturer, Eli Lilly. It used proximate cause language to support its decision, stating there were numerous policies in conflict and that a line had to be drawn somewhere in regard to liability. Not everyone who was injured by DES could recover. The court also stressed the value of pharmaceuticals to society.[81]

G. THE SUPREME COURT

In products liability cases, the U.S. Supreme Court tends to favor the corporation over the injured consumer. The best example of this is preemption.[82] Both *Cipollone v. Liggett Group*[83] and *Geier v. American Honda*[84] demonstrate the

---

77. Palsgraf v. The Long Island Railroad Co., 248 N.Y. 339 (N.Y. 1928). Almost all first-year law students read this case.

78. *Id.*

79. Strauss v. Belle Realty Co., 65 N.Y.2d 399, 405 (N.Y. 1985).

80. 77 N.Y.2d 377 (N.Y. 1991).

81. *Id.* at 391–92.

82. *See* Chapter 4, fn. 19.

83. *See* Chapter 4, fn. 26.

84. *See* Chapter 4, fn. 21.

Court's decisions tend to protect the corporate defendant by holding the state cause of action is preempted by a federal statute or regulation.

Other good examples include *Daubert v. Merrell Dow Pharmaceuticals*,[85] which gives the trial court enormous discretion to exclude an expert witness as unqualified, and *BMW v. Gore*, which allows courts to throw out punitive damages they consider too large.[86]

Citizens United v. Federal Election Committee (2010) is an excellent recent example of the Supreme Court dramatically favoring corporations. Historically, the goal of Congress has been to insure that each citizen gets one vote and no more.[87] The purpose of the McCain-Feingold Act was to severely limit the power of corporations to ensure citizens, not corporations, elect the government.[88]

This legislative history was ignored in January 2010, when the Supreme Court held that corporations and unions were entitled to free speech protection.[89] This means that from this point forward, corporations and unions will be able to spend unlimited amounts for advertising during elections to further gain control of government.[90] They will be able to use their financial fortunes to support their candidates and punish those candidates who did not accede to them while in office.[91]

Will *Citizens United* shift control of government further into the hands of the corporations? The composition of the Supreme Court majority in *Citizens United*—five to four—provides some insight into this question.[92] All five of the justices who voted in the majority were appointed by Republican presidents.[93] The vote was arguably their way of saying thanks. The answer is yes, *Citizens United* will likely toss substantial elective power into the outstretched hands of corporations[94] and further shift the control of government to corporations.

---

85. Daubert v. Merrell Dow Pharm., 509 U.S. 579 (1993).

86. BMW of North America, Inc. v. Gore, 517 U.S. 559 (1996). Note the dissent by Justices Scalia and Thomas in BMW.

87. *Democracy for Sale*, PITTSBURGH POST-GAZETTE, Jan. 24, 2010, at B2. United v. Federal Election Comm'n, Citizens 558 U.S. ____ (Jan. 21, 2010).

88. Erwin Chemerinsky, *A Stunning Example of Judicial Activism*, PITTSBURGH POST-GAZETTE, Jan. 24, 2010, at B3.

89. *Id.*

90. PITTSBURGH POST-GAZETTE, *supra* note 87.

91. *Id.*

92. Chemerinsky, *supra* note 88.

93. PITTSBURGH POST-GAZETTE, *supra* note 87. The five justices in the majority are Republicans who favor business. *Citizens United* arguably gives control of government to businesses (i.e., the powerful).

94. Chemerinsky, *supra* note 88.

H. CONGRESS, AGENCY FAILURE, LOBBYING, AND CRASHES: THE TOYOTA EXAMPLE

The quagmire Toyota found itself in at the end of 2009 and the start of 2010 reflects several themes of the book. For years, Toyota had expended substantial sums in lobbying Congress and NHTSA.[95] Why?

Toyota was sinking in a mire of three serious safety problems. The first was said to be sudden acceleration, caused by carpets sticking under the gas pedal. Now there are allegations the car's computer is involved, and electronic glitches that will neither allow the engine to shut off nor the brakes to stop the car. Nineteen people are alleged to have died in crashes caused by these alleged problems.[96] In the midst of this, a Toyota document surfaced that said Toyota saved $100 million by persuading NHTSA not to require a mandatory recall of cars with the carpet problem.

Now the reason for the substantial expenditures to lobby Congress and NHTSA has become clear. The "goodwill" created by Toyota has, so far, saved it $100 million in avoiding recalls and is at least equally valuable before Congress. As of February 24, 2010, the CEO of Toyota, Akio Toyoda, was being asked by a Congressional committee to explain the cause of the sudden acceleration. "Goodwill," earlier bought by Toyota, will likely prove very helpful before Congress.

Public safety will not be the sole issue before Congress or NHTSA. At the same time, questions are being raised whether NHTSA lacks the funds and expertise to deal with glitches in sophisticated vehicle computers.[97] Men and women in NHTSA and Congress will make decisions affecting the safety of the public, but their decisions will be shaped in part by the earlier lobbying efforts of Toyota.

---

95. *See* James R. Healey & Sharon Silk Carty, *Toyota Memo: Savings on Safety*, USA TODAY, Feb. 22, 2010, at 1A.

96. *Report: Toyota Brake Acceleration Inquiries*, Business, ATL. J.-CONST., Feb. 13, 2010, at A15. The WSJ suggests thirty-four deaths in the United States may have been caused by the acceleration problem. WALL STREET J., Feb. 26, 2010, at 64.

97. Peter Valdes–Dapena, "LaHood: Toyota Regulators Weren't 'Lap Dogs,'" CNN Money.com, Feb. 24, 2010.

CONCLUSION

Many of the laws today are designed and implemented by corporations and large interest groups. If we live under a rule of law, the rule involving financial matters was likely lobbied for by a powerful interest with a substantial stake in the outcome. This conclusion extends to courts, legislatures, and agencies at both the state and federal levels. Rule by the powerful, not the people, is neither a flaw nor an accident—it is intended by functional design.

TABLE OF CASES

INDEX